Henry Hart Milman

The History of Christianity

From the Birth of Christ to the Abolition of Paganism in the Roman Empire

Henry Hart Milman

The History of Christianity
From the Birth of Christ to the Abolition of Paganism in the Roman Empire

ISBN/EAN: 9783741180453

Manufactured in Europe, USA, Canada, Australia, Japa

Cover: Foto ©Lupo / pixelio.de

Manufactured and distributed by brebook publishing software (www.brebook.com)

Henry Hart Milman

The History of Christianity

THE
HISTORY OF CHRISTIANITY,

FROM THE BIRTH OF CHRIST TO THE ABOLITION OF
PAGANISM IN THE ROMAN EMPIRE.

By HENRY HART MILMAN, D.D.,

DEAN OF ST. PAUL'S.

IN THREE VOLUMES.—VOL. I.

A NEW AND REVISED EDITION.

LONDON:
JOHN MURRAY, ALBEMARLE STREET.
1867.

The Right of Translation is reserved.

PREFACE.

This new edition of the History of Christianity has been revised throughout. A few passages have been added, chiefly in the notes; a few slightly enlarged. In general, I have not found much, after a period of above twenty years, which I should wish to retract or to modify.

Some objection was raised on the first publication of the work against the commencement of the History of Christianity with the Life of Christ. I thought then, and still think, that life to be an integral and inseparable part of the History. It appeared to me necessary to the completeness of the history to trace it to its primal origin; to show that the Gospels, our only documentary authorities, offer a clear and distinct relation of that life, with no greater variation than might reasonably be expected from four separate and independent narratives, drawn up by different writers, at different times and places, and by one at least from a different point of view; that this relation accords in every respect with all that we know of the events, circumstances, manners, usages, opinions of the age and country; that its religious signification, and, in part, supernatural character, in no way conflict, but are rather in full and perfect harmony, with its simple truth and reality.

At all events, the reverence which had enshrined and set apart the life of Jesus in a kind of unapproachable sanctity had been then (and has since been) so ruthlessly invaded, as to force, as it were, others on that holy ground. In truth, advantage has been taken of that very secluding reverence to dismiss the whole Life of Christ from the domain of history; to make that reverence the source and parent of the whole, either supposing the religion, even Jesus himself, to be no more than the spontaneous growth of the opinions, thoughts, passions, ideal aspirations of the time; or a pure myth, the creation of the excited imagination of the believers; humanity, as it were, self superhumanised and deified; not what St. Paul asserts, "God in Christ, reconciling the world unto himself."

At the time of the publication of the History of Christianity these views had culminated in the famous work of Strauss,—a work, it must be acknowledged, of vast learning and unparalleled ingenuity. To the theory of Strauss, as far as I could understand it (for Strauss himself, as if appalled by his own conclusions, varied much in the successive editions of his book as to the result of his inquiries), I ventured to raise some objections, which seemed to me and to some others of weight and importance. I leave them as they stood.

Another work has now appeared, since the present edition was printed off, more brilliant and popular, in a language of universal currency, and in a style in which that language displays itself in all its captivating force, life, and distinctness. Yet I cannot but think this very perfection of style in some degree fatal to its pretensions. There are passages in which the vivid transparency betrays at once the perplexity of the writer and the inconceivable feebleness of his arguments. I cannot apprehend more lasting effect from the light, quick, and bright-flashing artillery of the Frenchman than from the more ponderous, and steadily-aimed culverins of the German. In one respect I had expected more from the wide and copious erudition of M. Renan. But I find no illustration, no allusion from the Jewish writers which was not familiar to me from Lightfoot, Schoetgen, Meuschen, and the great Talmudic scholars of the two last centuries. I suspect that they have exhausted the subject. As little new can be found or could be expected from the scenery and topography of Palestine, in like manner drained to the utmost by so many travellers before M. Renan. Even as to the style—may an Englishman venture to contrast it (by no means in its favour) not only with the dignity and solemnity of Pascal, but with the passionate earnestness of Rousseau: its "thin sentimentality" (this is not my own expression) reminds me more of 'Paul et Virginie' than, I will not say of the 'Pensées,' but even of the 'Vicaire Savoyard.' I cannot think that eventually the book will add to the high fame of M. Renan. To those who see in Christianity no more than a social revolution, a natural step in human progress, the beautiful passages on the transcendant humanity of Jesus (unhappily, not unleavened) may give satisfaction and delight; to those to whom Christianity is a *religion*, Jesus the author and giver of eternal life, it will fall dead, or be a grief and an offence.

As to the apostolic and immediate post-apostolic times, I have not neglected or closed my eyes against the labours of what are called the Tübingen School. I trust that it is from no blind, stubborn, or presumptuous prejudice that I read Baur and his disciples with wonder and admiration at their industry, sagacity, ingenuity; but without conviction. It seems to me that with them instead of the theory being the result of diligent and acute investigation, the theory is first made, and then the inferences or arguments sought out, discerned, or imagined, and wrought up with infinite skill to establish the foregone conclusion; at the same time with a contemptuous disregard or utter obtuseness to the difficulties of their own system. Their criticism will rarely bear criticism.

On one special point, discussed by writers of another character—the second imprisonment of St. Paul—I have added a note.

I have read a very able paper (in the 'Home and Foreign Review'), impugning my views (which are acknowledged to be those of most learned men of the day) on the connection of Christianity and what I have called Orientalism. Possibly some of my statements may have been somewhat too broad; but I have the satisfaction of finding that very recently that most distinguished Orientalist, M. Lassen, has given his sanction to the same views. The great difficulty seems to be as regards Buddhism. But of the ascetic and monastic institutions of Buddhism, so undeniably analogous to those of Christianity, the antiquity as well as the existence is incontestable. Yet their principle of estrangement from the world seems almost irreconcilable with the theory of Buddhism which has been wrought out by the later Orientalists, and the sum of which has been so well and so clearly expounded in the volume of M. Barthélemy St. Hilaire.

CONTENTS OF VOL. I.

BOOK I.

CHAPTER I.

Introduction — State and various forms of Pagan Religion, and of Philosophy .. .. Page 1

CHAPTER II.

Life of Jesus Christ — State of Judæa — The Belief in the Messiah 50

APPENDIX I.—Recent Lives of Christ 109

    "   II.—Origin of the Gospels 117

    "   III.—Influence of the more imaginative incidents of the early Evangelic History on the Maintenance and Propagation of the Religion .. 123

CHAPTER III.

Commencement of the Public Life of Jesus 127

CHAPTER IV.

Public Life of Jesus from the First to the Second Passover .. 165

CHAPTER V.

Second Year of the Public Life of Jesus .. .. Page 108

CHAPTER VI.

Third Year of the Public Life of Jesus 230

CHAPTER VII.

The Last Passover. — The Crucifixion 260

BOOK II.

CHAPTER I.

The Resurrection, and first Promulgation of Christianity .. 340

CHAPTER II.

Christianity and Judaism 377

CHAPTER III.

Christianity and Paganism 424

HISTORY OF CHRISTIANITY.

BOOK I.

CHAPTER I.

Introduction.—State and various forms of Pagan Religion, and of Philosophy.

THE reign of Augustus Cæsar is the most remarkable epoch in the history of mankind. For the first time, a large part of the families, tribes, and nations, into which the human race had gradually separated, were united under a vast, uniform, and apparently permanent, social system. The older Asiatic empires had, in general, owed their rise to the ability and success of some adventurous conqueror; and, when the master-hand was withdrawn, fell asunder; or were swept away to make room for some new kingdom or dynasty, which sprang up with equal rapidity, and in its turn experienced the same fate. The Grecian monarchy established by Alexander, as though it shared in the Asiatic principle of vast and sudden growth and as rapid decay, broke up at his death into several conflicting kingdoms; yet survived in its influence, and united, in some degree, Western Asia, Egypt, and Greece into one political system, in which the Greek language and manners predominated. But the monarchy of Rome was founded on principles as yet unknown; the kingdoms, which were won by the most unjustifiable aggression, were, for

[marginal note: Era of Augustus Cæsar.*]*

the most part, governed with a judicious union of firmness and conciliation, in which the conscious strength of irresistible power was tempered with the wisest respect to national usages. The Romans conquered like savages, but ruled like philosophic statesmen.* Till, from the Euphrates to the Atlantic, from the shores of Britain, and the borders of the German forests, to the sands of the African Desert, the whole Western world was consolidated into one great commonwealth, united by the bonds of law and government, by facilities of communication and commerce, and by the general dissemination of the Greek and Latin languages.

Roman Civilisation.

For civilisation followed in the train of Roman conquest: the ferocity of her martial temperament seemed to have spent itself in the civil wars: the lava flood of her ambition had cooled; and wherever it had spread, a rich and luxuriant vegetation broke forth. At least down to the time of the Antonines, though occasionally disturbed by the contests which arose on the change of dynasties, the rapid progress of improvement was by no means retarded. Diverging from Rome as a centre, magnificent and commodious roads connected the most remote countries; the free navigation of the Mediterranean united the most flourishing cities of the empire; the military colonies had disseminated the language and manners of the South in the most distant regions; the wealth and population of the African and Asiatic provinces had steadily increased; while, amid the forests of Gaul, the morasses of Britain, the sierras of Spain, flourishing cities arose; and the arts, the

---

* On the capture of a city, promiscuous massacre was the general order, which descended even to brute animals, until a certain signal. Polyb. x. 15. As to the latter point, I mean, of course, the general policy, not the local tyranny, which was often so capriciously, so blindly, so insolently exercised by the individual provincial governor.

luxuries, the order, and regularity of cultivated life were introduced into regions which, a short time before, had afforded a scanty and precarious subsistence to tribes scarcely acquainted with agriculture. The frontiers of civilisation seemed gradually to advance, and to drive back the still-receding barbarism:[b] while within the pale, national distinctions were dying away; all tribes and races met amicably in the general relation of Roman subjects or citizens, and mankind seemed settling down into one great federal society.[c]

About this point of time Christianity appeared. As Rome had united the whole Western world into one, as it might almost seem, lasting social system, so Christianity was the first religion which aimed at an universal and permanent moral conquest. The religions of the older world were content with their dominion over the particular people which were their several votaries. Family, tribal, national, deities were universally recognised; and as their gods accompanied the migrations or the conquests of different nations, the worship of those gods was extended over a wider surface, but rarely propagated among the subject races. To drag in triumph the divinities of a vanquished people was the last and most insulting mark of subjugation.[d] Yet, though the gods of the conquerors had thus manifested their superiority, and, in some cases, the subject nation

Appearance of Christianity.

The older Religions.

---

[b] Quæ sparsa congregaret imperia, ritusque molliret, et tot populorum discordes ferasque linguas sermonis commercio contraheret ad colloquia, et humanitatem homini daret. Plin. Nat. Hist. iii. 5.

[c] "Unum esse reipublicæ corpus, atque unius animo regendum." Such was the argument of Asinius Gallus, Tac. Ann. I. 12.

[d] Tot de diis, quot de gentibus triumphi. Tertullian. Compare Isaiah xlvi. 1, and Gesenius's note; Jer. xlviii. 7, xlix. 3; Hos. x. 5, 6; Dan. xi. 8.

might be inclined to desert their inefficient protectors who had been found wanting in the hour of trial; still the godhead even of the defeated divinities was not denied. Though their power could not withstand the mightier tutelar deity of the invaders; yet their right to a seat in the crowded synod of heaven, and their rank among the intermediate rulers of the world, were not called in question.* The conqueror might, indeed, take delight in showing his contempt, and, as it were, trampling under foot the rebuked and impotent deities of his subject; and thus religious persecution be inflicted by the oppressor, and religious fanaticism excited among the oppressed. Yet, if the temple was desecrated, the altar thrown down, the priesthood degraded or put to the sword, this was done in the fierceness of hostility, or the insolence of pride;ᶠ or from policy, lest the religion should become the rallying point of civil independence;ᵍ rarely, if ever, for the purpose of extirpating a false, or supplanting it by a true, system of belief; perhaps in no instance with the design of

---

* There is a curious passage in Lydus de Ostentis, a book which probably contains some parts of the ancient ritual of Rome. A certain aspect of a comet not merely foretold victory, but the passing over of the hostile gods to the side of the Romans: καὶ αὐτὰ δὲ τὰ θεῖα καταλείψουσι τοὺς πολεμίους, ὥστε ἐν περισσοῦ προστεθῆναι τοῖς νικῶσιν.—Lydus de Ostentis, lib. 12.

ᶠ Such was the conduct of Cambyses in Egypt. Xerxes had, before his Grecian invasion, shown the proud intolerance of his disposition, in destroying the deities of the Babylonians, and slaying their priesthood (Herod. i. 183, and Arrian, vii. 19,; though, in this case, the rapacity which fatally induced him to pillage and desecrate the temples of Greece may have combined with his natural arrogance. Herod. viii. 53.

ᵍ This was most likely the principle of the horrible persecution of the Jews by Antiochus Epiphanes, though a kind of heathen bigotry seems to have mingled with his strange character. 1 Macc. i. 41 et seq.; 2 Macc. vi.; Diod. Sic. xxxiv. 1; Hist. of the Jews, vol. I. p. 461.

promulgating the tenets of a more pure and perfect religion. A wiser policy commenced with Alexander. The deities of the conquered nations were treated with uniform reverence, the sacrilegious plunder of their temples punished with exemplary severity.[b]

Policy of Alexander;

According to the Grecian system, their own gods were recognised in those of Egypt and Asia. The foreign deities were called by Grecian names,[i] and worshipped with the accustomed offerings; and thus all religious differences between Macedonian, and Syrian, and Egyptian, and Persian, at once vanished away. On the same principle, and with equal sagacity, Rome, in this as in other respects, aspired to enslave the mind of those nations which had been prostrated by her arms. The gods of the subject nations were treated with every mark of respect: sometimes they were admitted within the walls of the conqueror, as though to render their allegiance, and rank themselves in peaceful subordination under the supreme divinity of the Roman Gradivus, or the Jupiter of the Capitol;[k] till, at length, they all met in

of Rome.

---

[b] Arrian, lib. vi. p. 431, 439 (Edit. Amst. 1668); Polyb. v, 10.

[i] Arrian, lib. iii. p. 158, vii. p. 464, and 486. Some Persian traditions, perhaps, represent Alexander as a religious persecutor; but these are of no authority against the direct statement of the Greek historians. "Alexandre brûle en Enfer pour avoir condamné au feu les Roshis" (the religious books of different nations), &c. From Anquetil du Perron. Sir W. Ouseley, On some Anecdotes of Alexander. (Transactions Royal Society of Literature, i. p. 5.) The Indian religious usages, and the conduct of some of their faquirs, excited the wonder of the Greeks.

[k] Solere Romanos Deos omnes urbium superatarum partim privatim per familias spargere, partim publicè consecrare. Arnob. lii. 38.

It was a grave charge against Marcellus, that, by plundering the temples in Sicily, he had made the state an object of jealousy (ἐπίφθονον), because not only men but gods were led in triumph. The older

the amicable synod of the Pantheon, a representative assembly, as it were, of the presiding deities of all nations, in Rome, the religious as well as the civil capital of the world.ᵐ The state, as Cicero shows in his Book of Laws, retained the power of declaring what forms of religion were permitted by the law (licitæ);ⁿ but this authority was rarely exercised with rigour, excepting against such foreign superstitions as were considered pernicious to the morals of the people,—in earlier times, the Dionysiac;⁰ in later, the Isiac and Serapic rites.ᵖ

---

citizens approved rather the conduct of Fabius Maximus, who left to the Tarentines their offended gods. Plut. Vit. Marc.

ᵐ According to Verrius Flaccus, cited by Pliny (xxviii. 2), the Romans used to invoke the tutelary deity of every place which they besieged, and bribed him to their side by promising greater honours. Macrobius has a copy of the form of Evocation (iii. 9)—a very curious chapter. The name of the tutelar deity of Rome was a secret. Pliny, Nat. Hist. iii. 5. Bayle, Art. Serapus. Plut. Quæst. Rom. Note on Hume's Hist. Nat. Rel. Essays, p. 450.

Roma triumphantis quotiens ducis inclita currum
Planibus excepit, tollens altaria Divûm
Addidit, et spoliis sublimet nova numina fecit.—Prudentius.

Compare Augustin de Cons. Evang. L. 18.

For the Grecian custom on this subject, see Thucyd. iv. 98. Philip, the king of Macedon, defeated by Flaminius in his wars with the Grecian states, paid little respect to the temples. His admiral Dicæarchus is said to have erected and sacrificed on two altars to Impiety and Lawlessness, 'Ασεβεία and Παρανομία. This fact would be incredible on less grave authority than that of Polybius, lib. xviii. 37. On the general respect to temples in war, comp. Grot. de Jur. Bell. et Pac. III. 12, § 6.

ⁿ The question is well discussed by Jortin, Discourses, p. 53, note. Dionysius Hal. distinguishes between religions permitted, and publicly received, lib. ii. vol. I. p. 275, edit. Reiske. Compare other quotations from Livy in Hartung, Religion der Römer (I. 231, et seqq.), showing the jealousy of foreign rites and ceremonies, especially in times of danger and disaster.

⁰ Livy, xxix. 12 et seqq.

ᵖ During the Republic, the temples of Isis and Serapis were twice ordered to be destroyed, Dion. xl. p. 142, xlii. p. 196, also liv. p. 525. Val. Max. I. 3. Prop. ii. 24. See La Bastie in Académ. des Inscrip. xv. 40. On the Roman law on this subject, compare Jortin, Discourses, p. 53; Gibbon, vol. I. p. 55, with Wenck's note.

Christianity proclaimed itself the religion, not of family, or tribe, or nation, but of universal man. It admitted within its pale, on equal terms, all ranks and all races. It addressed mankind as one brotherhood, sprang from one common progenitor, and raised to immortality by one Redeemer. In this respect Christianity might appear singularly adapted to become the religion of a great empire. At an earlier period in the annals of the world, it would have encountered obstacles apparently insurmountable, in passing from one province to another, in moulding hostile and jealous nations into one religious community. A fiercer fire was necessary to melt and fuse the discordant elements into one kindred mass, before its gentler warmth could penetrate and permeate the whole with its vivifying influence. Not only were the circumstances of the times favourable to the extensive propagation of Christianity, from the facility of intercourse between the most remote nations, the cessation of hostile movements, and the uniform system of internal police, but the state of mankind seemed imperiously to demand the introduction of a new religion, to satisfy those universal propensities of human nature which connect man with a higher order of things. Man, as history and experience teach, is essentially a religious being. There are certain faculties and modes of thinking and feeling apparently inseparable from his mental organisation, which lead him irresistibly to seek some communication with another and a higher world. But at the present juncture, the ancient religions were effete: they belonged to a totally different state of civilisation; though they retained the strong hold of habit and interest on different classes of society, yet the general mind was advanced beyond them; they could not supply the religious necessities of the age. Thus the world, peaceably united under one temporal monarchy, might be compared to a vast body without a soul. The throne of the human mind appeared vacant; among the rival competitors for its dominion, none advanced more than claims local, or limited to a certain class. Nothing less was required than a religion coextensive at least with the empire of Rome, and calculated for the advanced state of intellectual culture: and in Christianity this new element of society was found; which, in fact, incorporating itself with manners, usages, and laws, has been the bond which has held together, notwithstanding the internal feuds and divisions, the great European commonwealth; maintained a kind of federal relation between its parts; and stamped its peculiar character on the whole of modern history.

Christianity announced the appearance of its Divine Author as the era of a new moral creation;

Dissociating principle of old religions.

and if we take our stand, as it were, on the isthmus which separates the ancient from the modern world, and survey the state of mankind before and after the introduction of this new power into human society, it is impossible not to be struck with the total revolution in the whole aspect of the world. If from this point of view we look upward, we see the dissociating principle at work both in the civil and religious usages of mankind; the human race breaking up into countless independent tribes and nations, which recede more and more from each other as they gradually spread over the surface of the earth; and in some parts, as we adopt the theory of the primitive barbarism,ª or that of the de-

---

ª The notion that the primeval state of man was altogether barbarous and uncivilised, so generally prevalent in the philosophy of the two last centuries (for Dryden's line,

Runs wild in woods the noble savage ran,

generacy of man from an earlier state of culture, either remaining stationary at the lowest point of ignorance and rudeness, or sinking to it; either resuming the primeval dignity of the race, or rising gradually to a higher state of civilisation. A certain diversity of religion follows the diversity of race, of people, and of country. In no respect is the common nature of human kind so strongly indicated as in the universality of some kind of religion; in no respect is man so various, yet so much the same. All the religions of antiquity, multiform and countless as they appear, may be easily reduced to certain classes, and, independent of the traditions which they may possess in common, throughout

---

contains the whole theory of Rousseau), has encountered a strong reaction. It is remarkable that Niebuhr in Germany, and Archbishop Whately in this country, with no knowledge of each other's views, should at the same time call in question this, almost established theory. Dr. Whately's argument, that there is no instance in history of a nation self-raised from savage life, is very strong. I have been much struck by finding a very vigorous and lucid statement to the same effect, in an unpublished lecture of the late Lord Stowell (Sir William Scott), delivered when Professor of History at Oxford. The general bias, however, of later opinion certainly favours the progressive development from a ruder state. Mr. Darwin's theory would, of course, educe us from something lower than the lowest barbarism. All the theories of the progressive education of the human race tend to the same conclusion. So, too, the discoveries of human implements of the simplest kind, in not very recent geological formations (as to human remains, we have now the verdict of Sir C. Lyell; yet the question is again in suspense); the remarkable researches of the Northern antiquarians into the successive ages of flint, copper, and iron; the lacustrine cities so singularly traced in many parts of the world, which indicate a state of extremely imperfect civilisation. Yet this rude condition of the primitive inhabitants of Europe is by no means decisive against a high state of advancement in the primal stock in the East, including Egypt. The argument from language, according to that consummate master of the science, M. Max Müller, on the whole, as must be the case in all works which aspire to resolve language into its primitive elements, tends strongly towards slow and progressive development. Yet the more perfect structure, as it seems, of some of the earliest languages, must have its due weight in our general determination.

the whole, reigns something like a family resemblance. Whether all may be rightly considered as depravations of the same primitive form of worship; whether the human mind is necessarily confined to a certain circle of religious notions; whether the striking phenomena of the visible world, presented to the imagination of various people in a similar state of civilisation, will excite the same train of devotional thoughts and emotions,—the philosophical spirit, and extensive range of inquiry, which in modern times have been carried into the study of mythology, approximate in the most remarkable manner the religions of the most remote countries.[r] The same primary principles everywhere appear, modified by the social state, the local circumstances, the civil customs, the imaginative or practical character of the people.

---

[r] The best, in my opinion, and most comprehensive work on the ancient religions, is the (yet unfinished) translation of Creuzer's Symbolik, by M. de Guigniaut, Religions de l'Antiquité, Paris, 1825, 1835. It is far superior in arrangement, and does not appear to me so obstinately wedded to the symbolic theory as the original of Creuzer. The Aglaophamus of Lobeck, as might be expected from that distinguished scholar, is full of profound and accurate erudition. Yet I cannot but think that the Grecian polytheism will be better understood, when considered in connexion with the other religions of antiquity, than as an entirely independent system; and surely the sarcastic tone in which M. Lobeck speaks of the Oriental studies of his contemporaries is unworthy of a man of consummate learning. The work of the late M. Constant, Sur la Religion, extensive in research, ingenious in argument, and eloquent in style, is in my, perhaps partial, judgment, vitiated by an hostility to every kind of priesthood, better suited to the philosophy of the last than of the present century. M. Constant has placed the evils of sacerdotal influence in the strongest light, and disguised or dissembled its advantages. The ancient priestly castes, I conceive, attained their power over the rest of their race by their acknowledged superiority; they were the benefactors, and thence the rulers, of their people: *to retain their power*, as the people advanced, they resorted to every means of keeping men in ignorance and subjection, and so degenerated into the tyrants of the human mind. At all events, sacerdotal domination (and here M. Constant would have agreed with me) is altogether alien to genuine Christianity.

Each state of social culture has its characteristic theology, self-adapted to the intellectual and moral condition of the people, and coloured in some degree by the habits of life. In the rudest and most savage races we find a gross superstition, called by modern foreign writers Fetichism,ᵃ in which the shapeless stone, the meanest reptile, any object however worthless or insignificant, is consecrated by a vague and mysterious reverence, as the representative of an unseen Being. The beneficence of this deity is usually limited to supplying the wants of the day, or to influencing the hourly occurrences of a life, in which violent and exhausting labour alternates either with periods of sluggish and torpid indolence, as among some of the North American tribes; or, as among the Africans, with wild bursts of thoughtless merriment.ᵇ This Fetichism apparently survived in more polished nations, in the household gods, perhaps in the Teraphim, and in the sacred stones (the Bœtylia), which were thought either to have fallen from heaven, or were sanctified by immemorial reverence.

In the Oriental pastoral tribes, Tsabaism,ᵃ the simpler worship of the heavenly bodies, in general prevailed; which among the agricultural races

---

ᵃ The Fetiche of the African is the Manitou of the American Indian. The word Fetiche was first, I believe, brought into general use in the curious volume of the President De Brosses, Du Culte des Dieux Fétiches. The word was formed by the traders to Africa, from the Portuguese, Fetisso, chose fée, enchantée, divine, ou rendant des oracles. De Brosses, p. 18.

ᵇ Hume (History of Nat. Religion) argues that a pure and philosophical theism could never be the creed of a barbarous nation struggling with want.

ᵃ The astral worship of the East is ably and clearly developed in an Excursus at the end of Gesenius's Isaiah. I use Tsabaism in its popular sense. The proper signification and limitation of the word must be sought in the profoundly learned work of Chwolsohn, die SSabier und der SSabaismus, St. Petersburg, 1856.

grew up into a more complicated system, connecting the periodical revolutions of the sun and moon with the pursuits of husbandry. It was Nature-worship, simple in its primary elements, but branching out into mythological fables, rich and diversified in proportion to the poetic genius of the people. This Nature-worship in its simpler, probably its earlier form, appears as a sort of dualism, in which the two great antagonist powers, the creative and destructive, Light and Darkness, seem contending for the sovereignty of the world, and, emblematical of moral good and evil, are occupied in pouring the full horn of fertility and blessing, or the vial of wrath and misery, upon the human race. Subordinate to, or as a modification of, these two conflicting powers, most of the Eastern races concurred in deifying the active and passive powers of generation. The sun and the earth, Osiris and Isis, formed a second dualism. And it is remarkable how widely, almost universally extended throughout the earlier world, appears the institution of a solemn period of mourning about the autumnal, and of rejoicing about the vernal, equinox.[x] The suspension, or apparent extinction of the great

<small>*Marginal note: Nature-worship.*</small>

---

[x] Plutarch, de Iside et Osiride:— Φρύγες τὸν θεὸν οἴδμενοι χειμῶνος μὲν καθεύδειν, θέρους δ' ἐγρηγορέναι, τότε μὲν κατευνασμοὺς τότε δ' ἀνεγέρσεις Βακχεύοντες αὐτῷ τελοῦσι. Παφλαγόνες δὲ καταδεῖσθαι καὶ καθείργνυσθαι χειμῶνος, ἦρος δὲ ἀναλύεσθαι φάσκουσι.

[y] Bohlen (das Alte Indien, p. 139 et seq.) gives a long list of these festivals of the sun. Lobeck (I. 690) would altogether deny their symbolical character. It is difficult, however, to account for the remarkable similarity between the usages of so many distinct nations in the New World as well as the Old, in Peru and Florida, in Gaul and Britain, as in India and Syria, without some such common origin, or a common sentiment springing from a certain kindred and identity in human nature. See Picart's large work, Cérémonies et Coutumes Religieuses, passim.

Compare likewise Dr. Pritchard's valuable work on Egyptian Mythology; on the Deification of the Active and Passive Powers of Generation;

vivifying power of nature, Osiris or Iacchus; the destitution of Ceres, Isis, or the Earth, of her husband or her beautiful daughter, torn in pieces or carried away into their realms by the malignant powers of darkness; their reappearance in all their bright and fertilising energy; these, under different forms, were the great annual fast and festival of the early heathen worship.*

But the poets were the priests of this Nature-worship; and from their creative imagination arose the popular mythology, which gave its separate deity to every part of animate or inanimate being; and, departing still farther from the primitive allegory, and the symbolic forms under which the phenomena of the visible world were embodied, wandered into pure fiction; till Nature-worship was almost supplanted by religious fable: and hence, by a natural transition, those who discerned God in every thing, multiplied every separate part of creation into a distinct divinity. The mind fluctuated between a kind of vague and unformed pantheism, the deification of the whole of nature, or its animation by one pervading power or soul, and the deification of every object which impressed the mind with awe or admiration.* While every nation, every

Poets.

---

the Marriage of the Sun and the Earth, p. 40, and pp. 62-75, and Grimm, Deutsche Mythologie, p. 144, &c.

* Nam rudis ante illos, nullo discrimine, vita
  In speciem conversa, operum ratione carebat.
  Et manifesta novo pendebat lumine mundi.
  Tum siderum cursus, tum lata regendi
  Sideribus, &c.—MANIL. L. 67.

* Some able writers are of opinion that the reverse of this was the case—

that the variety was the primary belief; the simplification the work of a later and more intellectual age. On this point A. W. Schlegel observes, "The more I investigate the ancient history of the world, the more I am convinced that the civilised nations set out from a purer worship of the Supreme Being; that the magic power of Nature over the imagination of the successive human races, first, at a later period, produced polytheism, and, finally, altogether obscured the more

tribe, every province, every town, every village, every family, had its peculiar, local, or tutelar deity, there was a kind of common neutral ground on which they all met, a notion that the gods in their collective capacity exercised a general controlling providence over the affairs of men, interfered, especially on great occasions, and, though this belief was still more vague and more inextricably involved in fable, administered retribution in another state of being. And thus even the common language of the most polytheistic nations approached to monotheism.[b]

Wherever, indeed, there has been a great priestly

---

spiritual religious notions in the popular belief; while the wise alone preserved within the sanctuary the primeval secret. Hence mythology appears to me the last developed and most changeable part of the old religion. The divergence of the various mythologies, therefore, proves nothing against the descent of the religions from a common source. The mythologies might be locally formed, according to the circumstances of climate or soil; it is impossible to mistake this with regard to the Egyptian myths." Schlegel, p. 16. Preface to Pritchard's Egyptian Mythology. My own views, considering the question in a purely historical light, coincide with those of M. Schlegel; but the solution of this question mainly depends on the former one— the primitive rudeness or earlier civilisation of man.

[b] This is strikingly expressed by a Christian writer: — "Audio vulgus cum ad coelum manus tendunt, nihil aliud quam Deum dicunt, et Deus magnus est, et Deus verus est, et si Deus dederit. Vulgi iste naturalis sermo est, an Christiani confitentis oratio?" Min. Fel. Octavius. The same thought may be found in Cyprian, de Van. Idol., and Tertullian, Apolog.

There is nothing in this brief statement irreconcileable with the view of the common development of language and mythology, or rather the growth of mythology out of expanding language—expanded with such wonderful ingenuity and surpassing erudition by M. Max Müller, Oxford Essays, 1856. That theory accounts for the common origin and descent of the myths of the whole Arian race, the kindred and similitude of which have been generally admitted; whilst the passing of these myths in their second stage through the minds of poets explains their endless diversity, their departure from their original meaning, and the perpetual loss of the key to their interpretation.

caste, less occupied with the daily toils of life, and advanced beyond the mass of the people, the primitive Nature-worship has been perpetually brought back, as it were, to its original elements; and, without disturbing the popular mythological religion, furnished a creed to the higher and more thinking part of the community, less wild and extravagant.[c] In Persia the Magian order retained or acquired something like a pure theism, in which the Supreme Deity was represented under the symbol of the primal uncreated fire; and there Nature-worship, under the form of the two conflicting principles, preserved much more of its original simplicity than in most other countries. To the influence of a distinct sacerdotal order may be traced,[d] in India, the singular union of the sublimest

---

[c] This is nowhere more openly professed than in China. The early Jesuit missionaries assert that the higher class (the literatorum secta) despised the idolatry of the vulgar. One of the charges against the Christians was their teaching the worship of one God, which they had full liberty to worship themselves, to the common people:—"Non æque placere, rudem plebeculam rerum novarum cupiditate, cœli Dominum venerari." Trigault, Exped. in Sinas, pp. 438-573.

[d] "The learned Brahmins adore one God, without form or quality, eternal, unchangeable, and occupying all space; but they carefully confine these doctrines to their own schools, as dangerous; and teach in public a religion, in which, in supposed compliance with the infirmities and passions of human nature, the deity is brought more to a level with our prejudices and wants. The incomprehensible attributes ascribed to him are invested with sensible and even human forms. The mind, lost in meditation, and fatigued in the pursuit of something, which, being divested of all sensible qualities, suffers the thoughts to wander without finding a resting-place, is happy, they tell us, to have an object on which human feelings and human senses may again find repose. To give a metaphysical deity to ignorant and sensual men, absorbed in the cares of supporting animal existence, and entangled in the impediments of matter, would be to condemn them to atheism. Such is the mode in which the Brahmins excuse the gross idolatry of their religion." William Erskine, Bombay Transactions, I. 199. Compare Colebrooke, Asiat. Res. vii. 279; and other quotations in Bohlen, Das Alte Indien, I. 153, which indeed might be multiplied without end.

allegory, and a sort of lofty poetical religious philosophy, with the most monstrous and incoherent superstitions; and the appearance of the profound political religion of Egypt in strange juxtaposition with the most debasing Fetichism, the worship of reptiles and vegetables.*

Anthropo-morphism of the Greeks. From this Nature-worship arose the beautiful anthropomorphism of the Greeks, of which the Homeric poetry, from its extensive and lasting popularity, may in one sense be considered the parent. The primitive traditions and the local superstitions of the different races were moulded together in these songs, which, disseminated throughout Greece, gave a kind of federal character to the religion of which they were, in some sort, the sacred books. But the genius of the people had already assumed its bias: few, yet still some, vestiges remain in Homer of the earlier theogonic fables.† Conscious, as it were, and prophetic

---

Mr. Mill (Hist. of India), among the ablest and most uncompromising opponents of the high view of Indian civilisation, appears to me not to pay sufficient attention to this point.

* Heeren has conjectured, with his usual ingenuity, or rather perhaps has adopted from De Brosses, the theory, that the higher part of the Egyptian religion was that of a foreign and dominant caste; the worship of plants and brutes, the original undisturbed Fetichism of the primitive and barbarous African race. (Compare Von Hammer, Geschichte der Assassinen, p. 57.) On the whole, I prefer this theory to that of Cicero (Nat. Deor. i. 36), that it was derived from mere usefulness; to the political reason suggested by Plutarch (de Isid. et Osir.); to that of Porphyry (de Abst. iv. 9), which, however, is adopted, and, I think, made more probable, by Dr. Pritchard in his Egyptian Mythology, from the transmigration of the soul into beasts; of Marsham and Warburton, from hieroglyphics; of Lucian (de Astrol.) and Dupuis, from the connexion with astronomy; or, finally, that of Bohlen (Das Alte Indien, i. 188), who traces its origin to the consecration of particular animals to particular deities among their Indian ancestors.

† Nothing can be more groundless or unsuccessful than the attempt of later writers to frame an allegorical system out of Homer; the history and design of this change are admirably traced by Lobeck, Aglaophamus, i. 158.

of their future pre-eminence in all that constitutes the physical and mental perfection of our race, this wonderful people conformed their religion to themselves. The cumbrous and multiform idol, in which wisdom, or power, or fertility, was represented by innumerable heads or arms, or breasts, as in the Ephesian Diana, was refined into a being, only distinguished from human nature by its preterhuman development of the noblest physical qualities of man. The imagination here took another and a nobler course; it threw an ideal grandeur and an unearthly loveliness over the human form, and by degrees deities became men, and men deities, or, as the distinction between the godlike ($θεοείκελος$) and the divine ($θεῖος$) became more indistinct, were united in the intermediate form of heroes and demi-gods. The character of the people here, as elsewhere, operated on the religion; the religion reacted on the popular character. The religion of Greece was the religion of the Arts, the Games, the Theatre; it was that of a race, living always in public, by whom the corporeal perfection of man had been carried to the highest point. In no other country would the legislator have taken under his protection the physical conformation, in some cases the procreation, in all the development of the bodily powers by gymnastic education; and it required the most consummate skill in the sculptor to preserve the endangered pre-eminence of the gods, in whose images were embodied the perfect models of power and grace and beauty.[f]

---

[f] Maximus Tyrius (Dissert. viii.) defends the anthropomorphism of the Greeks, and distinguishes it from the symbolic worship of barbarians. "If the soul of man is the nearest and most like to God, God would not have enclosed in an unworthy tabernacle that which bears the closest resemblance to himself." Hence he argues that God ought to be represented under the noblest form, that of man.

The religion of Rome was political and military.[k] Springing originally from a kindred stock to that of earlier Greece, the rural Gods of the first cultivators of Italy,[l] it received many of its rites from that remarkable people, the Etruscans; and rapidly adapted itself, or was forced by the legislator into an adaptation to the character of the people.[b] Mars or Gradivus was the divine ancestor of the race.[m] The religious calendar was the early history of the people; a large part of the festivals was not so much the celebration of the various deities, as the commemoration of the great events in their annals.[n] The priesthood was united with the highest civil and military offices; and the great occupation of Roman worship seems to have been to secure the stability of her constitution, and still more, to give a religious character to her wars, and infuse a religious confidence of success into her legionaries. The great office of the diviners, whether augurs or aruspices, was to choose the fortunate day of battle; the Fetiales, religious officers, denounced war: the

---

[k] Dionysius Halicarn. compares the grave and serious character of the Roman as contrasted with the Greek religion. The Romans rejected many of the more obscene and monstrous fables of the Greeks. But it is as part of the civil polity that he chiefly admires the Roman religion, lib. II. c. 7.

[l] The Palilia and other rural rites. The statues of the goddesses Seja and Segesta, of seed and of harvest, stood in the great Circus in the time of Pliny, H. N. xviii. 2.

[b] Beaufort's République Romaine, t. I. ch. 5. Compare the recent and valuable work of Walter, Geschichte des Römischen Rechts, p. 177.

[m] Ex tanero motu cinxere Martem colonæ priores,
Hæc dederat studiis bellica turba suis.
After reciting the national deities of other cities, the religious poet of Rome proceeds,
Mars Latio venerandus erat; quia præsidet armis,
Arma ferm genti remoque decusque dabant.
Ovid, Fasti, iii. 10.

The month of Mars began the year. Ibid.

[n] Compare the proportion of Roman and of religious legend in the Fasti of Ovid. See, likewise, Constant, i. 21, &c. Also the section in Hartung, Vom Staat als Kirche, i. p. 205 et seqq.

standards and eagles possessed a kind of sanctity; the eagle was in fact a shrine.° The altar had its place in the centre of the camp, as the ark of God in that of the Israelites. The Triumph may be considered as the great religious ceremony of the nation; the god Terminus, who never receded, was, as it were, the deified ambition of Rome. At length Rome herself was impersonated and assumed her rank in heaven, as it were the representative of the all-conquering and all-ruling republic.

There was a stronger moral element in the Roman religion, than in that of Greece.^p In Greece the gods had been represented, in their collective capacity, as the avengers of great crimes; a kind of general retributive justice was assigned to them; they guarded the sanctity of oaths. But in the better days of the Republic, Rome had, as it were, deified her own virtues. Temples arose to Concord, to Faith, to Constancy, to Modesty (Pudor), to Hope. The Penates, the household deities, became the guardians of domestic happiness. Venus Verticordia presided over the purity of domestic morals,^q and Jupiter Stator over courage. But the true national character of the Roman theology is most remarkably shown in the various temples and various attributes assigned to the good Fortune of the city, who might appear the Deity of Patriotism.^r Even Peace was at length re-

Moral Element of Roman Religion.

° Ὁ γὰρ ἀετὸς ὀνομασμένος (ἐστὶ δὲ πρὸς μικρὸς) καὶ ἐν αὐτῷ ἀετὸς χρυσοῦς ἱδρυται. Dion. Cass. xl. c. 18. Gibbon, i. 18. Moyle's Works, ii. 66. Compare Tac. Ann. i. 39.

^p The distinction between the Roman and Greek religions is drawn with singular felicity in the two supplemental (in my opinion the most valuable and original), but unfortunately unfinished, volumes of M. Constant, Du Polytheisme Romain.

^q The most virtuous woman in Rome was chosen to dedicate her statue. Val. Max. viii. 15.

^r Constant, L. 16.

ceived among the gods of Rome. And as long as the worship of the heart continued to sanctify these impersonations of human virtues, their adoration tended to maintain the lofty moral tone; but so soon as that was withdrawn or languished into apathy, the deities became cold abstractions, without even that reality which might appear to attach itself to the other gods of the city: their temples stood, their rites were perhaps solemnised, but they had ceased to command, and no longer received, the active veneration of the people. What, in fact, is the general result of the Roman religious calendar, half a year of which is described in the Fasti of Ovid? There are festivals founded on old Italian and on picturesque Grecian legends; others commemorative of the great events of the heroic days of the Republic; others instituted in base flattery of the ruling dynasty; one ceremonial only, that of the Manes,[*] which relates to the doctrine of another life, and that preserved as it were from pride, and as a memorial of older times. Nothing can show more strongly the nationality of the Roman religion, and its almost complete transmutation from a moral into a political power.[†]

Religion of the Jews. Amidst all this labyrinth we behold the sacred secret of the divine Unity, preserved inviolate, though sometimes under the most adverse circumstances, and, as it were, perpetually hovering on the verge of extinction, in one narrow district of the world,

---

[*] II. 533. The Lemuria (Remuria) were instituted to appease the shade of Remus, V. 451, &c.

Ovid applies on another occasion his general maxim

Pro magnâ teste vetustas
Creditur: acceptam parce movere fidem.
Fasti, IV. 2—4.

[†] See the fine description of Majestas (Fasti, v. 25–52), who becomes at the end the tutelar deity of the senate and matrons, and presides over the triumphs of Rome.

the province of Palestine. Nor is it there the recondite treasure of a high and learned caste, or the hardly worked-out conclusion of the thinking and philosophical few, but the plain and distinct groundwork of the popular creed. Still, even there, as though in its earlier period, the yet undeveloped mind of man was unfit for the reception, or at least for the preservation of this doctrine, in its perfect spiritual purity; as though the Deity condescended to the capacities of the age, and it were impossible for the divine nature to maintain its place in the mind of man without some visible representative; a kind of symbolic worship still enshrines the one great God of the Mosaic religion. There is a striking analogy between the Shechinah[a] or luminous appearance which "dwelt between the cherubim," and the pure immaterial fire of the Theism, which approaches nearest to the Hebrew, that of the early Persians. Yet even here likewise is found the great indelible distinction between the religion of the ancient and of the modern world; the characteristic, which besides the general practice of propitiating the Deity, usually by animal sacrifices, universally prevails in the præ-Christian ages. The physical predominates over the moral character of the Deity. God is *Power* in the old religion; He is *Love* under the new.[x] Nor does his pure and essential spirituality, in the more complete faith of the Gospel, attach itself to, or exhibit

_{God under the old and the new Religion.}

---

[a] Even if the notion of a visible Shechinah was of a later period (note to Heber's Bampton Lectures, p. 278), God was universally believed to have a local and personal residence behind the veil, in the unapproachable Holy of Holies; and the imagination would thus be even more powerfully excited than by a visible symbol.

[x] Hartung, Religion der Römer, l. 10, has worked out this notion. This book did not come into my hands till after the publication of my first edition.

itself under any form. "God," says the Divine Author of Christianity, "is a Spirit, and they that worship him, must worship him in spirit and in truth." In the early Jewish worship, it was the physical power of the Deity which was chiefly and perpetually presented to the mind of the worshipper: he was their temporal king, the dispenser of earthly blessings, famine and plenty, drought and rain, discomfiture or success in war. The miracles recorded in the Old Testament, particularly in the earlier books, are amplifications, as it were, or new directions of the powers of nature; as if the object were to show that the deities of other nations were but subordinate and obedient instruments in the hand of the great self-existent Being, the Jehovah of Jewish worship.

Yet, when it is said that the physical rather than the moral character of the Deity *predominated*, it must not be supposed that the latter was altogether excluded. It is impossible entirely to dissociate the notion of moral government from that belief, or that propensity to believe, in the existence of a God, implanted in the human mind; and religion was too useful an ally not to be called in to confirm the consciously imperfect authority of human law. But it may be laid down as a principle that the nearer the nation approaches to barbarism, the childhood of the human race, the more earthly are the conceptions of the Deity; the moral aspect of the divine nature seems gradually to develope itself with the development of the human mind. It is at first, as in Egypt and India, the prerogative of the higher class; the vulgar are left to their stocks and their stones, their animals and their reptiles. In the republican states of Greece, the intellectual aristocracy of the philosophers, guarded by no such legally established distinction, rarely dared openly to assert their superiority, but concealed their more extended views behind a prudential veil, as a secret or esoteric doctrine, and by studious conformity to the national rites and ceremonies.

Gradually, however, as the period approaches in which the religion of civilisation is to be introduced into the great drama of human life, as we descend nearer towards the point of separation between the ancient and modern world, the human mind appears expanding. Polytheism is evidently relaxing its hold upon all classes: the monarch maintains his throne, not from the deep-rooted, or rational, or conscientious loyalty of his subjects, but from the want of a competitor; because mankind were habituated to a government which the statesman thought it might be dangerous, and the philosopher, enjoying perfect toleration, and rather proud of his distinctive superiority than anxious to propagate his opinions throughout the world, did not think it worth while, at the hazard of popular odium, to disturb. *[Preparation for new Religion seen in the Heathen World.]*

Judaism gave manifest indications of a preparation for a more essentially spiritual, more purely moral faith. The symbolic presence of the Deity (according to their own tradition [f]) ceased with the temple of Solomon; and the heathen world beheld with astonishment a whole race whose deity was represented under no visible form or likeness. The Prophets, in their spiritual as in their moral tone, rose high above the Law. The conqueror Pompey, who enters the violated temple, is filled with wonder at finding the sanctuary without image or emblem of the presiding deity;[g] *[Among the Jews.]*

---

[f] Hist. of the Jews, I. 423.   [g] Ib. ii. 47.

the poet describes them as worshipping nothing but the clouds and the divinity that fills the Heaven;[a] the philosophic historian, whose profounder mind seems struggling with hostile prejudices, defines, with his own inimitable compression of language, the doctrine, to the sublimity of which he has closed his eyes. "The worship of the Jews is purely mental; they acknowledge but one God—and that God supreme and eternal, neither changeable nor perishable."[b] The doctrine of another life (which derived no sanction from the Law, and was naturally obscured by the more immediate and intelligible prospect of temporal rewards and punishments) dawns in the prophetic writings; and from the apocryphal books and from Josephus, as well as from the writings of the New Testament, clearly appears to have become incorporated with the general sentiment. Retribution in another life has already taken the place of the immediate or speedy avenging or rewarding providence of the Deity in the land of Canaan.[c]

Judaism, however, only required to expand with the expansion of the human mind; its sacred records had preserved in its original simplicity the notion of the Divine Power; the pregnant definitions of the one great self-existing Being, the magnificent poetical amplifications of his might and providence were of all ages: they were eternal poetry, because they were eternal truth. If the moral aspect of the Divine nature was more obscurely intimated, and, in this respect, had assumed the character of a local or national Deity, whose love was confined to the chosen

---

[a] Nil præter nubes et cœli numen adorant. Jev. Sat. xiv. 9.

[b] Judæi mente sola, unumque numen intelligunt. . . . Summum illud et æternum, neque mutabile, neque interiturum. Tac. Hist. v. 5.

[c] See Chap. II., in which this question is resumed.

people, and displayed itself chiefly in the beneficence of a temporal sovereign: yet nothing was needed but to give a higher and more extensive sense to those types and shadows of universal wisdom; an improvement which the tendency of the age manifestly required; and which the Jews themselves, especially the Alexandrian school, had already attempted, by allegorising the whole annals of their people, and extracting a profound moral meaning from all the circumstances of their extraordinary history.[a]

But the progress of knowledge was fatal to the popular religion of Greece and Rome. The awe-struck imagination of the older race, which had listened with trembling belief to the wildest fables, the deep feeling of the sublime and the beautiful, which, uniting with national pride, had assembled adoring multitudes before the Parthenon or the Jove of Phidias, now gave place to cold and sober reason. Poetry had been religion—religion was becoming mere poetry. Humanizing the Deity, and bringing it too near the earth, naturally produced, in a less imaginative and more reflecting age, that familiarity which destroys respect. When man became more acquainted with his own nature, the less was he satisfied with deities cast in his own mould. In some respects the advancement of civilisation had no doubt softened and purified the old religions from their savage and licentious ten-

Effects of progress of knowledge upon polytheism.

Beneficial.

---

[a] Philo wrote for the unbelievers among his own people, and to conciliate the Greeks. (De Conf. Linguar. vol. i. p. 405.) The same principle which among the heathens gave rise to the system of Euhemerus, who resolved all mythology into history, and that of the other philosophers who attempted to reduce it to allegory, induced Philo, and no doubt his predecessor Aristobulus, thus to endeavour to accommodate the Mosaic history to an incredulous age, and to blend Judaism and Platonism into one harmonious system.

dencies. Human sacrifices had ceased,* or had retired to the remotest parts of Germany, or to the shores of the Baltic.† Though some of the secret rites were said

---

* Human sacrifices sometimes, but rarely, occur in the earlier periods of Grecian history. According to Plutarch, Vit. Arist. 9, and Vit. Themistoclis, three sons of Sandauke, sister of the king of Persia, were offered, in obedience to an oracle, to Bacchus Omestes. The blood-stained altar of Diana of Tauris was placed by the tragedians in a barbarous region. Prisoners were sometimes slain on the tombs of warriors in much later times, as in the Homeric age, even on that of Philopœmen. Plut. Vit. Philop. c. 21. Compare Tschirner, Fall des Heidenthums, p. 34.

Octavius is said (Suet. Vit. Octav.) to have sacrificed 300 Perugian captives on an altar sacred to the deified Julius (Divo Julio). This may be considered the sanguinary spirit of the age of proscriptions taking for once a more solemn and religious form. As to the libation of the blood of the gladiators (see Tertullian, Apolog. c. 9. Scorpiac. 7. Cyprian, De Spectaculis. Compare Porphyr. de Abstin. Lactant. 1-21) I should agree with M. Constant in ascribing this ceremony to the barbarity of the Roman amusements rather than to their religion. All public spectacles were, perhaps, to a certain degree religious ceremonies; but the gladiators were the victims of the sanguinary pleasures of the Roman people, not slain in honour of their gods. Constant, iv. 335. Tschirner, p. 45.

† Tac. Ann. i. 61. Tac. Germ. 10, 40. Compare on the gradual abolition of human sacrifices, Constant, iv. 330. The exception, which rests on the authority of Pliny, xxviii, 2, and of Plutarch, Vit. Maril, in init. Quæst. Rom. appears to me very doubtful. The prohibitory law of Lentulus, A.U. DCLVII., " minime Romano Sacro," lib. xiii. 57, and Livy's striking expression concerning the sacrifice, A.U. 536, said to be continued to a late period, as well as the edict of Tiberius, promulgated in the remoter provinces, indicate the general sentiment of the time. Non satis æstimari potest quantum Romanis debeatur, qui sustulere monstra in quibus hominem occidere religiosissimum erat, mandi vero saluberrimum. Plin. H. N. xxx. 1. See in Ovid, Fasti, iii. 341, the reluctance of Numa to offer human sacrifice. Hadrian issued an edict prohibiting human sacrifices; this was directed, according to Creuzer (Symb. i. 363), against the later Mithrine rites, which had reintroduced the horrible practice of consulting futurity in the entrails of human victims. The savage Commodus (Lamprid. in Comm.) offered a human victim to Mithra. The East, if the accounts are to be credited, continually reacted on the religion of Rome. Human sacrifices are said to have taken place under Aurelian (Aug. Hist. Vit. Aurel.), and even under Maxentius. I add, as the subject is of great interest and importance, and as the erroneous view is held in a book so justly popular as Giesler's Handbook of Church History, some further observations. " M. de

to be defiled with unspeakable pollutions,[f] yet this, if true, arose from the depravation of manners, rather than

Fontenelle is mistaken when he thinks the Romans prohibited the Carthaginians by treaty from offering any more human sacrifices. The original treaties between these powerful republics are still extant in Polybius and Livy. I need only refer to them. Gelon, tyrant of Syracuse, is indeed reported (though not on the very best authority) to have imposed that humane condition after the battle of Himera (V. Diodor. Sic. xi. 21, et Wesseling ad loc.). M. de Fontenelle is pleased to accuse the Romans of contradicting their own practice, since they sacrificed a man every year to Jupiter Latiaris. But I shall not believe upon the words only of Porphyry, Lactantius, and Prudentius, that human sacrifices were ever a regular part of Roman worship." Gibbon, Miscellaneous Works, v. 582.

Lord Stanhope has printed a correspondence between Sir Robert Peel and Lord Macaulay on this subject. Neither of these distinguished men had profoundly investigated the subject, nor were aware how much had been written upon it. Each wrote from his general reading. But two such men could not but arrive at the same just conclusion. Sir Robert uses the convincing argument, "Surely, if it had been the annual usage in Rome to offer human sacrifices to Jupiter, Cicero could never have uttered these words, 'Quidquam Gallis sanctum ac religiosum videri potest? Qui etiam si quando aliquo metu adducti, Deos placandos arbitrantur, humanis hostiis eorum aras funestant ut ne religionem quidem colere possint, nisi eam ipsam scelere violarint. Quis enim ignorat eos usque ad hunc diem retinere illam immanem ac barbaram consuetudinem hominum immolandorum?' Pro Fonteio, 10." Lord Macaulay replies by citing the description of the rites of Jupiter Latiaris from Dionysius Hal., from which it appears that the offerings were lambs, cheeses, and milk. "Now can anybody believe that Dionysius, who had been at Rome, could have written thus, if a human sacrifice had been part of the rites?" ... "But observe that Cicero himself had officiated as consul at the feast of Jupiter Latiaris. He described the solemnity incidentally in his poem on his own consulship. You will find the passage in the Book de Divinatione. He introduces Urania speaking to him—

Tu quoque cum tumulos Albano in monte nivales
Lustrasti, et lacte mactasti lacte Latinas.

This mention of milk equally agrees with Dionysius' account. But can you believe that on this occasion Cicero sacrificed a man, and then described it as performed 'lacte lacte'? In short, do you believe that Cicero ever sacrificed a man?"

Neither Sir Robert nor Lord Macaulay seems to have been aware of the Senatus Consultum of Lentulus, "ne homo immolaretur," Pliny, xxx. 1. That law was no doubt directed against the newly-subjugated and barbarous nations, Iberians, Gauls, and implies its long disuse in Rome, and that it was abhorrent to Roman feeling.

[f] The dissolute rites against which

from religion. The orgies of the Bona Dea were a profanation of the sacred rite, held up to detestation by the indignant satirist, not as among some of the early Oriental nations, the rite itself.

But with the tyranny, which could thus extort from reluctant human nature the sacrifice of all humanity and all decency, the older religions had lost their more salutary, and, if the expression may be ventured, their constitutional authority. They had been driven away, or silently receded from their post, in which indeed they had never been firmly seated, as conservators of public morals. The circumstances of the times tended no less to loosen the bonds of the ancient faith. Peace enervated the deities, as well as the soldiers of Rome: their occupation was gone;[b] the augurs read no longer the signs of conquest in the entrails of the victims; and though down to the days of Augustine,[f] Roman pride clung to the worship of the older and glorious days of the Republic, and denounced the ingratitude of forsaking gods, under whose tutelary sway Rome

Prejudicial

---

the Fathers inveigh were of foreign and Oriental origin—Isiac, Bacchanalian, Mithriac. Lobeck, I. 197. See Constant, vol. iv. c. 11. Compare the Confession of Hispala in Livy. I cannot refrain from transcribing an observation of M. Constant on these rites, which strikes me as extremely profound and just: "La mauvaise influence des fables licencieuses commence avec le mépris et le ridicule versé sur ces fables. Il en est de même des cérémonies. Des rites indécens peuvent être pratiqués par un peuple religieux avec une grande pureté de cœur. Mais quand l'incrédulité atteint ces peuples, ces rites sont pour lui la cause et la prétexte de la plus révoltante corruption." Du Polyth. Rom. II. 102.

[b] Our generals began to wage civil wars against each other, as soon as they neglected the auspices. Cic. Nat. Deor. ii. 3. This is good evidence to the fact; the cause lay deeper.

[f] This was the main argument of his great work, de Civitate Dei. It is nowhere more strongly expressed than in the oration of Symmachus to Theodosius. Hic cultus in leges meas orbem redegit; hæc sacra Annibalem a mœnibus, a Capitolio Sennonas repulerunt. This subject will frequently recur in the course of our History.

had become the empress of the world, yet the ceremonies had now no stirring interest; they were pageants in which the unbelieving aristocracy played their parts with formal coldness, the contagion of which could not but spread to the lower classes. The only novel or exciting rite of the Roman religion was that which probably tended more than any other, when the immediate excitement was over, to enfeeble the religious feeling, the deification [a] of the living, or the apotheosis of the dead emperor, whom a few years or perhaps a few days abandoned to the open execration or contempt of the whole people. At the same time that energy of mind, which had consumed itself in foreign conquest or civil faction, in carrying the arms of Rome to the Euphrates or the Rhine, or in the mortal conflict for patrician or plebeian supremacy, now that the field of military or civil distinction was closed, turned inward and preyed upon itself; or, compressed by the iron hand of despotism, made itself a vent in philosophical or religious speculations. The noble mind sought a retreat from the degradation of servitude in the groves of the Academy, or

---

[a] The deification of Augustus found some opponents. Nihil Deorum honoribus relictum, cum se templis et effigie numinum, per flamines et sacerdotes coli vellet. Tac. Ann. I. 10. The more sagacious Tiberius shrunk from such honours. In one instance, he allowed himself to be joined in divine honours with his mother and the senate, but in general he refused them. Tac. Ann. iv. 15, 37, v. 2. The very curious satire of Seneca, the Αποκολοκυντωσις, though chiefly aimed at Claudius, throws ridicule on the whole ceremony. Augustus, in his speech to the gods, says, Denique dum talea deos facitis, nemo vos deos esse credet. A later writer complains —Aliquanti pari libidine in coelestium numerum referuntur, egre exequiis digni. Aur. Victor, Cæsar, in Gallieno. M. Ranke, in the first chapter of whose admirable work (Die Römischen Papste) I am not displeased to find some coincidences of view, even of expression, with my own, seems to think that much of the strength of the old religion lay in the worship of the emperor. I am not disposed to think so ill of human nature.

attempted to find consolation for the loss of personal dignity, by asserting with the Stoic the dignity of human nature.[m]

Philosophy. But Philosophy aspired in vain to fill that void in the human mind, which had been created by the expulsion or secession of religion. The objects of Philosophy were twofold: either—1. To refine the popular religion into a more rational creed; or, 2. To offer itself as a substitute. With this first view it endeavoured to bring back the fables to their original meaning,[a] to detect the latent truth under the allegoric shell: but in many cases the key was lost, or the fable had wandered so far from its primary sense as to refuse all rational interpretation; and where the truth had been less encumbered with fiction, it came forth cold and inanimate. The philosopher could strip off the splendid robes in which the moral or religious doctrine had been disguised, but he could not instil into it the breath of life. The imagination refused the unnatural alliance of cold and calculating reason; and the religious feeling, when it saw the old deities reduced into ingenious allegories, sank into apathy; or vaguely yearned for

---

[m] Cicero, no doubt, speaks the language of many of the more elevated minds when he states that he took refuge in philosophy from the afflictions of life at that dark period of civil contention. Hortata etiam est, ut me ad hæc conferrem, animi ægritudo, magnâ et gravi commota injuriâ: cujus si majorem aliquam levationem reperire potuissem, non ad hæc potissimum confugissem. De Nat. Deor. i. 4.

[a] Πραγμάτων ὑπ' ἀνθρωπίνης ἀσθενείας οὐ καθορωμένων σαφὼς εὐσχημονέστερος ἑρμηνεὺς ὁ μῦθος. Max. Tyr., Dissert. X. The whole essay is intended to prove that poetry and philosophy held the same doctrine about the gods. This process, it should be observed, though it had already commenced, was not carried to its height until philosophy and polytheism coalesced again, from the sense of their common danger, and endeavoured to array a system composed of the most rational and attractive parts of both, against the encroachments of Christianity.

THE MYSTERIES.

some new excitement, which it knew not from what quarter to expect.

The last hopes of the ancient religion lay in the Mysteries. Of them alone the writers, about the time of the appearance of Christianity, speak with uniform reverence, if not with awe. They alone could bestow happiness in life, and hope in death.[c] In these remarkable rites[p] the primitive Nature-worship had survived under a less refined and less humanized form; the original and more simple symbolic forms (those of the first agricultural inhabitants of Greece[q]) had been retained by ancient reverence: as its allegory was less intricate and obscure,[r] it accommodated itself better with the advancing spirit of the age. It may indeed be questioned whether the Mysteries did not owe much of their influence to their secrecy, and to the impressive forms under which they shadowed forth their more recondite truths.[s] These, if they did not satisfy, yet kept the mind in a state of progressive and continued

The Mysteries.

---

[c] Neque solum cum lætitiâ vivendi rationem accipimus, sed etiam cum spe meliore moriendi. Cic. de Leg. ii. 14. The theory of Warburton on the Mysteries is now universally exploded; but neither, with the utmost deference to his erudition, can I enter altogether into the views of Lobeck. In my judgment his quotations do not bear him out, as to the publicity of the ceremonies; nor can I conceive that there was none, or scarcely any, secret.

——— Vetabo qui Cereris sacrum
Vulgarit arcanæ, sub iisdem
Sit trabibus, fragilemque mecum
Solvat phaselum.—Hor. Carm. iii. 2.

[p] The theories of Maier, Warburton, Plass &c, Boulanger, Dupuis, Meiners,

Villoison, P. Knight, Heeren, St. Croix, Creuzer, may be found briefly stated, Lobeck, L. 6, 8.

[q] Quibus explicatis, ad rationem que revocatis, rerum magis natura cognoscitur, quam deorum. Cic. de Nat. Deor. L. 42.

[r] See Varro's View of the Eleusinian Mysteries, preserved by Augustine, De Civ. Dei, vii. 15.

[s] Ἀγρυπνία σημείοτης ἐπὶ τελετῶν καὶ νῦν διὰ τοῦτο τυντελοῦται τὰ μυστήρια, καὶ ἄβατα συλᾶται διὰ τοῦτο ὁρᾶττεται, καιροὶ καὶ τόποι πρὸντειν εἰδότες ἀξιοτεωρίαν ἵκοον. Synes. de Prov. Compare the splendid passage in Dio. Chrys. Orat. 12.

excitement. They were, if it may be so said, a great religious drama, in which the initiated were at once spectators and actors; where the fifth act was designedly delayed to the utmost possible point, and of this still suspended catastrophe, the dramatis personæ, the only audience, were kept in studied ignorance.[t] The Mysteries had, perhaps, from an early period associated a moral[u] purport with their sacred shows; and with the progress of opinion, the moral would more and more predominate over the primitive religious meaning.[x] Yet the morality of the Mysteries was apparently that of the ancient Nature-worship of the East. It taught the immortality of the soul as a part of that vast system of nature, which, emanating from the Supreme Being, passed through a long course of deterioration or refinement, and at length returned and resolved itself into the primal source of all existence. But the Mysteries, from their very nature, could only act upon the public mind in a limited manner:[y] directly they ceased to be mysteries they lost their power.[z] Nor can it be doubted, that while

---

[t] Non semel quædam sacra traduntur: Eleusis servat, quod ostendat revisentibus. Rerum natura sacra sua non simul tradit. Initiatos nos credimus: in vestibulo ejus hæremus. Sen. Nat. Quæst. vii. 31. Ut opinionem suspendio cognitionis ædificent, atque ita tantam majestatem adhibere videantur, quantum præstruxerunt cupiditatem. Tert. adv. Valent. c. 1.

[u] Pindar, Frag. 116. Sophocles, Fragm. Luc. LVIII. Isoc. Pan. VII. Plato, Men.

[x] Even Lobeck allows this of the Eleusinian Mysteries—Sacerdotes interdum aliquid de metempsychosi νίκιασε largiar. l. 73.

[y] The Jews were forbidden to be initiated in the Mysteries. In the Greek text of the LXX., a text was interpolated or mistranslated (Deut. xxiii. 17), in which Moses, by an anachronism not uncommon in the Alexandrian school, was made distinctly to condemn these peculiar rites of paganism.

[z] Philo demands why, if they are so useful, they are not public: "Nature makes all her most beautiful and splendid works, her heaven and all her stars, for the sight of all; her seas, fountains, and rivers, the annual temperature of the air, and the winds, the innumerable tribes and races of

the local and public Mysteries, particularly the greatest of all, the Eleusinian, were pure and undefiled by licentiousness, and, if they retained any of the obscene symbols, disguised or kept them in the back ground; the private and moveable mysteries, which, under the conduct of vagabond priests, were continually flowing in from the East, displayed those symbols in unblushing nakedness, and gave occasion for the utmost licence and impurity.[a]

II. Philosophy as a substitute for religion was still more manifestly deficient. For, in the first place, it was unable, or condescended not, to reach the body of the people, whom the progress of civilisation was slowly bringing up towards the common level; and where it found or sought proselytes, it spoke without authority, and distracted with the multitude of its conflicting sects the patient but bewildered inquirer.[b] Philosophy maintained the aristocratic tone, which, while it declared that to a few elect spirits alone it was possible to communicate the highest secrets of knowledge, more particularly the mystery of the great Supreme Being, proclaimed it vain and unwise to attempt to elevate the many to such exalted speculations.[c] "The Father of

Philosophy.

---

animals, and fruits of the earth, for the common use of man—why then are the Mysteries confined to a few, and those not always the most wise and most virtuous?" This is the general sense of a long passage, vol. ii. p. 260. Ed. Mangey.

[a] The republic severely prohibited these practices, which were unknown in its earlier and better days. Dionys. Hal. ii. viii.

[b] 'Ὁρᾷς τὸ πλῆθος τῶν σωθημάτων; τῇ τις τράπηται; ποίον αὐτῶν καταλέξομεν; τίνι πεισθῶ τῶν παραγγελμάτων; Max. Tyr. xxiv. sub fin.

[c] Neander has likewise quoted several of the same authorities adduced in the following passage. See the translation of Neander, which had not been announced when the above was written. It is curious that Strabo remarks, on another point, the similarity of the Indian opinions to Platonism, and treats them all as μύθοι:— Παραπλέκουσι δὲ καὶ μύθους, ὥσπερ καὶ Πλάτων, περί τε ἀφθαρσίας ψυχῆς, καὶ τῶν καθ' ᾅδου κρίσεων καὶ ἄλλα τοιαῦτα. L. xv. p. 713.

the worlds," says Plato in this tone, "it is difficult to discover, and, when discovered, it is impossible to make him known to all." So, observes a German historian of Christianity, think the Brahmins of India. Plato might aspire to the creation of an imaginary republic, which, if it could possibly be realised, might stand alone, an unapproachable model of the physical and moral perfection of man; but the amelioration of the whole world, the simultaneous elevation of all nations, orders, and classes to a higher degree of moral advancement, would have been a vision from which even his imagination would have shrunk in despair. This remained to be conceived and accomplished by one who appeared to the mass of mankind in his own age, as a peasant of Palestine.

It cannot be denied that, to those whom it deigned to address, philosophy was sufficiently accommodating; and whatever the bias of the individual mind, the school was open, and the teacher at hand, to lead the inquirer, either to the luxurious gardens of Epicurus, or among the loftier spirits of the Porch. In the two prevalent systems of philosophy, the Epicurean and the Stoic, appears a striking assimilation to the national character of the two predominant races which constituted the larger part of the Roman world. The Epicurean, with its subtle metaphysics, its abstract notion of the Deity, its imaginative materialism, its milder and more pleasurable morals, and perhaps its propensity to degenerate into indolence and sensuality, was kindred and congenial to that of Greece, and the Grecian part of the Roman society. The Stoic, with its more practical character, its mental strength and self-confidence, its fatalism, its universally diffused and all-

Varieties of philosophic systems.

Epicureanism accordant to Greek character.

Stoicism to Roman.

governing Deity, the soul of the universe (of which the political power of the all-ruling republic might appear an image), bore the same analogy to that of Rome. While the more profound thinkers, who could not disguise from themselves the insufficiency of the grounds on which the philosophical systems rested, either settled into a calm and contented scepticism, or, with the Academics, formed an eclectic creed from what appeared the better parts of the rest. {Academics}

Such on all the great questions of religion, the divine nature, providence, the origin and future being of the soul,[d] was the floating and uncertain state of the human mind. In the department of morals, Philosophy nobly performed her part; but perhaps her success in this respect more clearly displayed her inefficiency. The height to which moral science was carried in the works of Cicero, Seneca, Epictetus, and Marcus Antoninus, while it made the breach still wider between the popular religion and the advanced state of the human mind, more vividly displayed the want of a faith, which would associate itself with the purest and loftiest morality; and remarry, as it were, those thoughts and feelings which connect man with a future state of being, to the practical duties of life.[e]

---

[d] Augustine, speaking of the great work of Varro, concludes thus:—In hac tota serie pulcherrimæ et subtilissimæ disputationis, vitam æternam frustra quæri et sperari, facillime apparet. Civ. Dei, vi. 3.

[e] Gibbon and many other writers (Law, Theory of Religion, 127, 130; Sumner, Evidences, p. 70) have adduced the well-known passages from Sallust and Cicero, which indicate the general state of feeling on the great question of the immortality of the soul. There is a striking passage in a writer whose works have lately come to light through the industry of Angelo Mai. The author is endeavouring to find consolation for the loss of a favourite grandson: Si maxime eæ animæ immortales constet, exit hoc philosophis disserendi argumentum, non ægrotibus desiderandi remedium. Front. de Nep. Ambs.

For while these speculations occupied the loftier and more thinking minds, what remained for the vulgar of the higher and of the lower orders? Philosophy had shaken the old edifice to its base; and even if it could have confined its more profound and secret doctrines within the circle of its own elect, if its contempt for the old fables of the popular creed had been more jealously guarded, it is impossible but that the irreligion of the upper order must work downwards upon the lower. When religion has, if not avowedly, yet manifestly, sunk into an engine of state policy, its most imposing and solemn rites will lose all their commanding life and energy. Actors will perform ill who do not feel their parts. "It is marvellous," says the Epicurean in Cicero, "that one soothsayer (Haruspex) can look another in the face without laughing." And when the Epicurean himself stood before the altar, in the remarkable language of Plutarch, "he hypocritically enacted prayer and adoration from fear of the many; he uttered words directly opposite to his philosophy. While he sacrifices, the ministering priest seems to him no more than a cook, and he departs uttering the line of Menander, 'I have sacrificed to Gods in whom I have no concern.'"[f]

Philosophy fatal to popular religion.

Unless indeed the literature as well as the philosophy of the age immediately preceding Christianity had been confined to the intellectual aristocracy, the reasoning spirit, which rejected with disdain the old imaginative fables, could not but descend at least as low as the rudiments of liberal education. When the gravest writers, like Polybius and Strabo,

Literature.

---

[f] Quoted also by Neander from Plutarch. (Non poss. suav. viv. sec. Epic.) I have adopted Reiske's reading of the latter clause.

find it necessary to apologise to their more learned and thinking readers for the introduction of those mythic legends which formed the creed of their ancestors; and to plead the necessity of avoiding offence, because such tales are still sacred among the vulgar, this deference shows rather the increasing indifference, than the strength of popular opinion. "Historians," says the former writer, "must be pardoned, if for the sake of maintaining piety among the many, they occasionally introduce miraculous or fabulous tales; but they must not be permitted on these points to run into extravagance." "Religion," he declares in another passage, " would perhaps be unnecessary in a commonwealth of wise men. But since the multitude is ever fickle, full of lawless desires, irrational passions and violence, it is right to restrain it by the fear of the invisible world, and such tragic terrors. Whence our ancestors appear to have introduced notions concerning the Gods, and opinions about the infernal regions, not rashly or without consideration. Those rather act rashly and inconsiderately who would expel them."[s] "It is impossible," observes the inquiring geographer, "to govern a mob of women, or the whole mixed multitude, by philosophic reasoning, and to exhort them to piety, holiness, and faith; we must also employ superstition with its fables and prodigies. For the thunder, the ægis, the trident, the torches, the serpents, the thyrsi of the Gods are fables, as is all the ancient theology; but the legislature introduced these things as bugbears to those who are children in understanding."[a] In short even when the Roman writers professed the utmost respect for the religious institutions of their country,

---

[s] Polyb. vi. 56.   [a] Strabo, lib. 1. p. 19.

there was a kind of silent protest against their sincerity. It was an evident, frequently an avowed, condescension to the prejudices of the vulgar. Livy admires the wisdom of Numa, who introduced the fear of the Gods, as a "most efficacious means of controlling an ignorant and barbarous populace."¹ Even the serious Dionysius judges of religion according to its usefulness, not according to its truth, as the wise scheme of the legislator, rather than as the revelation of the Deity.ᵏ Pausanias, while he is making a kind of religious survey of Greece, expressing a grave veneration for all the temples and rites of antiquity, frequently relating the miraculous intervention of the several deities,ᵐ is jealous and careful lest he should be considered a believer in the fables which he relates.ⁿ The natural consequence of this double doctrine was not unforeseen. "What," says the Academic in Cicero, "when men maintain all belief in the immortal Gods to have been invented by wise men for the good of the state, that religion might lead to their duty those who would not be led by reason, do they not sweep away the very foundations of all religion?"ᵒ

Future Life. The mental childhood of the human race was passing away, at least it had become wearied of its old toys.ᵖ The education itself, by which, accord-

---

¹ H. n. i. 19.
ᵏ Ant. Rom. ii. 8, 9.
ᵐ Bœotica, 25; Laconica, 4.
ⁿ Τοῦτον τὸν λόγον, καὶ ὅσα ἐοικότα εἴρηται, οὐκ ἀποδεχόμενος γράφω, γράφω δὲ οὐδὲν ἧσσον. Corinth. xvii. In another place he repeats that he gives the popular legend as he finds it. Arcad. viii.
ᵒ De Nat. Deor. i. 42. Compare the chapter of the De Civitate Dei, vi. 10, in which Augustine, after citing some remarkable passages from Seneca, concludes—Sed ille quem philosophiæ quasi liberum fecerat, quia illustris populi Romani senator erat, colebat quod repudiabat, agebat quod arguebat, quod culpabat, adorabat.

ᵖ Gibbon has a striking sentence in his juvenile Essai sur la Littérature (Misc. Works, iv. 61); "Les Romains étaient éclairés: cependant ces mêmes

ing to these generally judicious writers, the youthful mind was to be impregnated with reverential feelings for the objects of national worship, must have been coldly conducted by teachers conscious that they were practising a pious fraud upon their disciples, and perpetually embarrassed by the necessity of maintaining the gravity befitting such solemn subjects, and of suppressing the involuntary smile, which might betray the secret of their own impiety. One class of fables seems to have been universally exploded even in the earliest youth, those which related to another life. The picture of the unrivalled satirist may be overcharged, but it corresponds strictly with the public language of the orator, and the private sentence of the philosopher:

> The silent realm of disembodied ghosts,
> The frogs that croak along the Stygian coasts;
> The thousand souls in one crazed vessel steer'd,
> Not boys believe, save boys without a beard.*

Even the religious Pausanias speaks of the immortality of the soul as a foreign doctrine, introduced by the Chaldeans and the Magi, and embraced by some of the Greeks, particularly by Plato.* Pliny, whose Natural History opens with a declaration that the universe is the sole Deity, devotes a separate chapter to a contemptuous exposure of the idle notion of the im-

---

Romains ne furent pas choqués de voir réunir dans la personne de César un dieu, un prêtre, et un athée." He adds atheist, as disbelieving with the Epicureans the providence of God.

* Esse aliquid manes et subterranea regna, Et contum, et Stygio ranas in gurgite nigrant Atque una transire vadum tot millia cymba. Nec pueri credunt nisi qui nondum ære lavantur.—Pro Sat. ii. 149.

Nisi forte ineptiis ac fabulis du-cimur, ut existimemus apud inferos impiorum supplicia perferre . . . . . quæ si falsa sunt, id quod omnes intelligunt.—Cic. Pro Cluent. c. 61. Nemo tam puer est ut Cerberum timeat, et tenebras et larvarum habitum nudis ossibus cohærentem. Mors nos aut consumit aut emittit. Sen. Ep. 24.

* Messeniaca, c. xxxii.

mortality of the soul, as a vision of human pride, and equally absurd, whether under the form of existence in another sphere, or under that of transmigration.*

Reception of Foreign Religions. We return then again to the question, what remained for minds thus enlightened beyond the poetic faith of their ancestors, yet not ripe for philosophy? how was the craving for religious excitement to be appeased, which turned with dissatisfaction or disgust from its accustomed nutriment? Here is the secret of the remarkable union between the highest reason and the most abject superstition which characterises the age of Imperial Rome. Every foreign religion found proselytes in the capital of the world; not only the pure and rational theism of the Jews, which had made a progress, the extent of which it is among the most difficult questions in history to estimate: but the Oriental rites of Phrygia, and the Isiac and Serapic worship of Egypt, which, in defiance of the edict of the magistrate[t] and the scorn of the philosopher, maintained their ground in the capital, and were so widely propagated among the provinces, that their vestiges may be traced in the remote districts of Gaul[u] and Britain;[x] and at a later period the reviving Mithriac Mysteries, which in the same manner made their way into the western provinces of the empire.[y] In the capital itself, every thing that was new, or secret,

---

* Lib. vii. 55.
[t] See ante, p. 6.
[u] As late as the time of Julian, the son of a German king had changed his barbarous name of Agenario for that of Serapion, having been instructed in certain mysteries in Gaul. Amm. Marcell. xvi. c. 12.
[x] I have been informed that in some recent excavations at York, vestiges of Isiac worship have been discovered. The passage in Pliny, xxx. 1, refers probably to Druidical magic. Britannia hodieque eam attonite celebrat tantis cæremoniis ut dedisse Persis videri possit.
[y] Religions de l'Antiquité, I. 363; and note⁹, p. 743.

or imposing, found a welcome reception among a people that listened with indifference to philosophers who reasoned, and poets who embodied philosophy in the most attractive diction. For in Rome, poetry had forsworn the alliance of the old imaginative faith. The irreligious system of Euhemerus[a] had found a translator in Ennius; that of Epicurus was commended by the unrivalled powers of Lucretius. Virgil himself, who, as he collected from all quarters the beauties of ancient poetry, so he inlaid in his splendid tessellation the noblest images of the poetic faith of Greece: yet, though at one moment he transfuses mythology into his stately verse, with all the fire of an ardent votary, at the next he appears as a pantheist, and describes the Deity but as the animating soul of the universe.[a] An occasional fit of superstition crosses over the careless and Epicurean apathy of Horace.[b] Astrology and witchcraft[c] led captive minds which

Poetry ceases to be religious.

---

[a] See quotation from Ennius, Cic. de Divinat. II. 50. Euhemerus, either of Messina in Sicily or of Messene in Peloponnesus (he lived in the time of Cassander king of Macedon), was of the Cyrenaic school of philosophy, and was employed on a voyage to the Red Sea by Cassander. But he was still more celebrated for his theologic innovation: he pretended to have discovered during this voyage on an island in the Eastern Ocean, called Panchaia, a register of the births and deaths of the gods inscribed on a golden column in the temple of the Triphylian Jupiter. Hence he inferred that all the popular deities were mere mortals deified on account of their fame, or their benefactions to the human race. Cic. de Nat. Deor. i. 42. Plut. de Isid. et Osir. p. 421; Brucker, i. 604.

[a] Æn. vi. 724. According to his Life by Donatus, Virgil was an Epicurean.

[b] Insanientis dum sapientiæ
Consultus erro, nunc retrorsum
Vela dare, atque iterare cursus
Cogor relictos.

And this because he heard thunder at noon-day.

[c] See the Canidia of Horace. According to Gibbon's just criticism, a "vulgar witch," the Erictho of Lucan, is "tedious, disgusting, but sometimes sublime." Note, ch. xxv. vol. iv. p. 239. It is the difference between the weird sisters in Macbeth and Middleton's "Witch," excepting of course the prolixity of Lucan.

boasted themselves emancipated from the idle terrors of the avenging gods. In the Pharsalia of Lucan, which manifestly soars far above the vulgar theology, where the lofty Stoicism elevates the brave man who disdains, above the gods who flatter, the rising fortunes of Cæsar; yet in the description of the witch Erictho evoking the dead (the only purely imaginative passage in the whole rhetorical poem), there is a kind of tremendous truth and earnestness, which show that if the poet himself believed not " the magic wonders which he drew," at least he well knew the terrors that would strike the age in which he wrote.

Superstitions. The old established traders in human credulity had almost lost their occupation, but their place was supplied by new empirics, who swarmed from all quarters. The oracles were silent, while astrology seized the administration of the secrets of futurity. Pompey, and Crassus, and Cæsar, all consulted the Chaldæans,[d] whose flattering predictions that they should die in old age, in their homes, in glory, so belied by their miserable fates, still brought not the unblushing science into disrepute. The repeated edicts which expelled the astrologers and "mathematicians" from Rome, were no less an homage to their power over the public mind, than their recall, the tacit permission to return, or the return in defiance of the insulted edict. Banished by Agrippa,[e] by Augustus,[f] by Tiberius,[g] by Claudius,[h] they are described in the inimitable language of Tacitus, as a race who, treacherous to those in power,

---

[d] Chaldæis sed major erit fiducia, quicquid Dixerit astrologus, credent de fonte relatum Hammonis; quoniam Delphis oracula cessant, Et genus humanum damnat caligo futuri. Juv. vi. 553.

[e] Dion. xlix. c. 43.
[f] Dion. lvi. c. 25.
[g] Tac. Ann. ii. 32.
[h] Tac. Ann. xii. 52.

fallacious to those who hope for power, are ever proscribed, yet will ever remain.[1] They were at length taken under the avowed patronage of Vespasian and his successors.[k] All these circumstances were manifest indications of the decay and of the approaching dissolution of the old religion. The elegiac poet had read, not without sagacity, the signs of the times.

> None sought the aid of foreign gods, while bow'd
> Before their native shrines the trembling crowd.[m]

And thus, in this struggle between the old household deities of the established faith, and the half-domiciliated gods of the stranger, undermined by philosophy, supplanted by still darker superstition, Polytheism seemed, as it were, to await its death-blow; and to be ready to surrender its ancient honours to the conqueror, whom Divine Providence should endow with sufficient authority over the human mind to seize upon the abdicated supremacy.

Such is the state in which the ancient world leaves the mind of man. On a sudden a new era commences; a rapid yet gradual revolution takes place in the opinions, sentiments, and principles of mankind; the void is filled; the connexion between religion and morals re-established with an intimacy of union yet unknown. The unity of the Deity becomes,

---

[1] Genus hominum, potentibus infidum, sperantibus fallax, quod in civitate nostrâ et vetabitur semper et retinebitur. Tac. Hist. L. 22.

[k] Tac. Hist. ii. 78. Suet. in Vesp. Dio. lxvii. Suet. in Dom. xiv. xv.

[m] Nulli cura fuit externos quærere Divos, Cum tremeret patrio pendula turba foro. Prop. iv. 1-17. Propertius may be considered in one sense the most religious poet of this period; his verses teem with mythological allusion, but it is poetical ornament rather than the natural language of piety; it has much of the artificial school of the Alexandrian Callimachus, his avowed model, nothing of the simplicity of faith which breathed in Pindar and Sophocles.

not the high and mysterious creed of a privileged sacerdotal or intellectual oligarchy, but the common property of all whose minds are fitted to receive it: all religious distinctions are annihilated; the jurisdictions of all local deities abolished; and imperceptibly the empire of Rome becomes one great Christian commonwealth, which even sends out, as it were, its peaceful colonies into regions beyond the limits of the Imperial power. The characteristic distinction of the general revolution is this: that the physical agency of the Deity seems to recede from the view, while the spiritual character is more distinctly unfolded; or rather, the notion of the Divine Power is merged in the more prevailing sentiment of his moral Goodness. The remarkable passage in the Jewish history, in which God is described as revealing himself to Elijah, "neither in the strong wind, nor in the earthquake, nor in the fire, but in the still small voice," may be considered, we will not say prophetic, but singularly significant of the sensations to be excited in the human mind by the successive revelations of the Deity.

The doctrine of the immortality of the soul partook in the same change with the notion of the Deity; it became at once popular, simple, and spiritual. It was disseminated throughout all orders of society: it admitted no aristocratic elysium of heroes and demi-gods, like that of the early Greeks;[a] it sepa-

Immortality of the soul.

---

[a] It is curious to see, in another mythology, the same martial aristocratic spirit which, in the earlier religions, excluded the ἀμενηνὰ κάρηνα, the inglorious vulgar, from the seats of bliss, where Achilles and Diomed pursued their warlike amusements. It was not proper to appear poor before Odin; and it is very doubtful whether a poor man was thought worthy of any place in his dwellings, unless he came from the field of battle in the bloody train of some great chieftain. Slaves at least were distinctly excluded, and after death turned away from the doors of Valhalla. Geijer, Hist. of Sweden, Germ. Transl. I. 103.

rated itself from that earlier and widely prevalent form, which it assumed in the theogonies of the Nature-worship, where the soul emanating from the source of Being, after one or many transmigrations, was reabsorbed into the Divine Essence. It announced the resurrection of all mankind to judgment, and the reunion of the spirit to a body, which, preserving the principle of identity, nevertheless should be of a purer and more imperishable nature. Such are the great primary principles, which became incorporated with the mind of man; and, operating on all human institutions, on the common sentiments of the whole race, form the great distinctive difference between the ancient and the modern, the European and the Asiatic world. During the dark ages there was a strong reaction of barbarism: in its outward form Christianity might appear to recede towards the polytheism of older times; and, as has been shown, not in a philosophic, but in a narrow polemic spirit of hostility to the Church of Rome, many of the rites and usages of heathenism were admitted into the Christian system; yet the indelible difference between the two periods remained. A higher sense and meaning was infused into these forms; God was considered in his moral rather than his physical attributes—as the Lord of the future as much or even more than of the present world. The saints and angels, who have been compared to the intermediate deities of the older superstitions, had, nevertheless, besides their tutelar power against immediate accidents and temporal calamities, an important influence over the state of the soul in the world to come; they assumed the higher office of ministering the hopes of the future, in a still greater degree than the blessings of the present life.

To the more complete development of this fact we

shall descend in the course of our History, which will endeavour to trace all the modifications of Christianity, by which it accommodated itself to the spirit of successive ages; and by this apparently almost skilful, but in fact necessary condescension to the predominant state of moral culture, of which itself formed a constituent element, maintained its uninterrupted dominion. It is the author's object, the difficulty of which he himself fully appreciates, to portray the genius of the Christianity of each successive age, in connexion with that of the age itself; entirely to discard all polemic views; to mark the origin and progress of all the subordinate diversities of belief; their origin in the circumstances of the place or time in which they appeared; their progress from their adaptation to the prevailing state of opinion or sentiment: rather than directly to confute error or to establish truth; in short, to exhibit the reciprocal influence of civilisation on Christianity, of Christianity on civilisation. To the accomplishment of such a scheme he is well aware, that besides the usual high qualifications of a faithful historian, is requisite, in an especial manner, the union of true philosophy with perfect charity, if indeed they are not one and the same. This calm, impartial, and dispassionate tone he will constantly endeavour, he dares scarcely hope, with such warnings on every side of involuntary prejudice and unconscious prepossession, uniformly to maintain. In the honesty of his purpose he will seek his excuse for all imperfection or deficiency in the execution of his scheme. Nor is he aware that he enters on ground preoccupied by any writers of established authority, at least in our own country, where the History of Christianity has usually assumed the form of a History of the Church, more or less controversial, and confined itself to annals of the internal feuds and divisions in the Christian community, and the variations in doctrine and discipline, rather than to its political and social influence. Our attention, on the other hand, will be chiefly directed to its effects on the social and even political condition of man, as it extended itself throughout the Roman world, and at length entered into the administration of government and of law; the gradual manner in which it absorbed and incorporated into the religious commonwealth the successive masses of population, which, after having overthrown the temporal polity of Rome, were subdued to the religion of the conquered people; the separation of the human race into the distinct castes of the clergy and laity; the former at first an aristocracy, afterwards a despotic monarchy: as Europe sank back into barbarism, the imaginative state of the human mind, the formation of a new poetic faith, a mythology, and a complete system of symbolical worship; the interworking of Christianity with barbarism, till they slowly grew into a kind of semi-barbarous heroic period, that of Christian chivalry; the gradual expansion of the system, with the expansion of the human mind; and the slow, perhaps not yet complete, certainly not general, development of a rational and intellectual religion. Throughout his work the author will equally, or as his disposition inclines, even more diligently, labour to show the good as well as the evil of each phasis of Christianity; since it is his opinion that, at every period, much more is to be attributed to the circumstances of the age, to the collective operation of certain principles which grew out of the events of the time, than to the intentional or accidental influence of any individual or class of men. Christianity, in short,

Christianity different in form in different periods of civilisation.

may exist in a certain form in a nation of savages as well as in a nation of philosophers,[*] yet its specific character will almost entirely depend upon the character of the people who are its votaries.[y] It must be considered, therefore, in constant connexion with that character; it will darken with the darkness, and brighten with the light, of each succeeding century; in an ungenial time it will recede so far from its genuine and essential nature as scarcely to retain any sign of its divine original: it will advance with the advancement of human nature, and keep up the moral to the utmost height of the intellectual culture of man.

Christianity not self-developed.

While, however, Christianity necessarily submitted to all these modifications, I strongly protest against the opinion, that the *origin* of the religion can be attributed, according to a theory adopted by many foreign writers, to the gradual and spontaneous development of the human mind.[q] Christ is as much beyond his own age, as his own age is beyond the darkest barbarism. The time, though fitted to receive, could not by any combination of prevalent opinions, or by any conceivable course of moral improvement, have

---

[*] Euseb. l. p. 20.

[y] Compare a very curious passage which expresses the same opinion in the commencement of the Ecc. Hist. of Eusebius: Οὐκ ἦν τε χωρὶς οἰδέ τε τῆν τοῦ Χριστοῦ πάντοφον, καὶ πάνδρετον διδασκαλίαν ὁ πᾶσι τῶν ἀνθρώπων βίος. Read the whole. By the accounts of Bruce, Salt, and recently of Pearce, the Christianity of Abyssinia may be adduced as an instance of the state to which it may be degraded among a people at a very low state of barbarism. All later accounts of Abyssinian Christianity fully confirm this. The conversions among the South Sea islanders, it will of course be remembered, were effected, and are still superintended, by strangers in a very different stage of civilization.

[q] This theory is sketched by no means with an unfair though unfriendly hand by Chateaubriand, Études sur l'Histoire; a book of which, I am constrained to add, the meagre performance contrasts strangely with the loftiness of its pretensions.

produced Christianity. The conception of the human character of Jesus, and the simple principles of the new religion, as they were in direct opposition to the predominant opinions and temper of his own countrymen, so they stand completely alone in the history of our race; and, as imaginary no less than as real, altogether transcend the powers of man's moral conception. Supposing the Gospels purely fictitious, or that, like the Cyropædia of Xenophon, they embody on a groundwork of fact the highest moral and religious notions to which man had attained, and show the utmost ideal perfection of the divine and human nature, they can be accounted for, according to my judgment, on none of the ordinary principles of human nature.' When we behold Christ standing in the midst of the wreck of old religious institutions, and building, or rather at one word commanding to arise, the simple and harmonious structure of the new faith, which seems equally adapted for all ages—a temple to which nations in the highest degree of civilisation may bring their offerings of pure hearts, virtuous dispositions, universal charity,—our natural emotion is the recognition of the Divine goodness, in the promulgation of this beneficent code of religion; and adoration of that Being in whom that Divine goodness is thus embodied and made comprehensible to the faculties of man. In the language of the apostle, "God is in Christ, reconciling the world unto himself."

' Dirons nous que l'histoire de l'Évangile est inventée à plaisir? Ce n'est pas ainsi qu'on invente; et les faits de Socrate, dont personne ne doute, sont bien moins attestés que ceux de Jésus Christ. Au fond c'est reculer la difficulté sans la détruire; il seroit plus inconcevable que plusieurs hommes d'accord eussent fabriqué ce livre, qu'il ne l'est qu'un seul en a fourni le sujet. Et l'Évangile a des caractères de vérité si frappans, si parfaitement inimitables, que l'inventeur en seroit plus étonnant que le héros. Rousseau, Emile, liv. iv.

' 2 Cor. v. 19

CHAPTER II.

Life of Jesus Christ — State of Judæa — The Belief in the Messiah.

THE history of Christianity without the life of its Divine Author appears imperfect and incomplete, particularly considering the close connexion of that life, not only with the more mysterious doctrines, but with the practical, and even political influence of the religion; for even its apparently most unimportant incidents have, in many cases, affected most deeply the opinions and feelings of the Christian world. The isolation of the history of Christ in a kind of sacred seclusion has no doubt a beneficial effect on the piety of the Christian, which delights in contemplating the Saviour, undisturbed and uncontaminated by less holy associations; but it has likewise its disadvantages, in disconnecting his life from the general history of mankind, of which it forms an integral and essential part. Had the life of Christ been more generally considered as intimately and inseparably connected with the progress and development of human affairs, with the events and opinions of his time, works would not have been required to prove his existence, scarcely perhaps the authenticity of his history. The real historical evidence of Christianity is the absolute necessity of his life, to fill up the void in the annals of mankind, to account for the effects of his religion in the subsequent history of man.

Yet to write the life of Christ, though at first sight it may appear the most easy, is perhaps the most difficult task which an historian can undertake. Many Lives have been composed with a devotional, none at least to my knowledge, in this country,[a] with an historic design; none in which the author has endeavoured to throw himself completely back into the age when Jesus of Nazareth began to travel as the teacher of a new religion through the villages of Galilee; none which has attempted to keep up a perpetual reference to the circumstances of the times, the habits and national character of the people, and the state of public feeling; and thus, identifying itself with the past, to show the origin and progress of the new faith, as it slowly developed itself, and won its way through the adverse elements which it encountered in Judæa and the adjacent provinces. To depart from the evangelic simplicity in the relation of the facts would not merely offend the reverential feelings of the reader, but tend likewise to destroy the remarkable harmony between the facts and doctrines, which characterises the narrative of the Gospels, and on which their authenticity, as genuine historical documents, might to an intelligent mind be safely rested. The three first Gospels, unless written at a very early period, could scarcely have escaped the controversial, or at least argumentative tone, which enters into the later Christian writings, and with which the relation of St. John is imbued.[b] The plan then which the author will pursue, will be to presume, to a certain degree, on the reader's acquaintance with the subject on which he enters: he will not think it necessary to relate at length all the discourses or even all the acts of Christ, but rather to interweave the historic

---

[a] See Appendix I., on the recent Lives of Christ.
[b] See Appendix II., on the Origin of the Gospels.

illustration with the main events, disposed, as far as possible, in the order of time, and to trace the effect which each separate incident, and the whole course of the life of Jesus, may be supposed to have produced upon the popular mind. In short, it will partake, in some degree, of the nature of an historical comment, on facts which it will rather endeavour to elucidate, than to draw out to their full length.

The days of the elder Herod were drawing to a close.
State of Judæa.— Herod the Great. His prosperous and magnificent reign was ending in darkness and misery, such as the deepest tragedy has rarely ventured to imagine. His last years had revealed the horrible, the humiliating secret, that the son, at whose instigation he had put to death the two noble and popular princes, his children by Mariamne the Asmonean, had almost all his life been overreaching him in that dark policy, of which he esteemed himself the master; and now, as a final return for his unsuspecting confidence, had conspired to cut short the brief remainder of his days. Almost the last, and the most popular exercise of Herod's royal authority, was to order the execution of the perfidious Antipater.
Intrigues and death of Antipater. Fearful times! when the condemnation of a son by a father, and that father an odious and sanguinary tyrant, could coincide with the universal sentiment of the people! The attachment of the nation to the reigning family might have been secured, if the sons of Mariamne, the heiress of the Asmonean line, had survived to claim the succession. The foreign and Idumean origin of the father might have been forgotten in the national and splendid descent of the mother. There was, it would seem, a powerful Herodian party, attached to the fortunes of the ruling house; but the body of the nation now looked with ill-concealed

aversion to the perpetuation of the Idumean tyranny in the persons of the sons of Herod. Yet to those who contemplated only the political signs of the times, nothing remained but the degrading alternative, either to submit to the line of Herod, or to sink into a Roman province. Such was to be the end of their long ages of national glory, such the hopeless termination of the national independence. But, notwithstanding the progress of Grecian opinions and manners, with which the politic Herod had endeavoured to counterbalance the turbulent and unruly spirit of the religious party, the great mass of the people, obstinately wedded to the law and to the institutions of their fathers, watched with undisguised jealousy the denationalising proceedings of their king. This stern and inextinguishable enthusiasm had recently broken out into active resistance, in the conspiracy to tear down the golden eagle, which Herod had suspended over the gate of the Temple.[c] The signal for this daring act had been a rumour of the king's death; and the terrific vengeance, which, under a temporary show of moderation, Herod had wreaked on the offenders, the degradation of the High-priest, and the execution of the popular teachers, who were accused of having instigated the insurrection, could not but widen the breach between the dying sovereign and the people. The greater part of the nation looked to the death of Herod with a vague hope of liberation and independence, which struck in with the more peculiar cause of excitement predominant in the general mind.

For the principle of this universal ferment lay deeper

[c] Hist. of the Jews, vol. II. p. 87.

than in the impatience of a tyrannical government, which burdened the people with intolerable exactions, or the apprehension of national degradation if Judæa should be reduced to the dominion of a Roman proconsul. It was the confidence in the immediate coming of the *Messiah*, which was working with vague and mysterious agitation in the hearts of all orders.[d] The very danger to which Jewish independence was reduced, was associated with this exalted sentiment; the nearer the ruin, the nearer the restoration of their Theocracy. For there is no doubt, that among other predictions, according to the general belief, which pointed to the present period, a very ancient interpretation of the prophecy, which declared that the sceptre, the royal dominion, should not depart from the race of Israel until the coming of the Shiloh, one of the titles uniformly attributed to the Messiah, connected the termination of the existing polity with the manifestation of the Deliverer.[e] This expectation of a wonderful

---

[d] Whoever is curious in such inquiries will find a fearful catalogue of calamities which were to precede, according to the Rabbinical authorities, the coming of the Messiah, either in Lightfoot's Harmony, vol. v. p. 180 (8vo. edit.), or in Schoetgen, Horæ Hebraicæ, vol. ii. p. 509, or Eisenmenger, das entdecktes Judenthum, ii. p. 711. The notion may have been grounded on the last chapter of the Prophecy of Daniel. Compare Bertholdt, c. 13.—The Rabbins deliver, "In the first year of that week (of years), that the Son of David is to come, shall that be fulfilled, 'I will rain upon one city, but I will not rain upon another.'" Amos, iv. 7.—"The second year the arrows of famine shall be sent forth. The third, the famine shall be grievous, and men and women and children, holy men and men of good works, shall die; and there shall be a forgetfulness of the Law among those that learn it. The fourth year fulness and not fulness. The fifth year great fulness: they shall eat, and drink, and rejoice, and the Law shall return to its scholars. The sixth year, voices." (The gloss is, "a fame shall be spread that the Son of David comes," or "they shall sound with the trumpet.") "The seventh year, wars; and in the going out of that year, the Son of David shall come." Lightfoot, xi. 421.

[e] Casaubon Exercit. anti-Baron. ii.

revolution to be wrought by the sudden appearance of some great mysterious person, had been so widely disseminated, as to excite the astonishment, perhaps the jealousy of the Romans, whose historians, Suetonius and Tacitus, as is well known, bear witness to the fact. "Among many," writes the latter, "there was a persuasion, that in the ancient books of the priesthood it was written, that at this precise time, the East should become mighty, and that the sovereigns of the world should issue from Judæa." "In the East, an ancient and consistent opinion prevailed, that it was fated there should issue, at this time, from Judæa, those who should obtain universal dominion."

Yet no question is more difficult than to ascertain the origin, the extent, the character of this belief, as it prevailed at the time of our Saviour's coming;—how far it had spread among the surrounding nations; or how far, on the other hand, the original Jewish creed, formed from the authentic prophetical writings, had become impregnated with Oriental or Alexandrian notions. It is most probable, that there was no consistent, uniform, or authorised opinion on the subject. All was vague and indefinite; and in this vagueness and indefiniteness lay much of its power over the general mind. Whatever purer or loftier notions concerning the great Deliverer and Restorer might be imparted to wise and holy men,

---

* 2 Esdras, vi. 25.
* Tac. Hist. v. 13.
* Suet. Ves. p. 4.
* The Jewish opinions concerning the Messiah have been examined with great diligence and accuracy by Professor Bertholdt, in his Christologia Judæorum. Bertholdt is what may be called a moderate Rationalist. To his work, and to Lightfoot, Schoetgen, Meuschen, and Eisenmenger, I am indebted for most of my Rabbinical quotations.

in whatever sense we understand that "Abraham rejoiced to see the day" of the Messiah, the intimations on this subject in the earlier books of the Old Testament, though distinctly to be traced along its whole course, are few, brief, and occurring at long intervals. But from the time, and during the whole period of the Prophets, this mysterious Being becomes gradually more prominent. The future dominion of some great king, to descend from the line of David, to triumph over all his enemies, and to establish an universal kingdom of peace and happiness, of which the descriptions of the golden age in the Greek poets are but a faint and unimaginative transcript: the promise of the Messiah, in short, comes more distinctly forward. As early as the first chapters of Isaiah, he appears to assume a title and sacred designation, which at least approaches near to that of the Divinity;[k] and in the later prophets, not merely does this leading characteristic maintain its place, but under the splendid poetical imagery, drawn from existing circumstances, there seems to lie hid a more profound meaning, which points to some great and general moral revolution, to be achieved by this mysterious Being.

Tradition. But their sacred books, the Law and the Prophets, were not the clear and unmingled source of the Jewish opinions on this all-absorbing subject. Over this, as over the whole system of the Law, tradition had thrown a veil; and it is this traditionary notion of the Messiah, which it is necessary here to

---

[k] Such is the opinion of Rosenmüller (on Isaiah ix. 5. Compare likewise, on Psalm xlv. 7). On a point much contested by modern scholars, Gesenius, in his note on the same passages, espouses the opposite opinion. Neither of these authors, it may be added, discusses the question on theological, but purely on historical and critical grounds.

develope: but from whence tradition had derived its apparently extraneous and independent notions, becomes a much more deep and embarrassing question.[a] It is manifest from the Evangelic history,[b] that although there was no settled or established creed upon the subject, yet there was a certain conventional language: particular texts of the sacred writings were universally recognised, as bearing reference to the Messiah; and there were some few characteristic credentials of his title and office, which would have commanded universal assent.

There are two quarters from which the Jews, as they ceased to be an insulated people, confined in the narrow tract of Palestine, and by their captivity and migrations became more mingled with other races, might insensibly contract new religious notions, the East and the West, Babylonia and Alexandria. The latter would be the chief, though not

Foreign connexions of the Jews.

---

[a] Bertholdt, p. 8.

[b] The brief intimations in the Gospels are almost the only absolutely certain authorities for the nature of this belief, at that particular period, except, perhaps, the more genuine part of the Apocrypha. Josephus, though he acknowledges the existence and the influence of this remarkable feature in the national character, is either inclined to treat it as a popular delusion, or to warp it to his own purposes, its fulfilment in the person of Vespasian. For his own school, Philo is a valuable witness; but among the Alexandrian Jews, the belief in a personal Messiah was much more faint and indistinct than in Palestine. The Rabbinical books, even the oldest Targumim or comments on the Sacred Writings, are somewhat suspicious from the uncertainty of their date: still, in this as in other points of coincidence, where their expressions are similar to those of the Christian records, there seems so manifest an improbability that these should have been adopted after the two religions had assumed as hostile position towards each other, that they may be fairly considered as vestiges of an earlier system of opinions, retained from ancient reverence, and indelible even by implacable animosity. It is far more likely that Christianity should speak the current language of the time, than that the Synagogue should interpolate their own traditionary records, with terms or notions borrowed from the Church.

perhaps the only channel through which the influence of Grecian opinions would penetrate into Palestine;[*] and of the Alexandrian notions of the Messiah, we shall hereafter adduce two competent representatives, the author of the Book of Wisdom and Philo. But the East no doubt made a more early, profound, and lasting impression on the popular mind of the Jews. Unfortunately in no part does history present us with so melancholy a blank, as in that of the great Babylonian settlement of the people of Israel. Yet its importance in the religious, and even in the civil, affairs of the nation cannot but have been very considerable. It was only a small part of the nation which returned with the successive remigrations under Ezra and Nehemiah to their native land; and, though probably many of the poorer classes had remained behind at the period of the Captivity, and many more returned singly or in small bodies, yet on the other hand it is probable, that the tide of emigration, which at a later time was perpetually flowing from the valleys of Palestine into Egypt, Syria, Asia Minor, and even more remote regions, would often take the course of the Euphrates, and swell the numbers of the Mesopotamian colony.[p] In the great contest between Alexander and the Persian monarchy, excepting from some rather suspicious stories in Josephus, we hear less than we might expect of this race of Jews.[q] But as we approach the

Babylonia.

---

[*] Even as early as the reign of Antiochus the Great, certain Jews had attempted to introduce Grecian manners, and had built a Grecian school or gymnasium at Jerusalem. 1 Macc. i. 11, 16; 2 Macc. ii. 4, 11, 12.

[p] I have examined this question much more at length, with the aid of some recent Jewish writers, in the new edition of the History of the Jews.

[q] There may be truth in the observation of St. Croix: "Les Grecs et les Romains avoient tant de haine et de

era of Christianity, and somewhat later, they emerge rather more into notice. While the Jews were spreading in the West, and no doubt successfully disseminating their Monotheism in many quarters, in Babylonia their proselytes were kings; and the later Jewish Temple beheld an Eastern queen (by a singular coincidence, of the same name with the celebrated mother of Constantine, the patroness of Christian Jerusalem) lavishing her wealth on the structure on Mount Moriah, and in the most munificent charity to the poorer inhabitants of the city. The name of Helena, queen of the Adiabeni, was long dear to the memory of the Jews; and her tomb was one of the most remarkable monuments near the walls of the city. Philo not only asserts that Babylon and other Eastern satrapies were full of his countrymen,[r] but intimates that the apprehension of their taking up arms in behalf of their outraged religion and marching upon Palestine, weighed upon the mind of Petronius, when commanded, at all hazards, to place the statue of Caligula in the Temple.[s] It appears from some hints of Josephus, that during the last war, the

---

mépris pour le peuple Juif, qu'ils affectoient n'en pas parler dans leurs écrits." (Historiens d'Alex. p. 555.) This, however, would apply only to the later writers, which are all we now possess; but if in the contemporary historians there had been much more, it would probably, at least if to the credit of his countrymen, have been gleaned by Josephus.

[r] See on the numbers of the Jews in the Asiatic provinces, particularly Armenia, at a later period (the conquest of Armenia by Sapor, A. D. 367), St. Martin's additions to Le Beau's Hist. du Bas Empire. The death of this valuable writer, it is to be feared, will deprive the learned world of his promised work on the History of the Birth and Death of Jesus Christ, which was to contain circumstantial accounts of the Jews beyond the Euphrates.

Of the different races of Jews mentioned in the Acts, as present in Jerusalem, four are from this quarter:— Parthians, Medes, Elamites, dwellers in Mesopotamia.

[s] Leg. ad Caium, vol. ii. p. 578, Edit. Mangey.

revolted party entertained great hopes of succour from that quarter;¹ and there is good ground for supposing that the final insurrection in the time of Hadrian was connected with a rising in Mesopotamia.² At the same period the influence of this race of Jews on the religious character of the people is no less manifest. Here was a chief scene of the preaching of the great apostle:³ and we cannot but think, that its importance in early Christian history, which has usually been traced almost exclusively in the West, has been much underrated. Hence came the mystic Cabala⁴ of the Jews, the chief parent of those gnostic opinions, out of which grew the heresies of the early Church: here the Jews, under the Prince of the Captivity, held their most famous schools, where learning was embodied in the Babylonian Talmud; and here the most influential heresiarch, Manes,

---

¹ Dion (or Xiphilin) asserts that they received considerable succours from the East. L. lxvi. c. 4.

² Hist. of Jews, ii. 422, &c.

³ Nothing but the stubborn obstinacy of controversy could have thrown a doubt on the plain date in the first Epistle of St. Peter (v. 13). Philo in two places (ii. p. 578, 587), Josephus in one (Ant. xviii. 9, 8), expressly name *Babylon* as the habitation of the great Eastern settlement. It is not certain whether the city was then entirely destroyed (Gesenius on Isaiah, xiii. 22), but in fact the name was extended to the province or satrapy. But it was equally the object of the two great conflicting parties in Christianity to identify Rome with Babylon. This fact established, the Roman Catholic had an unanswerable argument to prove the contested point of St. Peter's residence in the Western metropolis; Babylon therefore was decided to mean pagan Rome. The Protestant at once concurred; for if Rome was Babylon, it was the mystic spiritual Babylon of the Apocalypse. The whole third chapter of the Second Epistle of St. Peter (assuming its authenticity, and my view rather favours that authenticity) appears to me full of Oriental allusions, and the example of Balaam seems peculiarly appropriate if written in that region. Lucan's "Cumque superba foret Babylon spolianda" may indeed be mere poetic licence, or may allude to Seleucia.

⁴ Cabala is used here in its most extensive sense. See Chiarini, p. 97. In this sense it is used by Maimonides. See Hist. of Jews.

attempted to fuse into one system the elements of Magianism, Cabalism, and Christianity. Having thus rapidly traced the fortunes of this great Jewish colony, we must reascend to the time of its first establishment.

From a very early period the Jews seem to have possessed a Cabala, a traditionary comment or interpretation of the sacred writings. Whether it existed before the Captivity, it is impossible to ascertain; it is certain that many of their books, even those written by distinguished prophets, Nathan, and Gad, and Iddo, were lost at that disastrous time. But whether they carried any accredited tradition to Babylonia, it seems evident, from the Oriental cast which it assumed, that they either brought it from thence on their return to their native land, or received it subsequently during their intercourse with their Eastern brethren.* Down to the Captivity the Jews of Palestine had been in contact only with the religions of the neighbouring nations, which, however differently modified, appear to have been essentially the same, a sort of Nature-worship, in which the host of Heaven, especially the sun and moon, under different names, Baal and Moloch, Astarte and Mylitta, and probably as symbols or representatives of the active and passive powers of nature, no doubt with some distinction of their attributes, were the predominant objects. These religions had long degenerated into cruel or licentious superstitions; and the Jews, in falling off to the idolatry of their neighbours, or introducing foreign rites into their own religious system, not merely offended against the great primal distinction of their faith, the Unity of the Godhead, but sunk from the pure, humane, and compara-

---

* Mosheim, De Rebus Christ. B. 18.

tively civilised institutes of their lawgiver, to the loose and sanguinary usages of barbarism. In the East, however, they encountered a religion of a far nobler and more regular structure:[a] a religion which offered no temptation to idolatrous practices; for the Magian rejected, with the devout abhorrence of the followers of Moses, the exhibition of the Deity in the human form; though it possessed a rich store of mythological and symbolical figures, singularly analogous to those which may be considered the poetic machinery of the later Hebrew prophets.[b] The religion of Persia seems to have held an intermediate rank between the Pantheism of India, where the whole universe emanated from the Deity, and was finally to be reabsorbed into the Deity, and the purer Theism of the Jews, which asserted the one omnific Jehovah, and seemed to place a wide and impassable interval between the nature of the Creator and that of the created being. In the Persian system, the Creation owed its existence to the conflicting powers of evil and good. These were subordinate to, or proceeding from, the Great Primal Cause (Zeruane Akerene), Time without bounds,[c] which in

---

[a] In Asiâ Persarum religionem cæteris esse nobiliorem. Mosheim, Inst. p. 58, and Grot. de Ver. ii. 10.

[b] This, it may be observed, has no connexion whatever with the originality or authority of these predictions. It should be borne in mind, that in these visions it is the moral or religious meaning alone which can be the object of faith, not the figures through which that meaning is conveyed. There is no reason why the images of Daniel and Ezekiel should not be derived from, or assimilate to, the prevalent forms around them, as well as those of the rustic Amos be chiefly drawn from pastoral or rural life. See, e. g., Chiarini's curious theory about the chariot of Ezekiel. Preface to Talmud. p. 90 and 101. Compare Hist. of the Jews and the quotations in the notes.

[c] So translated by Du Perron and Kleuker. There is a learned dissertation of Foucher on this subject. Acad. des Ins. vol. xix. According to Bohlen it is analogous to the Sanskrit Sarvam akarsaam, the Uncreated

fact appears, as Gibbon observes, rather as a metaphysical abstraction, than as an active and presiding deity. The Creation was at once the work and the dominion of the two antagonist creators, who had balanced against each other in perpetual conflict a race of spiritual and material beings, light and darkness, good and evil. This Magianism, subsequent to the Jewish Captivity,[d] and during the residence of the captives in Mesopotamia, either spread with the conquests of the Persians, from the regions farther to the east, Aderbijan and Bactria, or was first promulgated by Zoroaster, who is differently represented as the author or as the reformer of the faith. From the remarkable allusions or points of coincidence between some of the Magian tenets and the Sacred Writings,[e] Hyde and Prideaux laboured to prove that Zoroaster[f] had been a pupil of Daniel, and derived those notions, which seem more nearly allied to the purer Jewish faith, from his intercourse with the Hebrew prophet, who held a high station

---

Whole: according to Fred. Schlegel, Sarvam akharyam, the Unum Indivisibile. I cannot quite understand Dr. Haag on this subject. He considers, p. 21, that this notion owes its rise to Anquetil du Perron's ignorance of the Zend grammar; yet, p. 264, he acknowledges that the doctrine of Zarvam akaranam was commonly believed in Persia during the times of the Sassanids, and is accepted by all modern doctors as an incontrovertible fact, p. 264. Compare the Greek and Armenian accounts, p. 9, 10. Dr. Haag seems to think this a heresy, that Zoroaster's own original creed was Monotheism (Ahura Mazdao).

The One God, p. 256. But I think that he hardly proves his point.

[d] The appearance of the Magian order, before the conquest of Babylon by the Medo-Persian Kings, is an extremely difficult question. Nebuchadnezzar's army was attended (Jer. xxxix. 3) by Nergal-sharezer, the Rabmag, רב מג (Archimagus). Compare Bertholdt, Daniel Excurs. iii.

[e] Isaiah xlvii. 7.

[f] The name of Zoroaster (Zerotosh) has been deduced from words signifying "the star of gold," or "the star of splendour," and may have been a title or appellative.

under the victorious Medo-Persian monarchy.* But, in fact, there is such an originality and completeness in the Zoroastrian system, and in its leading principles, especially that of the antagonistic powers of good and evil, it departs so widely from the ancient and simple Theism of the Jews, as clearly to indicate an independent and peculiar source, at least in its more perfect development; if it is not, as we are inclined to believe, of much more ancient date, and native to a region much farther to the east than the Persian court, where Zoroaster, according to one tradition, might have had intercourse, in his youth, with the Prophet Daniel.

If, as appears to be the general opinion of the Continental writers who have most profoundly investigated the subject, we have authentic remains, or at least records, which, if of later date, contain the true principles of Magianism in the Liturgies

---

* The hypothesis which places Zoroaster under the reign of Darius Hystaspes, identified with the Gushtasp of Persian mythological history, is maintained by Hyde, Prideaux, Anquetil du Perron, Kleuker, Herder, Goerres, Malcolm, Von Hammer, and apparently by De Guignault. The silence of Herodotus appears to me among the strongest objections to this view.

Foucher, Tychsen, Heeren, and recently Holty, identify Gushtasp with Cyaxares I., and place the religious revolution under the previous Median dynasty.

A theory which throws Zoroaster much higher up into antiquity is developed with great ability by Rhode, in his Heilige Sage. The earlier date of the Persian prophet has likewise been maintained by Moyle, Gibbon, and Volney.

These views may in some degree be reconciled by the supposition that it was a reformation, not a primary development of the religion which took place under the Medo-Persian, or the Persian monarchy. The elements of the faith and the caste of the Magi were, I should conceive, earlier. The inculcation of agricultural habits on a people emerging from the pastoral life, so well developed by Heeren, seems to indicate a more ancient date. Consult also Gesenius on Isaiah, lxv. 5; Constant sur la Religion, ii. 187.

CHAP. II.   THE INSTITUTES OF THE ZENDAVESTA.   65

and Institutes of the Zendavesta;[h] it is by no means an improbable source in which we might discover the origin

---

[h] It may be necessary, in this country, briefly to state the question as to the authenticity or value of these documents. They were brought from the East by that singular adventurer, Anquetil du Perron. Sir W. Jones, in a letter, not the most successful of the writings of that excellent and accomplished man, being a somewhat stiff and laboured imitation of the easy irony of Voltaire, threw a shade of suspicion over the character of Du Perron, which in England has never been dispelled, and, except among Oriental scholars, has attached to all his publications. Ahmed, however, the antiquity of the Zendavesta, at least its value as a trustworthy record of the Zoroastrian tenets, has been generally acknowledged. If altogether spurious, these works must be considered as forgeries by Du Perron. But, I., they are too incomplete and imperfect for forgeries ; if it had been worth Du Perron's while to fabricate the Institutes of Zoroaster, we should, no doubt, have had something more elaborate than several books of prayers and treatises of different ages, from which it required his own industry and that of his German translator, Kleuker, to form a complete system. II. Du Perron must have forged the language in which the books are written, as well as the books themselves. But the Zend is universally admitted by the great Orientalists and historians of language to be a genuine and very curious branch of the Eastern dialects. (See Bopp, Vergleichende Grammatik.) It should be added, that the publication of the Zendavesta, in the original, has been commenced by M. Bournouf in Paris, and by M. Olshausen in Germany.

III. These documents may be considered as more modern compilations, of little greater authority than the Sadder, which Hyde translated from the modern Persian. That they are of the age of Zoroaster, it may be difficult to prove; but their internal evidence, and their coincidence with the other notices of the Persian religion, scattered among the writings of the Greeks and Romans (see Du Perron's and Kleuker's illustrations, especially the Persica of the latter), afford sufficient ground for supposing that they contain the genuine and unadulterated elements of the Zoroastrian faith, and, if not of primitive, are of very high antiquity. The traces of Mohammedanism, which Brucker (vol. vi. p. 68) supposed that he had detected, and which are apparent in the Sadder, are rather notions borrowed by Mohammed from the Jews; but whence obtained by the Jews is the question. Mr. Erskine, the highest authority on such subjects, considers the existing Zendavesta to have been compiled in the age of Ardeshir Babegan, the great restorer of the Magian faith. (Bombay Transactions.) In Professor Neuman's translation of Vartan there is a curious sentence, which seems to intimate that the books of the Magian faith either did not exist at that time, or were inaccessible to the generality.

IV. A thought has sometimes

VOL. I.   F

of those traditional notions of the Jews, which were extraneous to their earlier system, and which do not appear

---

crossed my own mind (it has been anticipated by Du Perron), whether they can be the sacred books of a sect formed from an union of Gnostic or Manichæan Christianity with the ancient Persian religion. But there is no vestige of purely Christian tradition; and those points in which Parseeism seems to coincide with Christianity are integral and inseparable parts of their great system. And against all such opinions must be weighed the learned paper of Professor Rask, who gives strong reasons for the antiquity both of the language and of the books. The language he considers the vernacular tongue of ancient Media. (Trans. of Asiatic Society, iii. 524.) Still, while I appeal to the Zendavesta as authority, I shall only adduce the more general leading principles of the faith, of which the antiquity appears certain; and rarely any tenet for which we have not corroborative authority in the Greek and Latin writers. The testimonies of the latter have been collected both by Du Perron and Kleuker.

I have not thought fit to cancel this note. But since the publication of this work, the study of the Zend language and of the Zendavesta has made great progress, first by Bournouf's invaluable Commentary on the Yaçna (then unknown to me), Paris, 1833; then by editions of the Zendavesta, more or less complete, lithographed in Paris by Bournouf, 1829-1843; by Brockhaus, in Leipsic, in Roman characters; by Spiegel, in Zend, 1851; by Westergaard, Copenhagen, 1852-4. Finally, Dr. Martin Haug, in four Essays, published last year in Bombay, has summed up the whole with consummate erudition and great perspicuity. All that is of importance may now be read in English. The result is the full recognition of the Zend as a genuine language; the sister, possibly the elder sister, of the Sanscrit (this had been already admitted by all the great masters of philological science, Bopp, Rask, Westergaard, Bournouf, Max Müller. My friend H. H. Wilson doubted; but I believe his doubts grew weaker, if they had not quite died away). Dr. Haug has wrought out the grammar, the structure, to a certain extent the literature, of the language. As to the religion of the Zendavesta, I cannot here enter into Dr. Haug's theory of the great schism which severed the primal Arian religion, which was Monotheistic, into Zoroastrianism and Brahminism, in which the Devas, the gods of the Brahminical Polytheism, became the devils of Zoroastrianism; the Asuras (the Ahuras), the god or gods of Zoroastrianism, the evil spirits of Brahminism. Bactria was the birth- and dwelling-place of Zoroastrianism, and India, the upper part of the Punjaub, of Brahminism. But the analysis of all the remaining sacred books of the Parsees is the most important and satisfactory part of Dr. Haug's work. I confess, indeed, that Dr. Haug's fine distinction between the religious and philosophical notions of Zoroaster is much too modern, too German, for me. But on the relative

to rest on their sacred records.¹ It is undoubtedly remarkable that among the Magian tenets we find so many of those doctrines about which the great schism in the Jewish popular creed, that of the traditionists and anti-traditionists, contended for several centuries. It has already been observed that in the later prophetic writings many allusions, and much of what may be called the poetic language and machinery, are strikingly similar to the main principles of the Magian faith. Nor can it be necessary to suggest how completely such expressions as the "children of light," and the "children of darkness," had become identified with the common language of the Jews at the time of our Saviour: and when our Lord proclaimed himself "the Light of the World," no doubt He employed a term familiar to the ears of the people, though, as usual, they might not clearly comprehend in what sense it was applicable to the Messiah, or to the purely moral character of the new religion.

It is generally admitted that the Jewish notions about the angels,ʰ one great subject of dispute in their synagogues, and what may be called The Angels.

---

ages and importance of the various fragments and books, which together form the Zendavesta, he is convincing and satisfactory. The primeval Yathas, fragments of songs or hymns (answering to the Vedas); he holds to be the sole original verse of Zaratushtra Spitama (Spitama is the name, Zaratushtra the title), and of his immediate successors. Then follow the Gathas and the Vendidads; the rest are much later. For my purpose, however, those tenets which were held in common by the Zoroastrians and the Jews of the Captivity are alone of importance. I find but little to retract or modify in the text.

¹ Mosheim has traced with brevity, but with his usual good sense and candour, this analogy between the traditional notions of the Jews and those of the Magians. De Reb. ante Const. M. ii. 7.

ʰ La doctrine de l'existence des anges, fondée sur la révélation, a été beaucoup modifiée par les opinions des peuples qui habitaient sur les rivages du fleuve Cobar, dans la Babylonie,

F 2

their Dæmonology, received a strong foreign tinge during their residence in Babylonia. The earliest books of the Old Testament fully recognize the ministration of angels; but in Babylonia ᵃ this simpler creed grew up into a regular hierarchy, in which the degrees of rank and subordination were arranged with almost heraldic precision. The seven great archangels of Jewish tradition correspond with the Amschaspands of the Zendavesta:ᵇ and in strict mutual analogy, both systems arrayed against each other a separate host of spiritual beings, with distinct powers and functions. Each nation, each individual had in one case his Ferver, in the other his guardian angel;ᶜ and was exposed to the

---

ᵃ et dans les autres pays de l'Orient, où les deux royaumes d'Israel et de Juda furent dispersés. Sous ce point de vue on peut regarder les *Mehestani*, ou les sectateurs de Zoroastre, comme ceux qui ont appris beaucoup des choses aux dépositaires de la tradition, et dont les maximes se retrouvent aujourd'hui dans les deux Talmuds. Chiarini, Le Talmud de Babylone, tom. i, p. 101.

ᵇ Even the traditionists among the Jews allowed that the names of the angels came from Babylon; they are nevertheless pure Hebrew or Chaldean. Mich-a-el (who is as God), Gabri-el, the Man of God. Gesen. Lex. in verb. Bellerman, über die Esser, p. 30. The transition from the primitive to the Babylonian belief may be traced in the apocryphal book of Tobit, no doubt of Eastern origin. On the Notions of Dæmons, see Jortin, Eccl. Hist. i. 181.

ᶜ Jonathan, the Chaldean paraphrast, on Gen. II. 7. "The Lord said to the seven angels that stand before him." Drusius, on Luke i. 19. Seven, however, seems to have been the number of perfection among the Jews from the earliest period. Old Testament, passim.

Six seems the sacred number with the Persians. The Amschaspands are usually reckoned six; but Oromasd is sometimes included to make up seven. See the Yesht of the Seven Amschaspands, in the Zendavesta of Du Perron or Kleuker. Compare also Foucher's Disquisition, translated in Kleuker, Anhang. i. p. 294. See also Haag's Celestial Council, p. 260.

ᵈ In the LXX. the doctrine of guardian angels is interpolated into the translation of Deut. xxxii. 8. Plato adopted the notion, either mediately, or immediately, from the East. Polit. et in Critiâ (in init.). Compare Max. Tyrius, xv. 17. Hostanes the Magian held the same opinions. Cypr. de Van. Idol., Min. Fel. Compare on the guardian angels of Zoroastrianism, Haag, pp. 190 et seqq.

malice of the hostile Dev or Dæmon. In apparent allusion to or coincidence with this system, the visions of Daniel represent Michael, the tutelar angel or intelligence of the Jewish people, in opposition to the four angels of the great monarchies; and even our Saviour seems to condescend to the popular language, when He represents the parental care of the Almighty over children, under the significant and beautiful image, "that in Heaven their angels do always behold the face of my Father which is in Heaven."[p]

The great impersonated Principle of Evil appears to have assumed much of the character of the antagonist power of darkness. The name itself of Satan,[q] which in the older poetical book of Job is assigned to a spirit of different attributes, one of the celestial ministers who assemble before the throne of the Almighty, and is used in the earlier books of the Old Testament in its simple sense of an adversary, became appropriated to the prince of the malignant spirits—the head and representative of the spiritual world, which ruled over physical as well as moral evil.

<small>Principle of Evil</small>

---

[p] Matt. xviii. 10.

[q] Schleusner, Lex., voc. SATAN. Dr. Russell, in a Dissertation prefixed to his Connexion of Sacred and Profane History, has traced the gradual development of this tenet. It is rather singular that in the work of Theodorus of Mopsuestia on Magianism (quoted Photii Bibliotheca, num. 81), Zervan is said to have produced τὸν 'Ορμίσ-δαν . . . καὶ τὸν Σατανᾶν. On the other side of this question may be consulted Rosenmüller on Job, ch. I., and Michaelis, Epimetron in Lowth, de sacra Poesi. Grimm, Deutsche Mythologie, p. 550, expresses himself nearly as in the text. Haag, however, asserts that a separate evil spirit, of equal powers with Ahura Mazdao and always opposed to him, is entirely strange to Zarathustra's theology, though the existence of such an opinion among the ancient Zoroastrians can be gathered from some later books, such as the Vendidad. There can, I think, be no doubt that it was the dominant doctrine in the times of which I write. Dr. Haag's primeval Zoroastrianism seems to me to be somewhat conjectural.

Even the notion of the one Supreme Deity had undergone some modification consonant to certain prevailing opinions of the time. Wherever any approximation had been made to the sublime truth of the one great First Cause, either awful religious reverence or philosophic abstraction had removed the primal Deity entirely beyond the sphere of human sense, and supposed that the intercourse of the Divinity with man, the moral government, and even the original creation, had been carried on by the intermediate agency, either in Oriental language of an Emanation, or in Platonic, of the Wisdom, Reason, or Intelligence of the one Supreme. This being was more or less distinctly impersonated, according to the more popular or more philosophic, the more material or more abstract notions of the age or people.[r]

Mediator. This was the doctrine from the Ganges, or even the shores of the Yellow Sea,[s] to the Ilissus; it was the fundamental principle of the Indian religion and Indian philosophy;[t] it was the basis of Zoroastrianism,[u] it was pure Platonism,[x] it was the Platonic

---

[r] It is curious to trace the development of this idea in the older and in the apocryphal books of the Old Testament. In the book of Proverbs, the Wisdom is little more than the great attribute of the Deity, an intellectual personification: in Ecclesiasticus it is a distinct and separate being, and " stands up beautiful " before the throne of God, xxiv. 1.

[s] M. Abel Rémusat says, of the three Chinese religions, " Parmi leurs dogmes fondamentaux, enseignés six siècles avant notre ère par Lao-tseu, un de leurs maîtres, est celui de l'existence de la raison primordiale, qui a créé le monde, le Logos des Platoniciens." Rech. Asiat. 2 sér. l. 38.

[t] In the Indian system Brahm, in the neuter, is the great Primal Spirit. See Baron W. Von Humboldt, über den Bhagavat Gita. Compare Bopp, Conjugations System, 290, 301.

[u] See above.

[x] Πᾶν τὸ δαιμόνιον μεταξύ ἐστι Θεοῦ καὶ θνητοῦ—Θεὸς δὲ ἀνθρώπῳ οὐ μίγνυται, ἀλλὰ διὰ τούτου πᾶσα ἐστὶ ἡ ὁμιλία. Plato, in Symp.

Judaism of the Alexandrian school. Many fine passages might be quoted from Philo, on the impossibility that the first self-existing Being should become cognizable to the sense of man; and even in Palestine, no doubt, John the Baptist, and our Lord himself, spoke no new doctrine, but rather the common sentiment of the more enlightened, when they declared that "no man had seen God at any time."[7] In conformity with this principle, the Jews, in the interpretation of the older Scriptures, instead of direct and sensible communication from the one great Deity, had interposed either one or more intermediate beings, as the channels of communication. According to one accredited tradition alluded to by St. Stephen, the Law was delivered "by the disposition of angels;"[z]—according to another, this office was delegated to a single angel, sometimes called the Angel of the Law,[a] at others the Metatron. But the more ordinary representative, as it were, of God to the sense and mind of man, was the Memra, or the Divine Word; and it is remarkable that the same appellation is found in the Indian,[b] the

The Word.

---

[7] John, i. 18. Compare John, i. 4, 18, vi. 46.

[z] Compare LXX. Transl. of Deut. xxxiii. 2, where the angels are interpolated. 'Ημῶν τὰ κάλλιστα τῶν δογμάτων καὶ τὰ ὁσιώτατα τῶν ἐν τοῖς νόμοις δι' ἀγγέλων παρὰ τοῦ θεοῦ μαθόντων. Joseph. Ant. xv. 5, 3. Compare Chiarini, i. 307. And on the traces of the Judæo-Alexandrian philosophy in the LXX. Dähne, Judisch-Alexandrinische Religions Philosophie, part ii. pp. 49-56.

[a] Compare Gal. iii. 19. Deus Mosen legem docuit: cum autem descrodisset, tanto timore perculsus est,

ut omnium obliviscoretur. Deus autem statim Jesifiam, Angelum legis, vocavit, qui ipsi legem tradidit bene ordinatam et custoditam, omnesque angeli amici ejus facti sunt. Jalkut Ruben, quoted by Wetstein and Schoetgen, in loco. See also Eisenmenger, 1-56. Two angels seem to be introduced in this latter tradition, the angelus Metatron, and Jesifia, angelus Legis.

Philo, de Præm., rationalises further, and considers the commandments communicated, as it were, by the air made articulate, ii. 405.

[b] It appears in the Indian system: Vach signifying speech. She is the

Persian, the Platonic, and the Alexandrian systems. By the Targumists, the earliest Jewish commentators on the Scriptures, this term had been already applied to the Messiah; nor is it necessary to observe the manner in which it has been sanctified by its introduction into the Christian scheme. From this remarkable uniformity of conception, and coincidence of language, has sometimes been assumed a common tradition, generally disseminated throughout the race of man. I should be content with receiving it as the general acquiescence of the human mind in the necessity of some mediation between the pure spiritual nature of the Deity and the

---

active power of Brahma, proceeding from him: she speaks a hymn in the Vedas, in praise of herself as the supreme and universal soul. (Colebrooke, in Asiatic Researches, viii. p. 402.) La première parole, que proféra le Créateur, ce fut Oum: Oum parut avant toutes choses, et il s'appelle le premier-né du Créateur. Oum ou Prana, parol au par éther renfermant en soi toutes les qualités, tous les élémens, est le nom, le corps de Brahm, et par conséquent infini comme lui, créateur et maître de toutes choses. Brahm méditant sur le Verbe divin y trouva l'eau primitive. Oupnek-Hat. quoted in De Guignaut, p. 644.

Origen, or rather the author of the Philosophoumena inserted in his works, was aware of this fact. Ἀυτοί (Brachmanes) τὸν θεὸν φῶς εἶναι λέγουσιν οὐχ ὁποῖόν τις ὁρᾷ, οὐδ' οἷον ἥλιος καὶ πῦρ· ἀλλὰ ἐστιν αὐτοῖς ὁ Θεὸς λόγος, οὐχ ὁ ἔναρθρος, ἀλλὰ ὁ τῆς γνώσεως, δι' οὗ τὰ κρύπτα τῆς γνώσεως μυστήρια ὁρᾶται σοφοῖς. De Brachman.

According to a note, partly by M. le Normant, partly by M. Champollion, in Chateaubriand (Etudes sur l'Histoire), Thoth is, in the hieroglyphical language of Egypt, the World.

In the Persian system the use of the term Honover is by no means consistent; strictly speaking it occupies only a third place. Ormuzd, the Good Principle, created the external universe by his Word (Honover); in another sense the great primal spirit is the Word; in another, the Principle of Good.

It is by the latter, as may be seen in the works of Lightfoot, Schoetgen, and other Talmudic writers, and in Bertholdt (Christologia Judaica), that it is applied to the Messiah, not by Philo, who, as will appear, scarcely, if ever, notices a personal Messiah.

Dr. Burton (in his Bampton Lectures) acknowledges, of course, the antiquity of the term, and suggests the most sensible mode of reconciling this fact with its adoption into Christianity.

intellectual and moral being of man, of which the sublimest and simplest, and therefore the most natural development, was the revelation of God in Christ—in the inadequate language of our version of the original "the brightness of (God's) glory, and the express image of his person."[f]

No question has been more strenuously debated than the knowledge of a future state, entertained by the earlier Jews. At all events it is quite clear, that before the time of Christ, not merely the immortality of the soul, but what is very different, a final resurrection,[g] had become completely interwoven with the popular belief. Passages in the later prophets, Daniel and Ezekiel, particularly a very remarkable one in the latter, may be adduced as the first distinct authorities on which this belief might be grounded. It appears, however, in its more perfect development, soon after the return from the Captivity. As early as the revolt of the Maccabees, it was so deeply rooted in the public mind, that we find a solemn ceremony performed for the dead.[h] From henceforth it became the leading article of the great schism between the traditionists and the anti-traditionists, the Pharisees and the Sadducees: and in the Gospels we cannot but discover at a glance its almost universal prevalence. Even the Roman historian was struck by its influence on the indomitable character of the people.[i] In the Zoroastrian religion, a resurrection holds a place no less prominent, than in the

<small>[marginal note: Future State.]</small>

---

[f] Ἀπαύγασμα τῆς δόξης καὶ χαρακτὴρ τῆς ὑποστάσεως αὐτοῦ. Hebrews i. 3.

[g] It is singular how often this material point of difference has been lost sight of in the discussions on this subject.

[h] 2 Macc. xii. 44.

[i] Animasque prælio et suppliciis peremptorum æternas putant. Tac. Hist. v. 5.

later Jewish belief.[k] On the day of the final triumph of the Great Principle of Light, the children of light are to be raised from the dead, to partake in the physical splendour, and to assume the moral perfection of the subjects of the triumphant Principle of Good. In the same manner, the Jews associated together the coming of the Messiah with the final resurrection. From many passages, quoted by Lightfoot, I select the following: "The righteous, whom the Lord shall raise from the dead in the days of the Messiah, when they are restored to life, shall not again return to their dust, neither in the days of the Messiah, nor in the following age, but their flesh shall remain upon them."[m]

Out of all these different sources, from whence they derived a knowledge of a future state, the passages of their prophets in their own sacred writings (among which that in the book of Daniel, from its coincidence with the Zoroastrian tenet, might easily be misapplied), and the Oriental element, the popular belief of the Palestinian Jews had moulded up a splendid though confused vision of the appearance of the Messiah, the simultaneous regeneration of all things, the resurrection of the dead, and the reign of the Messiah upon earth. All these events were to take place at once, or to follow close upon each other. In many passages, the

---

[k] Hyde, de Vet. Pers. Relig. 537 and 293. Beausobre, Hist. du Manicheisme, l. 204. 'Αναβιώσεσθαι κατὰ τοὺς Μάγους τοὺς ἀνθρώπους καὶ ἔσεσθαι ἀθανάτους. Theopomp. apud Diog. Laert. Kleuker's Zendavesta and Anhang. part II. p. 110. Boundehesch, cis. xxxi. &c. Compare Gesenius on Isaiah xxvi. 19. On the Zoroastrian Resurrection and Palingenesis see Haag. p. 268. The idea of a future life and immortality of the soul is expressed very distinctly already in the Gathas, and pervades the whole later Zend literature. The belief in a life to come is one of the chief dogmas of the Zendavesta, p. 205.

[m] Lightfoot, v. 255, x. 495, xi. 353.

language of the Apostles clearly intimates that they were as little prepared to expect a purely religious renovation, at the coming of the Messiah, as the rest of their countrymen; and throughout the Apostolic age, this notion still maintained its ground, and kept up the general apprehension, that the final consummation was immediately at hand.[a] It is no doubt impossible to assign their particular preponderance to these several elements, which combined to form the popular belief: yet, even if many of their notions entirely originated in the Zoroastrian system, it would be curious to observe how, by the very calamities of the Jews, Divine Providence adapted them for the more important part which they were to fill in the history of mankind; and to trace the progressive manner in which the Almighty prepared the development of the more perfect and universal system of Christianity.

For, with whatever Oriental colouring Jewish tradition might invest the image of the great Deliverer, in Palestine it still remained rigidly national and exclusive. If the Jew concurred with the worshipper of Ormuzd in expecting a final restoration of all things through the agency of a Divine Intelligence,[b] that Being, according to the promise to their fathers, was to be

Messiah national.

---

[a] Compare 2 Esdras vi. 24, 25.

[b] The Persians long preserved the notion of a restoration of the law of Zoroaster by a kind of Messiah. "Suivant les traditions des Parses, rapportées dans la Zerdouscht-nameh et dans le Djamaspi-nameh, Pashoutan, l'un des personnages destinés à faire refleurir la religion de Zoroastre, et l'empire des Perses dans les derniers temps, demeure en attendant ce moment dans le Kanguédez, pays qui paroît répondre en partie à Khorassan. Il en sortira à l'ordre, qui lui sera apporté par un ized (i. e. spiritus celestis) nommé Serosch, et reviendra dans l'Iran. Par l'efficace des paroles sacrées de l'Avesta, il mettra en fuite les barbares, qui désoloient ce pays, y rétablira la religion dans toute sa pureté, et y fera remaître l'abondance, le bonheur, et la paix." Silvestre de Sacy, sur div. Ant. de la Perse, p. 95.

intimately connected with their race; he was to descend from the line of David; he was to occupy Sion, the holy city, as the centre of his government; he was to make his appearance in the temple on Mount Moriah; he was to reassemble all the scattered descendants of the tribes, to discomfit and expel their barbarous and foreign rulers. The great distinction between the two races of mankind fell in completely with their hereditary prejudices: the children of Abraham were, as their birthright, the children of light; and even the doctrine of the resurrection was singularly harmonised with that exclusive nationality. At least the first resurrection ᵖ was to be their separate portion; ᵍ it was to summon them, if not all, at least the more righteous, from Paradise, from the abode of departed spirits; and under their triumphant king they were to enjoy a thousand years of glory and bliss upon the recreated and renovated earth.ʳ

ᵖ 2 Esd. xi. 10-31. All Israelites (says the Mischna, Tract. Sanh. c. xi. 12) shall partake in the life to come—except those who deny the resurrection of the dead (the Sadducees?) and that the law came from heaven, and the Epicureans. R. Akiba added, he who reads foreign books—Aba Schaul, he who pronounces the ineffable name (Jehovah). Three kings and four private individuals have no share in the life to come:—the kings, Jeroboam, Ahab, Manasseh; the four private men, Balaam, Doeg, Achitophel, ——?

ᵍ It is good (says the martyred youth in the book of Maccabees) being put to death by men, to be raised up again by him; as for thee, thou shalt have no resurrection to life. 2 Macc. ⁊. 14; all. 44; also 2 Esd. ii. 23.

Compare the speech of Josephus, Hist. of the Jews, vol. ii. p. 267. Quotations might be multiplied from the Rabbinical writers.

ʳ Tanchuma, fol. 255. Quot sunt dies Messiæ? R. Eliezer, filius R. Jose, Galilæus, dixit Messiæ tempora sunt mille anni, secundum dictum Jer. xxiii. 4. Dies enim Dei mille est annorum. Bertholdt, p. 38.

The holy blessed God will renew the world for a thousand years—quoted by Lightfoot, iii. 37. If I presume to treat the millennium as a fable "of Jewish dotage," I may remind my readers that this expression is taken from what once stood as an Article (the forty-first) of our Church. See Collier for the Articles in Edward the Sixth's reign. Atque de hujus in his terris regno, mille annos duraturo

We pass from the rich poetic impersonations, the fantastic but expressive symbolic forms of the East, to the colder and clearer light of Grecian philosophy, with which the Western Jews, especially in Alexandria, had endeavoured to associate their own religious truths. The poetic age of Greece had long passed away before the two nations came into contact; and the same rationalising tendency of the times led the Greek to reduce his religion, the Jew the history of his nation, to a lofty moral allegory.* Enough of poetry remained in the philosophic system, adopted in the great Jewish Alexandrian school, that of Plato, to leave ample scope for the imagination: and indeed there was a kind of softened Orientalism, probably derived by Plato from his master Pythagoras, by Pythagoras from the East, which readily assimilated with the mystic interpretations of the Egypto-Jewish theology. The Alexandrian notions of the days of the Messiah are faintly shadowed out in the book "of the Wisdom of Solomon,"† in terms which occasionally remind us of some which occur in the New Testament. The righteous Jews, on account of their acknowledged moral and religious superiority, were to "judge the nations," and have "dominion over all people." But the more perfect development of these views is to be found in the works of Philo. This writer, who, however inclined to soar into the cloudy realms of mysticism, often rests in the middle region of the moral

---

ejusdemque deliciis et voluptatibus, de bellis ejus cum terribili quodam adversario quem Antichristum dicebant, de victoriis deoique earumque fructibus mirabilia narrabant somnia, quorum deinde pars ad Christianos transferebatur. Mosheim, II. 8.

* This was the kingdom of heaven, the kingdom of God—of Christ, or emphatically "the kingdom." See Kuinoel, vol. I. p. 61, Schoetgen, Hor. Heb. p. 1147.
* Compare Bertholdt, ch. vi.
† Wisdom III. 8; v. 16; viii. 14.

sublime, and abounds in passages which would scarcely do discredit to his Athenian master, had arrayed a splendid vision of the perfectibility of human nature, in which his own nation was to take the most distinguished part. From them knowledge and virtue were to emanate through the universal race of man. The whole world, convinced at length of the moral superiority of the Mosaic institutes, interpreted, it is true, upon the allegorical system, and so harmonised with the sublimest Platonism of the Greeks, was to submit in voluntary homage, and render allegiance to the great religious teachers and examples of mankind." The Jews themselves, thus suddenly regenerated to more than the primitive purity and loftiness of their Law (in which the Divine Reason, the Logos, was as it were embodied), were to gather together from all quarters, and under the guidance of a more than human being, unseen to all eyes but those of the favoured nation [a] (such was the only vestige of the Messiah), to reassemble in their native land. There the great era of virtue, and peace, and abundance, productiveness of the soil, prolificness in the people, in short, of all the blessings promised in the book of Deuteronomy, was to commence and endure for ever. This people was to be invincible, since true valour is inseparable from true virtue. By a singular inference, not out of character with allegoric interpreters who, while they refine the plainest facts and precepts to a more subtle and mystic meaning, are apt to take that which is evidently figurative in a literal sense, the very wild beasts, in awe and wonder at this pure and passionless race, who shall have ceased to rage against each other with bestial ferocity,

<small>Reign of Messiah according to Alexandrian Jews.</small>

---

[a] E. g. Vita Mosis, ii.; Opera, ii. p. 141.   [b] De Exerc. ii. 433, 436.

were to tame their savage hostility to mankind.[y] Thus the prophecy of Isaiah, to which Philo seems to allude, though he does not adduce the words, was to be accomplished to the letter; and that paradisiacal state of amity between brute and man, so beautifully described by Milton, perhaps from this source, was finally to be renewed. And as the Jewish philosopher, contrary to most of his own countrymen and to some of the Grecian sects, denied the future dissolution of the world by fire, and asserted its eternity,[z] he probably contemplated the everlasting duration of this peaceful and holy state.

Such, for no doubt the Alexandrian opinions had penetrated into Palestine, particularly among the Hellenist Jews—such were the vast, incoherent, and dazzling images with which the future teemed to the hopes of the Jewish people.[a] They admitted either a part or the whole of the common belief, as accorded with their tone of mind and feeling. Each region, each rank, each sect; the Babylonian, the Egyptian, the Palestinian, the Sama-

Belief different according to character of the believer.

---

[y] De Præm. ii. p. 422.

[z] De Mundi Incorruptibilitate, passim.

[a] The following passages from the apocryphal books may be consulted; I do not think it necessary to refer to all the citations which might be made from the Prophets:—The "faithful prophet" is mentioned, 1 Macc. xiv. 41; the discomfiture of the enemies of Israel, Judith xvi. 17; universal peace, Ecclesiast. l. 23, 24; the reassembling of the tribes, Tobit xiii. 13-18. Baruch ii. 34, 35; the conversion of many nations, Tobit xiii. 11, xiv. 6, 7: see particularly the second apocryphal book of Esdras, which, although manifestly Judæo-Christian, is of value as illustrating the opinions of the times,—" Thou madest the world for our sakes; as for the other people, which also come of Adam, thou hast said that they are nothing, but be like unto spittle; and hast likened the abundance of them unto a drop that falleth from a vessel. . . . . If the world now be made for our sakes, why do we not possess an inheritance with the world? how long shall this endure?" 2 Esdras vi. 56-59.

ritan; the Pharisee, the Lawyer, the Zealot, arrayed the Messiah in those attributes which suited his own temperament. Of that which was more methodically taught in the synagogue or the adjacent school, the populace caught up whatever made the deeper impression. The enthusiasm took an active or contemplative, an ambitious or a religious, an earthly or a heavenly tone, according to the education, habits, or station of the believer; and to different men the Messiah was man or angel, or more than angel; he was king,[b] conqueror, or moral reformer; a more victorious Joshua, a more magnificent Herod, a wider-ruling Cæsar, a wiser Moses,[c] a holier Abraham;[d] an Angel, the Angel of the Covenant, the Metatron, the Mediator between God and man;[e] Michael, the great tutelar archangel of the nation, who appears by some to have been identified with the mysterious Being who led them forth from Egypt; he was the Word of God;[f] an Emanation from the Deity; himself partaking of the

---

[b] The Gospels, passim; 2 Esdras xii. 32.

[c] Thou wilt proclaim liberty to thy people, the house of Israel, by the hand of Messias, as thou didst by the hand of Moses and Aaron, on the day of the Passover. Chald. Par. on Lament. ii. 22, quoted by Lightfoot, v. 181.

Among others to the same purport, the following, of a later date, is curious. Moses came out of the wilderness, and King Messias out of the midst of Rome; the one spake in the head of a cloud, and the other spake in the head of a cloud, and the Word of the Lord speaking between them, and they walking together. Targ. Jer. on Exod. xii.

[d] "Behold, glorious shall be my servant King Messiah, exalted, lofty, and very high: more exalted than Abraham, for it is written of him, I have lifted up my hand to the Lord (Gen. xiv. 22); and more exalted than Moses, for it is written of him, He saith of me, Take him unto thy bosom, for he is greater than the fathers." Jalkut Shamuni; see Bertholdt, 101.

Some of the titles of the Messiah, recognised by general belief and usage, will be noticed as they occur in the course of the History.

[e] Sohar, quoted by Bertholdt, p. 121, 133.

[f] Many of the quotations about the Memra, or divine Word, may be found in Dr. Pye Smith's work on the Messiah.

divine nature. While this was the religious belief, some there were, no doubt, of the Sadducaic party, or the half-Græcised adherents of the Herodian family, who treated the whole as a popular delusion; or, as Josephus with Vespasian, would not scruple to employ it as a politic means for the advancement of their own fortunes. While the robber chieftain looked out from his hill-tower to see the blood-red banner of him whom he literally expected to come "from Edom with dyed garments from Bozrah," and "treading the wine-press in his wrath," the Essene in his solitary hermitage, or monastic fraternity of husbandmen, looked to the reign of the Messiah, when the more peaceful images of the same prophet would be accomplished, and the Prince of Peace establish his quiet and uninterrupted reign.

In the body of the people, the circumstances of the times powerfully tended both to develope more fully, and to stamp more deeply into their hearts, the expectation of a temporal deliverer, a conqueror, a king. As misgovernment irritated, as exaction pressed, as national pride was wounded by foreign domination, so enthusiasm took a fiercer and more martial turn: as the desire of national independence became the predominant sentiment, the Messiah was more immediately expected to accomplish that which lay nearest to their hearts. The higher views of his character, and the more unworldly hopes of a spiritual and moral revolution, receded further and farther from the view; and as the time approached in which the Messiah was to be born, the people in general were in a less favourable state of mind to listen to the doctrines of peace, humility, and love, or to recognise that Messiah in a being so entirely divested of temporal power or splendour. In the ruling party, on the other hand, as will hereafter appear, the dread of this inflammable state of the public mind, and the dangerous position of affairs, would confirm that jealousy of innovation inseparable from established governments. Every tendency to commotion would be repressed with a strong hand, or at least the rulers would be constantly on the watch, by their forward zeal in condemning all disturbers of the public peace, to exculpate themselves with their foreign masters from any participation in the tumult. Holding, no doubt, with devout, perhaps with conscientious earnestness, the promised coming of the Messiah as an abstract truth, and as an article of their religious creed, their own interests, their rank and authority, were so connected with the existing order of things, political prudence would appear so fully to justify more than ordinary caution, that while they would have fiercely resented any imputation on their want of faith in the divine promises, it would have been difficult, even by the most public and imposing "signs," to have satisfied their cool incredulity.

With all these elements of political and religious excitement stirring through the whole fabric of society, it would be difficult to conceive a nation in a more extraordinary state of suspense and agitation than the Jews about the period of the birth of Christ. Their temporal and religious fortunes seemed drawing to an immediate issue. Their king lay slowly perishing of a lingering and loathsome disease; and his temper, which had so often broken out into paroxysms little short of insanity, now seemed to be goaded by bodily and mental anguish to the fury of a wild beast. Every day might be anticipated the spectacle of the execution of his eldest son, now on his way from Rome, and known to have been detected in his unnatural treasons. It seemed that even yet the royal authority and the stern fanaticism of the religious party, which had, for many years, lowered upon each other with hostile front, might grapple in a deadly struggle. The more prudent of the religious leaders could scarcely restrain the indignant enthusiasm of their followers, which broke out at once on the accession of Archelaus; while, on the other hand, the almost incredible testamentary cruelty, by which Herod commanded the heads of the principal Jewish families to be assembled in the Hippodrome, at the signal of his death, to be cut down in a promiscuous massacre, may reasonably be ascribed to remorseless policy, as well as to frantic vengeance. He might suppose that, by removing all opponents of weight and influence, he could secure the peaceable succession of his descendants, if the Emperor, according to his promise, should ratify the will, by which he had divided his dominions among his surviving sons.[f]

In the midst of this civil confusion, that great event took place, which was to produce so total a revolution in the state of all mankind. However striking the few incidents which are related of the birth of Christ, when contemplated distinct and separate from the stirring transactions of the times, and through the atmosphere, as it were, of devotional feelings, which at once seem to magnify and harmonise them; yet, for this very reason, we are perhaps scarcely capable of judging the effect which such events actually produced, and the relative magnitude in which they appeared to the contemporary generation. For if we endeavour to cast ourselves back into the period to which these incidents belong, and place ourselves, as it were, in the

---

[f] Compare Hist. of the Jews, vol. ii. p. 88.

midst of the awful political crisis, which seemed about to decide at once the independence or servitude of the nation, and might, more or less, affect the private and personal welfare of each family and individual, it will by no means move our wonder, that the commotion excited by the appearance of the Magians in Jerusalem, and the announcement of the birth of the Christ, should not have made a more deep impression on the public mind, and should have passed away, it should seem, so speedily from the popular remembrance. In fact, even if generally credited, the intelligence that the Messiah had appeared in the form of a new-born infant, would rather perhaps have disappointed, than gratified, the high-wrought expectation, which looked for an instant, an immediate deliverance, and would be too impatient to await the slow development of his manhood. Whether the more considerate expected the Deliverer suddenly to reveal himself in his maturity of strength and power, may be uncertain: but the last thing that the more ardent and fiery looked for, particularly those who supposed that the Messiah would partake of the divine or superhuman nature, was his appearance as a child; the last throne to which they would be summoned to render their homage, would be the cradle of a helpless infant.[b]

Nor is it less important, throughout the early history of Christianity, to seize the spirit of the times. Events which appear to us so extraordinary, that we can scarcely conceive that they should either fail in exciting a powerful sensation, or ever be obliterated from the popular remembrance, in their own day might pass off as of little more than ordinary occur-

Belief in preternatural interpositions.

---

[b] "When Christ cometh, no man knoweth whence he is." John vii. 27.

rence. During the whole life of Christ, and the early propagation of the religion, it must be borne in mind that they took place in an age, and among a people, which superstition had made so familiar with what were supposed to be preternatural events, that wonders awakened no emotion, or were speedily superseded by some new demand on the ever-ready belief. The Jews of that period not only believed that the Supreme Being had the power of controlling the course of nature, but that the same influence was possessed by multitudes of subordinate spirits, both good and evil. Where the pious Christian in the present day would behold the direct agency of the Almighty, the Jews would invariably have interposed an angel as the author or ministerial agent in the wonderful transaction. Where the Christian moralist would condemn the fierce passion, the ungovernable lust, or the inhuman temper, the Jew discerned the workings of diabolical possession. Scarcely a malady was endured, or crime committed, but it was traced to the operation of one of these myriad dæmons, who watched every opportunity of exercising their malice in the sufferings and the sins of men.

Yet the first incident in Christian history, the annunciation of the conception and birth of John the Baptist,[1] as its wonderful circumstances took place in a priestly family, and on so public a scene as the Temple, might be expected to excite the public attention in no ordinary degree. The four Levitical families who returned from the Captivity had been distributed into twenty-four courses, one of which came into actual office in the Temple every week: they had assumed the old names, as if descended

Conception and birth of John the Baptist (A.C. 5).

---

[1] Luke i. 5-22.

in direct lineage from the original heads of families; and thus the regular ministrations of the priesthood were reorganised on the ancient footing, coeval with the foundation of the Temple. In the course of Abia, the eighth in order,[a] was an aged priest, named Zachariah. The officiating course were accustomed to cast lots for the separate functions. Some of these were considered of higher dignity than others, which were either of a more menial character, or at least were not held in equal estimation. Nearly the most important was the watching and supplying with incense the great brazen altar, which stood within the building of the Temple, in the first or Holy Place. Into this, at the sound of a small bell, which gave notice to the worshippers at a distance, the ministering priest entered alone. And in the sacred chamber, into which the light of day never penetrated, but where the dim fires of the altar, and the chandeliers, which were never extinguished, gave a solemn and uncertain light, still more bedimmed by the clouds of smoke arising from the newly fed altar of incense, no doubt, in the pious mind, the sense of the more immediate presence of the Deity, only separated by the veil, which divided the Holy Place from the Holy of Holies, would constantly have awakened the most profound emotions. While the priest was employed within the gates, the multitude of worshippers in the adjacent court awaited his return; for it would seem, that the offering of incense was considered emblematic of the prayers of the whole

---

[a] As each came into office twice in the year, and there is nothing to indicate whether this was the first or second period, it appears to me quite impossible to calculate the time of the year in which this event took place. Of this ordering of the courses, observes Lightfoot, both Talmuds speak largely. iiL 21.

nation; and though it took place twice every day, at morning and evening, the entrance and return of the priest from the mysterious precincts were watched by the devout with something of awful anxiety.

This day, to the general astonishment, Zachariah, to whom the function had fallen, lingered far beyond the customary time. For it is said of the high-priest's annual entrance into the Holy of Holies, that he usually stayed within as short a time as possible, lest the anxious people should fear, that on account of some omission in the offering, or guilt in the minister, or perhaps in the nation, of which he was the federal religious head, he might have been stricken with death. It may be supposed, therefore, that even in the subordinate ceremonies there was a certain ordinary time, after which the devouter people would begin to tremble, lest their representative, who in their behalf was making the national offering, might have met with some sinister or fatal sign of the divine disfavour. When at length Zachariah appeared he could not speak; and it was evident that in some mysterious manner he had been struck dumb, and to the anxious inquiries he could only make known by signs that something awful and unusual had taken place within the sanctuary. At what period he made his full relation of the wonderful fact which had occurred does not appear; but it was a relation of absorbing interest both to the aged man himself, who, although his wife was far advanced in years, was to be blessed with offspring; and to the whole people, as indicating the fulfilment of one of the preliminary signs which were universally accredited as precursive of the Messiah.

In the vision of Zachariah, he had beheld an angel standing on the right side of the altar, who announced that his prayer was heard,[m] and that his barren house was to be blessed; that his aged wife should bear a son, and that son be consecrated from his birth to the service of God, and observe the strictest austerity; that he was to revive the decaying spirit of religion, unite the disorganised nation, and above all, should appear as the expected harbinger, who was to precede and prepare the way for the approaching Redeemer. The angel proclaimed himself to be the messenger of God (Gabriel), and both as a punishment for his incredulity, and a sign of the certainty of the promise, Zachariah was struck dumb, but with an assurance that the affliction should remain only till the accomplishment of the divine prediction in the birth of his son.[n] If, as has been said, the vision of Zachariah was in any manner communicated to the assembled people (though the silence of the evangelist makes strongly against any such supposition), or even to his kindred the officiating priesthood, it would no doubt have caused a great sensation, falling in, as it would, with the prevailing tone of the public mind. For it was the general belief that some messenger would, in the language of Isaiah, "prepare the way of the Lord;" and the last words which had, as it were, sealed the book of prophecy, intimated, as many supposed, the *personal* reappearance of Elijah, the greatest, and, in popular opinion, a sort of representative of the whole prophetic community. The ascetic life to which the infant prophet was to be dedicated, according to the

---

[m] Grotius and many other writers are of opinion that by this is meant, not the prayer of Zachariah for offspring, but the general national prayer, offered by him in his ministerial function, for the appearance of the Messiah.

[n] According to Josephus, Ant. xiii. 18, Hyrcanus, the high-priest, heard a voice from heaven, while he was offering on the altar of incense.

Nazaritish vow of abstinence from all wine or strong drink, was likewise a characteristic of the prophetic order, which, although many, more particularly among the Essenes, asserted their inspired knowledge of futurity, was generally considered to have ceased in the person of Malachi, the last whose oracles were enrolled in the sacred canon.°

It does not appear that dumbness was a legal disqualification for the sacerdotal function, for Zachariah remained among his brethren, the priests, till their week of ministration ended. He then returned to his usual residence in the southern part of Judæa, most probably in the ancient and well-known city of Hebron,ᵖ which was originally a Levitical city; and although the sacerdotal order had not resumed the exclusive possession of their cities at the return from the Captivity, it might lead the priestly families to settle more generally in those towns; and Hebron, though of no great size, was considered remarkably populous in proportion to its extent. The divine promise began to be accomplished; and during the five first months of her pregnancy, Elizabeth, the wife of Zachariah, concealed herself, either avoiding the curious inquiries of her neighbours in these jealous and perilous

Return of Zachariah to Hebron.

° The mythic interpreters (see Strauss, p. 138) assert that this "short poem," as they call it, was invented out of the passages in the Old Testament relating to the births of Isaac, Samson, and Samuel, by a Judaizing Christian, while there were still genuine followers of John the Baptist, in order to conciliate them to Christianity. This is admitting very high antiquity for the passage; and unless it coincided with their own traditions, was it likely to have any influence upon that sect?

ᵖ Yet, as there seems no reason why the city of Hebron should not be named, many of the most learned writers, Valesius, Reland, Harenberg, Kuinoel, have supposed that Jutta (the name of a small city) is the right reading, which, being little known, was altered into a city (of) Judah.

times, or in devotional retirement, rendering thanks to the Almighty for the unexpected blessing.[t]

It was on a far less public scene that the birth of Christ, of whom the child of Zachariah was to be the harbinger, was announced to the Virgin Mother. The families which traced their descent from the house of David had fallen into poverty and neglect. When, after the return from the Babylonian captivity, the sovereignty had been assumed, first by the high-priests of Levitical descent, subsequently by the Asmonean family, who were likewise of the priestly line, and finally, by the house of Herod, of Idumean origin, but engrafted into the Maccabean line by the marriage of Herod with Mariamne, it was the most obvious policy to leave in the obscurity into which they had sunk, that race which, if it should produce any pretendant of the least distinction, he might advance an hereditary claim, as dear to the people as it would be dangerous to the reigning dynasty. The whole descendants of the royal race seem to have sunk so low, that even the popular belief, which looked to the line of David, as that from which the Messiah was to spring,[u] did not invest them with sufficient importance to awaken the jealousy or suspicion of the rulers. Joseph, a man

---

[t] Luke i. 23-25.

[u] This opinion revived so strongly in the time of Domitian, as, according to the Christian historian, to awaken the apprehension of the Roman emperor, who commanded diligent search to be made for all who claimed descent from the line of David. It does not appear how many were discovered, as Eusebius relates the story merely for the purpose of showing that the descendants of our Lord's brethren were brought before the Emperor, and dismissed as simple labourers, too humble to be regarded with suspicion. Many families of this lineage may have perished in the exterminating war of Titus, between the birth of Christ and this inquiry of Domitian. In later times the Prince of the Captivity, with what right it would be impossible to decide, traced his descent from the line of the ancient kings. Conf. Casaubon, Exercit. Anti-Baron. ii. p. 17.

THE ANNUNCIATION.

descended from this royal race, had migrated, for some unknown reason, to a distance from the part of the land inhabited by the tribe of Benjamin, to which, however, they were still considered to belong. He had settled in Nazareth, an obscure town in Lower Galilee, which, independent of the general disrepute in which the whole of the Galilean provinces were held by the inhabitants of the more holy district of Judæa, seems to have been marked by a kind of peculiar proverbial contempt. Joseph had been betrothed to a virgin of his own race, named Mary; but according to Jewish usage, some time was to elapse between the betrothment and the espousals. In this interval took place the annunciation of the divine conception to the Virgin.[a] In no part is the singular simplicity of the Gospel narrative more striking than in the relation of this incident; and I should be inclined, for this reason alone, to reject the notion that these chapters were of a later date.[b] So early does that remarkable characteristic of the evangelic writings develope itself; the manner in which they relate, in the same calm and equable tone, the most extraordinary and most trivial events; the apparent absence either of wonder in the writer, or the desire of producing a strong effect on the mind of the reader.[c] To illustrate this,

---

[a] Luke I. 26, 38.

[b] I cannot discover any great force in the *critical* arguments adduced to disjoin these preliminary chapters from the rest of the narrative. There is a very remarkable evidence of their authenticity in the curious apocryphal book (the Ascensio Isaiæ, published from the Æthiopic by Archbishop Lawrence). Compare Gesenius, Jesaias, Einleitung, p. 50. This writing marks its own date, the end of the reign of Nero, with unusual certainty, and contains distinct allusions to these facts, as forming integral parts of the life of Christ. The events were no doubt treasured in the memory of Mary, and might by her be communicated to the Apostles.

[c] I may be in error, but this appears to me the marked and perceptible *internal* difference between the genuine and apocryphal Gospels. The latter are *mythic*, not merely in the matter, but also in their style.

no passage can be more striking than the account of her vision,—" And the angel came in unto her, and said, Hail thou that art highly favoured, the Lord is with thee: blessed art thou among women. And when she saw him, she was troubled at his saying, and cast in her mind what manner of salutation this should be. And the angel said unto her, Fear not, Mary: for thou hast found favour with God. And, behold, thou shalt conceive in thy womb, and bring forth a Son, and shalt call his name JESUS. He shall be great, and shall be called the Son of the Highest: and the Lord God shall give unto him the throne of his father David: and he shall reign over the house of Jacob for ever; and of his kingdom there shall be no end. Then said Mary unto the angel, How shall this be, seeing I know not a man? And the angel answered and said unto her, The Holy Ghost shall come upon thee, and the power of the Highest shall overshadow thee: therefore also that holy thing which shall be born of thee shall be called the Son of God. And, behold, thy cousin Elizabeth, she hath also conceived a son in her old age; and this is the sixth month with her, who was called barren. For with God nothing shall be impossible. And Mary said, Behold the handmaid of the Lord; be it unto me according to thy word. And the angel departed from her."

The Incarnation of the Deity, or the union of some part of the Divine Essence with a material or human body, is by no means an uncommon religious notion, more particularly in the East. Yet, in the doctrine as subsequently developed by Christianity, there seems the same important difference which characterises the whole system of the ancient and modern religions. It is in the former a mythological impersonation of the Power, in Christ it is the Goodness of the Deity, which, associating itself with a human form, assumes the character of a representative of the human race; in whose person is exhibited a pure model of moral perfection, and whose triumph over evil is by the slow and gradual progress of enlightening the mind, and softening and purifying the heart. The moral purpose of the descent of the Deity is by no means excluded in the religions in which a similar notion has prevailed, as neither is that of divine power, though confining itself to acts of pure beneficence, from the Christian scheme. This seems more particularly the case, if we may state any thing with certainty concerning those half-mythological, half-real personages, the Buddh, Gautama, or Somana Codom of the remoter East.[1] In these systems likewise the overbearing excess of human wickedness demands the interference, and the restoration of a better order of things is the object, which vindicates the presence of the embodied Deity; yet there is invariably a greater or less connexion with the Oriental cosmogonical systems; it is the triumph of mind over matter, the termination of the long strife between the two adverse principles. The Christian scheme, however it may occasionally admit the current language of the

---

[1] The characteristic of the Buddhist religion, which in one respect may be considered (I deprecate misconstruction) the Christianity of the remoter East, seems an union of political with religious reformation; its end to substitute purer morality for the wild and multifarious idolatry into which Brahminism had degenerated, and to break down the distinction of castes. But Buddhism appears to be essentially monastic; and how different the superstitious regard for life in the Buddhist from the enlightened humanity of Christianity! See Mahony, in Asiat. Research. vii. p. 40.

M. Klaproth has somewhere said, that, "next to the Christian, no religion has contributed more to ennoble the human race than the Buddha religion." Compare likewise the very judicious observations of Wm. Humboldt, Über die Kawi Sprache, p. 95.

time, as where Christ is called the "Light of the World," yet in its scope and purport stands clear and independent of all these physical notions: it is original, inasmuch as it is purely, essentially, and exclusively a moral revelation; its sole design to work a moral change; to establish a new relation between man and the Almighty Creator, and to bring to light the great secret of the immortality of man.

Hence the only deviation from the course of nature was the birth of this Being from a pure virgin.[r] Much has been written on this subject; but it is more consistent with our object to

---

[r] According to a tradition known in the West at an early period, and quoted by Jerome (Adv. Jovin. c. 26), Buddh was born of a virgin. So were the Fohi of China and the Shaka of Thibet, no doubt the same, whether a mythic or a real personage. The Jesuits in China were appalled at finding in the mythology of that country, the counterpart of the "Virgo Deipara." (Barrow's Travels in China, I.) There is something extremely curious in the appearance of the same religious notions in remote, and apparently quite disconnected countries, where it is impossible to trace the secret manner of their transmission. Certain incidents, for example, in the history of the Indian Crishna, are so similar to those of the life of Christ, that De Guignant is almost inclined to believe that they are derived from some very early Christian tradition. In the present instance, however, the peculiar sanctity attributed to virginity in all countries, where the ascetic principle is held in high honour as approximating the pure and passionless human being to the Divinity, might suggest such an origin for a Deity in human form. But the birth of Buddh seems purely mythic: he was born from Maia, the virgin goddess of the imaginative world—as it were the Phantasia of the Greeks, who was said by some to have given birth to Homer. The Shaka of Thibet was born from the nymph Lhamoghinpral. Georgi. Alph. Tibet. Compare Rosenmüller, das Alte und Neue Morgenland, v. iv.; on Buddh and his birth, Bohlen, I. 312.

I am inclined to think that the Jews, though partially orientalised in their opinions, were the people among whom such a notion was least likely to originate of itself. Marriage by the mass of the people was considered in a holy light; and there are traces that the hopes of becoming the mother of the Messiah, was one of the blessings which, in their opinion, belonged to marriage; and after all, before we admit the originality of these notions in some of the systems to which they

point out the influence of this doctrine upon the human mind, as hence its harmony with the general design of Christianity becomes more manifest.

We estimate very inadequately the influence or the value of any religion, if we merely consider its dogmas, its precepts, or its opinions. The impression it makes, the emotions it awakens, the sentiments which it inspires, are perhaps its most vital and effective energies. From these, men continually act; and the character of a particular age is more distinctly marked by the predominance of these silent but universal motives, than by the professed creed, or prevalent philosophy, or, in general, by the opinions of the times. Thus, none of the primary facts in the history of a widely-extended religion can be without effect on the character of its believers. The images perpetually presented to the mind, work, as it were, into its most intimate being, become incorporated with the feelings, and thus powerfully contribute to form the moral nature of the whole race. Nothing could be more appropriate than that the martial Romans should derive their origin from the nursling of the wolf, or from the god of war; and whether those fables sprung from the national temperament, or contributed to form it, however these fierce images were enshrined in the national traditions, they were at once the emblem and example of that bold and relentless spirit which gradually developed itself, until it had made the Romans the masters of the world. The circumstances of the birth of Christ were as strictly

---

belong, we must ascertain (the most intricate problem in the history of Eastern religious opinions) their relative antiquity, as compared with the Nestorian Christianity, so widely prevalent in the East, and the effects of this form of Christianity on the more remote Oriental creeds. Jerome's testimony is the most remarkable.

in unison with the design of the religion. This incident seemed to incorporate with the general feeling the deep sense of holiness and gentleness, which was to characterise the followers of Jesus Christ. It was the consecration of sexual purity and maternal tenderness. No doubt by falling in, to a certain degree, with the ascetic spirit of Oriental enthusiasm, the former incidentally tended to confirm the sanctity of celibacy, which for so many ages reigned paramount in the Church; and in the days in which the Virgin Mother was associated with her divine Son in the general adoration, the propensity to this worship was strengthened by its coincidence with the better feelings of our nature, especially among the female sex. Still the substitution of these images for such as formed the symbols of the older religions, was a great advance towards that holier and more humane tone of thought and feeling, with which it was the professed design of the new religion to imbue the mind of man.[a]

Visit to Elizabeth. In the marvellous incidents which follow, the visit of the Virgin Mother to her cousin[a] Elizabeth,[b] when the joy occasioned by the miraculous conception seemed to communicate itself to the child of

---

[a] The poetry of this sentiment, is beautifully expressed by Wordsworth:—

Mother! whose virgin bosom was uncrost
With the least shade of thought to sin allied;
Woman, above all women glorified,
Our tainted Nature's solitary boast;
Purer than foam on central ocean tost,
Brighter than Eastern skies at daybreak strewn
With fancied roses, than th' unblemish'd moon
Before her wane begins on heaven's blue coast,
Thy Image falls to earth. Yet some, I ween,

Not unforgiven the suppliant knee might bend,
As to a visible power, in whom did blend
All that was mixed and reconciled in thee
Of mother's love with maiden purity,
Of high with low, celestial with terrene.

[a] Elizabeth must have been further removed than a first cousin; for as it is clear that Mary, as well as her husband, was of the line of David, and Elizabeth of the priestly line, the connexion must have been formed in a preceding generation.

[b] Luke i. 30, 36.

which the latter was pregnant, and called forth her ardent expressions of homage: and in the Magnificat, or song of thanksgiving, into which, like Hannah in the older Scriptures, the Virgin broke forth, it is curious to observe how completely and exclusively consistent every expression appears with the state of belief at that period; all is purely Jewish, and accordant with the prevalent expectation of the national Messiah:[c] there is no word which seems to imply any acquaintance with the unworldly and purely moral nature of the redemption, which was subsequently developed. It may perhaps appear too closely to press the terms of that which was the common, almost the proverbial, language of the devotional feelings: yet the expressions which intimate the degradation of the mighty from their seat, the disregard of the wealthy, the elevation of the lowly and the meek, and respect to the low estate of the poor, sound not unlike an allusion to the rejection of the proud and splendid royal race, which had so long ruled the nation, and the assumption of the throne of David by one born in a more humble state.[d]

After the return of Mary to Nazareth, the birth of John the Baptist excited the attention of the whole of Southern Judæa to the fulfilment of the rest of the prediction.[e] When the child is about to be named, the dumb father interferes; he writes on a tablet the name by which he desires him to be called,

Birth of John the Baptist.

---

[c] Agreeing so far, as the fact, with Strauss, I should draw a directly opposite inference, the high improbability that this remarkable *keeping*, this pure Judaism, without the intervention of Christian notions, should have been maintained, if this passage had been invented or composed after the complete formation of the Christian scheme.

[d] Neander in his recently published work has made similar observations on the Jewish notions in the Song of Simeon. Leben Jesu, p. 26.

[e] Luke i. 57, 80.

and instantaneously recovers his speech. It is not unworthy of remark that, in this hymn of thanksgiving, the part which was to be assigned to John in the promulgation of the new faith, and his subordination to the unborn Messiah, are distinctly announced. Already, while one is but a new-born infant, the other scarcely conceived in the womb of his mother, they have assumed their separate stations: the child of Elizabeth is announced as the prophet of the Highest, who shall go "before the face of the Lord, to prepare his ways." Yet even here the Jewish notion predominates: the first object of the Messiah's coming, is that the children of Israel "should be saved from their enemies and from the hand of all that hate them; that they, being delivered from the hand of their enemies, might serve him without fear."[f]

Journey to Bethlehem. As the period approaches at which the child of Mary is to be born, an apparently fortuitous circumstance summons both Joseph and the Virgin Mother from their residence in the unpopular town of Nazareth, in the province of Galilee, to Bethlehem, a small village to the south of Jerusalem.[g] Joseph on the discovery of the pregnancy of his betrothed, being a man of gentle[h] character, had been willing to spare her the rigorous punishment enacted by the law in such

---

[f] Even the expression the "remission of sins," which to a Christian ear may bear a different sense, to the Jew would convey a much narrower meaning. All calamity being a mark of the divine displeasure, was an evidence of sin; every mark of divine favour therefore an evidence of divine forgiveness. The expression is frequently used in its Jewish sense in the book of Maccabees. 1 Macc. iii. 8; 2 Macc. viii. 5, 27, and 29; vii. 98. Le Clerc has made a similar observation (note in loc.), but is opposed by Whitby, who however does not appear to have been very profoundly acquainted with Jewish phraseology.

[g] Matt. i. 18, 25.

[h] Grotius, in loc. from Chrysostom.

DECREE OF AUGUSTUS.

cases, and determined on a private dissolution of the marriage.¹ A vision, however, warned him of the real state of the case, and he no longer hesitated, though abstaining from all connexion, to take her to his home; and accordingly, being of the same descent, she accompanied him to Bethlehem. This town, as the birthplace of David, had always been consecrated in the memory of the Jews with peculiar reverence; and no prediction in the Old Testament appears more distinct, than that which assigns for the nativity of the great Prince, who was to perpetuate the line of David, the same town which had given birth to his royal ancestor.ᵏ

The decree of the Emperor Augustus,ᵐ in obedience to which the whole population of Palestine was to be enrolled and registered, has been, and still remains, an endless subject of controversy.ⁿ One

Decree of Augustus.

---

¹ A bill of divorce was necessary, even when the parties were only betrothed, and where the marriage had not actually been solemnised. It is probable that the Mosaic Law, which in such cases adjudged a female to death (Deut. xx. 23-25), was not at this time executed in its original rigour. It appears from Abarbanel (Buxtorf, de Divort.) that in certain cases a betrothed maiden might be divorced without stating the cause in the bill of divorce. This is the meaning of the word λάθρα, *secretly.* Grotius, in loc.

ᵏ Micah v. 2.

ᵐ Luke ii. 1, 7.

ⁿ The great difficulty arises from the introduction of the name of Cyrenius as the governor, under whose direction the enrolment, or, as it is no doubt mistranslated in our version, the taxation, took place. But it is well known that Cyrenius did not become governor of Syria till several years later. The most usual way of accounting for this difficulty, adopted by Lardner and Paley, is the natural one of supposing that Cyrenius conducted the transaction, while holding a subordinate situation in the province, of which he afterwards became governor, and superintended a more regular taxation. But Mr. Greswell has recently adduced strong reasons for questioning whether Cyrenius could have been at this time in Palestine; and I agree with him, that such a census must have been made by the native authorities under Herod. The alternative remains either to suppose some error in the Gospel of St. Luke, as it now stands; or to adopt another version. That followed by Mr. Gres-

point seems clear, that the enrolment must have been of the nature of a population-census; for any property, possessed by Joseph or Mary, must have been at Nazareth; and the enrolment, which seems to have included both husband and wife, was made at the place where the genealogical registers of the tribes were kept. About this period Josephus gives an account of an oath of allegiance and of fidelity, to Cæsar and to the interests of the reigning sovereign, which was to be taken by the whole Jewish nation. The affair of this oath is strangely mingled up with predictions of a change of dynasty, and with the expected appearance of a great king, under whose all-powerful reign the most extraordinary events were to take place. Six thousand of the Pharisees, the violent religious party, resolutely refused to take the oath. They were fined, and their fine discharged by the low-born wife of Pheroras, the brother of Herod, into whose line certain impostors or enthusiasts, pretending to the gift of prophecy, had declared that the succession was to pass." An eunuch, Bagoas, to whom

---

well, notwithstanding his apparent authorities, sounds to me quite irreconcileable with the genius of the Greek language. There cannot perhaps be found a more brief and satisfactory summary of the different opinions on this subject, than in the common book, Elsley's Annotations on the Gospels. Tholuck, in his answer to Strauss, has examined the question at great length, pp. 102-198. Neander fairly admits the possibility of a mistake in a point of this kind, on the part of the Evangelists, Leben Jesu, p. 19. With him I am at a loss to conceive how Dr. Strauss can imagine a myth in such a plain prosaic sentence.

The Essay of Zumpt of Berlin (Commentatio de Syriâ Romanorum provinciâ a Cæsare Augusto ad 'i. Vespasianum) has thrown unexpected light on this question. Zumpt shows very strong grounds for believing that Cyrenius (Quirinus) was twice Procurator of Syria, once precisely at this time.

* Though inclined to agree with Lardner in supposing that the census or population-return mentioned by St. Luke was connected with the oath of fidelity to Augustus and to Herod, I cannot enter into his notion, that the whole circumstantial and highly credible statement of Josephus is but

they had promised peculiar and miraculous advantages during the reign of the great predicted king,[p] was implicated in this conspiracy, and suffered death, with many of the obstinate Pharisees and of Herod's kindred. It is highly probable that the administration of the oath of allegiance in Josephus, and the census in St. Luke, belong to the same transaction; for if the oath was to be taken by all the subjects of Herod, a general enrolment would be necessary throughout his dominions; and it was likely, according to Jewish usage, that this enrolment would be conducted according to the established divisions of the tribes.[q] If, however, the expectation of the Messiah had penetrated even into the palace of Herod; if it had been made use of in the intrigues and dissensions among the separate branches of his family; if the strong religious faction had not scrupled to assume the character of divinely-inspired prophets, and to proclaim an immediate change of dynasty, the whole conduct of Herod, as described by the evangelists, harmonises in a most singular manner with the circumstances of the times. Though the birth of Jesus might appear to Herod but as an insignificant episode in the more dangerous tragic plot which was unfolding itself in his own family, yet his jealous apprehension at the very name of a new-born native king, would seize at once on the most trifling cause of suspicion; and the judicial

---

a maliciously disguised account of the incidents which took place at the birth of Christ. Lardner's Works, vol. I. (4to. edit.) p. 152.

[p] Independent of the nature of this promise, on which I am intentionally silent, the text of Josephus (Ant. xvii. 2, 6) is unintelligible as it stands, nor is the emendation, proposed by Ward,

a friend of Lardner's, though ingenious, altogether satisfactory. Lardner, ib.

[q] The chronological difficulties in this case do not appear to me of great importance, as the whole affair of the oath may have occupied some time, and the enrolment may have taken place somewhat later in the provinces than in the capital.

massacre of many of the most influential of the Pharisees, and of his own kindred in Jerusalem, which took place on the discovery of this plot, was a fitting prelude for the slaughter of all the children under a certain age in Bethlehem.

Birth of Christ.
But whether the enrolment, which summoned Joseph and Mary to the town where the registers of their descent were kept, was connected with this oath of fidelity to the emperor and the king; or whether it was only a population-return, made by the command of the emperor, in all the provinces where the Roman sovereignty or influence extended,[r] it singularly contributed to the completion of the prophecy to which we have alluded, which designated the city of David as the birthplace of the Messiah. Those who claimed descent from the families whose original possessions were in the neighbourhood of Bethlehem, crowded the whole of the small town; and in the stable of the inn or caravansera was born THE CHILD, whose moral doctrines, if adopted throughout the world, would destroy more than half the misery by destroying all the vice and mutual hostility of men; and who has been for centuries the object of adoration, as the Divine Mediator between God and man, throughout the most civilised and enlightened nations of the earth. Of this immediate epoch only one incident is recorded; but in all the early history of Christianity,

---

[r] This view is maintained by Tholuck, and seems to receive some support from the high authority of Savigny, writing on another subject: it is supported by passages of late writers, Isidore and Cassiodorus, "Augusti siquidem temporibus orbis Romanus agris divisus ponsuque descriptus est, ut possessio sua nulli haberetur incerta, quam pro tributorum susceperat quantitate solvenda." Of itself the authority of Cassiodorus, though a sensible writer, would have no great weight; but he may have read many works unknown to us on this period of history, of which we possess singularly imperfect information.

nothing is more beautiful, nor in more perfect unison with the future character of the religion, than the first revelation of its benign principles, by voices from heaven to the lowly shepherds.* The proclamation of "Glory to God, Peace on earth and good will towards men," is not made by day, but in the quiet stillness of the night;' not in the stately temple of the ancient worship, but among the peaceful pastures; not to the religious senate of the Jewish people, or to the priesthood arrayed in all the splendour of public ministration, but to peasants employed on their lowly occupation.°

In eight days, according to the law, the child was initiated into the race of Abraham, by the rite of circumcision: and when the forty days of purification, likewise appointed by the statute, are over, the Virgin Mother hastens to make the customary presentation of the first-born male in the Temple. Her offering is that of the poorer Jewish females, who, while the more

---

* Luke ii. 8, 20.

† Neander has well observed that the modesty of this quiet scene is not in accordance with what might be expected from the fertility and boldness of mythic invention.

° The year in which Christ was born is still contested. There is even more uncertainty concerning the time of the year, which learned men are still labouring to determine. Where there is and can be no certainty, it is the wisest course to acknowledge our ignorance, and not to claim the authority of historic truth for that which is purely conjectural. The two ablest modern English writers who have investigated the chronology of the life of Christ, Dr. Burton and Mr. Greswell, have come to opposite conclusions, one contending for the spring, the other for the autumn. Even if the argument of either had any solid ground to rest on, it would be difficult (would it be worth while?) to extirpate the traditionary belief, so beautifully embodied in Milton's Hymn:—

It was the winter wild
When the heaven-born child, &c.

Were the point of the least importance, we should, no doubt, have known more about it. "Quid tandem refert annum et diem exorti luminis, ignorare quum apparuisse illud, et cæcis hominum mentibus illuxisse constet, neque sit, quod obsistat nobis, ne splendore ac calore ejus utamur."—Mosheim de Reb. Christ., p. 62. There is a good essay in the Opuscula of Jablonski, iii. 317, on the origin of the festivity of Christmas Day.

wealthy made an oblation of a lamb, were content with the least costly, a pair of turtle doves, or two young pigeons.* Only two persons are recorded as having any knowledge of the future destiny of the child,—Anna, a woman endowed with a prophetical character, and the aged Simeon. That Simeon⁷ was not the celebrated master of the schools of Jewish learning, the son of Hillel, and the father of Gamaliel, is fairly inferred from the silence of St. Luke, who, though chiefly writing for the Greek converts, would scarcely have omitted to state distinctly the testimony of so distinguished a man to the Messiahship of Jesus. There are other insurmountable historical objections.ᶻ Though occurrences among the more devout worshippers in the Temple were perhaps less likely to reach the ear of Herod than those in any other part of the city, yet it was impossible that the solemn act of recognising the Messiah in the infant son of Mary, on so public a scene, by a man whose language and conduct were watched by the whole people, could escape observa-

Simeon.

---

* Luke ii. 21, 39.

⁷ This was the notion of Lightfoot, who, though often invaluable as interpreting the New Testament from Jewish usages, is sometimes misled by his Rabbinism into fanciful analogies and illustrations. Hist. Jews, ii. 403, note.

ᶻ Our first and not least embarrassing difficulty in harmonising the facts recorded in the several Gospels, is the relative priority of the presentation in the Temple and the visit of the Magians to Bethlehem. On one side there appears no reason for the return of the parents and the child, after the presentation, to Bethlehem, where they appear to have had no friends, and where the object of their visit was most probably effected: on the other hand, it is still more improbable, that, after the visit of the Magians, they should rush, as it were, into the very jaws of danger, by visiting Jerusalem, after the jealousy of Herod was awakened. Yet in both cases, it should be remembered that Bethlehem was but six miles, or two hours' journey, from Jerusalem. Reland, Palestina, p. 424. See, on one side, Schleiermacher's Essay on St. Luke, p. 47, though I entirely dissent on the point from the explanation of this author; on the other, Hug's Introduction.

tion. Such an acknowledgment, by so high an authority, would immediately have been noised abroad; no prudence could have suppressed the instantaneous excitement. Besides this, if alive at this time, Simeon ben Hillel would have presided in the court of inquiry, summoned by Herod, after the appearance of the Magi. The most remarkable point in the benediction of Simeon is the prediction that the child, who it would have been supposed would have caused unmingled pride and joy, should also be the cause of the deepest sorrow to his mother; and of the most fearful calamities, as well as of glory, to the nation.[a]

<small>His benediction.</small>

The intercommunion of opinions between the Jewish and Zoroastrian religions throws great light on the visit of the Magi, or Wise Men, to Jerusalem. The impregnation of the Jewish notions about the Messiah with the Magian doctrines of the final triumph of Ormusd, makes it by no means improbable that, on the other side, the national doctrines of the Jews may have worked their way into the popular belief of the East, or at least into the opinions of those among the Magian hierarchy, who had come more immediately into contact with the Babylonian Jews.[b] From them they may have adopted the expectation of the Great Principle of Light in a human form, and descending, according to ancient prophecy, from the race of Israel; and thus have been prepared to set forth, at the first appearance of the luminous body, by which they were

<small>The Magi.</small>

---

[a] Matt. ii. 1-12.
[b] The communication with Babylonia at this period was constant and regular; so much so, that Herod fortified and garrisoned a strong castle, placed under a Babylonian commander, to protect the caravans from this quarter from the untameable robbers of the Trachonitis, the district east of the Jordan and of the Sea of Tiberias.

led to Judæa.^c The universal usage of the East, never to approach the presence of a superior, particularly a sovereign, without some precious gift, is naturally exemplified in their costly but portable offerings of gold, myrrh, and frankincense.^d

The appearance of these strangers in Jerusalem at this critical period, particularly if considered in connexion with the conspiracy in the family of Herod and among the religious faction, as it excited an extraordinary sensation through the whole city, would reawaken all the watchfulness of the monarch. The assemblage of the religious authorities, in order that they might judicially declare the place from which the Messiah was expected, might be intended not merely to direct the ministers of the royal vengeance to the quarter from whence danger was to be apprehended, but to force the acknowledged interpreters of the sacred

Magi in Jerusalem.

---

^c What this luminous celestial appearance was, has been debated with unwearied activity. I would refer more particularly to the work of Ideler, Handbuch der Chronologie, ii. 399. There will be found, very clearly stated, the opinion of Kepler (adopted by Bishop Munter), which explains it as a conjunction between Jupiter and Saturn.

For my own part, I cannot understand why the words of St. Matthew, relating to such a subject, are to be so rigidly interpreted; the same latitude of expression may be allowed on astronomical subjects as necessarily must be in the Old Testament. The vagueness and uncertainty, possibly the scientific inaccuracy, seem to me the inevitable consequences of the manner in which such circumstances must have been preserved, as handed down and subsequently reduced to writing by simple persons, awe-struck under such extraordinary events.

^d It is the general opinion that the Magi came from Arabia. Pliny and Ptolemy (Grotius, in loc.) name Arabian Magi; and the gifts were considered the produce of that country. But in fact gold, myrrh, and frankincense, are too common in the East, and too generally used as presents to a superior, to indicate, with any certainty, the place from whence they came. If, indeed, by Arabia be meant not the peninsula, but the whole district reaching to the Euphrates, this notion may be true; but it is more probable that they came from beyond the Euphrates.

writings to an authoritative declaration as to the circumstances of the Messiah's birth; so, if any event should occur, contrary to their version of the prophecies, either to commit them on the side of the ruling powers, or altogether to invalidate the expectation, that was dangerously brooding in the popular mind. The subtlety of Herod's character is as strikingly exhibited in his pretended resolution to join the Magians in their worship of the new-born king, as his relentless decision, when the Magians did not return to Jerusalem, in commanding the general massacre of all the infants under the age of two years, in Bethlehem and its district.*

Egypt, where, by divine command, the parents of Jesus took refuge, was but a few days' journey, on a line perpetually frequented by regular caravans; and in that country, those who fled from Palestine could scarcely fail to meet with hospitable reception, among some of that second nation of Jews, who inhabited Alexandria and its neighbourhood.†

Flight into Egypt.

---

* The murder of the Innocents is a curious instance of the reaction of legendary extravagance on the plain truth of the evangelic history. The Greek church canonised the 14,000 Innocents; and another notion, founded on a misinterpretation of Revelations (xiv. 3), swelled the number to 144,000. The former, at least, was the common belief of the Church, though even in our Liturgy the latter has in some degree been sanctioned, by retaining the chapter of Revelations as the epistle for the day. Even later, Jeremy Taylor, in his Life of Christ, admits the 14,000 without scruple, or rather without thought. The error did not escape the notice of the acute adversaries of Christianity, who, impeaching this extravagant tale, attempted to bring the evangelic narrative into discredit. Voss, I believe, was the first divine who pointed out the monstrous absurdity of supposing such a number of infant children in so small a village. Matt. ii. 13-18.

† Some of the Rabbinical stories accuse Jesus of having brought "his enchantments" out of Egypt. (Lightfoot, ii. 45.) There is no satisfactory evidence as to the antiquity of these notions, or, absurd as they are, they might be some testimony to the authenticity of this part of the Chris-

On their return from Egypt, after the death of Herod (which took place in the ensuing year, though the parents of Jesus did not leave Egypt till the accession of Archelaus), Joseph, justly apprehensive that the son might inherit the jealousy and relentless disposition of the father, of which he had already given fearful indications, retired to his former residence in Galilee, under the less suspicious dominion of Herod Antipas." There the general prejudice against Galilee might be their best security; and the universal belief that it was in Judæa that the great king was to assume his sovereignty, would render their situation less perilous; for it was the throne of the monarch of Judah, the dominion of the ruler in Jerusalem, rather than the government of the Galilean tetrarch, which would have been considered in danger from the appearance of the Messiah.

---

tian history. See also Eisenmenger, i. p. 150.

The Jewish fiction of the birth of Jesus is at least as old as the time of Celsus (Origen contra Cels. 1), but bears the impress of hostile malice, in assigning as his parent a Roman soldier. This is the fable which was perpetuated from that time by Jewish animosity, till it assumed its most obnoxious form in the Toldoth Jesu. How much more natural and credible than the minute detail which so obviously betrays later and hostile invention, the vague inquiry of his own compatriots—"Is not this the carpenter's son?" Matt. xiii. 55.

The answer of Origen to this Jewish invention is sensible and judicious. The Christians, if such a story had been true, would have invented something more directly opposed to the real truth; they would not have agreed so far with the relation, but rather carefully suppressed every allusion to the extraordinary birth of Jesus. 'Εδύναντο γὰρ ἄλλως ψευδοποιῆσθαι διὰ τὸ σφόδρα παράδοξον τῆς ἱστορίαν, καὶ μὴ ὥσπερ) ἀκουσίως συγκατατίθεσθαι ὅτι οὐκ ἀπὸ συνήθων ἀνθρώποις γάμων ὁ Ἰησοῦς ἐγεννήθη. Contra Cels. l. 32.

⁵ Matt. xi. 19, 23. Luke xi. 40.

APPENDIX TO CHAPTER II.

I.

RECENT LIVES OF CHRIST.

At the time when this part of the present work was written, the ultra-rationalist work of Professor Paulus, the Leben Jesu (Heidelberg, 1828), was the most recent publication. Since that time have appeared, the Life of Jesus, Das Leben Jesu, by Dr. D. F. Strauss (2nd edition, Tubingen, 1837), and the counter publication of Neander, Das Leben Jesu (Berlin, 1837); to say nothing of a great number of controversial pamphlets and reviews, arising out of the work of Dr. Strauss.

This work (consisting of two thick and closely printed volumes of nearly 800 pages each) is a grave and elaborate exposition of an extraordinary hypothesis, which Dr. Strauss offers, in order to reconcile Christianity with the advancing intelligence of mankind, which is weary and dissatisfied with all previous philosophical and rationalist theories. Dr. Strauss solemnly declares, that the essence of Christianity is entirely independent of his critical remarks. "The supernatural birth of Christ, his miracles, his resurrection and ascension, remain eternal truths, however *their reality, as historical facts, may be called in question.*"* He refers to a dissertation at the close of his work, "to show that the doctrinal contents of the Life of Jesus are uninjured; and that the calmness and cold-bloodedness with which his criticism proceeds in its dangerous operations can only be explained by his conviction, that it is not in the least prejudicial to Christian faith." That dissertation, which opens (t. ii. p. 691) with a singularly eloquent description of the total destruction which this remorseless criticism has made in the ordinary grounds of

---

* Christi übernatürliche Geburt, seine Wunder, seine Auferstehung und Himmelfahrt bleiben ewige Wahrheiten, so sehr ihre Wirklichkeit als historische Facta angezweifelt werden mag. Vorrede, xii.

Christian faith and practice, I have read with much attention. But what resting-place it proposes to substitute for Christian faith, I have been unable to discover; and must acknowledge my unwillingness to abandon the firm ground of historical evidence, to place myself on any sublime but unsubstantial cloud which may be offered by a mystic and unintelligible philosophy. Especially as I find Dr. Strauss himself coolly contemplating at the close of his work the desolating effects of his own arguments, looking about in vain for the unsubstantial tenets which he has extirpated by his uncompromising logic; and plainly admitting, that if he has shattered to pieces the edifice of Christianity, it is not his fault.

But Christianity will survive the criticism of Dr. Strauss.

I would, however, calmly consider the first principles of this work, which appear to me, in many respects, singularly narrow and unphilosophical—by no means formed on an extensive and complete view of the whole case, and resting on grounds which, in my judgment, would be subversive of all history.

The hypothesis of Dr. Strauss is, that the whole history of our Lord, as related in the Gospels, is mythic, that is to say, a kind of imaginative amplification of certain vague and slender traditions, the germ of which it is now impossible to trace. These myths are partly what he calls historical, partly philosophic, formed with the design of developing an ideal character of Jesus, and of harmonising that character with the Jewish notions of the Messiah. In order to prove this, the whole intermediate part of the work is a most elaborate, and it would be uncandid not to say, a singularly skilful examination of the difficulties and discrepancies in the Gospels; and a perpetual endeavour to show in what manner and with what design each separate myth assumed its present form.

Arguing on the ground of Dr. Strauss, I would urge the following objections, which appear to me fatal to his whole system:—

First, The hypothesis of Strauss is unphilosophical, because it assumes dogmatically the principal point in dispute. His first canon of criticism is (t. i. p. 103), that wherever there is anything supernatural, angelic appearance, miracle, or interposition of the Deity, there we may presume a myth. Thus he concludes, both against the supernaturalists, as they are called in Germany, and the general mass of Christian believers of all sects in this country, that any recorded interference with the ordinary and experienced order of causation must be unhistorical and untrue; and even against the rationalists, that these wonders did not even *apparently* take place, having been supposed to be miraculous, from the *superstition* or ignorance of physical causes among the spectators: they cannot be even the honest, though mistaken, reports of eye-witnesses.

But secondly, The *belief* in some of those supernatural events, *e.g.* the resurrection, is indispensable to the existence of the religion. To suppose that this belief grew up, after the religion was formed; to assume these primary facts as after-thoughts, seems to me an absolute impossibility. But if they, or any one of them, were integral parts of the religion from its earliest origin, though they may possibly have been subsequently embellished, or unfaithfully recorded in the Gospels, their supernatural character is no evidence that they are so.

Thirdly, Besides this inevitable inference, that the religion could not have subsequently invented that which was the foundation of the religion,—that these things *must have been* the belief of the first Christian communities,—there is distinct evidence in the Acts of the Apostles (though Dr. Strauss, it seems, would involve that book in the fate of the Gospels), in the apostolical Epistles, and in every written document and tradition, that they were so. The general harmony of those three distinct classes of records, as to the main preternatural facts in the Gospels, proves incontestably that they were not the slow growth of a subsequent period, embodied in narratives composed in the second century.

For fourthly, Dr. Strauss has by no means examined the evidence for the early existence of the Gospels with the rigid diligence which characterises the rest of his work. I think he does not fairly state that the early notices of the Gospels, in the works of the primitive Fathers, show not only their existence but their general reception among the Christian communities, which imply both a much earlier composition and some strong grounds for their authenticity. As to the time when the Gospels were composed, his argument seems to me self-destructive. The later he supposes them to have been written, the more impossible (considering that the Christians were then so widely disseminated in Europe and Asia) is their accordance with each other in the same design or the same motives for fiction: if he takes an earlier date, he has no room for his long process of mythic development. In one place he appears to admit that the three first Gospels, at least, must have been completed between the death of our Lord and the destruction of Jerusalem, less than forty years. (I myself consider their silence, or rather the obscure and confused prophetic allusions to that event, as absolutely decisive on this point, with regard to all the four.) But is it conceivable that in this narrow period, this mythic spirit should have been so prolific, and the primitive simplicity of the Christian history have been so embellished, and then universally received by the *first* generation of believers?

The place, as well as the period, of their composition, is encumbered with difficulties according to this system. Where were they written? If all, or rather the three first, in Palestine, whence their general acceptance without direct and acknowledged authority? If in different parts of the world, their general acceptance is equally improbable; their similarity of design and object, altogether unaccountable.

Were they written with this mythic latitude by Judaising or Hellenising Christians? If by Judaising, I should expect to find far more of Judaism, of Jewish tradition, usage, and language, as appears to have been the case in the Ebionitish Gospel; if by Hellenising, the attempt to frame the myths in accordance with Jewish traditions is inconceivable.[b] They Judaise too little for the Petrine Christians (that is, those who considered the Gospel in some sort a re-enactment of the Mosaic Law), too much for the followers of St. Paul, who rejected the Law.

The other canons of Dr. Strauss seem to me subversive of all history. Everything extraordinary or improbable, the prophetic anticipations of youthful ambition, complete revolution in individual character (he appears to allude to the change in the character of the Apostles after the resurrection, usually, and in my opinion justly, considered as one of the strongest arguments of the truth of the narrative), though he admits that this canon is to be applied with caution, are presumptive of a mythic character.

---

[b] Dr. Strauss, for instance, asserts all the passages relating to the miraculous birth of Christ (the first chapters of St. Matthew and St. Luke), and those which relate His baptism in St. John, to have proceeded from two distinct classes of Christians, differing materially, or rather directly opposed to each other in their notions of the Messiah, a Judaising and an anti-doctic sect. See vol. i. pp. 448-448. We must find time not merely for the growth and development of both notions, but for their blending into one system, and the general adoption of that system by the Christian communities.

If discrepancies in the circumstances between narratives of the same events, or differences of arrangement in point of time, particularly among rude and inartificial writers, are to be admitted as proofs of this kind of fiction, all history is mythic; even the accounts of every transaction in the daily papers, which are never found to agree precisely in the minute details, are likewise mythic.

To these which appear to me conclusive arguments against the hypothesis of Dr. Strauss, I would add some observations, which to my mind are general maxims, which must be applied to all such discussions.

No religion is in its origin mythic. Mythologists embellish, adapt, modify, idealise, clothe in allegory or symbol, received and acknowledged truths. This is a later process, and addressed to the imagination, already excited and prepared to receive established doctrines or opinions in this new form. But in Christianity (according to Dr. Strauss's hypothesis) what was the first impulse, the germ of all this high-wrought and successful idealisation?—Nothing more than the existence of a man named Jesus, who obtained a few followers, and was put to death as a malefactor, without any pretensions on his part to a superior character, either as a divine or a divinely commissioned being, or as the expected Messiah of the Jews. Whatever, extorted by the necessity of the case, is added to this primary conception of the character of Jesus, in order sufficiently to awaken the human mind to a new religion connected with his name, belief of his miraculous powers, of his resurrection, of his Messiahship, even of his more than human virtue and wisdom, tends to verify the delineation of his character in his Gospels, as the original object of admiration and belief to his followers; and to anticipate and preclude, as it were, its being a subsequent mythic invention.

Can the period in which Jesus appeared be justly considered a mythic age? If by mythic age (and I do not think Dr. Strauss very rigid and philosophical in the use of the term) be meant an age in which there was a general and even superstitious belief, in wonders and prodigies, mingled up with much cool incredulity, this cannot be denied. The prodigies which are related by grave historians, as taking place at the death of Cæsar; those which Josephus, who is disposed to rationalise many of the miracles of the early history of his people, describes during the capture of Jerusalem, are enough, out of the countless instances which could be adduced,[*] to determine the question. But if the term mythic be more properly applied to that idealisation, that investing religious doctrines in allegory or symbol; above all, that elevating into a deity a man only distinguished for moral excellence (the deification of the Roman emperors was a political act), this appears to me to be repugnant to the genius of the time and of the country. Among the Jewish traditions in the Talmud, there is much fable, much parable, much apologue; as far as I can discern, nothing strictly speaking mythic. Philo's is a kind of poetico-philosophic rationalism. The later legends, of Simon Magus, Alexander in Lucian, and Apollonius of Tyana, are subsequent inventions, after the imaginative impulse given by Christianity, possibly imitative of the Gospels.

I would be understood, however, as laying least stress upon this argument, as this tendency to imaginative excitement and creation does not depend so much on the age as on the state of civilisation, which perhaps in the East has never become completely exempt from this tendency.

But I cannot admit the spurious Gospels, which seem to me the manifest offspring of Gnostic and heretical sects, and to have been composed at periods which historical criticism might designate from internal evidence, though clearly *mythical*, to involve the genuine Gospels in the same proscription. To a discriminating and unprejudiced mind, I would rest the distinction between mythical and non-mythical on the comparison between the apocryphal and canonical Gospels.[*]

Neander, in my opinion, has exercised a very sound judgement in declining direct controversy with Dr. Strauss; for controversy, even conducted in the calm and Christian spirit of Neander, rarely works conviction, except in those who are already convinced. He has chosen the better course of giving a fair and candid view of the opposite side of the question, and of exhibiting the accordance of the ordinary view of the origin and authority of the Gospels with sound reason and advanced philosophy. He has dissembled no difficulties, and appealed to no passions. It affords me much satisfaction to find that, although my plan did not require or admit of such minute investigation, I have anticipated many of the conclu-

---

[*] The nearest approach to the mythic, would, perhaps, be the kind of divine character assumed by Simon Magus among the Samaritans, and alluded to in the Acts.

sions of Neander. In many respects the point of view, from which I have looked at the subject, is altogether different; and, as I have preferred to leave my own work in its original form, though some of the difficulties and discrepancies on which Dr. Strauss dwells may, I trust, be reasonably accounted for in the following chapters of my work, this will be only incidentally; the full counter-statement, prepared with constant reference to Dr. Strauss's book, must be sought in the work of Neander.

It accords even less with the design of my work, which is rather to trace the influence and effect of Christian opinions, than rigidly to investigate their origin or to establish their truth, to notice the various particular animadversions on Dr. Strauss which might suggest themselves; yet I have added some few observations on certain points, when they have crossed the course of my narrative.

The best answer to Strauss is to show that a clear, consistent, and probable narrative can be formed out of that of the four Gospels, without more violence, I will venture to say, than any historian ever found necessary to harmonise four contemporary chronicles of the same events; and maintaining a general accordance with the history, customs, habits, and opinions of the times, altogether irreconcileable with the poetic character of mythic history.

The inexhaustible fertility of German speculation has now displayed itself in another original and elaborate work, Die Evangelische Geschichte, Kritisch und Philosophisch bearbeitet, Von Ch. Hermann Weisse. 2 Bände. Leipsic, 1838. Dr. Weisse repudiates the theory of Strauss. If he does not bring us to the cold and dreary conclusion of Strauss, or land us on the Nova Zembla of that writer, he leaves us enveloped in a vague and indistinct mist, in which we discern nothing clear, distinct, or satisfactory.

The critical system of Weisse rests on two leading points:—The assumption of the Gospel of St. Mark as the primitive Gospel,—a theory which has been advanced before, but which no writer has wrought out with so much elaborate diligence as Weisse;—and a hostility which leads to the virtual rejection of the Gospel of St. John as almost entirely spurious. With regard to St. Mark's Gospel he receives the tradition of Papias, that it was written from the dictation, or at least from information obtained from St. Peter. St. Matthew's was formed from the incorporation of the Gospel of the Hebrews with the λογια, a collection of speeches attributed to our Lord. As to St. John's, he submits it to the test of his own arbitrary, and it appears to me, however they may be called critical, very narrow and unphilosophical laws of probability.

The theory by which Weisse would reconcile and harmonise what he retains of the evangelic history with what he considers the highest philosophy, I must confess my inability to comprehend, and must plead as my excuse, that he admits it to be unintelligible to those who are not acquainted with some of his former philosophical works, which I have not at my command. What I do comprehend it would be impossible to explain, as the philosophical language of Germany would, if retained, be entirely without meaning to most readers, and is untranslatable into a foreign tongue.

Weisse retains a much larger and more solid substratum of historic fact than Strauss; and though he may be called a mythic interpreter, his mythic system seems to me entirely different from that of Strauss. With the latter the historic facts are, in general, pure fictions, wrought out of preconceived Jewish notions; with Weisse they are symbolic rather than mythic. In some cases they arise from the mistake of symbolic action for real fact; as, for instance, the notion of the feeding the multitudes in the desert arose out of the mystic language of the Saviour, relating to spiritual nourishment by the bread of life. In other parts he adopts the language of Vico, which has found so much favour in Germany, but which I confess, when gravely applied to history, and followed out to an extent, I conceive, scarcely anticipated by its author, appears to me to be one of the most monstrous improbabilities which has ever passed current under the garb of philosophy. Individual historical characters are merely symbols of the age in which they live,—ideal personifications, as it were, of the imagination, without any actual or personal existence. Thus the elder Herod (Weisse is speaking of the massacre of the Innocents) is the symbol, the representation of worldly power. And so the tyrant of the Jews is sublimated into an allegory.

Weisse, however, in his own sense, distinctly asserts the divinity of the religion and of our Lord himself.

I mention this book for several reasons:—First, because, although it is written in a tone of bold, and, with us it would seem, presumptuous speculation, and ends, in my opinion, in a kind of unsatisfactory mysticism, it contains much profound and extremely beautiful thought.

Secondly, because in its system of interpretation it seems to me to bear a remarkable resemblance to that of Philo and the better part of the Alexandrian school,—it is to the New Testament, what they were to the Old.

Lastly, to show that the German mind itself has been startled by the conclusions to which the stern and remorseless logic of Strauss has pushed on the historical criticism of rationalism; and that, even where there is no tendency to return to the old system of religious interpretation, there is not merely strong discontent with the new, but a manifest yearning for a loftier and more consistent harmony between the religion of the Gospels and true philosophy, than has yet been effected by any of the remarkable writers who have attempted this reconciliation.

(It is hardly worth the space to notice such writers as Feuerbach and Bruno Bauer, who reproach Strauss with his timid orthodoxy. As far as I can judge, they have been repudiated with contemptuous silence even in Germany. The work of Strauss has been translated into French and into English. In England, I suspect, its number of readers has been extremely limited; but it is impossible to trace its indirect effect.—1863.)

APPENDIX II.

ORIGIN OF THE GOSPELS.

THE question concerning the origin of the three first Gospels, both before and subsequent to the publication of Bishop Marsh's Michaelis, has assumed every possible form; and it may be safely asserted, that no one victorious theory has gained anything like a general assent among the learned. Every conceivable hypothesis has found its advocates; the priority of each of the Evangelists has been maintained with erudition and ingenuity; each has been considered the primary authority, which has been copied by the others. The hypothesis of one or more common sources, from which all three derived their materials (the view supported with so much learning and ability by the Bishop of Peterborough), has in its turn shared the common fate.

This inexhaustible question, though less actively agitated, still continues to occupy the attention of Biblical critics in Germany.

I cannot help suspecting that the best solution of this intricate problem lies near the surface.* The incidents of the Saviour's life and death, the contents of the Gospels, necessarily formed a considerable part of the oral teaching, or, if not of the oral teaching, of oral communication, among the first propagators of Christianity.[b] These incidents would be repeated and dwelt upon with different degrees of frequency, and perhaps distinctness, according to their relative importance. While, on the other hand, from the number of teachers scattered at least through Palestine, and probably in many other parts of the Roman empire, many varieties of expression, much of that unintentional difference of colouring which every narrative receives by frequent repetition, would unavoidably arise; on the other, there would be a kind of sanctity attributed to the precise expressions of the Apostles, if recollected, which would insure on many points a similarity, a perfect identity, of language. We cannot suppose but that these incidents and events in the life of Christ, these parables and doctrines delivered by himself, thus orally communicated in the course of public teaching and in private, received

---

* It would be difficult to point out a clearer and more satisfactory exposition of any controversy, than that of this great question in Biblical criticism, by Mr. Thirlwall, now Bishop Thirlwall, in his Preface to Schleiermacher's Essay on St. Luke.

[b] I have considered the objections urged by Hug, and more recently with great force by Weisse (p. 20 et seq.), to this theory, the more important of which resolve themselves into the undoubted fact, that it was a *creed*, and not a *history*, which, in all the accounts we have in the Acts of the Apostles and elsewhere, formed the subject of oral teaching. This is doubtless true; but, resting as the creed did upon the history, containing no doubt in its primitive form a very few simple articles, would it not necessarily awaken curiosity as to the historic facts? and would not that curiosity demand, as it were, to be satisfied? The more belief warmed into piety, the more insatiably would it require, and the more would the teacher be disposed, to gratify this awakened interest and eagerness for information on every point that related to the Redeemer. The formal public teaching no doubt confined itself to the enforcement of the creed, and to combating Jewish or heathen objections, and confuting Judaism or idolatry. But in private intercourse, when the minds of both instructor and hearer were exclusively full of these subjects, would not the development of the history, in more or less detail, be a necessary and unavoidable consequence? I subscribe to the maxim that Christianity is essentially a historical religion. Its creed, all but the transcendental articles, is history.

with such zealous avidity, treasured as of such inestimable importance, would be perpetually written down, if not as yet in continuous narratives, in numerous and accumulating fragments, by the Christian community, or by some one or more distinguished members of it. They would record, as far as possible, the *ipsissima verba* of the primitive teacher, especially if an apostle or a personal follower of Jesus. But these records would still be liable to some inaccuracy, from misapprehension or infirmity of memory; and to some discrepancy, from the inevitable variations of language in oral instruction or communication frequently repeated, and that often by different teachers. Each community or church, each intelligent Christian would thus possess a more or less imperfect Gospel, which he would preserve with jealous care, and increase with zealous activity, till it should be superseded by some more regular and complete narrative, the authenticity and authority of which he might be disposed to admit. The Evangelists who, like St. Luke, might determine to write "in order," either to an individual like Theophilus, to some single church, or to the whole body of Christians, "those things which were most surely believed among them," would naturally have access to, would consult, and avail themselves of many of those private or more public collections. All the three, or any two, might find many coincidences of expression (if indeed some expressions had not already become conventional and established, or even consecrated forms of language, with regard to certain incidents), which they would transfer into their own narrative; on the other hand, incidents would be more or less fully developed, or be entirely omitted in some, while retained in others.

Of all points on which discrepancies would be likely to arise, there would be none so variable as the chronological order and consecutive series of events. The primitive teacher, or communicator, of the history of the life and death of Jesus, would often follow a doctrinal rather than a historical connexion; and this would, in many instances, be perpetuated by those who should endeavour to preserve in writing that precious information communicated to them by the preacher. Hence the discrepancies and variations in order and arrangement, more especially, as it may be said without irreverence, these rude and simple historians, looking more to religious impression than to historic precision, may have undervalued the importance of rigid chronological narrative. Thus, instead of one or two primary, either received or unauthoritative, sources of the

Gospels, I should conceive that there would be many, almost as many as there were Christian communities, all in themselves imperfect, but contributing more or less to the more regular and complete narratives extant in our Gospels. The general necessity, particularly as the Apostles and first followers were gradually withdrawn from the scene, would demand a more full and accurate narrative; and these confessedly imperfect collections would fall into disuse, directly that the want was supplied by regular Gospels, composed by persons either considered as divinely commissioned, or at least as authoritative and trustworthy writers. The almost universal acceptance of these Gospels is the guarantee for their general conformity with these oral, traditional, and written records of the different communities, from which if they had greatly differed, they would probably have been rejected; while the same conformity sufficiently accounts for the greater or less fulness, the variation in the selection of incidents, the silence on some points, or the introduction of others, in one Gospel alone. Whether or not either of the Evangelists saw the work of the other, they made constant use of the same or similar sources of information, not merely from their own personal knowledge, but likewise from the general oral teaching and oral communications of the Apostles and first preachers of Christianity, thus irregularly and incompletely, but honestly and faithfully, registered by the hearers. Under this view, for my own part, I seem rationally to avoid all embarrassment with the difficulties of the subject. I am not surprised at exact coincidences of thought or language, though followed by, or accompanied with, equally remarkable deviations and discrepancies. I perceive why one is brief and the other full; why one omits, while another details, minute circumstances. I can account for much apparent and some real discrepancy. I think that I discern, to my own satisfaction, sufficient cause for diversity in the collocation of different incidents: in short, admitting these simple principles, there flows a natural harmony from the whole, which blends and reunites all the apparent discords which appear to disturb the minds of others.

There is one point which strikes me forcibly in all these minute and elaborate arguments, raised from every word and letter of the Gospels, which prevails throughout the whole of the modern German criticism. It is, that following out their rigid juridical examination, the most extreme rationalists are (unknowingly) influenced by the theory of the strict inspiration of the Evangelists. Weisse himself has drawn very ably a distinction between juridical and historical truth, that is, the sort of legal truth which we should require in a court of justice, and that which we may expect from ordinary history. But in his own investigations he appears to me constantly to lose sight of this important distinction; no cross-examination in an English court of law was ever so severe as that to which every word and shade of expression in the Evangelists is submitted. Now this may be just in those who admit a rigid verbal inspiration; but those who reject it, and consider the Evangelists merely as ordinary historians, have no right to require more than ordinary historic accuracy. The Evangelists were, either—

I. Divinely inspired in their language and expressions as well as in the facts and doctrines which they relate. On this theory the inquirer may reasonably endeavour to harmonise discrepancies; but if he fails, he must submit in devout reverence, and suppose that there is some secret way of reconciling such contradictions, which he wants acuteness or knowledge to comprehend.

II. We may adopt a lower view of inspiration, whether of suggestion or superintendence, or even that which seems to have been generally received in the early ages, the inflexible love of truth, which, being inseparable from the spirit of Christianity, would of itself be a sufficient guarantee for fidelity and honesty. Under any of these notions of inspiration (the definition of which word is, in fact, the real difficulty), there would be much latitude for variety of expression, of detail, of chronological arrangement. Each narrative (as the form and the language would be uninspired) would bear marks of the individual character, the local circumstances, the education, the character of the writer.

III. We may consider the Evangelists as ordinary historians, credible merely in proportion to their means of obtaining accurate knowledge, their freedom from prejudice, and the abstract credibility of their statements. If, however, so considered (as is invariably the case in the German school of criticism), they should undoubtedly have all the privileges of ordinary historians, and indeed of historians of a singularly rude and inartificial class. They would be liable to all the mistakes into which such writers might fall; nor would trifling inaccuracies impeach the truth of their general narrative. Take, for instance, the introduction of Cyrenius, in relation to the census in the beginning of St. Luke's Gospel. In common historical

inquiry, it would be concluded that the author had made a mistake *
as to the name, his general truth would remain unshaken, nor would
any one think of building up a hypothesis on so trivial and natural
an inaccuracy. But there is scarcely a work of this school without
some such hypothesis. I confess that I am constantly astonished at
the elaborate conclusions which are drawn from trifling discrepancies
or inaccuracies in those writers, from whom is exacted a precision of
language, a minute and unerring knowledge of facts incident to, but
by no means forming constituent parts of, their narrative, which is
altogether inconsistent with the want of respect in other cases shown
to their authority. The Evangelists must have been either entirely
inspired, or inspired as to the material parts of their history, or altogether
uninspired. In the latter, and indeed in the more moderate
view of the second case, they would have a right to the ordinary
latitude of honest narrators; they would, we may safely say, be read,
as other historians of their inartificial and popular character always
are; and so read, it would be impossible, I conceive, not to be surprised
and convinced of their authenticity, by their *general* accordance
with all the circumstances of their age, country, and personal
character.

---

* Non nos debere arbitrari mentiri quemquam, si pluribus rem quam audierant vel viderunt reminiscentibus, non eodem modo atque eisdem verbis, eandem tamen rem fuerit indicata: aut sive mutetur ordo verborum, sive alia pro aliis, quae tamen idem valeant, verba proferantur, sive aliquid vel quod recordanti non occurrit, vel quod ex aliis quae dicuntur possit intelligi minus dicatur, sive aliorum quae magis dicere statuit narrandorum gratia, ut congruus temporis modus sufficiat, aliquid sibi non totum explicandum, sed ex parte tangendum quisque suscipiat; sive ad illuminandam declarandamque sententiam, nihil quidem rerum, verborum tamen aliquid addat, cui auctoritas narrandi concessa est, sive rem bene tenens, non assequatur quamvis id conetur, memoriter etiam verba quae audivit ad integrum enuntiare. Augustin. De Consensu. Evangelist. ii. 28. Compare the whole passage, which coincides with the general view of the Fathers as to this question, in c. 50. St. Augustine seems to admit an inspiration of guidance or superintendence. In one passage he seems to go farther, but to plunge (with respect be it spoken) into inextricable nonsense, iii. 30; see also 48.

APPENDIX III.

INFLUENCE OF THE MORE IMAGINATIVE INCIDENTS OF THE EARLY EVANGELIC HISTORY ON THE PROPAGATION AND MAINTENANCE OF THE RELIGION.

A CURIOUS fact occurs to those who trace the progress of religious opinion, not merely in the popular theology, but in the works of those, chiefly foreign writers, who indulge in bolder speculations on these subjects. Many of these are men of the profoundest learning, and it would be the worst insolence of uncharitableness to doubt, with the most sincere and ardent aspirations after truth. The fact is this :—Certain parts of the evangelic history, the angelic appearances, the revelations of the Deity addressed to the senses of man (the Angelo-phaniai and Theophaniai, as they have been called)—with some, though not with all this class of writers, everything miraculous, appears totally inconsistent with historic truth. These incidents, being irreconcileable with our actual experience, and rendered suspicious by a multitude of later fictions, which are rejected in the mass by most Protestant Christians, cannot accord with the more subtle and fastidious intelligence of the present times. Some writers go so far as to assert that it is impossible that an inquiring and reasoning age should receive these supernatural facts as historical verities. But if we look back, we find that precisely these same parts of the sacred narrative were dearest to the believers of a more imaginative age; and they are still dwelt upon by the general mass of Christians, with that kind of ardent faith, which refuses to break its old alliance with the imagination. It was by this very supernatural agency, if I may so speak, that the doctrines, the sentiments, the moral and religious influence of Christianity, were implanted in the mind, on the first promulgation of the Gospel, and the reverential feeling thus excited, most powerfully contributed to maintain the efficacy of the religion for at least seventeen centuries. That which is now to many incredible, not merely commanded the belief, but made the purely moral and spiritual part of Christianity, to which few of these writers now refuse their assent, credible.

An argument which appears to me of considerable weight arises out of these considerations. Admit, as even the rationalist and mythic interpreters seem to do, though in vague and metaphysical terms, the divine interposition, or at least the prearrangement, and effective though remote agency of the Deity, in the introduction of Christianity into the world. These passages in general are not the vital and essential truths of Christianity, but the vehicle by which these truths were communicated; a kind of language by which opinions were conveyed, and sentiments infused, and the general belief in Christianity implanted, confirmed, and strengthened. As we cannot but suppose that the state of the world, as well during, as subsequent to the introduction of Christianity, the comparative rebarbarisation of the human race, the long centuries in which mankind was governed by imagination, rather than by severe reason, were within the design, or at least the foreknowledge, of all-seeing Providence; so from the fact that this mode of communication with mankind was for so long a period so effective, we may not unreasonably infer its original adoption by Divine Wisdom. This language of poetic incident, and, if I may so speak, of imagery, interwoven as it was with the popular belief, infused into the hymns, the services, the ceremonial of the Church, embodied in material representation by painting or sculpture, was the vernacular tongue of Christianity, universally intelligible, and responded to by the human heart, throughout these many centuries. Revelation thus spoke the language, not merely of its own, but of succeeding times; because its design was the perpetuation as well as the first propagation of the Christian religion.

Whether then these were actual appearances or impressions produced on the mind of those who witnessed them, is of slight importance. In either case they are real historical facts; they partake of poetry in their form, and, in a certain sense, in their groundwork, but they are imaginative, not fictitious; true, as relating that which appeared to the minds of the relators exactly as it did appear.*

---

* This, of course, does not apply to facts which must have been either historical events or direct fictions, such as the resurrection of Jesus. The reappearance of an actual and well-known bodily form, cannot be refined into one of those airy and unsubstantial appearances which may be represented to, or may exist solely through, the imaginative faculty. I would strictly maintain this important distinction.

Poetry, meaning by poetry such an imaginative form, and not merely the form, but the subject-matter of the narrative, as, for instance, in the first chapters of St. Matthew and St. Luke, was the appropriate and perhaps necessary intelligible dialect; the vehicle for the more important truths of the Gospel to later generations. The incidents, therefore, were so ordered, that they should thus live in the thoughts of men; the revelation itself was so adjusted and arranged in order that it might insure its continued existence throughout this period.[b] Could, it may be inquired, a purely rational or metaphysical creed have survived for any length of time during such stages of human civilisation?

I am aware that this may be considered as carrying out what is called *accommodation* to an unprecedented extent; and that the whole system of what is called accommodation is looked upon with great jealousy. It is supposed to compromise, as it were, the truth of the Deity, or at least of the revelation; a deception, it is said, or at least an illusion, is practised upon the belief of man.

I cannot assent to this view.

From the necessity of the case there must be some departure from the pure and essential spirituality of the Deity, in order to communicate with the human race,—some kind of condescension from the Infinite and inconceivable state of Godhead, to become cognisable, or to enter into any kind of relation with material and dimly-mental man. All this is in fact *accommodation*; and the adaptation of any appropriate means of addressing, for his benefit, man in any peculiar state of intelligence, is but the wise contrivance, the indispensable condition, which renders that communication either possible,

---

[b] By all those who consider the knowledge of these circumstances to have reached the Evangelists (by whatever notion of inspiration they may be guaranteed) through the ordinary sources of information, from the reminiscences of Mary herself, or from those of other contemporaries, it would be expected that these remote incidents would be related with the greatest indistinctness, without mutual connexion or chronological arrangement, and different incidents be preserved by different Evangelists. This is precisely the case: the very marvellousness of the few circumstances thus preserved accounts in some degree for their preservation, and at the same time for the kind of dimness and poetic character with which they are clothed. They are too slight and wanting in particularity to give the idea of invention: they seem like a few scattered fragments preserved from oral tradition.

or at least effective to its manifest end. Religion is one great system of accommodation to the wants, to the moral and spiritual advancement of mankind; and I cannot but think that as it has so efficaciously adapted itself to one state of the human mind, so it will to that mind during all its progress; and it is of all things the most remarkable in Christianity, that it has, as it were, its proper mode of addressing with effect every age and every conceivable state of man. Even if (though I conceive it impossible) the imagination should entirely wither from the human soul, and a severer faith enter into an exclusive alliance with pure reason, Christianity would still have its moral perfection, its rational promise of immortality—its approximation to the one pure, spiritual, incomprehensible Deity, to satisfy that reason, and to infuse those sentiments of dependence, of gratitude, of love to God, without which human society must fall to ruin, and the human mind, in humiliating desperation, suspend all its noble activity, and care not to put forth its sublime and eternal energies.

CHAPTER III.

Commencement of the Public Life of Jesus.

NEARLY thirty years had passed away since the birth in Bethlehem, during which period there is but one incident recorded, which could direct the public attention to the Son of Mary.[a] All religious Jews made their periodical visits to the capital at the three great festivals, especially at the Passover. The more pious women, though exempt by the law from regular attendance, usually accompanied their husbands or kindred. It is probable that, at the age of twelve, the children, who were then said to have assumed the rank of "Sons of the Law," and were considered responsible for their obedience to the civil and religious institutes of the nation, were first permitted to appear with their parents in the metropolis, to be present, and, as it were, to be initiated in the religious ceremonies.[b] Accordingly,

Period to the assumption of public character.

---

[a] There is no likelihood that the extant apocryphal Gospel of the Infancy contains any traditional truth. This work, in my opinion, was evidently composed with a controversial design, to refute the sects which asserted that Jesus was no more than an ordinary child, and that the divine nature descended upon him at his baptism. Hence his childhood is represented as fertile in miracles as his manhood; miracles which are certainly puerile enough for that age. But it is a curious proof of the vitality of popular legends, that many of these stories are still current, even in England, in our Christmas carols, and in this form are disseminated among our cottages.

[b] "A child was free from presenting himself in the Temple at the three feasts until (according to the school of Hillel) he was able, his father taking him by the hand, to go up with him into the mount of the Temple." Lightfoot. i. 71. See also Wetstein, in loc.

at this age, Jesus went up with his parents at the festival to Jerusalem;[a] but on their return, after the customary residence of seven days, they had advanced a full day's journey without discovering that the youth was not to be found in the whole caravan, or long train of pilgrims, which probably comprised all the religious inhabitants of the populous northern provinces. In the utmost anxiety they returned to Jerusalem, and, after three days,[b] found Him in one of the chambers, within the precincts of the Temple, set apart for public instruction. In these schools the wisest and most respected of the Rabbis, or teachers, were accustomed to hold their sittings, which were open to all who were desirous of knowledge. Jesus was seated, as the scholars usually were; and at his familiarity with the Law, and the depth and subtilty of his questions, the learned men were in the utmost astonishment: the phrase may, perhaps, bear the stronger sense—they were "in an ecstasy of admiration." This incident is strictly in accordance with Jewish usage. The more promising youths were encouraged to the early development and display of their acquaintance with the Sacred Writings, and the institutes of the country. Josephus, the historian, relates, that in his early youth he was an object of wonder for his precocious knowledge, with the Wise Men, who took delight in examining and developing his proficiency in the subtler questions of the Law. Whether the impression of the transcendent promise of Jesus was as deep and lasting as it was vivid, we have no information; for without reluctance, with no more than a brief and mys-

---

[a] Luke ii. 41, 52.
[b] According to Grotius, they had advanced one day's journey towards Galilee, returned the second, and found him the third: in loc.

terious intimation that public instruction was the business imposed upon him by his Father, he returned with his parents to his remote and undistinguished home. The Law, in this, as in all such cases, harmonising with the eternal instincts of nature, had placed the relation of child and parent on the simplest and soundest principles. The authority of the parent was unlimited, while his power of inflicting punishment on the person, or injuring the fortunes of the child by disinheritance, was controlled; and while the child, on the one hand, was bound to obedience by the strongest sanctions, on the other the duty of maintaining and instructing his offspring was as rigidly enforced upon the father. The youth then returned to the usual subjection to his parents; and, for nearly eighteen years longer, we have no knowledge that Jesus was distinguished among the inhabitants of Nazareth, except by his exemplary piety, and by his engaging demeanour and conduct, which acquired him the general good-will. The Law, as some suppose, prescribed the period of thirty years for the assumption of the most important functions; and it was not till he had arrived at this age that Jesus again emerged from his obscurity;* nor does it appear improbable that John had previously commenced his public career at the same period in his life.

During these thirty years most important revolutions had taken place in the public administration of affairs in Judæa, and a deep and sullen change had been slowly working in the popular mind. The stirring events which had rapidly succeeded

Political Revolutions during the prevailing period.

---

* Or entering on his thirtieth year. According to the Jewish mode of computation, the year, the week, or the day which had commenced was included in the calculation. Lightfoot.

each other, were such as no doubt might entirely obliterate any transient impressions made by the marvellous circumstances which attended the birth of Jesus, if indeed they had obtained greater publicity than we are inclined to suppose. As the period approached, in which the new Teacher was to publish his mild and benignant faith, the nation, wounded in their pride, galled by oppression, infuriated by the promulgation of fierce and turbulent doctrines more congenial to their temper, became less and less fit to receive any but a warlike and conquering Messiah. The reign of Archelaus, or rather the interregnum, while he awaited the ratification of his kingly powers from Rome, had commenced with a bloody tumult, in which the royal soldiery had attempted to repress the insurrectionary spirit of the populace. The Passover had been interrupted—an unprecedented and ill-omened event!—and the nation, assembled from all quarters, had been constrained to disperse without the completion of the sacred ceremony.ᶠ After the tyrannical reign of Archelaus as ethnarch, for more than nine years, he had been banished into Gaul, and Judæa was reduced to a Roman province, under a governor (procurator) of the equestrian order, who was subordinate to the President of Syria. But the first Roman governors, having taken up their residence in Herod's magnificent city on the coast, Cæsarea, the municipal government of Jerusalem had apparently fallen into the hands of the native authorities. The Sanhedrin of seventy-one, composed of the chief priests and men learned in the Law, from a court of judicature, to which their functions were chiefly confined, while the executive was

Reign of Archelaus.

Reduction to a Roman province.

Sanhedrin.

ᶠ Hist. of the Jews, ii. 96.

administered by the kings, had become a kind of senate. Pontius Pilate, the first of the Roman governors, who, if he did not afflict the capital with the spectacle of a resident foreign ruler, seems to have visited it more frequently, was the first who introduced into the city the "idolatrous" standards of Rome, and had attempted to suspend certain bucklers, bearing an image of the emperor, in the palace of Herod.[a] In his time, the Sanhedrin seems to have been recognised as a sort of representative council of the nation. But the proud and unruly people could not disguise from itself the humiliating consciousness that it was reduced to a state of foreign servitude. Throughout the country the publicans, the farmers or collectors of the tribute to Rome, a burden not less vexatious in its amount[b] and mode of collection than offensive to their feelings, were openly exercising their office. The chief priest was perpetually displaced at the order of the Roman prefect, by what might be jealous or systematic policy, but which had all the appearance of capricious and insulting violence.[i] They looked abroad, but without hope. The country had, without any advantage, suffered all the evils of insurrectionary anarchy. At the period between the death of Herod and the accession of his sons, adventurers of all classes had taken up arms, and some of the lowest, shepherds and slaves, whether hoping to strike in with the popular feeling, and if successful at first, to throw the whole nation on their side, had not scrupled to assume the title and ensigns of

The publicans.

Insurrections.

---

[a] Hist. of the Jews, ii. 120.
[b] About this period Syria and Judæa petitioned for a remission of tribute, which was described as intolerably oppressive. Tac. Ann. ii. 42.
[i] There were twenty-eight, says Josephus, from the time of Herod to the burning of the Temple by Titus. Ant. xx. 8.

K 2

royalty. These commotions had been suppressed; but the external appearance of peace was a fallacious evidence of the real state of public feeling. The religious sects which had long divided the nation, those of the Pharisees and Sadducees, no longer restrained by the strong hand of power, renewed their conflicts: sometimes one party, sometimes the other, obtained the high priesthood, and predominated in the Sanhedrin; while from the former had sprung up a new faction, in whose tenets the stern sense of national degradation which rankled in the hearts of so many, found vent and expression.

The sect of Judas the Gaulonite, or as he was called, the Galilean, may be considered the lineal inheritors of that mingled spirit of national independence and of religious enthusiasm, which had in early days won the glorious triumph of freedom from the Syro-Grecian kings, and had maintained a stern though secret resistance to the later Asmoneans, and to the Idumean dynasty. Just before the death of Herod, it had induced the six thousand Pharisees to refuse the oath of allegiance to the king and to his imperial protector, and had probably been the secret incitement in the other acts of resistance to the royal authority. Judas the Galilean openly proclaimed the unlawfulness, the impiety of God's people submitting to a foreign yoke, and thus acknowledging the subordination of the Jewish theocracy to the empire of Rome. The payment of tribute which began to be enforced on the deposition of Archelaus, according to his tenets, was not merely a base renunciation of their liberties, but a sin against their God. To the doctrines of this bold and eloquent man, which had been propagated with dangerous rapidity and success, frequent allusions are found in the Gospels.

Though the Galileans slain by Pilate may not have been of this sect, yet probably the Roman authorities would look with more than usual jealousy on any appearance of tumult arising in the province which was the reputed birthplace of Judas; and the constant attempts to implicate Jesus with this party appear in their insidious questions about the lawfulness of paying tribute to Cæsar. The subsequent excesses of the Zealots, who were the doctrinal descendants of Judas, and among whom his own sons assumed a dangerous and fatal pre-eminence, may show that the jealousy of the rulers was not groundless; and indicate, as will hereafter appear, under what unfavourable impressions with the existing authorities, on account of his coming from Galilee, Jesus was about to enter on his public career.

Towards the close of this period of thirty years, though we have no evidence to fix a precise date, while Jesus was growing up in the ordinary course of nature, in the obscurity of the Galilean town of Nazareth, which lay to the north of Jerusalem, at much the same distance to the south John had arrived at maturity, and suddenly appeared as a public teacher, at first in the desert country in the neighbourhood of Hebron; but speedily removed, no doubt for the facility of administering the characteristic rite, from which he was called the Baptist, at all seasons, and with the utmost publicity and effect.[b] In the southern desert of Judæa the streams are few and scanty, probably in the summer entirely dried up. The nearest large body of water was the Dead Sea. Besides that the western banks of this great lake are mostly rugged and precipitous, natural feeling, and still more the religious awe of the people, would have

---

[b] Matt. iii. 1-12; Mark i. 2-8; Luke iii. 1-18.

shrunk from performing sacred ablutions in those fetid, unwholesome, and accursed waters.ᵃ But the banks of the great national stream, the scene of so many miracles, offered many situations, in every respect admirably calculated for this purpose. The Baptist's usual station was near the place, Bethabara, the ford of the Jordan, which tradition pointed out as that where the waters divided before the ark, that the chosen people might enter into the promised land. Here, though the adjacent region towards Jerusalem is wild and desert, the immediate shores of the river offer spots of great picturesque beauty.ᵇ The Jordan has a kind of double channel. In its summer course the shelving banks, to the top of which the waters reach at its period of flood, are covered with acacias and other trees of great luxuriance; and amid the rich vegetation and grateful shade afforded by these scenes, the Italian painters, with no less truth than effect, have delighted to represent the Baptist surrounded by listening multitudes, or performing the solemn rite of initiation. The teacher himself partook of the ascetic character of the more solitary of the Essenes, all of whom retired from the tumult and licence of the city; some dwelt alone in remote hermitages, and not rarely pretended to a prophetic character. His raiment was of the coarsest texture, of camel's hair; his girdle (an ornament often of the greatest richness in Oriental costume, of the finest linen or cotton, and embroidered with silver or gold) was of untanned leather; his food

---

ᵃ The Aulon, or Valley of the Jordan, is mostly desert. Διαιρεῖται τὴν Γεννήσαρ μέσην, ἔπειτα πολλὴν ἀναμετρούμενος ἐρημίαν εἰς τὴν Ἀσφαλτῖτιν ἔπεισι λίμνην. Joseph. B. J. iii. 10, 7.

ᵇ Compare on the scene of John's Teaching and Baptism the eloquent passage in Stanley, p. 304, &c., 1st edition.

the locusts[a] and wild honey, of which there is a copious supply both in the open and the wooded regions, in which he had taken up his abode.

No question has been more strenuously debated than the origin of the rite of baptism. The practice of the external washing of the body, as emblematic of the inward purification of the soul, is almost universal. The sacred Ganges cleanses all moral pollution from the Indian; among the Greeks and Romans even the murderer might, it was supposed, wash the blood "clean from his hands;"[b] and in many of their religious rites, lustrations or ablutions, either in the running stream or in the sea, purified the candidate for divine favour, and made him fit to approach the shrines of the gods. The perpetual similitude and connexion between the uncleanness of the body and of the soul, which ran through the Mosaic Law and had become interwoven with the common language and sentiment, the formal enactment of washing in many cases, which either required the cleansing of some unhealthy taint, or more than usual purity, must have familiarised the mind with the mysterious effects attributed to such a rite; and of all the Jewish sects, that of the Essenes, to which no doubt popular opinion associated the Baptist, were most frequent and scrupulous in their ceremonial ablutions. It is strongly asserted on the one hand, and denied with equal confidence on the other, that baptism was in general use among the Jews as a distinct and

Baptism.

---

[a] That locusts are no uncommon food is so well known from all travellers in the East, that it is unnecessary to quote any single authority. There is a kind of bean, called in that country the locust-bean, which some have endeavoured to make out to have been the food of John.

[b] Ah nimium faciles, qui tristia crimina cædis
Tolli flumineâ posse putatis aquâ.
Ovid.

formal rite; and that it was by this ceremony that the Gentile proselytes, who were not yet thought worthy of circumcision, or perhaps refused to submit to it, were imperfectly initiated into the family of Israel.* Though there does not seem very conclusive evidence in the earlier Rabbinical writings to the antiquity, yet there are perpetual allusions to the existence of this rite, at least at a later period; and the argument, that after irreconcileable hostility had been declared between the two religions, the Jews would be little likely to borrow their distinctive ceremony from the Christians, applies with more than ordinary force. Nor, if we may fairly judge from the very rapid and concise narrative of the Evangelists, does the public administration of baptism by John appear to have excited astonishment as a new and unprecedented rite.

For, from every quarter, all ranks and sects crowded to the teaching and to partake in the mystic ablutions performed by the Baptist. The stream of the Jordan reflected the wondering multitudes of every class and character, which thronged around him with that deep interest and high-wrought curiosity, which could not fail to be excited, especially at such a crisis, by one who assumed the tone and authority of a divine commission, and seemed, even if he were not hereafter to break forth in a higher character, to renew in his person the long silent and interrupted race of the ancient prophets. Of all those prophets Elijah was held in the most profound reverence by the descendants of Israel.' He was the representative of their great race

---

* Lightfoot, Harmony of Evang. iii. 38, iv. 407, &c. Dansius, in Menachem, Talmudka, &c. Schoetgen and Wetstein, in loc.

' Some of the strange notions about Elias may be found in Lightfoot, Harm. of Evang. iv. 399. Compare Ecclesiast. xlviii. 10, 11. " Elias,

of moral instructors and interpreters of the Divine Will, whose writings (though of Elijah nothing remained) had been admitted to almost equal authority with the Law itself, were read in the public synagogues, and with the other sacred books formed the canon of their Scripture. A mysterious intimation had closed this hallowed volume of the prophetic writings, announcing, as from the lips of Malachi, on which the fire of prophecy expired, a second coming of Elijah, which it would seem popular belief had construed into the personal reappearance of him who had ascended into heaven in a car of fire. And where, and at what time, and in what form was he so likely to appear as in the desert, by the shore of the Jordan, at so fearful a crisis in the national destinies, and in the wild garb and with the mortified demeanour so frequent among the ancient seers? The language of the Baptist took the bold, severe, and uncompromising tone of those delegates of the Most High. On both the great religious factions he denounced the same maledictions, from both demanded the same complete and immediate reformation. On the people he inculcated mutual charity; on the publicans, whom he did not

---

who is written of for reproofs in these times, to appease the anger of him that is ready for wrath (or before wrath, προθύμων, or πρὸ θύμων), to turn the heart of the father to the son, and to restore the tribes of Jacob. Blessed are they that see thee, and are adorned with love; for we too shall live the life." In the English translation the traditionary allusion is obscured. "In that day, when the Lord shall deliver Israel, three days before the coming of the Messiah, Elias shall come, and shall stand on the mountains of Israel mourning and wailing concerning them, and saying, How long will ye stay in the dry and wasted land? And his voice shall be heard from one end of the world to the other; and after that he shall say unto them, Peace cometh to the world, as it is written (Isaiah lii. 7), How beautiful upon the mountains are the feet of him that bringeth good tidings, that publisheth peace!" Jalkut Schamuni, fol. 53, c. 6. Quoted in Bertholdt. See other quotations. Schoetgen, Hor. Heb. ll. 533, 534. Justin. Dial. cum Tryph.

exclude from his followers, justice; on the soldiery[a] humanity, and abstinence from all unnecessary violence and pillage. These general denunciations against the vices of the age, and the indiscriminate enforcement of a higher moral and religious standard, though they might gall the consciences of individuals, or wound the pride of the different sects; yet, as clashing with no national prejudice, would excite no hostility, which could be openly avowed; while the fearless and impartial language of condemnation was certain to secure the wonder, the respect, the veneration, of the populace.

But that which no doubt drew the whole population in such crowds to the desert shores of the Jordan, was the mysterious yet distinct assertion, that the "kingdom of Heaven was at hand"[b]— that kingdom of which the belief was as universal as of the personal coming of the Messiah; and as variously coloured by the disposition and temperament of every class and individual, as the character of the sovereign who was thus to assume dominion. All anticipated the establishment of an earthly sovereignty, but its approach thrilled the popular bosom with mingled emotions. The very prophecy which announced the previous appearance of Elijah, spoke of the "great and dreadful

<small>Expectation of the Messiah.</small>

---

[a] Michaelis has very ingeniously observed that these men are described not merely as soldiers (στρατιῶται), but as on actual service (στρατευόμενοι); and has conjectured that they were part of the forces of Herod Antipas, who was at this time at war, or preparing for war, with Aretas, king of Arabia. Their line of march would lead them to the ford of the Jordan.

[b] This phrase is discussed by Kuinoel, vol. i. page 33. According to its Jewish meaning, it was equivalent to the kingdom of the Messiah (the kingdom of God, or of Heaven—Schoutgen, Hor. Hebr. p. 1147), which was to commence and endure for ever, when the Law was to be fully restored, and the immutable theocracy of God's chosen people re-established for eternity. In its higher Christian signification it assumed the sense of the moral dominion to be exercised by Christ over his subjects in this life; that dominion which is to be continued over his faithful in the state of immortal existence beyond the grave.

day of the Lord," and, as has been said, according to the current belief, fearful calamities were to precede the glorious days of the Messiah: nor was it till after a dark period of trial, that the children of Abraham, as the prerogative of their birth, the sons of God,[u] the inheritors of his kingdom, were to emerge from their obscurity; their theocracy to be re-established in its new and more enduring form; the dead, at least those who were to share in the first resurrection, their own ancestors, were to rise; the solemn judgement was to be held; the hostile nations were to be thrust down to hell; and those only of the Gentiles, who should become proselytes to Judaism, were to be admitted to this earthly paradisincal state.[x]

---

[u] Compare Justin Martyr (Dial. 433), ed. Thirlby. Grotius on Matt. x. 28, xiv. 2. James, ii. 14. Whitby on Acts i. 23. Jortin's Discourses, page 26.

[x] See Wetstein, in loc. The following passage closely resembles the language of John: "Whose fan is in his hand, and he will throughly purge his floor, and gather his wheat into the garner; but he will burn up the chaff with unquenchable fire." Matt. iii. 12. The Jer. Talmud adduces Isaiah xvi. 12. "The morning cometh and also the night; it shall be morning to Israel, but night to the nations of the world." (Taanith, fol. 64, l.) "The threshing is come: the straw they cast into the fire, the chaff unto the wind, but preserve the wheat in the floor, and every one that sees it, takes it and kisses it. So the nations of the world say, The world was made for our sakes: but Israel say to them, Is it not written, But the people shall be as the burning of the lime-kiln, but Israel in the time to come (i.e. the time of the Messiah) shall be left only; as it is said, The Lord shall be with him alone, and there shall be no strange God." Mid. Tell, on Psalm ii. Lightfoot, iii. 47.

Some of these and similar expressions may belong to the period of the obstinate, we may surely add, the patriotic struggle of the Jews against the tyranny of Rome, after what Tacitus terms their "hatred of the human race" had been embittered by years of contempt and persecution; and while, in Gibbon's language, "their dreams of prophecy and conquest" were kept alive by the bold resistance to Titus, and the successes of Barcochab under Hadrian. But there can be little doubt, that pride had already drawn these distinctions between themselves and the rest of mankind, which were deepened by the sense of persecution, and cherished as

The language of the Baptist at once fell in with and opposed the popular feeling; at one instant it raised, at the next it crossed their hopes. He announced the necessity of a complete moral change, while he repudiated the claims of those who rested their sole title to the favours of God on their descent from the chosen race, for "God even of the stones could raise up children to Abraham." But, on the other hand, he proclaimed the immediate, the instant coming of the Messiah; and on the nature of the kingdom, though he might deviate from the ordinary language, in expressly intimating that the final separation would be made not on national but moral grounds—that the bad and good, even of the race of Israel, were to be doomed according to their wickedness or virtue—yet there was nothing which interfered with the prevailing belief in the personal temporal reign of the Son of David.

The course of our History will show how slowly Christianity attained the purely moral and spiritual notion of the change to be wrought by the coming of Christ, and how perpetually this inveterate Judaism has revived in the Christian Church, where, in days of excitement, the old Jewish tenet of the personal reign of the Messiah

---

the only consolation of degradation and despair.

Le Judaisme est un système de misanthropie, qui ne veut à tous les peuples de la terre sans aucune exception. . . . . . Il n'étend l'amour du prochain qu'aux seuls Juifs, tandis que le Mosaisme l'étend à tous les hommes, sans aucune distinction (vide note). Il commande en outre qu'on envisage tous les autres peuples de la terre comme dignes de haine et de mépris, pour la seule raison qu'ils n'ont pas été, ou qu'ils ne sont pas Juifs. Chiarini, Préface to Translation of Talmud, p. 55.

Passages of the Talmud will certainly bear out this harsh conclusion: but I think better of human nature than to suppose that this sentiment was not constantly counteracted by the humane feelings to which affliction would subdue hearts of better mould, or which would be infused by the gentler spirit of the genuine religion of Moses.

has filled the mind of the enthusiast. Nor were the Jews likely to be more embarrassed than mankind in general by the demand of high moral qualifications; for while one part would look on their own state with perfect complacency and satisfaction, another would expect to obtain from Heaven, without much effort or exertion on their own part, that which Heaven required. God who intended to make them happy would first make them virtuous.

Such was the general excitement at the appearance, the teaching, and the baptizing of John. So great was the influence which he had obtained throughout the country, that, as we shall speedily see, a formal deputation from the national authorities was commissioned to inquire into his pretensions, and to ascertain whether he limited himself to those of a prophet, or laid claim to the higher title of "the Christ." And the deep hold which he had taken upon the popular feeling is strongly indicated by the fact, that the rulers did not dare, on the occasion of a question proposed to them at a much later period, by Jesus, openly to deny the prophetic mission of John, which was not merely generally acknowledged, but even zealously asserted by the people. *Imputation of the priesthood concerning the pretensions of John.*

How long the preaching of John had lasted before the descent of the Son of Mary to the shores of the Jordan, rests on somewhat uncertain evidence.ᶠ We can decide with as little confidence on some other more interesting questions. There is no precise information, whether any or what degree of intercourse had been kept up between the family of Zachariah and that of Joseph, who resided at a considerable distance from

---

ᶠ Matt. iii. 13-17; Mark i. 9, 11; Luke iii. 21, 23; John i. 15, 18.

each other, and were not likely to meet, unless at the periodical feasts; nor how far John might be previously acquainted with the person of Jesus.¹ But it is undoubtedly a remarkable fact in the history of Christianity, that from the very first appearance of Jesus on the shores of the Jordan, unquestionably before He had displayed his powers, or openly asserted his title to the higher place, John should invariably retain his humbler relative position. Such was his uniform language from the commencement of his career; such it continued to the end. Yet at this period the power and influence of John over the public mind were at their height; Jesus, humanly speaking, was but an unknown and undistinguished youth, whose qualifications to maintain the higher character were as yet untried. John, however, cedes at once the first place: in the strongest language* he declares himself immeasurably inferior to him, who stood among the crowd, unmarked and unregarded; whatever his own claims, whatever the effects of his initiatory rite, Jesus

margin: Avowed inferiority of John to Jesus.

---

¹ The discrepancies between the different Evangelists as to the language of John, on several occasions, with regard to Jesus, appear to me characteristic of the dim and awe-struck state of the general mind, which would extend to the remembrance and the faithful record of such incidents. It is assumed, I think without warrant, that John himself must have had a distinct or definite notion of the Messiahship of Jesus; he may have applied some of the prophetic or popular sayings supposed to have reference to the Messiah, without any precise notion of their meaning; and his conception of the Messiah's character, and of Jesus himself, may have varied during different passages of his own life. If the whole had been more distinct and systematic, it would be more liable, according to my judgement, to suspicion. The account of John in Josephus is just as his character would be likely to appear to a writer of the disposition and in the situation of the Jewish historian.

* The remarkable expression, "whose shoe's latchet I am not worthy to unloose," is illustrated by a passage in the Talmud. (Tract. Kiddushin, xxi. 2.) "Every office a servant will do for his master, a scholar should perform for his teacher, excepting loosing his sandal thong."

was at once to assume a higher function, to administer a more powerful and influential baptism.[b] This has always appeared to me one of the most striking incidental arguments for the truth of the Evangelic narrative, and consequently of the Christian faith. The recognition appears to have been instant and immediate. Hitherto, the Baptist had insisted on the purification of all who had assembled around him; and, with the commanding dignity of a Heaven-commissioned teacher, had rebuked, without distinction, the sins of all classes and all sects. In Jesus alone, by his refusal to baptize him, he acknowledges the immaculate purity, while his deference assumes the tone of homage, almost of adoration.[c]

Jesus, however, perhaps to do honour to a rite which was hereafter to be that of initiation into the new religion, insists on submitting to the usual ablution. As he went up out of the water, which wound below in its deep channel, and was ascending the shelving shore, a light shone around with the rapid and undulating motion of a dove, typifying the descent of the Holy Spirit on the Son of Man; and a voice was heard from heaven, which recognised him as the Son of God, well pleasing to the Almighty Father of the Universe. This light could scarcely have been seen, or the voice heard, by more than the Baptist and the Son of

Baptism of Jesus.

---

[b] Strauss (I. 396) argues that this concession of the higher place by the ascetic John (and asceticism, he justly observes, is the most stern and unyielding principle in the human character) is so contrary to the principles of human nature, and to all historical precedent, that the whole must be fictitious; a singular canon, that every thing extraordinary and unprecedented in history must be untrue. I suspect the common phrase, "truth is strange —stranger than fiction," to be founded on deeper knowledge of human nature, and of the events of the world.

[c] The more distinct declarations of inferiority contained in several passages are supposed by most harmonists of the Gospels to have been made after the baptism of Jesus.

Mary himself,[d] as no immediate sensation appears to have been excited among the multitudes, such as must have followed this public and miraculous proclamation of his sacred character; and at a subsequent period, Jesus seems to have appeared among the followers of John, unrecognised, or at least unhonoured, until He was pointed out by the Baptist, and announced as having been proclaimed from Heaven at his baptism. The calmness and comparatively unimposing peacefulness of this scene, which may be described as the inauguration of this "greater than Moses," in his office as founder of a new religion, is strikingly contrasted with the terrific tempests and convulsions of nature at the delivery of the Law on Sinai, and harmonises with the general tone and character of the new faith. The image of the Dove, the universal symbol of innocence and peace,[e] even if purely illustrative, is beautifully in keeping with the gentler character of the whole transaction.

Temptation of Jesus.

The Temptation of Jesus is the next event in the history of his life;[f] and here, at the opening, as it were, of his career, appears shadowed out the sort of complex character under which Christianity

---

[d] This appears from John i. 32. Neander (Leben Jesu, p. 69) represents it as a symbolic vision.

It may be well to observe that this explanation of voices from heaven, as a mental perception, not as real articulate sounds but as inward impressions, is by no means modern, or what passes under the unpopular name of rationalism. There is a very full and remarkable passage in Origen cont. Celsum, l. 48, on this point. He is speaking of the offence which may be given to the simple, who from their great simplicity are ready on every occasion to shake the world, and cleave the compact firmament of heaven. Κἂν προσκόπτῃ τὸ τοιοῦτον τοῖς ἁπλουστέροις, οἳ διὰ πολλὴν ἁπλότητα κινοῦσι τὸν κόσμον, σχίζοντες τὸ τηλικοῦτον σῶμα ἡνωμένον τοῦ παντὸς οὐρανοῦ. See likewise in Suicer's Thesaur., voc. φώνη, the passages from St. Basil and Gregory of Nyssa.

[e] Ennius apud Cic. de Div. l. 48 Tibull. l. 8, 9.

[f] Matt. iv. 1, 11; Mark iv. 12, 13; Luke iv. 1-13.

represents its Divine Author, as a kind of federal representative of mankind. On the interpretation of no incident in the Gospels, do those who insist on the literal acceptation of the Evangelists' language, and those who consider that, even in the New Testament, much allowance is to be made for the essentially allegoric character of Oriental narrative, depart so far asunder.[f] While the former receive the whole as a real scene, the latter suppose that the truth lies deeper; and that some, not less real, though less preternatural transaction, is related, either from some secret motive, or, according to the genius of Eastern narrative, in this figurative style. As pretending to discover historical facts of much importance in the life of Christ, the latter exposition demands our examination. The Temptation, according to one view, is a parabolic description of an actual event;[h] according to another, of a kind of inward mental trial, which continued during the public career of Jesus. In the first theory, the Tempter was nothing less than the high priest, or one of the Sanhedrin, delegated by their authority to discover the real pretensions of Jesus. Having received intelligence of the testimony borne to Jesus by John, this person was directed to follow him into the wilderness, where he first demanded,

---

[f] Some of the older writers, as Theodore of Mopsuestia, explained it as a vision; to this notion Le Clerc inclines. Schleiermacher treats it as a parable, p. 58. Those who are most scrupulous in departing from the literal sense, cannot but be embarrassed with this kind of personal conflict with a Being, whom the devil must have known, according to their own view, to have been divine. This is one of those points which will be differently understood, according to the tone and cast of mind of different individuals. I would therefore deprecate the making either interpretation an article of faith, or deciding with dogmatic certainty on so perplexing a passage.

[h] This theory, differently modified, is embraced by Herman Von der Hardt, by the elder Rosenmüller (Schol. in loc.), and by Kuinoel.

as the price of his acknowledgment by the public authorities, some display of miraculous power, such as should enable him, like Moses, to support the life of man by a preternatural supply of food in the wilderness. He then held out to him the splendid prospects of aggrandisement, if he should boldly place himself, as a divinely commissioned leader, at the head of the nation; and even led him in person to the pinnacle of the Temple, and commanded him to cast himself down, as the condition, if he should be miraculously preserved, of his formal recognition by the Sanhedrin. To this view, ingenious as it is, some obvious objections occur;—the precise date apparently assigned to the transaction by the Evangelists, and the improbability that, at so early a period, he would be thought of so much importance by the ruling powers; the difficulty of supposing that, even if there might be prudential motives to induce St. Matthew, writing in Judæa, to disguise, under this allegoric veil, so remarkable an event in the history of Christ, St. Luke, influenced by no such motives, would adopt the same course. Though, indeed, it may be replied, that if the transaction had once assumed, it would be likely to retain, its parabolic dress; still, it must seem extraordinary that no clearer notice of so wonderful a circumstance should transpire in any of the Christian records. Nor does it appear easily reconcileable with the cautious distance at which the authorities appear to have watched the conduct of Jesus, thus, as it were, at once to have committed themselves, and almost placed themselves within his power.

The second theory is embarrassed with fewer of these difficulties, though it is liable to the same objection, as to the precise date apparently assigned to the incident. According to this view, at one particular period of his life, or at several times, the earthly and temporal thoughts, thus parabolically described as a personal contest with the Principle of Evil, passed through the mind of Jesus, and arrayed before him the image constantly present to the minds of his countrymen, that of the author of a new temporal theocracy. For so completely were the suggestions in unison with the popular expectation, that ambition, if it had taken a human or a worldly turn, might have urged precisely such displays of supernatural power as are represented in the temptations of Jesus. On no two points, probably, would the Jews have so entirely coincided, as in expecting the Messiah to assume his title and dignity, before the view of the whole people, and in the most public and imposing manner; such, for instance, as, springing from the highest point of the Temple, to have appeared floating in the air, or preternaturally poised upon the unyielding element; any miraculous act, in short, of a totally opposite character to those more private, more humane, and, if we may so speak, more unassuming signs, to which he himself appealed as the evidences of his mission. To be the lord of all the kingdoms, at least of Palestine, if not of the whole world, was, according to the same popular belief, the admitted right of the Messiah. If then, as the history implies, the Saviour was tried by the intrusion of worldly thoughts, whether according to the common literal interpretation, actually urged by the Principle of Evil, in his proper person, or, according to this more modified interpretation of the passage, suggested to his mind, such was the natural turn which they might have taken.

But, however interpreted, the moral purport of the scene remains the same — the intimation that the strongest and most lively impressions were made upon the mind of Jesus, to withdraw him from the purely religious end of his being upon earth, to transform him from the author of a moral revolution to be slowly wrought by the introduction of new principles of virtue, and new rules for individual and social happiness, to the vulgar station of one of the great monarchs or conquerors of mankind; to degrade him from a being who was to offer to man the gift of eternal life, and elevate his nature to a previous fitness for that exalted destiny, to one whose influence over his own generation might have been more instantaneously manifest, but which could have been as little permanently beneficial as that of any other of those remarkable names, which, especially in the East, have blazed for a time and expired.

From the desert, not improbably supposed to be that of Quarantania, lying between Jericho and Jerusalem, where tradition, in Palestine unfortunately of no great authority, still points out the scene of this great spiritual conflict, and where a mountain,[1] commanding an almost boundless prospect of the valleys and hills of Judæa, is shown as that from whence Jesus looked down unmoved on the kingdoms of the earth, the Son of Man returned to the scene of John's baptism.

In the mean time the success of the new prophet, the Baptist, had excited the attention, if not the jealousy, of the ruling authorities of the Jews. The solemn deputation appeared to inquire into his pretensions. The Pharisees probably at this time predominated in the great council, and the delegates, as of this sect, framed their questions in accordance with the popular traditions, as well as with the prophetic

Deputation from Jerusalem to John.

---

[1] The best description of this mountain is in the Travels of the Abbé Mariti. Compare Stanley, p. 302.

writings:[k] they inquire whether he is the Christ, or Elias, or *the prophet*.[m] John at once disclaims his title to the appellation of the Christ; nor is he Elijah, personally returned, according to the vulgar expectation;[n] nor Jeremiah, to whom tradition assigned the name of "the prophet," who was to rise from the dead at the coming of the Messiah, in order, it was supposed, to restore the tabernacle, the ark, and the altar of incense, which he was said to have concealed in a cave on the destruction of the Temple by Nebuchadnezzar, and which were to be brought again to light at the Messiah's coming.[o]

The next day John renewed his declaration that he was the harbinger,[p] described in the Prophet Isaiah, who, according to the custom in the progresses of Oriental monarchs, was to go before, and cutting through mountains and bridging valleys, to make a wide and level way for the advance of the Great King. So John was to remove some of the moral impediments for the reception of Christ. At the same time, as Jesus mingled undistinguished among the crowd, without directly designating him, the Baptist declared the actual presence of the mightier teacher who was about to appear. The next day, in the more private circle of his believers, John did not scruple to point out more distinctly the person of the Messiah.[q] *Jesus designated by John as the Messiah.* The occasion of his remarkable speech (it has been suggested with much probability) was the passing of large flocks of sheep and lambs, which, from the rich

---

[k] The Sanhedrin alone could judge a tribe, the high priest, or a prophet (Sanhedrin Paroch. 1.). Hence "a prophet could not perish out of Jerusalem." Luke xiii. 33. Lightfoot, Harm. Ev.

[m] John i. 19-28.
[n] Wetstein. Nov. Test. in loc.
[o] 2 Macc. ii. 4-8; xv. 14.
[p] John i. 29-34.
[q] John i. 35, 36.

pastoral districts beyond the river, crossed the Jordan at the ford, and were driven on to the metropolis, to furnish either the usual daily sacrifices or those for the approaching Passover. The Baptist, as they were passing, glanced from them to Jesus, declared him to be that superior Being, of whom he was but the humble harbinger, and described him as "the Lamb of God,* which taketh away the sins of the world." Unblemished and innocent as the meek animals that passed, like them he was to go up as a sacrifice to Jerusalem, and in some mysterious manner to "take away" the sins of mankind. Another title, by which he designated Jesus yet more distinctly as the Messiah, was that of the "Son of God," one of the appellations of the Deliverer

---

* Supposing (as is the general opinion) that this term refers to the expiatory sacrifice of Christ, according to the analogy between the death of Jesus and the sacrificial victims, subsequently developed by the Apostles (and certainly the narrower sense maintained by Grotius and the modern learned writers (see Rosenmüller and Kuinoel in loc.) is by no means satisfactory), to the bearers of John at this time such an allusion must have been as unintelligible as the intimations of Jesus about his future sufferings to his disciples. Indeed, if understood by John himself in its full sense, it is difficult to reconcile it with the more imperfect views of the Messiah evinced by his doubt during his imprisonment. To the Jews in general it can have conveyed no distinct meaning. That the Messiah was to be blameless, was strictly accordant with their notions, and " his taking away sins" bore an intelligible Jewish sense; but taking them away by his own sacrifice, was a purely Christian tenet, and but obscurely and prophetically alluded to before the death of Christ. How far the Jews had any notion of a suffering Messiah (afterwards their great stumbling-block) is a most obscure question. The Chaldaic paraphrast certainly refers, but in very vague and contradictory language (Isaiah lii. 13 et seq.), to the Messiah. See on one side Schoetgen, Hor. Heb. ii. 161, and Danzius, De Ἀἐργῳ, in Meuschen; on the other, Rosenmüller and Gesenius on Isaiah. The notion of the double Messiah, the suffering Messiah the son of Joseph, and the triumphant, the son of David (as in Pearson on the Creed, vol. ii.), is of most uncertain date and origin; but nothing, in my opinion, can be more incredible than that it should have been derived, as Bertholdt would imagine, from the Samaritan belief. Bertholdt, c. 29.

most universally admitted, though, no doubt, it might bear a different sense to different hearers.

Among the more immediate disciples of John this declaration of their master could not but excite the strongest emotions; nor can anything be more characteristic of the feelings of that class among the Jews than the anxious rapidity with which the wonderful intelligence is propagated, and the distant and awe-struck reverence with which the disciples slowly present themselves to their new master. The first of these were, Andrew, the brother of Simon (Peter), and probably the author of the narrative, St. John.[a] Simon, to whom his brother communicates the extraordinary tidings, immediately follows, and on him Jesus bestows a new name, expressive of the firmness of his character. All these belonged to the same village, Bethsaida, on the shore of the lake of Gennesaret. On the departure of Jesus, when He is returning to Galilee, He summons another, named Philip. Philip, like Andrew, hastens away to impart the tidings to Nathanael, not improbably conjectured to be the apostle Bartholomew (the son of Tolmai or Ptolemy), a man of blameless character, whose only doubt is, whether the Messiah could come from a town of such proverbial disrepute as Nazareth.[b] But the doubts of Nathanael are removed by the preternatural knowledge displayed by Jesus of an incident which he could not have witnessed; and this fifth disciple, in like manner, does homage to the Messiah, under his titles "the Son of God, the King of Israel." Yet this proof of more than human knowledge, Jesus declares to be as nothing in comparison with the more striking signs of the Divine protection

First disciples of Jesus.

---

[a] John i. 37-42.   [b] John i. 43-51.

and favour, which he asserts, under the popular and significant image of the perpetual intervention of angels, that his chosen followers are hereafter to witness.

<small>Jesus commences his career as a Teacher.</small> Jesus had now commenced his career: disciples had attached themselves to this new master, and his claim to a divine mission must necessarily be accompanied by the signs and wonders which were to ratify the appearance of the Messiah. Yet even his miraculous powers had nothing of the imposing, the appalling, or public character, looked for, no doubt, by those who expected that the appeal would be made to their senses and their passions, to their terror and their hope, not to the more tranquil emotions of gratitude and love. But of this more hereafter.

<small>First miracle. Anti-Essenian.</small> The first miracle of Jesus was the changing the water into wine, at the marriage feast at Cana in Galilee.[a] This event, however, was not merely remarkable as being the first occasion for the display of supernatural power, but as developing in some degree the primary principles of the new religious revelation. The attendance of Jesus at a marriage festival, his contributing to the festive hilarity, more particularly his sanctioning the use of wine on such occasions, at once separated and set him apart from that sect with which he was most likely to be confounded. John, no doubt, passed with the vulgar for a stricter Essene, many of whom, it has been before said, observed the severest morality, and, in one great point, differed most widely from all their brethren. They disregarded the ceremonies of the Law, even the solemn national festivals, and depreciated sacrifices. Shut up, in short, in their own monastic establishments, they had substituted

---
[a] John ii. 1-11.

observances of their own for those of the Mosaic institutes. In all these points, John, who nowhere appears to have visited Jerusalem, at least after his assumption of the prophetic office (for his presence there would doubtless have excited much commotion), followed the Essenian practice. Like them he was severe, secluded, monastic, or rather eremitical in his habits and language. But among the most marked peculiarities of the Essenian fraternity was their aversion to marriage. Though some of the less rigid of their communities submitted to this inevitable evil, yet those who were of higher pretensions, and doubtless of higher estimation, maintained inviolable celibacy, and had fully imbibed that Oriental principle of asceticism, which proscribed all indulgence of the gross and material body as interfering with the purity of the immaculate spirit. The perfect religious being was he who had receded to the utmost from all human passion; who had withdrawn his senses from all intercourse with the material world, or rather had estranged his mind from all objects of sense, and had become absorbed in the silent and ecstatic contemplation of the Deity.[a] This mysticism was the vital principle of the Essenian observances in Judæa, and of those of the Therapeutæ, or Contemplatists, in Egypt, the lineal ancestors of the Christian monks and hermits. By giving public countenance to a marriage ceremony,

---

[a] It may be worth observing (for the connexion of Jesus with the Essenes has been rather a favourite theory) that his illustrations so perpetually drawn from the marriage rite, and from the vineyard, would be in direct opposition to Essenian phraseology. All these passages were peculiarly embarrassing to the Gnostic ascetics. "Noluit Marcion sub imagine Domini a nuptiis redeuntis Christum cogitari ' detestatorem nuptiarum.'" Marcion rejected from his Gospel, Luke xiv. 7-11. See the Gospel of Marcion by Hahn in Thilo, Cod. Apoc. Nov. Testam. p. 444 and 449.

still more by sanctioning the use of wine on such occasions (for wine was likewise proscribed by Essenian usage), Jesus thus, at the outset of his career, as he afterwards placed himself in direct opposition to the other prevailing sects, so he had already receded from the practice of these recluse mystics, who formed the third, and though not in numbers, yet in character and influence, by no means unimportant religious party.

After this event in Cana,[f] Jesus, with his mother, his brethren, and some of his disciples, took up their abode, not in their native town of Nazareth, but in the village of Capernaum,[a] which was situated not far from the rising city of Tiberias, on the shore of the beautiful lake, the Sea of Gennesaret. It was called the Village of Comfort, or the Lovely Village, from a spring of delicious water, and became afterwards the chief residence of Jesus, and the great scene of his wonderful works.[a]

The Passover approached,[b] the great festival[c] which

---

[f] Maundrell places Cana north-west of Nazareth; it was about a day's journey from Capernaum. Josephus (De Vita Sua) marched all night from Cana, and arrived at Tiberias in the morning.

[a] John ii. 12.

[a] Among the remarkable and distinctive peculiarities of the Gospel of St. John, is the much greater length at which he relates the events which occurred during the earlier visits of Jesus to Jerusalem, about which the other Evangelists are either entirely silent or extremely brief. I cannot help suspecting a very natural reason for this fact, that John was the constant companion of his Master during these journeys, and that the other apostles were much less constant in their attendance upon him during these more distant excursions, especially at the earlier period. The Gospel of St. John (some few passages omitted) might be described as the acts of Jesus in Jerusalem and its neighbourhood.

[b] John ii. 13.

[c] Many writers suppose that about half a year passed between the baptism of Jesus and this Passover. This is possible; but it appears to me that there is no evidence whatever as to the length of the period.

assembled not only from all parts of Palestine, but even from remoter regions, the more devout Jews, who at this period of the year constantly made their pilgrimage to the Holy City: regular caravans came from Babylonia and Egypt; and, as we shall explain hereafter, considerable numbers from Syria, Asia Minor, and the other provinces of the Roman empire. There can be no doubt that at least vague rumours of the extraordinary transactions which had already excited public attention towards Jesus of Nazareth, must have preceded his arrival at Jerusalem. The declaration of the Baptist, although neither himself nor many of his immediate disciples might attend the feast, could not but have transpired. Though the single miracle wrought at Cana might not have been distinctly reported at Jerusalem—though the few disciples who may have followed him from Galilee, having there disseminated the intelligence of his conduct and actions, might have been lost in the multitude and confusion of the crowded city—though, on the other hand, the impressions thus made, would be still further counterbalanced by the general prejudice against Galilee, more especially against a Galilean from Nazareth—still the Son of Mary, even at his first appearance in Jerusalem, seems to have been looked on with a kind of reverential awe. His actions were watched; and though both the ruling powers, and, as yet apparently, the leading Pharisees kept aloof, though he is neither molested by the jealousy of the latter, nor excites the alarm of the former, yet the mass of the people already observed his words and his demeanour with anxious interest. The conduct of Jesus tended to keep up this mysterious uncertainty so likely to work on the imagination of a people thus ripe for religious excitement. He is said to have performed "many miracles," but these, no doubt, were still of a private, secret, and unimposing character; and on all other points he maintains the utmost reserve, and avoids with the most jealous precaution any action or language which might directly commit him with the rulers or the people.

One act alone was public, commanding, and authoritative. The outer court of the Temple had become, particularly at the period of the greatest solemnity, a scene of profane disorder and confusion. As the Jews assembled from all quarters of the country, almost of the world, they were under the necessity of purchasing the victims for their offerings on the spot; and the rich man who could afford a sheep or an ox, or the poor man who was content with the humbler oblation of a pair of doves, found the dealer at hand to supply his wants. The traders in sheep, cattle, and pigeons, had therefore been permitted to establish themselves within the precincts of the Temple in the court of the Gentiles;[4] and a line of shops (tabernæ) ran along the outer wall of the inner court. Every Jew made an annual payment of a half-shekel to the Temple; and as the treasury, according to ancient usage, only received the coin of Palestine,[*] those who came from

The Temple a Mart.

---

[4] John II. 14, 25.

[*] According to Hug, "the ancient imposts which were introduced before the Roman dominion were valued according to the Greek coinage; *e.g.* the taxes of the Temple, Matt. xvii. 24. Joseph. B. J. vii. 6, 6. The offerings were paid in these, Mark xii. 42; Luke xxi. 2. A payment which proceeded from the Temple treasury, was made according to the ancient national payment by weight, Matt. xxvi. 15. [This is very doubtful.] But in common business, trade, wages, sale, &c., the assis and denarius and Roman coin were usual, Matt. x. 29; Luke xii. 6; Matt. xx 2; Mark xiv. 5; John xii. 5, vi. 7. The more modern state taxes are likewise paid in the coin of the nation which exercises at the time

distant provinces were obliged to change their foreign money, the relative value of which was probably liable to considerable fluctuation. It is evident from the strong language of Jesus, that not only a fair and honest, but even a questionable and extortionate traffic was conducted within the holy precincts. Nor is it impossible, that even in the Temple courts trade might be carried on less connected with the religious character of the place. Throughout the East, the periodical assemblages of the different tribes of the same descent at some central temple is intimately connected with commercial views.* The neighbourhood of the Holy Place is the great fair or exchange of the tribe or nation. Even to the present day, Mecca, at the time of the great concourse of worshippers at the tomb of the Prophet, is a mart for the most active traffic among the merchant pilgrims, who form the caravans from all quarters of the Mahometan world.†

We may conceive how the deep and awful stillness, which ought to have prevailed within the inner courts, dedicated to the adoration of the people—how the quiet prayer of the solitary worshipper, and the breathless silence of the multitude, while the priests were performing the more important ceremonies, either offering the national sacrifice, or entering the Holy Place, must have been interrupted by the close neighbourhood of this disorderly market. How dissonant must have been the noises of the bleating sheep, the lowing cattle, the clamours and disputes, and all the tumult and confusion thus crowded into a space of no great extent. No doubt

---

the greatest authority, Matt. xxi. 19; Mark xi. 15; Luke xix. 24." Vol. i. page 14. After all, however, some of these words may be translations.

* Heeren, Ideen, passim.
† Burckhardt, Travels in Arabia.

the feelings of the more devout must long before have been shocked by this desecration of the holy precincts; and when Jesus commanded the expulsion of all these traders out of the court of the Temple, from the almost unresisting submission with which they abandoned their lucrative posts, at the command of one invested with no public authority, and who could have appeared to them no more than a simple Galilean peasant, it is clear that this assertion of the sanctity of the Temple must have been a popular act with the majority of the worshippers.[h] Though Jesus is said personally to have exerted himself, assisting with a light scourge probably in driving out the cattle, it is not likely that if he had stood alone, either the calm and commanding dignity of his manner, or even his appeal to the authority of the Sacred Writings, which forbade the profanation of the Temple as a place of merchandise, would have overpowered the sullen obstinacy of men engaged in a gainful traffic, sanctioned by ancient usage. The same profound veneration for the Temple, which took such implacable offence at the subsequent language of Jesus, would look with unallayed admiration on the zeal for "the Father's House." That House would not brook the intrusion of worldly pursuits or profane noises within its hallowed gates.

Of itself, then, this act of Jesus might not amount to the assumption of authority over the Temple of God:

---

[h] I think these considerations make it less improbable that this event should have taken place on two separate occasions, and under similar circumstances. The account of St. John places the incident at this period of our Lord's life; the other Evangelists during his last visit to Jerusalem. For my own part, I follow St. John without hesitation: even if it were an error in chronological arrangement in one or other of the Evangelists, my faith in the historical reality of the event would not be in the least shaken.

it was, perhaps, no more than a courageous zealot for the Law might have done;[1] but, combined with the former mysterious rumours about his character and his miraculous powers, it invested him at once with the awful character of one, in whose person *might* appear the long-desired, the long-expected Messiah. The multitude eagerly throng around him, and demand some supernatural sign of his divine mission. The establishment of the Law had been accompanied, according to the universal belief, with the most terrific demonstrations of Almighty power—the rocking of the earth, the blazing of the mountain. Would the restoration of the Theocracy in more ample power, and more enduring majesty, be unattended with the same appalling wonders? The splendid images in the highly figurative writings of the Prophets, the traditions, among the mass of the people equally authoritative, had prepared them to expect the coming of the Messiah to be announced by the obedient elements. It would have been difficult, by the most signal convulsions of nature, to have come up to their high-wrought expectations. Private acts of benevolence to individuals, preternatural cures of diseases, or the restoration of disordered faculties, fell far beneath the notions of men, blind, in most cases, to the moral beauty of such actions. They required public, if we may so speak, national miracles, and those of the most stupendous nature. To their demand, Jesus calmly answered by an obscure and somewhat oracular allusion to the remote event of his own resurrection, the one great "sign" of Christianity, to which it is remarkable

Expectations raised by this event.

---

[1] Legally only the magistrate (i. e. the Sanhedrin), or a Prophet, could rectify abuses in the Temple of God. A Prophet must show his commission by some miracle or prediction. Grotius and Whitby.

that the Saviour constantly refers, when required to ratify his mission by some public miracle.[b] The gesture, by which he probably confined his meaning to the temple of his body, which, though destroyed, was to be raised up again in three days, was seen, indeed, by his disciples, yet even by them but imperfectly understood; by the people in general his language seemed plainly to imply the possible destruction of the Temple. An appalling thought, and feebly counterbalanced by the assertion of his power to rebuild it in three days!

This misapprehended speech struck on the most sensitive chord in the high-strung religious temperament of the Jewish people. Their national pride, their national existence, were identified with the inviolability of the Temple. Their passionate and zealous fanaticism on this point can scarcely be understood unless after the profound study of their history. In older times, the sad and loathsome death of Antiochus Epiphanes, in more recent, the fate of Crassus, perishing amid the thirsty sands of the desert, and of Pompey, with his headless trunk exposed to the outrages of the basest of mankind on the strand of Egypt, had been construed into manifest visitations of the Almighty, in revenge for the plunder and profanation of his Temple. Their later history is full of the same spirit; and even in the horrible scenes of the fatal siege by Titus, this indelible passion survived all feelings of nature or of humanity. The fall of the Temple was like the bursting of the heart of the nation.

From the period at which Herod the Great had begun to restore the dilapidated work of Zorobabel, forty-six years had elapsed, and still the magnificence of the

---

[b] Compare Matt. xii. 40.

king, or the wealth and devotion of the principal among the people, had found some new work on which to expend those incalculable riches, which, from these sources, the tribute of the whole nation, and the donations of the pious, continued to pour into the Temple treasury. And this was the building of which Jesus, as he was understood, could calmly contemplate the fall, and daringly promise the immediate restoration. To their indignant murmurs, Jesus, it may seem, made no reply. The explanation would, perhaps, have necessarily led to a more distinct prediction of his own death and resurrection than it was yet expedient to make, especially on so public a scene. But how deeply this mistaken speech sunk into the popular mind, may be estimated from its being adduced as the most serious charge against Jesus at his trial; and the bitterest scorn, with which he was followed to his crucifixion, exhausted itself in a fierce and sarcastic allusion to this supposed assertion of power. Their expectations disappointed.

Still, although with the exasperated multitude the growing veneration for Jesus might be checked by this misapprehended speech, a more profound impression had been made among some of the more thinking part of the community. Already one, if not more members, of the Sanhedrin, began to look upon him with interest, perhaps with a secret inclination to espouse his doctrines. That one, named Nicodemus, determined to satisfy himself by a personal interview, as to the character and pretensions of the new Teacher.[m] Nicodemus had hitherto been connected with the Pharisaic party, and he dreaded the jealousy of that powerful sect, who, though not yet in declared Nicodemus.

---

[m] John iii. 1, 21.

VOL. I.

hostility against Jesus, watched, no doubt, his motions with secret aversion; for they could not but perceive that he made no advances towards them, and treated with open disregard their minute and austere observance of the literal and traditionary law, their principles of separation from the "unclean" part of the community, and their distinctive dress and deportment. The popular and accessible demeanour of Jesus showed at once that he had nothing in common with the spirit of this predominant religious faction. Nicodemus, therefore, chooses the dead of the night to obtain his secret interview with Jesus; he salutes him with a title, that of Rabbi, assumed by none but those who were at once qualified and authorised to teach in public; and he recognises at once his divine mission, as avouched by his wonderful works. But, with astonishment almost overpowering, the Jewish ruler hears the explanation of the first principles of the new religion. When the heathen proselyte was admitted into Judaism, he was considered to be endowed with new life: he was separated from all his former connexions; he was born again to higher hopes, to more extended knowledge, to a more splendid destiny.[a] But now, even the Jew of the most unimpeachable descent from Abraham, the Jew of the highest estimation so as to have been chosen into the court of Sanhedrin, and one who had maintained the strictest obedience to the law, required, in order to become a member of the new community, a change no less complete. He was to pass through the

---

[a] A Gentile proselyted, and a slave set free, is as a child new born; he must know no more of his kindred. Maimonides. Lightfoot, Harm. Ev. This notion of a second moral birth is by no means uncommon in the East. The Sanscrit name of a Brahmin is dwija, the twice born. Bopp. Gloss. Sanscr.

ceremony emblematic of moral and spiritual purification. To him, as to the most unclean of strangers, baptism was to be the mark of his initiation into the new faith; and a secret internal transmutation was to take place by divine agency in his heart, which was to communicate a new principle of religious life. Without this, he could not attain to that which he had hitherto supposed either the certain privilege of his Israelitish descent, or at least of his conscientious adherence to the Law. Eternal life, Jesus declared, was to depend solely on the reception of the Son of God, who, he not obscurely intimated, had descended from heaven, was present in his person, and was not universally received, only from the want of moral fitness to appreciate his character. This light was too pure to be admitted into the thick darkness which was brooding over the public mind, and rendered it impenetrable by the soft and quiet rays of the new doctrine. Jesus, in short, almost without disguise or reservation, announced himself to the wondering ruler as the Messiah, while, at the same time, He enigmatically foretold his rejection by the people. The age was not ripe for the exhibition of the Divine Goodness in his person; it still yearned for a revelation of the terrible, destructive, revengeful *Power* of the Almighty—a national deity which should embody, as it were, the prevailing sentiments of the nation. Nor came He to fulfil that impious expectation of Jewish pride—the condemnation of the world, of all Gentile races, to the worst calamities, while on Israel alone his blessings were to be showered with exclusive bounty.*

---

* Quæ sequuntur inde a versiculo decimo septimo propria ad Judæos spectant, et haud dubie dicta sunt a Domino contra opinionem illam impiam et in genus humanum iniquam, cum existimarent Messiam non nisi

He came as a common benefactor—as an universal Saviour—to the whole human race. Nicodemus, it may seem, left the presence of Jesus, if not a decided convert, yet impressed with still deeper reverence. Though never an avowed disciple, yet, with other members of the Sanhedrin, he was only restrained by his dread of the predominant party: more than once we find him seizing opportunities of showing his respect and attachment for the teacher, whose cause he had not courage openly to espouse; and, perhaps, his secret influence, with that of others similarly disposed, may, for a time, have mitigated or obstructed the more violent designs of the hostile Pharisees.

Thus ended the first visit of Jesus to Jerusalem since his assumption of a public character. His influence had, in one class probably, made considerable, though secret, progress; with others, a dark feeling of hostility had been more deeply rooted; while this very difference of sentiment was likely to increase the general suspense and interest, as to the future development of his character. As yet, it appears, unless in that most private interview with Nicodemus, he had not openly avowed his claim to the title of the Messiah: an expression of St. John,^p "he did not trust himself to them," seems to imply the extreme caution and reserve which He maintained towards all the converts which He made during his present visit to Jerusalem.

Judaicum populum liberaturum, reliquas vero gentes omnes suppliciis atrocissimis affecturum, penitusque perditurum esse. Titman. Mel. in Joan. p. 128.

^p John ii. 24, οὐκ ἐπίστευεν ἑαυτόν: he did not trust himself to them, he did not commit himself.

CHAPTER IV.

Public Life of Jesus from the First to the Second Passover.

ON the dispersion of the strangers from the metropolis, at the close of the Passover, Jesus, with his more immediate followers, passed a short time in Judæa, where such multitudes crowded to the baptism administered by his disciples, that the adherents of John began to find the concourse to their master somewhat diminished. The Baptist had removed his station to the other side of the Jordan, and fixed himself by a stream, which afforded a plentiful supply of water, near the town of Salim, in Peræa. The partisans of John, not it might seem without jealousy, began to dispute concerning the relative importance of the baptism of their master, and that of him whom they were disposed to consider his rival. But these unworthy feelings were strongly repressed by John. In terms still more emphatic he reasserted his own secondary station: he was but the paranymph, the humble attendant on the bridegroom, Christ the bridegroom himself: his doctrine was that of earth, that of Christ was from heaven; in short, he openly announces Jesus as the Son of the Almighty Father, and as the author of everlasting life.[a]

The career of John was drawing to a close. His now station in Peræa was within the dominions of Herod Antipas. On the division of the

---
[a] John iii. 22, 36.

Jewish kingdom at the death of Herod the Great, Galilee and Perea had formed the tetrarchate of Antipas. This Herod was engaged in a dangerous war with Aretas, king of Arabia Petræa, whose daughter he had married. But having formed an incestuous connexion with the wife of his brother, Herod Philip, his Arabian queen indignantly fled to her father, who took up arms to revenge her wrongs against her guilty husband.[b] How far Herod could depend in this contest on the loyalty of his subjects, was extremely doubtful. It is possible he might entertain hopes that the repudiation of a foreign alliance, ever hateful to the Jews, and the union with a branch of the Asmonean line (for Herodias was the grand-daughter of Herod the Great and of Mariamne), might counterbalance in the popular estimation the injustice and criminality of his marriage with his brother's wife.[c] The influence of John (according to Josephus) was almost unlimited. The subjects, and even the soldiery, of the tetrarch had crowded with devout submission around the Prophet. On his decision might depend the wavering loyalty of the whole province. But John denounced with open indignation the royal incest, and declared the marriage with a brother's wife to be a flagrant violation of the Law. Herod, before long, ordered him to be seized and imprisoned in the strong fortress of Machærus, on the remote border of his Transjordanic territory.

Jesus, in the mean time, apprehensive of the awaken-

---

[b] Luke iii. 19; Matt. xiv. 3, 5; Mark vi. 17, 20.

[c] This natural view of the subject appears to me to harmonise the accounts in the Gospels with that of Josephus. Josephus traces the persecution of the Baptist to Herod's dread of popular tumult and insurrection, without mentioning the real cause of that dread, which we find in the Evangelic narrative.

ing jealousy of the Pharisees, whom his increasing success inflamed to more avowed animosity, left the borders of Judæa, and proceeded on his return to Galilee.[d] The nearer road lay through the province of Samaria.[e] The mutual hatred between the Jews and Samaritans, ever since the secession of Sanballat, had kept the two races not merely distinct, but opposed to each other with the most fanatical hostility. *Jesus passes through Samaria. Hostility of Jews and Samaritans.* This animosity, instead of being allayed by time, had but grown the more inveterate, and had recently been embittered by acts, according to Josephus, of wanton and unprovoked outrage on the part of the Samaritans. During the administration of Coponius, certain of this hateful race, early in the morning on one of the days of the Passover, had stolen into the Temple at Jerusalem, and defiled the porticoes and courts by strewing them with dead men's bones—an abomination the most offensive to the Jewish principles of cleanliness and sanctity.[f] Still later, they had frequently taken advantage of the position in which their district lay, directly between Judæa and Galilee, to interrupt the concourse of the religious Galileans to the capital.[g] Jealous that such multitudes should pass their sacred mountain, Gerizim, to worship in the Temple at Jerusalem, they often waylaid the incautious pilgrim, and thus the nearest road to Jerusalem had become extremely insecure. Our History will show how calmly Jesus ever pursued his course through these conflicting elements of society, gently endeavoured to allay the implacable schism, and set the example of that mild

---

[d] Matt. iv. 12; Mark i. 14; Luke iv. 14.
[e] John iv. 1. 32.
[f] Hist. of the Jews, ii. 118.
[g] Ibid., 123.

and tolerant spirit, so beautifully embodied in his precepts. He passed on in quiet security through the dangerous district; and it is remarkable that here, safe from the suspicious vigilance of the Pharisaic party, among these proscribed aliens from the hopes of Israel, He more distinctly and publicly than He had hitherto done, avowed his title as the Messiah, and developed that leading characteristic of his religion, the abolition of all local and national deities, and the promulgation of one comprehensive faith, in which the great Eternal Spirit was to be worshipped by all mankind in "spirit and in truth."

There was a well[h] near the gates of Sichem, a name which by the Jews had been long perverted into the opprobrious term Sichar.[i] This spot, according to immemorial tradition, the Patriarch Jacob had purchased, and here were laid the bones of Joseph, his elder son, carried from Egypt, to whose descendant, Ephraim, this district had been assigned. Sichem lay in a valley between the two famous mountains Ebal and Gerizim, on which the Law was read, and ratified by the acclamations of the assembled tribes; and on the latter height stood the rival temple of the Samaritans, which had so long afflicted the more zealous Jews by its daring opposition to the one chosen sanctuary on Mount Moriah. The well bore the name of the Patriarch; and while his disciples entered the town to purchase

---

[h] Tradition still points to this well, about a mile distant from the walls of Sichar, which Maundrell supposes to have extended farther. A church was built over it by the Empress Helena, but it is now entirely destroyed. "It is dug in a firm rock, and contains about three yards in diameter, and thirty-five in depth, five of which we found full of water." Maundrell, p. 82.

[i] From a Hebrew word meaning a "lie" or an "idol." The name had no doubt grown into common use, as it could not be meant by the Evangelists in an offensive sense.

provisions,[a] a traffic from which probably few, except the disciples of Christ, would not have abstained,[m] except in extreme necessity, Jesus reposed by its margin. It was the sultry hour of noon, about twelve o'clock,[o] when a woman, as is the general usage in the East, where the females commonly resort to the wells or tanks to obtain water for all domestic uses, approached the well. Jesus, whom she knew not to be her countryman, either from his dress, or perhaps his dialect or pronunciation, in which the inhabitants of the Ephraimitish district of Samaria differed both from the Jews and Galileans, to her astonishment, asked her for water to quench his thirst. For in general the lip of a Jew, especially a Pharisaic Jew, would have shrunk in disgust from the purest element in a vessel defiled by the hand of a Samaritan. Drawing, as usual, his similitudes from the present circumstances, Jesus excites the wonder of the woman by speaking of living waters at his command, waters which were to nourish the soul for everlasting life: he increases her awe by allusions which show more than mortal knowledge of her own private history (she was living in concubinage, having been married to five husbands), and at length clearly

---

[a] According to the traditions they might buy of them, use their labour, or say Amen to their benedictions (Beracoth, l. 8), lodge in their towns, but not receive any gift or kindness from them. Buxtorf, Lex Talm. 1370. Lightfoot in loc.

[m] Probably the more rigid would have refrained, even from this permitted intercourse, unless in cases of absolute necessity.

[o] This is the usual opinion. Dr. Townson, in his ingenious argument to prove that the hours of John are not Roman or Jewish but Asiatic, adduces this passage, as in his favour, the evening being the usual time at which the women resort to the wells. On the other hand it is observed that noon was the usual time of dinner among the Jews, and the disciples probably entered the town for provisions for that meal.

announces that the local worship, both on Gerizim and at Jerusalem, was to give place to a more sublime and comprehensive faith. The astonished woman confesses her belief that, on the coming of the Messiah, truths equally wonderful may be announced. Jesus, for the first time, distinctly and unequivocally declares himself to be the Messiah.° On the return of the disciples from the town, their Jewish prejudices are immediately betrayed at beholding their master thus familiarly conversing with a woman of the hateful race: on the other hand, the intelligence of the woman runs rapidly through the town, and the Samaritans crowd forth in eager interest to behold and listen to the extraordinary teacher.

The nature and origin of the Samaritan belief in the Messiah is even a more obscure question than that of the Jews.ᵖ That belief was evidently more clear and defined than the vague expectation

---

° Le Clerc observes that Jesus spoke with more freedom to the woman of Samaria, as he had no fear of sedition, or violent attempts to make him a king. On John iv. 26.

ᵖ Bertholdt, ch. vii., which contains extracts from the celebrated Samaritan letters, and references to the modern writers who have translated them, and discussed their purport. Quæ vero fuerit spei Messianæ ratio neque ex hoc loco, neque ex ullo alio antiquiore monumento accuratius intelligi potest, et ex recentiorum demum Samaritanorum epistolis innotuit. Atque his testibus prophetam quemdam illustrem venturum esse sperant, cui observaturi sint populi ac creditori in illum, et in legem et in montem Garizim, qui fidem Mosaicam erecturus sit, tabernaculum restituturus in monte Garizim, populum suum breviturus, postea moriturus et sepeliendus apud Josephum (i. e. in tribu Ephraim). Quo tempore venturus sit, id semini præter Deum cognitum esse. Gesenius in his note to the curious Samaritan poems which he has published (p. 75), proceeds to say that his name is to be Hasch-hab or Hat-hab, which he translates conversor (converter), as converting the people to a higher state of religion. The Messiah ben Joseph of the Rabbies, Gesenius observes, is of a much later date. Quotations concerning the latter may be found in Eisenmenger, ii. 720.

which prevailed throughout the East; still it was probably, like that of the Jews, by no means distinct or definite. It is generally supposed that the Samaritans, admitting only the Law, must have rested their hope solely on some ambiguous or latent prediction in the books of Moses, who had foretold the coming of another and a mightier prophet than himself. But though the Samaritans may not have admitted the authority of the prophets as equal to that of the Law—though they had not installed them in the regular and canonised code of their sacred books, it does not follow that they were unacquainted with them, or that they did not listen with devout belief to the more general promises, which by no means limited the benefits of the Messiah's coming to the local sanctuary of Jerusalem, or to the line of the Jewish kings. There appear some faint traces of a belief in the descent of the Messiah from the line of Joseph, of which, as belonging to the tribe of Ephraim, the Samaritans seem to have considered themselves the representatives.[e] Nor is it improbable, from the subsequent rapid progress of the doctrines of Simon Magus, which were deeply impregnated with Orientalism,[f] that the Samaritan notion of the Messiah had already a strong Magian or Babylonian tendency. On the other hand, if their expectations rested on less

---

[e] We still want a complete and critical edition of the Samaritan chronicle (the Liber Josuæ), which may throw light on the character and tenets of this remarkable branch of the Jewish nation. Though in its present form a comparatively modern compilation, it appears to me, from the fragments hitherto edited, to contain manifest vestiges of very ancient tradition. See an abstract at the end of Hottinger's Dissertationes anti Morinianæ. This defect has now been supplied by a complete critical edition by Joynboll. I do not find, however, the value of the work to the historian much increased by the publication of the whole. (1863.)

[f] Mosheim, ii. 19.

definite grounds, the Samaritans were unenslaved by many of those fatal prejudices of the Jews, which so completely secularised their notions of the Messiah, and were free from that rigid and exclusive pride which so jealously appropriated the divine promises. If the Samaritans could not pretend to an equal share in the splendid anticipations of the ancient prophets, they were safer from their misinterpretation. They had no visions of universal dominion; they looked not to Samaria or Sichem to become the metropolis of some mighty empire. They had some legend of the return of Moses to discover the sacred vessels concealed near Mount Gerizim,* but they did not expect to see the banner raised, and the conqueror go forth to beat the nations to the earth and prostrate mankind before their re-established theocracy. They might even be more inclined to recognise the Messiah in the person of a purely religious reformer, on account of the overbearing confidence with which the rival people announced their hour of triumph, when the Great King should erect his throne on Sion, and punish all the enemies of the chosen race, among whom the " foolish people," as they were called, " who dwelt at Sichem,"† would not be the last to incur the terrible vengeance. A Messiah who would disappoint the insulting hopes of the Jews would, for that very reason, be more acceptable to the Samaritans.

The Samaritan commonwealth was governed, under the Roman supremacy, by a council or sanhedrin. But

---

* Hist. of the Jews, II. 123.
† There be two manner of nations which my heart abhorreth, and the third is no nation. They that sit upon the mountain of Samaria, and they that dwell among the Philistines, and that foolish people that dwell at Sichem. Ecclesiast. l. 25, 26.

this body had not assumed the pretensions of a divinely inspired hierarchy; nor had they a jealous and domineering sect, like that of the Pharisees, in possession of the public instruction, and watching every new teacher who did not wear the garb, or speak the Shibboleth of their faction, as guilty of an invasion of their peculiar province. But, from whatever cause, the reception of Jesus among the Samaritans, was strongly contrasted with that among the Jews. They listened with reverence, and entreated him to take up his permanent abode within their province; and many among them distinctly acknowledged him as the Messiah and Saviour of the world.

[margin: Samaritan Sanhedrin.]

Still a residence, longer than was necessary in the infected air, as the Jews would suppose it, of Samaria, would have strengthened the growing hostility of the ruling powers, and of the prevailing sect among the Jews. After two days, therefore, Jesus proceeded on his journey, re-entered Galilee, and publicly assumed, in that province, his office as the teacher of a new religion. The report of a second, a more public, and more extraordinary miracle than that before performed in the town of Cana, tended to establish the fame of his actions in Jerusalem, which had been disseminated by those Galileans who had returned more quickly from the Passover, and had excited a general interest to behold the person of whom such wonderful rumours were spread abroad.ª The nature of the miracle, the healing a youth who lay sick at Capernaum, about twenty-five miles distant from Cana, where he then was; the station of the father, at whose entreaty he restored the son to health (he was probably on the

[margin: Second miracle in Galilee.]

ª Matt. iv. 13, 17; Mark i. 14, 15; Luke iv. 14, 15; John iv. 43–45.

household establishment of Herod), could not fail to raise the expectation to a higher pitch, and to prepare the inhabitants of Galilee to listen with eager deference to the new doctrines.[x]

One place alone received the Son of Mary with cold and inhospitable unconcern, and rejected his claims with indignant violence — his native town of Nazareth. The history of this transaction is singularly true to human nature.[y] Where Jesus was unknown, the awe-struck imagination of the people, excited by the fame of his wonderful works, beheld him already arrayed in the sanctity of a prophetical, if not of a divine, mission. Nothing intruded on their thoughts to disturb their reverence for the commanding gentleness of his demeanour, the authoritative persuasiveness of his language, the holiness of his conduct, the celebrity of his miracles: He appeared before them in the pure and unmingled dignity of his public character. But the inhabitants of Nazareth had to struggle with old impressions, and to exalt their former familiarity into a feeling of deference or veneration. In Nazareth he had been seen from his childhood; and though gentle, blameless, popular, nothing had occurred, up to the period of his manhood, to place him so much above the ordinary level of mankind. His father's humble station and employment had, if we may so speak, still farther undignified the person of Jesus to the mind of his fellow-townsmen. In Nazareth Jesus was still "the carpenter's son." We think, likewise, that we discover in the language of the Nazarenes

---

[x] John iv. 46-54.
[y] Luke iv. 16-30. There appears to be an allusion (John iv. 44) to this incident, which may have taken place before the second miracle.

something of local jealousy against the more favoured town of Capernaum. If Jesus intended to assume a public and distinguished character, why had not his dwelling place the fame of his splendid works? Why was Capernaum honoured, as the residence of the new prophet, rather than the city in which he had dwelt from his youth?

It was in the synagogue of Nazareth, where Jesus had hitherto been a humble and devout listener, that he stood up in the character of a Teacher. *Jesus in the synagogue.* According to the usage, the chazan or minister of the synagogue,[a] whose office it was to deliver the volume of the Law or the Prophets appointed to be read to the person to whom that function had fallen, or who might have received permission from the rulers of the synagogue to address the congregation, gave it into the hands of Jesus. Jesus opened on the passage in the beginning of the 16th chapter of Isaiah,[b] by universal consent applied to the coming of the Messiah, and under its beautiful images describing with the most perfect truth the character of the new religion. It spoke of good tidings to the poor, of consolation in every sorrow, of deliverance from every affliction :—" He hath anointed

---

[a] It is said that on the Sabbath the Law was read in succession by seven persons—a priest, a Levite, and five Israelites—and never on any other day by less than three. The Prophets were read by any one; in general by one of the former readers, whom the minister might summon to the office.

[b] It is of some importance to the chronology of the life of Christ, to ascertain whether this pericope or portion was that appointed in the ordinary course of reading, or one selected by Jesus. But we cannot decide this with any certainty; nor is it clear that the distribution of the lessons, according to the ritual of that period, was the same with the present liturgy of the Jews. According to that, the 16th chapter of Isaiah would have been read about the end of August. Macknight and some other harmonists lay much stress on this point.

me to preach the Gospel to the poor; he hath sent me to heal the broken hearted; to preach deliverance to the captives, and recovering of sight to the blind; to set at liberty them that are bound." It went on, as it were, to announce the instant fulfilment of the prediction, in the commencement of the "acceptable year of the Lord;" but before it came to the next clause, which harmonised ill with the benign character of the new faith, and spoke of "the day of vengeance," He broke off and closed the book. He proceeded, probably at some length, to declare the immediate approach of these times of wisdom and peace.

The whole assembly was in a state of pleasing astonishment at the ease of his delivery, and the sweet copiousness of his language; they could scarcely believe that it was the youth whom they had so often seen, the son of a humble father, in their streets, and who had enjoyed no advantages of learned education. Some of them, probably either by their countenance, or tone, or gesture, expressed their incredulity, or even their contempt, for Joseph's son; for Jesus at once declared his intention of performing no miracle to satisfy the doubts of his unbelieving countrymen:—"No prophet is received with honour in his own country." This avowed preference of other places before the dwelling of his youth; this refusal to grant to Nazareth any share in the fame of his extraordinary works, embittered perhaps by the suspicion that the general prejudice against their town might be strengthened, at least not discountenanced, as it might have been, by the residence of so distinguished a citizen within their walls—the reproof so obviously concealed in the words and conduct of Jesus, mingled no doubt with other fanatical motives, wrought the whole assembly to such a pitch of frenzy, that they expelled Jesus from the synagogue. Nazareth lies in a valley, from which a hill immediately rises; they hurried him up the slope, and were preparing to cast him down from the abrupt cliff on the other side, when they found that the intended victim of their wrath had disappeared.[b]

Jesus retired to Capernaum, which from this time became, as it were, his head-quarters.[c] This place was admirably situated for his purpose, both from the facility of communication, as well by land as by the lake, with many considerable and flourishing towns, and of escape into a more secure region, in case of any threatened persecution. It lay towards the northern extremity of the lake or sea of Gennesaret.[d] On the land side it was a centre from which the circuit of both Upper and Lower Galilee might begin. The countless barks of the fishermen employed upon the lake, many of whom became his earliest adherents, could transport him with the utmost ease to any of the cities on the western bank; while, if danger approached from Herod or the ruling powers of Galilee, he had but to cross to the opposite shore, the territory, at least at the commencement of his career, of Philip, the most just and popular of the sons of Herod, and which on his death reverted to the Roman government. Nor was it an unfavourable circumstance, that he had most likely secured the powerful protection of the officer attached to the court of Herod, whose son he had healed, and who probably resided at Capernaum.

Capernaum the chief residence of Jesus.

---

[b] But see Stanley, p. 159. The abrupt cliff is *above* the town.

[c] Luke iv. 31, 32.

[d] This is the usual position of Capernaum, but it rests on very uncertain grounds, and some circumstances would induce me to adopt Lightfoot's opinion, that it was much nearer to the southern end of the lake. Compare Robinson, iii. 284; Stanley, 370.

The first act of the Saviour's public career was the permanent attachment to his person, and the investing in the delegated authority of teachers of the new religion, four out of the twelve who afterwards became the Apostles. Andrew and Peter were, as before stated, originally of Bethsaida, at the north-eastern extremity of the lake, but the residence of Peter appears to have been at Capernaum. James and John were brothers, the sons of Zebedee.* All these men had united themselves to Jesus, immediately after his baptism; the latter, if not all the four, had probably attended upon him during the festival in Jerusalem, but had returned to their usual avocations. Jesus saw them on the shore of the lake,—two of them were actually employed in fishing, the others at a little distance were mending their nets. At the well-known voice of their master, confirmed by the sign of the miraculous draught of fishes,† which impressed Peter with so much awe, that he thought himself unworthy of standing in the presence of so wonderful a Being, they left their ships and followed Him into the town; and though they appear to have resumed their humble occupations, on which, no doubt, their livelihood depended, it would seem that from this time they might be considered as the regular attendants of Jesus.

The reception of Jesus in the synagogue of Capernaum was very different from that which he encountered in Nazareth. He was heard on the regular day of teaching, the Sabbath, not only undisturbed, but with increasing reverence and awe.‡ And,

---

* Matt. iv. 22; Mark i. 17-20; Luke v. 1-11.
† This supposes, as is most probable, that Luke v. 1-11 refers to the same transaction.
‡ Luke iv. 31-38; Mark i. 21, 22.

indeed, if the inhabitants of Nazareth were offended, and the Galileans in general astonished at the appearance of the humble Jesus in the character of a public teacher, the tone and language which he assumed was not likely to allay their wonder. The remarkable expression, "He speaks as one having authority, and not as the scribes," seems to imply more than the extraordinary power and persuasiveness of his language.

The ordinary instructors of the people, whether under the name of scribes, lawyers, or Rabbis, rested their whole claim to the public attention on the established Sacred Writings. They were the conservators, and perhaps personally *ordained* interpreters of the Law, with its equally sacred traditionary comment; but they pretended to no authority, not originally derived from these sources. They did not stand forward as legislators, but as accredited expositors of the Law; not as men directly inspired from on high, but as men who, by profound study and intercourse with the older wise men, were best enabled to decide on the dark, or latent, or ambiguous sense of the inspired writings; or who had received, in regular descent, the more ancient Cabala, the accredited tradition. Although, therefore, they had completely enslaved the public mind, which reverenced the sayings of the masters or Rabbis equally with the original text of Moses and the Prophets; though it is quite clear that the spiritual Rabbinical dominion, which at a later period established so arbitrary a despotism over the understanding of the people, was already deeply rooted, still the basis of their supremacy rested on the popular reverence for the Sacred Writings. "It is written," was the sanction of all the Rabbinical decrees, however those decrees might misinterpret the real meaning of the Law, or "add burdens to the neck of the people," by no means intended by the wise and humane lawgiver.

Jesus came forth as a public teacher in a new and opposite character. His authority rested on no previous revelation, excepting as far as his divine commission had been foreshown in the Law and the Prophets. He prefaced his addresses with the unusual formulary, "I say unto you." Perpetually displaying the most intimate familiarity with the Sacred Writings, instantly silencing or baffling his adversaries by adducing, with the utmost readiness and address, texts of the Law and the Prophets according to the accredited interpretation, yet his ordinary language evidently assumed a higher tone. He was the direct, immediate representative of the wisdom of the Almighty Father; he appeared as equal, as superior, to Moses; as the author of a new revelation, which, although it was not to destroy the Law, was in a certain sense to supersede it, by the introduction of a new and original faith. Hence the implacable hostility manifested against Jesus, not merely by the fierce, the fanatical, the violent, or the licentious, by all who might take offence at the purity and gentleness of his precepts, but by the better and more educated among the people, the Scribes, the Lawyers, the Pharisees. Jesus at once assumed a superiority not merely over these teachers of the Law, this acknowledged religious aristocracy, whose reputation, whose interests, and whose pride were deeply pledged to the maintenance of the existing system, but he set himself above those inspired teachers, of whom the Rabbis were but the interpreters. Christ uttered commandments which had neither been registered on the tablets of stone, nor defined in the more minute enactments in the book of Leviticus. He superseded at once by his simple word all that they had painfully learned, and regularly taught as the eternal, irrepealable word of God, perfect, complete, enduring no addition. Hence their perpetual endeavours to commit Jesus with the multitude, as disparaging or infringing the ordinances of Moses; endeavours which were perpetually baffled on his part, by his cautious compliance with the more important observances, and, notwithstanding the general bearing of his teaching towards the development of a higher and independent doctrine,[h] his uniform respect for the letter as well as the spirit of the Mosaic institutes. But as the strength of the Rabbinical hierarchy lay in the passionate jealousy of the people about the Law, they never abandoned the hope of convicting Jesus on this ground, notwithstanding his extraordinary works, as a false pretender to the character of the Messiah. At all events, they saw clearly that it was a struggle for the life and death of their authority. Jesus acknowledged as the Christ, the whole fabric of their power and influence fell at once. The traditions, the Law itself, the skill of the Scribe, the subtilty of the Lawyer, the profound study of the Rabbi, or the teacher in the synagogue and in the school, became obsolete; and the pride of superior wisdom, the long-enjoyed deference, the blind obedience with which the people had listened to their decrees, were gone by for ever. The whole hierarchy were to cede at once their rank and estimation to an humble and uninstructed peasant from Galilee, a region scorned by the better educated for its rudeness and ignorance,[i]

<small>Causes of the hostility of the ordinary teachers.</small>

<small>[h] Compare the whole of the Sermon on the Mount, especially Matt. v. 20-45—the parables of the leaven and the grain of mustard-seed—the frequent intimations of the comprehensiveness of the "kingdom of God," as contrasted with the Jewish theocracy.

[i] See in the Compendium of the Talmud by Pinner of Berlin, intended</small>

and from Nazareth, the most despised town in the despised province. Against such deep and rooted motives for animosity, which combined and knit together every feeling of pride, passion, habit, and interest, the simple and engaging demeanour of the Teacher, the beauty of the precepts, their general harmony with the spirit however they might expand the letter of the Law, the charities they breathed, the holiness they inculcated, the aptitude and imaginative felicity of the parables under which they were couched, the hopes they excited, the fears they allayed, the blessings and consolations they promised, all which makes the discourses of Jesus so confessedly superior to all human morality, made little impression on this class, who in some respects, as the most intellectual, might be considered as in the highest state of advancement, and therefore most likely to understand the real spirit of the new religion. The authority of Jesus could not coexist with that of the Scribes and Pharisees; and this was the great principle of the fierce opposition and jealous hostility with which he was in general encountered by the best instructed teachers of the people.

In Capernaum, however, no resistance seems to have been made to his success: the synagogue was open to him on every Sabbath; and wonderful cures, that of a demoniac in the synagogue itself, that of Simon's wife's mother, and of many others within the same town, established and strengthened his growing influence.[k] From

as a kind of preface to an edition and translation of the whole Talmudical books, the curious passage (p. 60) from the Erubin, in which the Jews and Galileans are contrasted. The Galileans did not preserve the pure speech, therefore did not preserve pure doctrine—the Galileans had no teacher, therefore no doctrine—the Galileans did not open the book, therefore they had no doctrine.

[k] Mark i. 23-28; Luke iv. 33-37; Matt. viii. 14, 15; Mark i. 29-31; Luke iv. 28-39.

Capernaum He set forth to make a regular progress through the whole populous province of Galilee, which was crowded, if we are to receive the account of Josephus, with flourishing towns and cities, beyond almost any other region of the world.ᵃ According to the statement of this author, the number of towns, and the population of Galilee, in a district of between fifty and sixty miles in length, and between sixty and seventy in breadth, was no less than 204 cities and villages, the least of which contained 15,000 souls.ᵃ Reckoning nothing for smaller communities, and supposing each town and village to include the adjacent district, so as to allow of no scattered inhabitants in the country, the population of the province would amount to the incredible number of 3,060,000. Of these, probably, much the larger proportion were of Jewish descent, and spoke a harsher dialect of the Aramaic than that which prevailed in Judæa, though in many of the chief cities there was a considerable number of Syrian Greeks and of other foreign races.ᵇ Each of these towns had one or more synagogues, in which the people met for the ordinary purposes of worship, while the more religious attended regularly at the festivals in Jerusalem. The province of Galilee with Peræa formed the tetrarchate of Herod Antipas, who, till his incestuous marriage, had treated

---

ᵃ Matt. iv. 23-25; Mark I. 32-39; Luke iv. 40-44.

ᵃ Josephi Vita, ch. xlv. B. J. L. III. c. III. 2.

ᵇ According to Strabo, Galilee was full of Egyptians, Arabians, and Phœnicians, lib. xvi. Josephus states of Tiberias in particular, that it was inhabited by many strangers; Scythopolis was almost a Greek city. In Cæsarea, and many of the other towns, the most dreadful conflicts took place, at the commencement of the war, between the two races. Hist. of the Jews, II. 173-181.

the Baptist with respect, if not with deference, and does not appear at first to have interfered with the proceedings of Jesus. Though at one time decidedly hostile, he appears neither to have been very active in his opposition, nor to have entertained any deep or violent animosity against the person of Jesus even at the time of His final trial. No doubt Jerusalem and its adjacent province were the centre and stronghold of Jewish religious and political enthusiasm; the pulse beat stronger about the heart than at the extremities. Nor, whatever personal apprehensions Herod might have entertained of an aspirant to the name of the Messiah, whom he might suspect of temporal ambition, was he likely to be actuated by the same jealousy as the Jewish Sanhedrin, of a teacher who confined himself to religious instruction.[p] Herod's power rested on force, not on opinion; on the strength of his guards and the protection of Rome, not on the respect which belonged to the half-religious, half-political pre-eminence of the rulers in Jerusalem. That which made Jesus the more odious to the native government in Judæa, his disappointment of their hopes of a temporal Messiah, and his announcement of a revolution purely moral and religious, would allay the fears and secure the indifference of Herod. To him Christianity, however imperfectly understood, would appear less dangerous than fanatical Judaism. The Pharisees were in considerable numbers, and possessed much influence over the minds of the Galileans;[q] but it was in Judæa that this

---

[p] The supposition of Grotius, adopted by Mr. Greswell, that Herod was absent at Rome during the interval between the imprisonment and the death of John, and therefore during the first progress of Jesus, appears highly probable.

[q] Luke v. 17.

overwhelming faction completely predominated, and swayed the public opinion with irresistible power. Hence the unobstructed success of Jesus in this remoter region of the Holy Land, and the seeming wisdom of selecting that part of the country where, for a time at least, he might hope to pursue unmolested his career of blessing. During this first progress he appears to have passed from town to town uninterrupted, if not cordially welcomed. Either astonishment, or prudent caution, which dreaded to offend his numerous followers; or the better feeling which had not yet given place to the fiercer passions; or a vague hope that Jesus might yet assume all that they thought wanting to the character of the Messiah, not only attracted around him the population of the towns through which he passed, but as he approached the borders, the inhabitants of Decapolis (the district beyond the Jordan), of Judæa, and even of Jerusalem, and the remoter parts of Peræa, thronged to profit both by his teaching, and by the wonderful cures which were wrought on all who were afflicted by the prevalent diseases of the country.*

Jesus passes unmolested through Galilee.

How singular the contrast (familiarity with its circumstances, or deep and early reverence, prevents us from appreciating it justly) between the peaceful progress of the Son of Man, on the one hand healing maladies, relieving afflictions, restoring their senses to the dumb or blind; on the other gently instilling into the minds of the people those pure, and humane, and gentle principles of moral goodness, to which the wisdom of ages has been able to add nothing; and every other event to which it can be compared, in the history of human kind!

---

* Matt. iv. 25.

Compare the men who have at different periods wrought great and beneficial revolutions in the civil or the moral state of their kind; or those mythic personages, either deified men or humanised deities, which appear as the parents, or at some marked epoch in the history of different nations, embodying the highest notions of human nature or divine perfection to which the age or the people have attained—compare all these, in the most dispassionate spirit, with the impersonation of the divine goodness in Jesus Christ. It seems a conception, notwithstanding the progress in moral truth which had been made among the more intellectual of the Jews, and the nobler reasoners among the Greeks, so completely beyond the age, so opposite to the prevalent expectations of the times, as to add no little strength to the belief of the Christian in the divine origin of his faith. Was the sublime notion of the Universal Father, the God of Love, and the exhibition of as much of the divine nature as is intelligible to the limited faculties of man, his goodness and beneficent power, in the "Son of Man," first developed in the natural progress of the human mind among the peasants of Galilee?[*] Or, as the Christian asserts with more faith, and surely not less reason, did the great Spirit, which created and animates the countless worlds, condescend to show this image and reflection of his own inconceivable nature, for the benefit of one race of created beings, to restore them to, and prepare them for, a higher and eternal state of existence?

The synagogues, it has been said, appear to have been open to Jesus during the whole of his progress through Galilee; but it was not within the narrow walls of these

<small>Comparison with authors of other revolutions.</small>

---

[*] Compare the observations at the end of the first chapter.

buildings that he confined his instructions. It was in the open air, in the field, or in the vineyard, on the slope of the hill, or by the side of the lake, where the deck of one of his followers' vessels formed a kind of platform or tribune, that he delighted to address the wondering multitudes. His language teems with allusions to external nature, which, it has often been observed, seem to have been drawn from objects immediately around him. It would be superfluous to attempt to rival, and unjust to an author of remarkable good sense and felicity of expression, to alter the language in which this peculiarity of Christ's teaching has already been described:—" In the spring our Saviour went into the fields and sat down on a mountain, and made that discourse which is recorded in St. Matthew, and which is full of observations arising from the things which offered themselves to his sight. For when he exhorted his disciples to trust in God, he bade them behold the fowls of the air, which were then flying about them, and were fed by Divine Providence, though they did 'not sow nor reap, nor gather into barns.' He bade them take notice of the lilies of the field which were then blown, and were so beautifully clothed by the same power, and yet 'toiled not' like the husbandmen who were then at work. Being in a place where they had a wide prospect of a cultivated land, he bade them observe how God caused the sun to shine, and the rain to descend upon the fields and gardens, even of the wicked and ungrateful. And he continued to convey his doctrine to them under rural images, speaking of good *trees* and corrupt *trees*—of wolves in *sheep's clothing*—of grapes not growing upon thorns, nor figs on thistles—of the folly of casting precious things to dogs and swine—of good measure pressed down, and shaken together, and running over. Speaking at the same time to the people, many of whom were fishermen and lived much upon fish, he says, *What man of you will give his son a serpent, if he ask a fish?* Therefore when he said in the same discourse to his disciples, *Ye are the light of the world; a city that is set on a hill, and cannot be hid*, it is probable that he pointed to a city within their view, situated upon the brow of a hill. And when he called them *the salt of the earth*, he alluded, perhaps, to the husbandmen, who were manuring the ground: and when he compared every person who observed his precepts, to a man who built a house upon a rock, which stood firm; and every one who slighted his word, to a man who built a house upon the sand, which was thrown down by the winds and floods—when he used this comparison, 'tis not improbable that he had before his eyes houses standing upon high ground, and houses standing in the valley in a ruinous condition, which had been destroyed by inundations."[1]

<small>Sermon on the Mount.</small> It was on his return to Capernaum, either at the close of the present or of a later progress through Galilee, that among the multitudes who had gathered around him from all quarters, he ascended an eminence, and delivered in a long continuous address the memorable Sermon on the Mount.[2] It is not my

---

[1] Jortin's Discourses. The above is quoted and the idea is followed out at greater length and with equal beauty in Bishop Law's Reflections on the Life of Christ, at the end of his Theory of Religion.

[2] Scarcely any passage is more perplexing to the harmonist of the Gospels than the Sermon on the Mount, which appears to be inserted at two different places by St. Matthew and St. Luke. That the same striking truths should be delivered more than once in nearly the same language, or even that the same commanding situation should be more than once selected, from which to address the people, appears not altogether improbable; but

design to enter at length on the trite, though in my opinion by no means exhausted, subject of Christian morality. I content myself with indicating some of those characteristic points which belong, as it were, to the historical development of the new religion, and cannot be distinctly comprehended unless in relation to the circumstances of the times:—I. The morality of Jesus was not in unison with the temper or the feelings of his age. II. It was universal morality, adapted for the whole human race, and for every period of civilisation. III. It was morality grounded on broad and simple principles, which had hitherto never been laid down as the basis of human action.

<small>Principles of Christian morality.</small>

<small>1. Not in unison with the age.</small>

I. The great principle of the Mosaic theocracy was the strict apportionment of temporal happiness or calamity, at least to the nation, if not to the individual, according to his obedience or his rebellion against the divine laws. The natural consequence of this doctrine seemed to be, that prosperity was the invariable sign of the divine approval, adversity of disfavour. And this, in the time of our Lord, appears to have been carried to such an extreme, that every malady, every infirmity, was an evidence of sin in the individual, or a punishment inherited from his guilty forefathers. The only question which arose about the man born blind was, whether his affliction was the consequence of his own or his parents'

---

the difficulty lies in the accompanying incidents, which are almost the same, and could scarcely have happened twice. No writer who insists on the chronological order of the Evangelists has, in my judgment, removed the difficulty. On the whole, though I have inserted my view of Christian morality, as derived from this memorable discourse, in this place, I am inclined to consider the chronology of St. Luke more accurate. Matt. v. vi. vii.; Luke vi. 20, to the end.

criminality: he bore in his calamity the hateful evidence that he was accursed of God. This principle was perpetually struggling with the belief in a future state, and an equitable adjustment of the apparent inequalities in the present life, to which the Jewish mind had gradually expanded; and with the natural humanity, inculcated by the spirit of the Mosaic Law, towards their own brethren. But if the miseries of this life were an evidence of the divine anger, the blessings were likewise of his favour.[a] Hence the prosperous, the wealthy, those exempt from human suffering and calamity, were accustomed to draw even a more false and dangerous line of demarcation than in ordinary cases, between themselves and their humble and afflicted brethren. The natural haughtiness which belonged to such superiority, acquired, as it were, a divine sanction; nor was any vice in the Jewish character more strongly reproved by Jesus, or more hostile to his reception as the Messiah. For when the kingdom of Heaven should come—when the theocracy should be restored in more than its former splendour—who so secure in popular estimation of its inestimable blessings as those who were already marked and designated by the divine favour? Among the higher orders the expectation of a more than ordinary share in the promised blessings might practically be checked from imprudently betraying itself, by the natural timidity of those who have much to lose, and by their reluctance to hazard any political convulsion. Yet nothing could be more inexplicable, or more con-

---

[a] Compare Mosheim, ii. 12. He considers this feeling almost exclusively prevalent among the Sadducees; but from many passages of our Lord's discourses with the Pharisees, it would seem to have been almost universal. Pauperes et miseros existimare debebant Deum criminibus et peccatis offendisse, justamque ejus ultionem sentire.

trary to the universal sentiment, than that Jesus should disregard the concurrence of, and make no particular advances towards those who formed the spiritual as well as the temporal aristocracy of the nation—those whose possession of the highest station seemed, in a great degree, to prove their designation for such eminence by the Almighty. "Have any of the rulers believed in him?"[y] was the contemptuous, and, as they conceived, conclusive argument against his claims, adduced by the Pharisees. Jesus not only did not condescend to favour, he ran directly counter to this prevailing notion. He announced that the kingdom of Heaven was peculiarly prepared for the humble and the afflicted; his disciples were chosen from the lowest order; and it was not obscurely intimated that his ranks would be chiefly filled by those who were undistinguished by worldly prosperity. Yet, on the other hand, there was nothing in his language to conciliate the passions of the populace, no address to the envious and discontented spirit of the needy to inflame them against their superiors. Popular as he was, in the highest sense of the term, nothing could be further removed than the Prophet of Nazareth from the demagogue. The "kingdom of Heaven" was opened only to those who possessed and cultivated the virtues of their lowly station—meekness, humility, resignation, peacefulness, patience; and it was only because these virtues were most prevalent in the humbler classes, that the new faith was addressed to them. The more fierce and violent of the populace rushed into the ranks of the zealot, and enrolled themselves among the partisans of Judas the Galilean. They thronged around the robber chieftain, and secretly propagated that fiery spirit

---

[y] John vii. 48.

of insurrection which led, at length, to the fatal war. The meek and peaceful doctrines of Jesus found their way only into meek and peaceful hearts; the benevolent character of his miracles touched not those minds which had only imbibed the sterner, not the humaner, spirit of the Mosaic Law. Thus it was lowliness of character, rather than of station, which qualified the proselyte for the new faith—the absence, in short, of all those fierce passions which looked only to a conquering, wide-ruling Messiah: and it was in elevating these virtues to the highest rank, which to the many of all orders was treason against the hopes of Israel and the promises of God, that Jesus departed most widely from the general sentiment of his age and nation. He went still further; he annihilated the main principle of the theocracy—the administration of temporal rewards and punishments in proportion to obedience or rebellion—a notion which, though, as we have said, by no means justified by common experience, and weakened by the growing belief in another life, nevertheless still held its ground in the general opinion. Sorrow, as in one sense the distinguishing mark and portion of the new religion, became sacred; and the curse of God was, as it were, removed from the afflictions of mankind. His own disciples, He himself, were to undergo a fearful probation of suffering, which could only be secure of its reward in another life. The language of Jesus confirmed the truth of the anti-Sadducaic belief of the greater part of the nation, and assumed the certainty of another state of existence, concerning which, as yet, it spoke the current language; but which it was hereafter to expand into a more simple and universal creed, and mingle, if it may be so said, the sense of immortality with all the feelings and opinions of mankind.

II. Nor was it to the different classes of the Jews alone that the universal precepts of Christian morality expanded beyond the narrow and exclusive notions of the age and people. Jesus did not throw down the barrier which secluded the Jews from the rest of mankind, but he shook it to its base. Christian morality was not that of a sect, a race, or a nation, but of universal man: though necessarily delivered at times in Jewish language, couched under Jewish figures, and illustrated by local allusions, in its spirit it was diametrically opposite to Jewish. However it might make some provisions suited only to the peculiar state of the first disciples, yet in its essence it may be said to be comprehensive as the human race, immutable as the nature of man. It had no political, no local, no temporary precepts; it was, therefore, neither liable to be abrogated by any change in the condition of man, nor to fall into disuse, as belonging to a past and obsolete state of civilisation. It may dwell within its proper kingdom, the heart of man, in every change of political relation—in the monarchy, the oligarchy, the republic. It may domesticate itself in any climate, amid the burning sands of Africa, or the frozen regions of the North; for it has no local centre, no temple, no Caaba, no essential ceremonies impracticable under any conceivable state of human existence. In fact it is, strictly speaking, no Law; it is no system of positive enactments; it is the establishment of certain principles, the enforcement of certain dispositions, the cultivation of a certain temper of mind, which the conscience is to apply to the ever-varying exigencies of time and place. This appears to me to be the distinctive peculiarity of Christian morals, a characteristic in itself most remarkable, and singularly so when we find this free and comprehenaive system emanating from that of which the mainspring was its exclusiveness.

III. The basis of this universality in Christian morals was the broad and original principles upon which it rested. If we were to glean from the later Jewish writings, from the beautiful aphorisms of other Oriental nations, which we cannot fairly trace to Christian sources, and from the Platonic and Stoic philosophy, their more striking precepts, we might find, perhaps, a counterpart to almost all the moral sayings of Jesus. But the same truth is of different importance as an unconnected aphorism, and as the groundwork of a complete system. No doubt the benevolence of the Creator had awakened grateful feelings, and kindled the most exquisite poetry of expression, in the hearts and from the lips of many before the coming of Christ; no doubt general humanity had been impressed upon mankind in the most vivid and earnest language. But the Gospel first placed these two great principles as the main pillars of the new moral structure: God the universal Father, mankind one brotherhood; God made known through the mediation of his Son, the image, and humanized type and exemplar of his goodness; mankind of one kindred, and therefore of equal rank in the sight of the Creator, and to be united in one spiritual commonwealth. Such were the great principles of Christian morals, shadowed forth at first, rather than distinctly announced, in condescension to the prejudices of the Jews, who, if they had been found worthy of appreciating the essential spirit of the new religion—if they had received Jesus as the promised Saviour—might have been collectively and nationally the religious parents and teachers of mankind.

Such was the singular position of Jesus with regard

to his countrymen: the attempt to conciliate them to the new religion was to be fairly made; but the religion, however it might condescend to speak their language, could not forfeit or compromise, even for such an end, its primary and essential principles. Jesus therefore pursues his course, at one time paying the utmost deference to, at another unavoidably offending, the deep-rooted prejudices of the people. The inveterate and loathsome nature of the leprosy in Syria, the deep abhorrence with which the wretched victim of this disease was cast forth from all social fellowship, is well known to all who are even slightly acquainted with the Jewish Law and usages. One of these miserable beings appealed, and not in vain, to the mercy of Jesus.* He was instantaneously cured; but Jesus, whether to authenticate the cure, and to secure the readmission of the outcast into the rights and privileges of society from which he was legally excluded,* or more probably lest he should be accused of interfering with the rights or diminishing the dues of the priesthood, enjoined him to preserve the strictest secrecy concerning the cause of his cure; to submit to the regular examination of his case by the appointed authorities, and on no account to omit the customary offering. The second incident was remarkable for its publicity, as having taken place in a crowded house, in the midst of many of the Scribes, who were, at this period at

{margin: Conduct of Jesus with regard to his countrymen.}
{margin: Healing the leper.}
{margin: Second miracle.}

, Matt. viii. 2-4; Mark i. 40-45; Luke v. 12-16.

I have retained what may be called the moral connexion of this cure with the Sermon on the Mount; if the latter be inserted, as in St. Luke, after the more solemn inauguration of the Twelve, this incident will retain, perhaps, its present place, but lose this moral connexion. See Luke v. 12-15.

* I am inclined to adopt the explanation of Grotius, that "the testimony" was to be obtained from the priest, before he knew that he had been healed by Jesus, lest, in his jealousy, he should declare the cure imperfect.

least, not friendly to Jesus.[b] The door of the house being inaccessible on account of the crowd, the sick man was borne in his couch along the flat terrace roofs of the adjacent buildings (for in the East the roofs are rarely pointed or shelving) and let down through an aperture, which was easily made, and of sufficient dimensions to admit the bed into the upper chamber,[c] where Jesus was seated in the midst of his hearers. Jesus complied at once with their request to cure the afflicted man, but made use of a new and remarkable expression, "Thy sins are forgiven thee." This phrase, while it coincided with the general notion that such diseases were the penalties of sin, nevertheless as assuming to the Lord an unprecedented power, that which seems to belong to the Deity alone, struck his hearers, more especially the better instructed, the Scribes, with astonishment. Their wonder, however, at the instantaneous cure, for the present, overpowered their indignation, yet no doubt the whole transaction tended to increase the jealousy with which Jesus began to be beheld.

The third incident[d] jarred on a still more sensitive chord in the popular feeling. On no point were all orders among the Jews so unanimous as in their contempt and detestation of the publicans. Strictly speaking the persons named in the Evangelists were not publicans. These were men of property, not below the equestrian order, who farmed the public revenues. Those in question were the agents of these contractors, men, often freed slaves, or of low birth and station, and throughout the Roman world proverbial for their extortions, and in Judæa still more hateful, as

The publicans

---

[b] Matt. ix. 2-8; Mark ii. 1-12; Luke v. 18-26.

[c] Or they may merely have enlarged the door of communication with the

terrace roof.

[d] Matt. ix. 9; Mark ii. 13, 14; Luke v. 27, 28.

among the manifest signs of subjugation to a foreign dominion. The Jew who exercised the function of a publican was, as it were, a traitor to the national independence. One of these, Matthew, otherwise called Levi, was summoned from his post as collector, perhaps at the port of Capernaum, to become one of the most intimate followers of Jesus; and the general astonishment was still farther increased by Jesus entering familiarly into the house, and even partaking of food with men thus proscribed by the universal feeling; and though not legally unclean, yet no doubt held in even greater abhorrence by the general sentiment of the people.

Thus ended the first year of the public life of Jesus. The fame of his wonderful works; the authority with which he delivered his doctrines; among the meeker and more peaceful spirits the beauty of the doctrines themselves; above all, the mystery which hung over his character and pretensions, had strongly excited the interest of the whole nation. From all quarters, from Galilee, Peræa, Judæa, and even the remoter Idumea, multitudes approached him with eager curiosity. On the other hand, his total secession from, or rather his avowed condemnation of, the great prevailing party, the Pharisees, while his doctrines seemed equally opposed to the less numerous yet rival Sadducaic faction; his popular demeanour, which had little in common with the ascetic mysticism of the Essenes; his independence of the ruling authorities; above all, notwithstanding his general deference for the Law, his manifest assumption of a power above the Law, had no doubt, if not actively arrayed against him, yet awakened to a secret and brooding animosity, the interests and the passions of the more powerful and influential throughout the country.

CHAPTER V.

Second Year of the Public Life of Jesus.

<small>A. D. 28.

Passover. Jesus in Jerusalem.

Change in popular sentiment.</small>

THE second year of the public life of Christ opened, as the first, with his attendance at the Passover.[a] He appeared again amidst the assembled population of the whole race of Israel, in the place where, by common consent, the real Messiah was to assume his office, and to claim the allegiance of the favoured and chosen people of God.[b] It is clear that a considerable change had taken place in the popular sentiment, on the whole, at least with the ruling party, unfavourable to Jesus of Nazareth. The inquisitive wonder, not unmingled with respect, which on the former occasion seemed to have watched his words and actions, had turned to an unquiet and jealous vigilance, and a manifest anxiety on the part of his opponents to catch some opportunity of weakening his influence over the people. The misapprehended speech concerning the demolition and restoration of the Temple probably rankled in the recollection of many; and rumours no

---

<small>[a] My language on this point is to be taken with some latitude, as a certain time elapsed between the baptism of Jesus and the first Passover.

I adopt the opinion that the feast, in the 5th chapter of St. John (verse 1), was a Passover. This view is not without objection, namely, the long interval of nearly a whole year, which would be overleaped at once by the narrative of St. John. But if this Gospel was intended to be generally supplementary to the rest, or, as it seems, intended especially to relate the transactions in Jerusalem, omitted by the other Evangelists, this total silence on the intermediate events in Galilee would not be altogether unaccountable.

[b] John v. 1-15.</small>

doubt, and those most likely inaccurate and misrepresented, must have reached Jerusalem, of the mysterious language in which he had spoken of his relation to Jehovah, the Supreme Being. The mere fact that Galilee had been chosen, rather than Jerusalem or Judæa, for his assumption of whatever distinguished character he was about to support, would work, with no doubtful or disguised animosity, among the proud and jealous inhabitants of the metropolis. Nor was his conduct, however still cautious, without further inevitable collision with some of the most inveterate prejudices of his countrymen. The first year the only public demonstration of his superiority had been the expulsion of the buyers and sellers from the Temple, and his ambiguous and misinterpreted speech about that sacred edifice. His conversation with Nicodemus had probably not transpired, or at least not gained general publicity; for the same motives which would lead the cautious Pharisee to conceal his visit under the veil of night, would induce him to keep within his own bosom the important and startling truths, which perhaps he himself did not yet clearly comprehend, but which at all events were so opposite to the principles of his sect, and so humiliating to the pride of the ruling and learned oligarchy.

During his second visit, however, at the same solemn period of national assemblage, Jesus gave a new cause of astonishment to his followers, of offence to his adversaries, by an act which could not but excite the highest wonder and the strongest animadversion. This was no less than an assumption of authority to dispense with the observance of the Sabbath. Of all their institutes, which, after having infringed or neglected for centuries of

Breach of the Sabbath. Jewish reverence for the Sabbath.

cold and faithless service, the Jews, on the return from the Captivity, embraced with passionate and fanatical attachment, none had become so completely identified with the popular feeling, or had been guarded by such minute and multifarious provisions, as the Sabbath. In the early days of the Maccabean revolt against Antiochus, the insurgents, having been surprised on a Sabbath, submitted to be tamely butchered, rather than violate the sanctity of the day, even by defensive warfare. And though the manifest impossibility of recovering or maintaining their liberties against the inroads of hostile nations had led to a relaxation of the Law as far as self-defence, yet during the siege of Jerusalem by Pompey, the wondering Romans discovered, that although on the seventh day the garrison would repel an assault, yet they would do nothing to prevent or molest the enemy in carrying on his operations in the trenches. Tradition, "the hedge of the Law," as it was called, had fenced this institution with more than usual care: it had noted with jealous rigour almost every act of bodily exertion within the capacity of man, arranged them under thirty-nine heads, which were each considered to comprehend a multitude of subordinate cases, and against each and every one of these had solemnly affixed the seal of Divine condemnation. A Sabbath day's journey was a distance limited to 2,000 cubits, or rather less than a mile; and the carrying any burthen was especially denounced as among the most flagrant violations of the Law. This Sabbatic observance was the stronghold of Pharisaic rigour; and enslaved as the whole nation was in voluntary bondage to these minute regulations, in no point were they less inclined to struggle with the yoke, or wore it with greater willingness and pride.

THE MIRACLE AT BETHESDA.

There was a pool,[c] situated most likely to the north of the Temple, near the Sheep-gate, the same probably through which the animals intended for sacrifice were usually brought into the city. The place was called Beth-esda (the House of Mercy), and the pool was supposed to possess remarkable properties for healing diseases. At certain periods there was a strong commotion in the waters, which probably bubbled up from some chemical cause connected with their medicinal effects. Popular belief, or rather perhaps popular language, attributed this agitation of the surface to the descent of an angel;[d] for of course the regular descent of a celestial being, visible to the whole city, cannot for an instant be supposed. Around the pool were usually assembled a number of diseased persons, blind or paralytic, who awaited the right moment for plunging into the water, under the shelter of five porticoes, which had been built either by private charity, or at the public cost, for the general convenience. Among these lay one who had been notoriously afflicted for thirty-eight years by some disorder which deprived him of the use of his limbs.[e] It was in vain that he had watched an opportunity of relief; for as the sick person who first plunged into the water, when it became agitated, seems to have exhausted its virtues, this helpless and friendless sufferer

Healing of the sick man at the pool of Bethesda.

---

[c] John v. 1-15.
[d] The verse relating to the angel is rejected as spurious by many critics, and is wanting in some manuscripts. Perhaps it was silently rejected from a reluctance to depart from the literal interpretation; and, at the same time, the inevitable conviction that if taken literally the fact must have been notorious and visible to all who visited Jerusalem. Grotius, Lightfoot, Doddridge, in loc.
[e] We are not of course to suppose, as is assumed by some of the mythic interpreters, that the man had been all this time waiting for a cure at this place.

was constantly thrust aside, or supplanted by some more active rival for the salutary effects of the spring. Jesus saw and had compassion on the afflicted man, commanded him to rise, and, that he might show the perfect restoration of his strength, to take up the pallet on which he had lain, and to bear it away. The carrying any burthen, as has been said, was specifically named as one of the most heinous offences against the Law; and the strange sight of a man thus openly violating the statute in so public a place, could not but excite the utmost attention. The man was summoned, it would seem, before the appointed authorities, and questioned about his offence against public decency and the established law. His defence was plain and simple; he acted according to the command of the wonderful person who had restored his limbs with a word, but who that person was he had no knowledge; for, immediately after the miraculous cure, Jesus, in conformity with his usual practice of avoiding whatever might lead to popular tumult, had quietly withdrawn from the wondering crowd. Subsequently, however, meeting Jesus in the Temple, he recognised his benefactor, and it became generally known that Jesus was the author both of the cure and of the violation of the Sabbath. Jesus in his turn was called to account for his conduct.

The transaction bears the appearance, if not of a formal arraignment before the high court of the Sanhedrin, at least of a solemn and regular judicial inquiry. Yet, as no verdict seems to have been given, notwithstanding the importance evidently attached to the affair, it may be supposed either that the full authority of the Sanhedrin was wanting, or that they dared not, on such insufficient evidence, condemn with

Judicial investigation of the case.

severity one about whom the popular mind was at least divided. The defence of Jesus, though apparently not given at full length by the Evangelist, was of a nature to startle and perplex the tribunal: it was full of mysterious intimations, and couched in language about which it is difficult to decide how far it was familiar to the ears of the more learned. It appeared at once to strike at the literal interpretation of the Mosaic commandment, and at the same time to draw a parallel between the actions of Jesus and those of God.¹ On the Sabbath the beneficent works of the Almighty Father are continued as on any other day; there is no period of rest to Him whose active power is continually employed in upholding, animating, maintaining in its uniform and uninterrupted course the universe which He has created. The free course of God's blessing knows no pause, no suspension.² It is clear that the healing waters of Bethesda occasionally showed their salutary virtues on the Sabbath, and might thus be an acknowledged instance of the unremitting benevolence of the Almighty. In the same manner the benevolence of Jesus disdained to be confined by any distinction of days; it was to flow forth as constant and unimpeded as the Divine bounty. The indignant court heard with astonishment this aggravation of the offence. Not only had Jesus assumed the power of dispensing with the Law, but, with what appeared to them profane and

Defence of Jesus.

---

¹ John v. 16–47.

² If the sublime maxim which was admitted in the school of Alexandria had likewise found its way into the synagogues of Judæa, the speech of Jesus (My Father worketh hitherto, and I work) in its first clause appealed to principles acknowledged by his auditory. "God," says Philo, "never ceases from action, but as it is the property of fire to burn, of snow to chill, so to act (or to work) is the inalienable function of the Deity." De Alleg. lib. ii.

impious boldness, he had instituted a comparison between himself and the great Ineffable Deity. With one consent they determine to press with greater vehemence the capital charge. *Therefore the Jews sought the more to kill him, because he had not only broken the Sabbath, but said that God was his father, making himself equal with God.*

The second defence of Jesus was at once more full and explicit, and more alarming to the awe-struck assembly. It amounted to an open assumption of the title and offices of the Messiah—the Messiah in the person of the commanding and fearless, yet still, as they supposed, humble Galilean, who stood before their tribunal. It commenced by expanding and confirming that parallel, which had already sunk so deep into their resentful minds. The Son was upon earth, as it were, a representative of the power and mercy of the invisible Father—of that great Being who had never been comprehensible to the senses of man. *For what things soever he (the Father) doeth, those also doeth the Son likewise.* The Saviour proceeded to declare his divine mission and his claim to divine honour, his investment with power, not only over diseases, but over death itself. From thence he passed to the acknowledged offices of the Messiah, the resurrection, the final judgement, the apportionment of everlasting life. All these recognised functions of the Messiah were assigned by the Father to the Son, and that Son appeared in his person. In confirmation of these as yet unheard-of pretensions, Jesus declared that his right to honour and reverence rested not on his own assertion alone. He appealed to the testimony which had been publicly borne to his character by John the Baptist. The prophetic authority of John had been, if not universally, at least generally

Second defence of Jesus.

recognised; it had so completely sunk into the popular belief, that, as appears in a subsequent incident, the multitude would have resented any suspicion thrown even by their acknowledged superiors on one thus established in their respect and veneration, and perhaps further endeared by the persecution which he was now suffering under the unpopular tetrarch of Galilee. He appealed to a more decisive testimony, the public miracles which he had wrought, concerning which the rulers seem scarcely yet to have determined on their course, whether to doubt, to deny, or to ascribe them to dæmoniacal agency. Finally he appealed to the last unanswerable authority, the Sacred Writings, which they held in such devout reverence; and distinctly asserted that his coming had been prefigured by their great lawgiver, from the spirit at least, if not from the express letter of whose sacred laws they were departing, in rejecting his claims to the title and honours of the Messiah. *Had ye believed Moses, ye would have believed me, for he wrote of me.*

There is an air of conscious superiority in the whole of this address, which occasionally rises to the vehemence of reproof, to solemn expostulation, to authoritative admonition, of which it is difficult to estimate the impression upon a court accustomed to issue their judgements to a trembling and humiliated auditory. But of their subsequent proceedings we have no information,—whether the Sanhedrin hesitated or feared to proceed; whether they were divided in their opinions, or could not reckon upon the support of the people; whether they doubted their own competency to take so strong a measure without the concurrence or sanction of the Roman governor—at all events, no attempt was made to secure the person of

<small>Difficult position of the Sanhedrin.</small>

Jesus. He appears, with his usual caution, to have retired towards the safer province of Galilee, where the Jewish senate possessed no authority, and where Herod, much less under the Pharisaic influence, would not think it necessary to support the injured dignity of the Sanhedrin in Jerusalem; nor, whatever his political apprehensions, would he entertain the same sensitive terrors of a reformer who confined his views to the religious improvement of mankind.

But from this time commences the declared hostility of the Pharisaic party against Jesus. Every opportunity is seized of detecting him in some further violation of the religious statutes. We now perpetually find the Pharisees watching his footsteps, and, especially on the Sabbath, laying hold of every pretext to inflame the popular mind against his neglect or open defiance, of their observances. Nor was their jealous vigilance disappointed. Jesus calmly pursued on the Sabbath, as on every other day, his course of benevolence. A second and a third time, immediately after his public arraignment, that, which they considered the inexpiable offence, was renewed, and justified in terms which were still more repugnant to their inveterate prejudices.

Hostility of the Pharisaic party.

They follow him into Galilee.

The Passover was scarcely ended, and with his disciples he was probably travelling homewards, when the first of these incidents occurred. On the first Sabbath after the second day of unleavened bread, the disciples passing through a field of corn, and being hungry, plucked some of the ears of corn, and rubbing them in their hands, ate the grain.[b] This, according to

New violation of the Sabbath.

---

[b] Matt. xii. 1-8; Mark ii. 23-28; Luke vi. 1-5.

Jewish usage, was no violation of the laws of property, as, after the wave-offering had been made in the Temple, the harvest was considered to be ripe: and the humane regulation of the Lawgiver permitted the stranger, who was passing through a remote district, thus to satisfy his immediate wants. But it was the Sabbath, and the act directly offended against another of the multifarious provisions of Pharisaic tradition. The vindication of his followers by their Master took still higher ground. He not merely adduced the example of David, who in extreme want had not scrupled, in open violation of the Law, to take the shewbread, which was prohibited to all but the priestly order (he thus placed his humble disciples on a level with the great king, whose memory was cherished with the most devout reverence and pride), but he distinctly asserted his own power of dispensing with that which was considered the eternal, the irreversible commandment,—he declared himself Lord of the Sabbath.

Rumours of this dangerous innovation accompanied the Saviour into Galilee. Whether some of the more zealous Pharisees had followed him during his journey, or had accidentally returned at the same time from the Passover, or whether, by means of that intimate and rapid correspondence likely to be maintained among the members of an ambitious and spreading sect, they had already communicated their apprehensions of danger and their animosity against Jesus, they already seem to have arrayed against him in all parts the vigilance and enmity of their brethren. It was in the public synagogue in some town which he entered on his return to Galilee, in the face of the whole assembly, that a man with a withered hand recovered the strength of his limb at the command of Jesus on the Sabbath day.¹ And the multitude, instead of being inflamed by the zeal of the Pharisees, appear at least to have been unmoved by their angry remonstrances. They heard without disapprobation, if they did not openly testify their admiration, both of the power and goodness of Jesus; and listened to the simple argument with which he silenced his adversaries, by appealing to their own practice in extricating their own property, or delivering their own cattle from jeopardy, on the sacred day.ᵏ

The discomfited Pharisees endeavoured to enlist in their party the followers, perhaps the magistracy of Herod, and to organise a formidable opposition to the growing influence of Jesus. So successful was their hostility, that Jesus seems to have thought it prudent to withdraw for a short time from the collision. He passed towards the lake, over which he could at any time cross into the district which was beyond the authority both of Herod and of the Jewish Sanhedrin.ᵐ A bark attended upon him, which would transport him to any quarter he might desire, and on board of which he seems to have avoided the multitudes, which constantly thronged around, or seated on the deck addressed, with greater convenience, the crowding hearers who lined the shores. Yet concealment, or perhaps less frequent publicity, seems now to have been his object;ⁿ for when some of those insane persons, the dæmoniacs as they were called, openly address him by the title of Son of God, Jesus enjoins their silence,° as though he were yet unwilling openly to assume this title, which was fully equivalent

Jesus withdraws beyond the Sea of Galilee.

He retires from public view.

---

¹ Matt. xii. 9-14; Mark iii. 1-6; Luke vi. 6-11.
ᵏ Matt. xii. 15-21; Mark iii. 7-12.
ᵐ Mark iii. 7.
ⁿ Matt. xii. 10.
° Mark iii. 11-12.

to that of the Messiah; and which, no doubt, was already ascribed to him by the bolder and less prudent of his followers. The same injunctions of secrecy were addressed to others, who at this time were relieved or cured by the beneficent power; so that one Evangelist considers that the cautious and unresisting demeanour of Jesus, thus avoiding all unnecessary offence or irritation, exemplified that characteristic of the Messiah, so beautifully described by Isaiah,[p] "He shall neither strive nor cry, neither shall any man hear his voice in the streets; a bruised reed shall he not break, and smoking flax shall he not quench, till he send forth judgment unto victory."

This persecution, however, continues but a short time, and Jesus appears again openly in Capernaum and its neighbourhood. After a night passed in solitary retirement, he takes the decided step of organising his followers, selecting and solemnly inaugurating a certain number of his more immediate disciples, who were to receive an authoritative commission to disseminate his doctrines.[q] Hitherto he had stood, as it were, alone; though doubtless some of his followers had attended upon him with greater zeal and assiduity than others, yet he could scarcely be considered as the head of a regular and disciplined community. The twelve Apostles, whether or not selected with that view, could not but call to mind the number of the tribes of Israel. Of the earlier lives of these humble men little can be gathered beyond the usual avocations of some among them; and even tradition, for once, preserves a modest and almost total silence. They were of the lower,

Reappears at Capernaum.

Organisation of his followers.

[p] Matt. xii. 19, 20. [q] Mark iii. 13-19; Luke vi. 12-19.

though perhaps not quite the lowest, class of Galilean peasants. What previous education they had received we can scarcely conjecture; though almost all the Jews appear to have received some kind of instruction in the history, the religion, and the traditions of the nation.

The twelve Apostles. First among the twelve appears Simon, to whom Jesus, in allusion to the firmness of character which he was hereafter to exhibit, gave a name, or rather, perhaps, interpreted a name by which he was already known, Cephas,* the Rock; and declared that his new religious community was to rest on a foundation as solid as that name seemed to signify. Andrew his brother is usually associated with Peter. James and John* received the remarkable name of Boanerges, the Sons of Thunder, of which it is not easy to trace the exact force; for those who bore it do not appear remarkable among their brethren, either for energy or vehemence. The peculiar gentleness of the latter, both in character and in the style of his writings, would lead us to doubt the correctness of the interpretation generally assigned to the appellation. The two former were natives of one town, Bethsaida, the latter, either of Bethsaida or Capernaum, and all obtained their livelihood as fishermen on the Lake of Gennesaret, the waters of which were extraordinarily prolific in fish of

---

* The equivocal meaning of the word was, no doubt, evident in the original Aramaic dialect, spoken in Galilee. The French alone of modern languages exactly retains it. "Vous êtes Pierre, et sur cette pierre." The narrative of St. John ascribes the giving this appellative to an earlier period. See suprà, p. 151.

* John must have been extremely young when chosen as an apostle; there is so constant a tradition of his being alive at a late period in the first century, that the fact can scarcely be doubted. Jerome may perhaps have overstrained the tradition, "ut autem sciamus Johannem tum fuisse posterum, cum a Jesu electus est, manifestissimè docent ecclesiasticæ historiæ, quod usque ad Trajani vixerit imperium." Hieronym. in Jovin. L. I.

many kinds. Matthew or Levi, as it has been said, was a publican. Philip was likewise of Bethsaida. Bartholomew, the son of Tolmai or Ptolemy, is generally considered to have been the same with Nathanael, and was distinguished, before his knowledge of Jesus, by the blamelessness of his character, and, from the respect in which he was held, may be supposed to have been of higher reputation as of a better instructed class. Thomas or Didymus (for the Syriac and Greek words have the same signification, a twin) is remarkable in the subsequent history for his coolness and reflecting temper of mind. Lebbeus, or Thaddeus, or Judas the brother of James, are doubtless different names of the same person. Judas in Syriac is Thaddai. Whether Lebbaios is derived from the town of Lebba, on the seacoast of Galilee, or from a word denoting the heart, and therefore almost synonymous with Thaddai, which is interpreted the breast, is extremely doubtful. James was the son of Cleophas or Alpheus; concerning him and his relationship to Jesus there has been much dispute. His father Cleophas was married to another Mary, sister of Mary the mother of Jesus, to whom he would therefore be cousin-german. But whether he is the same with the James who in other places is named the brother of the Lord (the term of brother by Jewish usage, according to one opinion, comprehending these closer ties of kindred); and whether either of these two, or which, was the James who presided over the Christian community in Jerusalem, and whose cruel death is described by Josephus, must remain among those questions on which we can scarcely expect further information, and cannot therefore decide with certainty. Simon the Canaanite was so called, not, as has been supposed, from the town of Cana, still less from his

Canaanitish descent, but from a Hebrew word meaning a zealot, to which fanatical and dangerous body this apostle had probably belonged, before he joined the more peaceful disciples of Jesus. The last was Judas Iscariot, perhaps so named from a small village named Iscara, or more probably Carioth, situated in the tribe of Judah.

It was after the regular inauguration of the twelve in their apostolic office, that, according to St. Luke, the Sermon on the Mount was delivered, or some second outline of Christian morals repeated in nearly similar terms. Immediately after, as Jesus returned to Capernaum, a cure was wrought, both from its circumstances and its probable influence on the situation of Jesus, highly worthy of remark.[1] It was in favour of a centurion, a military officer of Galilean descent, probably in the service of Herod, and a proselyte to Judaism, for he could scarcely have built a synagogue for Jewish worship, unless a convert to the religion.[a] This man was held in such high estimation that the Jewish elders of the city, likewise it might seem not unfavourably disposed towards Jesus, interceded in his behalf. The man himself appears to have held the new teacher in such profound reverence, that in his humility he did not think his house worthy of so illustrious a guest, and expressed his confidence that a word from him would be as effective, even uttered at a distance, as the orders that he was accustomed to issue to his soldiery. Jesus not only complied with his request by restoring his servant to health, but took the opportunity of declaring that many Gentiles, from the most remote quarters,

Healing of the centurion's servant.

---

[1] St. Matthew as well as St. Luke places this cure as immediately following the Sermon on the Mount.

[a] Matt. viii. 5-13; Luke vii. 1-10.

would be admitted within the pale of the new religion, to the exclusion of many who had no title but their descent from Abraham. Still there was nothing, so far as in the earlier part of this declaration, directly contrary to the established opinions; for at least the more liberal Jews were not unwilling to entertain the splendid ambition of becoming the religious instructors of the world, provided the world did homage to the excellence and divine institution of the Law; and at all times the Gentiles, by becoming Jews, either as proselytes of the gate, if not proselytes by circumcision, might share in most, if not in all, the privileges of the chosen people. This incident was likewise of importance as still further strengthening the interest of Jesus with the ruling authorities and with another powerful officer in the town of Capernaum. A more extraordinary transaction followed. As yet Jesus had claimed authority over the most distressing and obstinate maladies; he now appeared invested with power over death itself. As he entered the town of Nain, between twenty and thirty miles from Capernaum, he met a funeral procession, accompanied with circumstances of extreme distress. It was a youth, the only son of a widow, who was borne out to burial; so great was the calamity that it had excited the general interest of the inhabitants. Jesus raises the youth from his bier, and restores him to the destitute mother.[x]

<small>Raising the widow's son.</small>

The fame of this unprecedented miracle was propagated with the utmost rapidity through the country; and still vague, yet deepening, rumours that a prophet had appeared; that the great event which held the whole nation in suspense was on the instant of fulfil-

---

[x] Luke vii. 11-18.

ment, spread throughout the whole province. It even reached the remote fortress of Machærus, in which John was still closely guarded, though it seems the free access of his followers was not prohibited.[y] John commissioned two of his disciples to inquire into the truth of these wonderful reports, and to demand of Jesus himself, whether he was the expected Messiah. But what was the design of John in this message to Jesus? The question is not without difficulty. Was it for the satisfaction of his own doubts, or those of his followers?[z] Was it that, in apprehension of his approaching death, he would consign his disciples to the care of a still greater instructor? Was it that he might attach them before his death to Jesus, and familiarise them with conduct, in some respects, so opposite to his own Essenian, if not Pharisaic, habits? He might foresee the advantage that would be taken by the more ascetic to alienate his followers from Jesus, as a teacher who fell far below the austerity of their own; and who, accessible to all, held in no respect those minute observances which the usage of the stricter Jews, and the example of their master, had arrayed in indispensable sanctity. Or was it that John himself, having languished for nearly a year in his remote prison, began to be impatient for the commencement of that splendid epoch,[a] of which the whole nation, even the Apostles of Jesus, both before and after the resurrection, had by no means abandoned their glorious, worldly, and Jewish notions? Was John, like the rest of the people, not yet exalted above those hopes which were inseparable from the national mind? If he is the King, why does he hesitate

---

[y] Matt. xi. 2-30; Luke vii. 17-35.
[z] Whitby, Doddridge, in loc.
[a] Hammond inclines to this view, as does Jortin, Discourses on the Truth of the Christian Religion.

to assume his kingdom? If the Deliverer, why so tardy to commence the deliverance? "If thou art indeed the Messiah (such may appear to have been the purport of the Baptist's message), proclaim thyself at once; assume thy state; array thyself in majesty; discomfit the enemies of holiness and of God! My prison doors will at once burst open; my trembling persecutors will cease from their oppressions. Herod himself will yield up his usurped authority; and even the power of Rome will cease to afflict the redeemed people of the Almighty!" What, on the other hand, is the answer of Jesus? It harmonises in a remarkable manner with this latter view. It declares at once, and to the disappointment of these temporal hopes, the purely moral and religious nature of the dominion to be established by the Messiah. He was found displaying manifest signs of more than human power, and to these peaceful signs he appeals as the conclusive evidence of the commencement of the Messiah's kingdom, the relief of diseases, the assuagement of sorrows, the restoration of their lost or decayed senses to the deaf or blind, the equal admission of the lowest orders to the same religious privileges with those more especially favoured by God. The remarkable words are added, "Blessed is he that shall not be offended in me;" he that shall not consider irreconcileable with the splendid promises of the Messiah's kingdom, my lowly condition, my calm and unassuming course of mercy and love to mankind, my total disregard of worldly honours, my refusal to place myself at the head of the people as a temporal ruler. Violent men, more especially during the disturbed and excited period since the appearance of John the Baptist, would urge on a kingdom of violence. How truly the character of the times is thus described, is apparent from the single fact, that shortly afterwards the people would have seized Jesus himself and forced him to assume the royal title, if he had not withdrawn himself from his dangerous adherents. This last expression, however, occurs in the subsequent discourse of Jesus, after his disciples had departed, when in those striking images he spoke of the former concourse of the people to the Baptist, and justified it by the assertion of his prophetic character. It was no idle object which led them into the wilderness, to see, as it were, "a reed shaken by the wind;" nor to behold any rich or luxurious object—for such they would have gone to the courts of their sovereigns. Still he declares the meanest of his own disciples to have attained some moral superiority, some knowledge, probably, of the real nature of the new religion, and of the character and designs of the Messiah, which had never been possessed by John. With his usual rapidity of transition, Jesus passes at once to his moral instruction, and vividly shows, that whether severe or gentle, whether more ascetic or more popular, the teachers of a holier faith had been equally unacceptable. The general multitude of the Jews had rejected both the austerer Baptist, and himself though of so much more benign and engaging demeanour. The whole discourse ends with the significant words, "My yoke is easy, and my burden is light."

<small>Contrast between Jesus and John the Baptist.</small> Nothing, indeed, could offer a more striking contrast to the secluded and eremitical life of John, than the easy and accessible manner with which Jesus mingled among all classes, even his bitterest opponents, the Pharisees. He accepts the invitation of one of these, and enters into his house to partake of refreshment.[b] Here a woman of dissolute

---

[b] Luke vii. 36-50; Luke xi. 14-26.

life found her way into the chamber where the feast was held; she sat at his feet, anointing him, according to Eastern usage, with a costly unguent, which was contained in a box of alabaster; she wept bitterly, and with her long locks wiped away the falling tears. The Pharisees, who shrunk not only from the contact, but even from the approach, of all whom they considered physically or morally unclean, could only attribute the conduct of Jesus to his ignorance of her real character. The reply of Jesus intimates that his religion was intended to reform and purify the worst, and that some of his most sincere and ardent believers might proceed from those very outcasts of society from whom Pharisaic rigour shrunk with abhorrence.

After this Jesus appears to have made another circuit through the towns and villages of Galilee. On his return to Capernaum, instigated, perhaps, by his adversaries, some of his relatives appear to have believed, or pretended to believe, that he was out of his senses; and, therefore, attempted to secure his person.[c] This scheme failing, the Pharisaic party, who had been deputed, it would seem, from Jerusalem to watch his conduct, endeavour to avail themselves of that great principle of Jewish superstition, the belief in the power of evil spirits, to invalidate his growing authority.[d] On the occasion of the cure of one of those lunatics, usually called dæmoniacs,[e] who was both dumb Dæmoniacs.

---

[c] Mark iii. 21.
[d] Matt. xii. 22-45; Mark iii. 19-30.
[e] I have no scruple in avowing my opinion on the subject of the dæmoniacs to be that of Joseph Mede, Lardner, Dr. Mead, Paley, and all the learned modern writers. It was a kind of insanity, not unlikely to be prevalent among a people peculiarly subject to leprosy and other cutaneous diseases; and nothing was more probable than that lunacy should take the turn and speak the language of the prevailing superstition of the times. As the belief in witchcraft made people fancy

and blind, they accused him of unlawful dealings with the spirits of evil. It was by a magic influence obtained by a secret contract with Beelzebub, the chief of the powers of darkness, or by secretly invoking his all-powerful name, that he reduced the subordinate dæmons to obedience. The answer of Jesus struck them with confusion. Evil spirits, according to their own creed, took delight in the miseries and crimes of men; his acts were those of the purest benevolence: how gross the inconsistency to suppose that malignant spirits would thus lend themselves to the cause of human happiness and virtue! Another more personal argument still farther confounded his adversaries. The Pharisees were professed exorcists;* if, then, exorcism, or the ejection of these

---

themselves witches, so the belief in possession made men of distempered minds fancy themselves possessed. The present case, indeed, seems to have been one rather of infirmity than lunacy: the afflicted person was blind and dumb; but such cases were equally ascribed to malignant spirits. There is one very strong reason, which I do not remember to have seen urged with sufficient force, but which may have contributed to induce our Lord to adopt the current language on this point. The disbelief in these spiritual influences was one of the characteristic tenets of the unpopular sect of the Sadducees. A departure from the common language, or the endeavour to correct this inveterate error, would have raised an immediate outcry against him from his watchful and malignant adversaries, as an unbelieving Sadducee. Josephus mentions a certain herb which had the power of expelling dæmons, a fact which intimates that it was a bodily disease. Kuinoel, in Matt. iv. 24, refers to the latter fact; shows that in Greek authors, especially Hippocrates, madness and dæmoniacal possessions are the same; and quotes the various passages in the New Testament where the same language is evidently held; as, among many others, John x. 20; Matt. xvii. 15; Mark v. 15. I have again the satisfaction of finding myself to have arrived at the same conclusion with Neander.

* The rebuking subordinate dæmons, by the invocation of a more powerful name, is a very ancient and common form of superstition. The later anti-Christian writers among the Jews attribute the power of Jesus over evil spirits to his having obtained the secret, and dared to utter the ineffable name, "the Sem-ham-phorash." To this name wonderful powers over the whole invisible world are attributed by the

evil spirits, necessarily implied unlawful dealings with the world of darkness, they were as open to the charge as he whom they accused. They had, therefore, the alternative of renouncing their own pretensions, or of admitting that those of Jesus were to be judged on other principles. It was, then, blasphemy against the Spirit of God to ascribe acts which bore the manifest impress of the divine goodness in their essentially beneficent character, to any other source but the Father of Mercies; it was an offence which argued such total obtuseness of moral perception, such utter incapacity of feeling or comprehending the beauty either of the conduct or the doctrines of Jesus, as to leave no hope that they would ever be reclaimed from their rancorous hostility to his religion, or be qualified for admission into the pale and to the benefits of the new faith.

The discomfited Pharisees now demand a more public and undeniable sign of his Messiahship,[s] which alone could justify the lofty tone assumed by Jesus. A second time Jesus obscurely alludes to the one great future sign of the new faith —his resurrection; and, refusing further to gratify their curiosity, he reverts, in language of more than usual energy, to the incapacity of the age and nation to discern the real and intrinsic superiority of his religion.

Pharisees demand a sign.

Jewish Alexandrian writers, Artapanus and Ezekiel the tragedian; and it is not impossible that the more superstitious Pharisees may have hoped to reduce Jesus to the dilemma either of confessing that he invoked the name of the prince of the demons, or secretly uttered that, which it was still more criminal to make use of for such a purpose, the mysterious and unspeakable Tetragrammaton. See Eisenmenger, i. 154. According to Josephus the art of exorcism descended from King Solomon. Antiq. viii. 2.

[s] Matt. xii. 38–45.

The followers of Jesus had now been organised into a regular sect or party. Another incident distinctly showed that he no longer stood alone; even the social duties, which up to this time he had, no doubt, discharged with the utmost affection, were to give place to the sublimer objects of his mission. While he sat encircled by the multitude of his disciples, tidings were brought that his mother and his brethren desired to approach him.[b] But Jesus refused to break off his occupation; he declared himself connected by a closer tie even than that of blood, with the great spiritual family of which he was to be the parent, and with which he was to stand in the most intimate relation. He was the chief of a fraternity not connected by common descent or consanguinity, but by a purely moral and religious bond; not by any national or local union, but bound together by the one strong but indivisible link of their common faith. On the increase, the future prospects, the final destiny of this community, his discourses now dwell, with frequent if obscure allusions.[i] His language more constantly assumes the form of parable. Nor was this merely in compliance with the genius of an Eastern people, in order to convey his instruction in a form more attractive, and therefore both more immediately and more permanently impressive; or by awakening the imagination, to stamp his doctrines more deeply on the memory, and to incorporate them with the feelings. These short and lively apologues were admirably adapted to suggest the first rudiments of truths which it was not expedient openly to announce. Though

Conduct of Jesus to his relatives.

Parables.

---

[b] Matt. xii. 46-49; Mark iii. 31-35.   [i] Matt. xiii.; Mark iv. 1-34; Luke viii. 1-18.

some of the parables have a purely moral purport, the greater part delivered at this period bear a more or less covert relation to the character and growth of the new religion; a subject which, avowed without disguise, would have revolted the popular mind, and clashed too directly with the inveterate nationality. Yet these splendid, though obscure, anticipations singularly contrast with occasional allusions to his own personal destitution: "The foxes have holes, and the birds of the air have nests, but the Son of Man hath not where to lay his head."[l] For with the growth and organisation of his followers he seems fully aware that his dangers increase; he now frequently changes his place, passes from one side of the lake to the other, and even endeavours to throw a temporary concealment over some of his most extraordinary miracles. During an expedition across the lake, he is in danger from one of those sudden and violent tempests which often disturb inland seas, particularly in mountainous districts. He rebukes the storm, and it ceases. On the other side of the lake, in the district of Gadara, occurs the remarkable scene of the dæmoniacs among the tombs, and the herd of swine; the only act in the whole life of Jesus in the least repugnant to the uniform gentleness of his disposition, which would shrink from the unnecessary destruction even of the meanest and most loathsome animals.[m] On his return

---

[l] Matt. viii. 18-27; Mark iv. 35-41; Luke viii. 22-25.

[m] The moral difficulty of this transaction has always appeared to me greater than that of reconciling it with the more rational view of dæmoniacism. Both are much diminished, if not entirely removed, by the theory of Kuinoel, who attributes to the lunatics the whole of the conversation with Jesus, and supposes that their driving the herd of swine down the precipice was the last paroxysm in which their insanity exhausted itself. Matt. viii. 28-34; Mark v. 1-20; Luke viii. 26-39.

from this expedition to Capernaum took place the healing of the woman with the issue of blood, and the raising of Jairus's daughter.ᵃ Concerning the latter, as likewise concerning the relief of two blind men,ᵇ he gives the strongest injunctions of secrecy, which, nevertheless, the active zeal of his partisans seems by no means to have regarded.

But a more decisive step was now taken than the organisation of the new religious community. The twelve Apostles were sent out to disseminate the doctrines of Jesus throughout the whole of Galilee.ᵖ They were invested with the power of healing diseases; with cautious deference to Jewish feeling, they were forbidden to proceed beyond the borders of the Holy Land, either among the Gentiles or the heretical Samaritans; they were to depend on the hospitality of those whom they might address for their subsistence; and he distinctly anticipates the enmity which they would perpetually encounter, and the dissension which would be caused, even in the bosom of families, by the appearance of men thus acting on a commission unprecedented and unrecognised by the religious authorities of the nation, yet whose doctrines were of such intrinsic beauty, and so full of exciting promise.

The Apostles sent out.

It was most likely this open proclamation, as it were, of the rise of a new and organised community, and the greater publicity which this simultaneous appearance of two of its delegates in the different towns of Galilee could not but give to the growing influence of Jesus, that first attracted the notice of the government. Up to this period Jesus, as a remarkable

Conduct of Herod.

ᵃ Luke viii. 40-56.
ᵇ Matt. xx. 27-31.
ᵖ Matt. x.; Mark vi. 7-13; Luke ix. 1-6.

man, must have been well known by general report; by this measure he stood in a very different character, as the chief of a numerous fraternity. There were other reasons, at this critical period, to excite the apprehensions and jealousy of Herod. During the short interval between the visit of John's disciples to Jesus and the present time, the Tetrarch had at length, at the instigation of his wife, perpetrated the murder of the Baptist. Whether his reluctance to shed unnecessary blood, or his prudence, had as yet shrunk from this crime, the condemnation of her marriage could not but rankle in the heart of the wife. The desire of revenge would be strengthened by a feeling of insecurity, and an apprehension of the precariousness of an union, declared, on such revered authority, null and void. As long as this stern and respected censor lived, her influence over her husband, the bond of marriage itself, might, in an hour of passion or remorse, be dissolved. The common crime would cement still closer, perhaps for ever, their common interests. The artifices of Herodias, who did not scruple to make use of the beauty and grace of her daughter to compass her end, had extorted from the reluctant king, in the hour of festive carelessness—the celebration of Herod's birthday—the royal promise, which, whether for good or for evil, was equally irrevocable.[q] The head of John the Baptist was the reward for the dancing of the daughter of Herodias.[r] Whether the mind of Herod, like that of

---

[q] Matt. xiv. 1-12; Mark vi. 14-29; Luke ix. 7-9.

[r] Josephus places the scene of this event in Macherus. Macknight would remove the prison of John to Tiberias. But the circumstances of the war may have caused the court to be held in this strong frontier town, and the feast may have been intended chiefly for the army, the "Chiliarchs" of St. Mark.

his father,[a] was disordered by his crime, and the disgrace and discomfiture of his arms contributed to his moody terrors; or whether some popular rumour of the reappearance of John, and that Jesus was the murdered prophet restored to life, had obtained currency; indications of hostility from the government seem to have put Jesus upon his guard.[b] For no sooner had he been rejoined by the Apostles, than he withdrew into the desert country about Bethsaida, with the prudence which he now thought fit to assume, avoiding any sudden collision with the desperation or the capricious violence of the Tetrarch.

But he now filled too important a place in the public mind to remain concealed so near his customary residence, and the scene of his extraordinary actions. The multitude thronged forth to trace his footsteps, so that five thousand persons had preoccupied the place of his retreat; and so completely were they possessed by profound religious enthusiasm, as entirely to have forgotten the difficulty of obtaining provisions in that desolate region. The manner in which their wants were preternaturally supplied, and the whole assemblage fed by five loaves and two small fishes, wound up at once the rising enthusiasm to the highest pitch. It could not but call to the mind of the multitude the memorable event in their annals, the feeding the whole nation in the desert by the multiplication of the manna.[c] Jesus then would no longer confine himself to those private and more

Jesus withdraws from Galilee.

The multitude fed in the desert.

---

[a] According to Josephus the Jews ascribed the discomfiture of Herod's army by Aretas, king of Arabia, to the wrath of Heaven for the murder of John.

[b] Matt. xiv. 13, 14; Mark vi. 30–34; Luke ix. 10, 11; John vi. 1, 2.
[c] Matt. xiv. 15–23; Mark vi. 35–45; Luke ix. 12–17; John vi. 3–14.

unimposing acts of beneficence, of which the actual advantage was limited to a single object, and the ocular evidence of the fact to but few witnesses. Here was a sign performed in the presence of many thousands, who had actually participated in the miraculous food. This then, they supposed, could not but be the long-desired commencement of his more public, more national, career. Behold a second Moses! behold a Leader of the people, under whom they could never be afflicted with want! behold at length the Prophet, under whose government the people were to enjoy, among the other blessings of the Messiah's reign, unexampled, uninterrupted plenty.[x]

Their acclamations clearly betrayed their intentions; they would brook no longer delay; they would force him to assume the royal title; they would proclaim him, whether consenting or not, the King of Israel.[y] Jesus withdrew from the midst of the dangerous tumult, and till the next day they sought him in vain. On their return to Capernaum, they found that He had crossed the lake, and entered the city the evening before. Their suspense, no doubt, had

---

[x] He made manna to descend for them, in which were all manner of tastes; and every Israelite found in it what his palate was chiefly pleased with. If he desired fat in it, he had it. In it the young men tasted bread; the old men, honey; and the children, oil. So it shall be in the world to come (the days of the Messias); he shall give Israel peace, and they shall sit down and eat in the garden of Eden; all nations shall behold their condition; as it is said, "Behold, my servants shall eat, but ye shall be hungry." Isaiah lxv. Rambam in Sanhed. cap. 10.

Many affirm that the hope of Israel is, that Messiah shall come and raise the dead; and they shall be gathered together in the garden of Eden, and shall eat and drink, and satiate themselves all the days of the world . . .; and that there are houses built all of precious stones, beds of silk, and rivers flowing with wine and spicy oil. Shemoth Rabba, sect. 25; Lightfoot in loc., vol. xii. 292.

[y] John vi. 15.

not been allayed by his mysterious disappearance on the other side of the lake. The circumstances under which He had passed over,ᶠ if communicated by the Apostles to the wondering multitude (and unless positively prohibited by their Master, they could not have kept silence on so wonderful an occurrence), would inflame still farther the intense popular agitation. While the Apostles were passing the lake in their boat, Jesus had appeared by their side, walking upon the waters.

When therefore Jesus entered the synagogue of Capernaum, no doubt the crisis was immediately expected: at length He will avow himself; the declaration of his dignity must now be made; and where with such propriety as in the place of the public worship, in the midst of the devout and adoring people?ᵃ The calm, the purely religious language of Jesus was a death-blow to these high-strung hopes. The object of his mission, he declared in explicit terms, was not to confer temporal benefits; they were not to follow him with the hope that they would obtain without labour the fruits of the earth, or be secured against thirst and hunger—these were mere casual and incidental blessings.ᵇ The real design of the new religion was the elevation of the moral and spiritual condition of man, described under the strong but not unusual figure of nourishment administered to the soul. During the whole of his address, or rather his conversation with the different parties, the popular opinion was in a state of fluctuation; or, as is probable, there were two distinct parties,—that of the populace, at first more favourable to Jesus; and that of the Jewish

---

ᶠ Matt. xiv. 24-33; Mark vi. 47-53; John vi. 16-21. ᵃ John vi. 22-71. ᵇ Ibid. 26-29.

leaders, who were altogether hostile. The former appear more humbly to have inquired what was demanded by the new Teacher in order to please God: of them Jesus required faith in the Messiah. The latter first demanded a new sign,^c but broke out into murmurs of disapprobation when "the carpenter's son" began in his mysterious language to speak of his descent, his commission, from his Father, his reascension to his former intimate communion with the Deity; still more when He seemed to confine the hope of everlasting life to those only who were fitted to receive it; to those whose souls would receive the inward nutriment of his doctrines. No word in the whole address fell in with their excited, their passionate hopes: however dark, however ambiguous his allusions, they could not warp or misinterpret them into the confirmation of their splendid views. Not only did they appear to discountenance the immediate, they gave no warrant to the remote, accomplishment of their visions of the Messiah's earthly power and glory.^d At all events the disappointment was universal; his own adherents, baffled and sinking at once from their exalted hopes, cast off their unambitious, their inexplicable Leader; and so complete appears to have been the desertion, that Jesus demanded of the Twelve, whether they too would abandon his cause, and leave him to his fate. In the name of the Apostles Peter replied, that they had still full confidence in his doctrines, as teaching the way to

---

^c John vi. 30.
^d There is some difficulty in placing the conversation with the Pharisees (Matt. xv. 1-20; Mark vii. 1-23), whether before or after the retreat of Jesus to the more remote district. The incident, though characteristic, is not of great importance, and seems rather to have been a private inquiry of certain members of the sect, than the public appeal of persons deputed for that purpose.

eternal life; they still believed him to be the promised Messiah, the Son of God. Jesus received this protestation of fidelity with apparent approbation, but intimated that the time would come when one even of the tried and chosen Twelve would prove a traitor.*

Thus the public life of Jesus closed its second year. On one side endangered by the zeal of the violent, on the other enfeebled by the desertion of so many of his followers, Jesus, so long as he spoke the current language about the Messiah, might be instantly taken at his word, and against his will be set at the head of a

---

* The wavering and uncertainty of the Apostles, and still more of the people, concerning the Messiahship of Jesus, is urged by Strauss as an argument for the later invention and inconsistency of the Gospels. It has always appeared to me one of those marks of true nature and of inartificial composition which would lead to a conclusion directly opposite. The first intimation of the deference and homage shown to him by John at his baptism, grows at once into a welcome rumour that the Christ has appeared. Andrew imparts the joyful tidings to his brother: "We have found the Messias, which is, being interpreted, the Christ;" so Philip, verse 46. But though Jesus in one part of the Sermon on the Mount speaks of himself as the future judge, in general his distinct assumption of that character is exclusively to individuals in private, to the Samaritan woman (John iv. 26-42), and in more ambiguous language, perhaps, in his private examination before the authorities in Jerusalem (John v. 46). Still the manner in which he assumed the title, and asserted his claims, was so totally opposite to Jewish expectation, he appeared to delay so long the open declaration of his Messiahship, that the populace constantly fluctuated in their opinion, now ready by force to make him a king (John vi. 15), immediately after this altogether deserting him, so that even the Apostles' faith is severely tried. (Compare with John vi. 69, Luke ix. 20, Matt. xvi. 16, Mark viii. 29, where it appears that rumours had become prevalent that though not the Messiah, he was either a prophet or a forerunner of the Messiah.) The real test of the fidelity of the Apostles was their adherence, under all the fluctuation of popular opinion, to this conviction, which at last, however, was shaken by that which most completely clashed with their preconceived notions of the Messiah, his ignominious death, and undisturbed burial.

As a corrective to Strauss on this point, I would recommend the work of one who will not be suspected of loose and inaccurate reasoning—Locke on the Reasonableness of Christianity.

daring insurrection; immediately that he departed from it, and rose to the sublimer tone of a purely religious teacher, he excited the most violent animosity even among many of his most ardent adherents. Thus his influence at one moment was apparently most extensive, at the next was confined to but a small circle. Still, however, it held the general mind in unallayed suspense; and the ardent admiration, the attachment of the few, who were enabled to appreciate his character, and the animosity of the many, who trembled at his progress, bore testimony to the commanding authority and the surprising works of Jesus of Nazareth.

CHAPTER VI.

Third Year of the public Life of Jesus.

Passover. THE third Passover had now arrived since Jesus of Nazareth had appeared as a public Teacher, but, as it would seem, "his appointed hour" was not yet come; and, instead of descending with the general concourse of the whole nation to the capital, he remains in Galilee, or rather retires to the remotest extremity of the country; and though he approaches nearer to the northern shore of the lake, never ventures down into the populous region in which he more usually fixed his residence. The avowed hostility of the Jews, and their determination to put him to death; the apparently growing jealousy of Herod, and the desertion of his cause, on one hand, by a great number of his Galilean followers, who had taken offence at his speech in the synagogue of Capernaum, with the rash and intemperate zeal of others who were prepared to force him to assume the royal title, would render his presence at Jerusalem, if not absolutely necessary for his designs, both dangerous and inexpedient.[a] But his absence from this Passover is still more remarkable, if, as appears highly probable, it was at this feast that the event occurred which is alluded to in

---

[a] The commencement of the 8th chapter of St. John's Gospel appears to me to contain a manifest reference to his absence from this Passover. "After these things Jesus walked in Galilee: for he would not walk in Jewry, because the Jews sought to kill him." (ver. 1.) The next verse, as it were, intimating that the Passover was gone by, says, "the Feast of Tabernacles was at hand."

St. Luke [b] as of general notoriety, and at a later period was the subject of a conversation between Jesus and his disciples,—the slaughter of certain Galileans in the Temple of Jerusalem by the Roman governor.[c] The reasons for assigning this fact to the period of the third Passover appear to have considerable weight. Though at all times of the year the Temple was open, not merely for the regular morning and evening offerings, but likewise for the private sacrifices of more devout worshippers, such an event as this massacre was not likely to have occurred, even if Pilate was present at Jerusalem at other times, unless the metropolis had been crowded with strangers, at least in numbers sufficient to excite some apprehension of dangerous tumult. For Pontius Pilate, though prodigal of blood if the occasion seemed to demand the vigorous exercise of power, does not appear to have been wantonly sanguinary. It is, therefore, most probable, that the massacre took place during some public festival; and if so, it must have been either at the Passover or Pentecost, as Jesus was present at both the later feasts of the present year, those of Tabernacles and of the Dedication: nor does the slightest intimation occur of any disturbance of that nature at either.[d] Who these Galileans were, whether they had been guilty of tur-

Massacre of the Galileans at the Passover.

---

[b] John vii. 1.
[c] Luke xiii. 1.
[d] The point of time at which the notice of this transaction is introduced in the narrative of St. Luke, may appear irreconcileable with the opinion that it took place so far back as the previous Passover. This circumstance, however, admits of an easy explanation. The period at which this fact is introduced by St. Luke was just before the last fatal visit to Jerusalem. Jesus had now expressed his fixed determination to attend the approaching Passover; he was actually on his way to the metropolis. It was precisely the time at which some who might take an interest in his personal safety, might think it well to warn him of his danger. These persons may have been actively

bulent and seditious conduct, or were the innocent victims of the governor's jealousy, there is no evidence. It has been suggested, not without plausibility, that they were of the sect of Judas the Galilean; and, however they may not have been formally enrolled as belonging to this sect, they may have been, in some degree, infected with the same opinions; more especially, as properly belonging to the jurisdiction of Herod, these Galileans would scarcely have been treated with such unrelenting severity, unless implicated, or suspected to be implicated, in some designs obnoxious to the Roman sway. If, however, our conjecture be right, had he appeared at this festival, Jesus might have fallen undistinguished in a general massacre of his countrymen, by the direct interference of the Roman governor, and without the guilt of his rejection and death being attributable to the rulers or the nation of the Jews. Speaking according to mere human probability, the Saviour of mankind might have been swept away by a stern act of Roman despotism.

Yet, be that as it may, during this period of the life of Jesus, it is most difficult to trace his course; his rapid changes have the semblance of concealment. At one time He appears at the extreme border of Palestine, the district immediately adjacent to

Concealment of Jesus.

ignorant of his intermediate visits to Jerusalem, which had been sudden, brief, and private. He had appeared unexpectedly; he had withdrawn without notice. They may have supposed, that having been absent at the period of the massacre in the remote parts of the country, he might be altogether unacquainted with the circumstances, or at least little impressed with their importance; or even, if not entirely ignorant, they might think it right to remind him of the dangerous commotion which had taken place at the preceding festival, and to intimate the possibility that under a governor so reckless of human life as Pilate had shown himself, and by recent circumstances not predisposed towards the Galilean name, he was exposing himself to most serious peril.

that of Tyre and Sidon; he then seems to have descended again towards Bethsaida, and the desert country to the north of the Sea of Tiberias; he is then again on the immediate frontiers of Palestine, near the town of Cæsarea Philippi, close to the fountains of the Jordan.

The incidents which occur at almost all these places coincide with his singular situation at this period of his life, and perpetually bear almost a direct reference to the state of public feeling at this particular time. His conduct towards the Greek or Syro-Phœnician woman may illustrate this.[*] Those who watched the motions of Jesus with the greatest vigilance, either from attachment or animosity, must have beheld him with astonishment, at this period when every road was crowded with travellers towards Jerusalem, deliberately proceeding in an opposite direction; thus, at the time of the most solemn festival, moving, as it were, directly contrary to the stream which flowed in one current towards the capital. There appears at one time to have prevailed, among some, an obscure apprehension which, though only expressed during one of his later visits to Jerusalem,[†] might have begun to creep into their minds at an earlier period; that, after all, the Saviour might turn his back on his ungrateful and inhospitable country, or at least not fetter himself with the exclusive nationality inseparable from their conceptions of the true Messiah. And here, at this present instant, after having excited their hopes to the utmost by the miracle which placed him, as it were, on a level with their lawgiver, and having afterwards afflicted them with bitter disappointment by his speech in the synagogue—here, at the season of the Passover,

The Syro-Phoenician woman.

---

[*] Matt. xv. 21-28; Mark vii. 24-30.   [†] John vii. 35.

He was proceeding towards, if not beyond, the borders of the Holy Land; placing himself, as it were, in direct communication with the uncircumcised, and imparting those blessings to strangers and aliens, which were the undoubted, inalienable property of the privileged race.

At this juncture, when He was upon the borders of the territory of Tyre and Sidon, a woman of heathen extraction,* having heard the fame of his miracles, determined to have recourse to him to heal her daughter, who was suffering under diabolic possession. Whether adopting the common title, which she had heard that Jesus had assumed, or from any obscure notion of the Messiah, which could not but have penetrated into the districts immediately bordering on Palestine, she saluted him by his title of Son of David, and implored his mercy. In this instance alone Jesus, who on all other occasions is described as prompt and forward to hear the cry of the afflicted, turns, at first, a deaf and regardless ear to her supplication: the mercy is, as it were, slowly and reluctantly wrung from him. The secret of this apparent, but unusual, indifference to suffering, no doubt lies in the circumstances of the case. Nothing would have been so repugnant to Jewish prejudice, especially at this juncture, as his admitting at once this recognition of his title, or his receiving and rewarding the homage of any stranger from the blood of Israel, particularly one descended from the accursed race of Canaan. The conduct of the Apostles shows their harsh

---

* She is called in one place a Canaanite, in another a Syro-Phœnician and a Greek. She was probably of Phœnician descent, and the Jews considered the whole of the Phœnician race as descended from the remnant of the Canaanites who were not extirpated. She was a Greek as distinguished from a Jew; for the Jews divided mankind into Jews and Greeks, as the Greeks did into Greeks and Barbarians.

and Jewish spirit. They are indignant at her pertinacious importunity; they almost insist on her peremptory dismissal. That a stranger, a Canaanite, should share in the mercies of their Master, does not seem to have entered into their thoughts: the brand of ancient condemnation was upon her: the hereditary hatefulness of the seed of Canaan marked her as a fit object for malediction, as the appropriate prey of the evil spirits, as without hope of blessing from the God of Israel. Jesus himself at first seems to countenance this exclusive tone. He declares that he is sent only to the race of Israel; that dogs (the common and opprobrious term by which all religious aliens were described) could have no hope of sharing in the blessings jealously reserved for the children of Abraham. The humility of the woman's reply, "Truth, Lord, yet the dogs eat of the crumbs which fall from their masters' table," might almost disarm the antipathy of the most zealous Jew. That the Gentiles might receive a kind of secondary and inferior benefit from their Messiah, was by no means in opposition to the vulgar belief; it left the Jews in full possession of their exclusive religious dignity, while it was rather flattering to their pride than debasing to their prejudices, that, with such limitation, the power of their Redeemer should be displayed among Gentile foreigners. By his condescension, therefore, to their prejudices, Jesus was enabled to display his own benevolence, without awakening, or confirming if already awakened, the quick suspicion of his followers.

After this more remote excursion, Jesus appears again, for a short time, nearer his accustomed residence; but still hovering, as it were, on the borders, and lingering rather in the wild mountainous region to the north and east of the lake, than

Jesus still in partial concealment.

descending to the more cultivated and populous districts to the west.ʰ But here his fame follows him; and even in these desert regions, multitudes, many of them bearing their sick and afflicted relatives, perpetually assemble around him.ⁱ His conduct displays, as it were, a continual struggle between his benevolence and his caution. He seems as if he could not refrain from the indulgence of his goodness, while at the same time he is aware that every new cure may reawaken the dangerous enthusiasm from which he had so recently withdrawn himself. In the hill country of Decapolis, a deaf and dumb man is restored to speech; he is strictly enjoined, though apparently without effect, to preserve the utmost secrecy. A second time the starving multitude in the desert appeal to his compassion. They are again miraculously fed; but Jesus, as though remembering the immediate consequences of the former event, dismisses them at once, and crossing in a boat to Dalmanutha or Magdala, places, as it were, the lake between himself and their indiscreet zeal, or irrepressible gratitude.ᵏ At Magdala he again encounters some of the Pharisaic party, who were, perhaps, returned from the Passover. They reiterate their perpetual demand of some sign which may satisfy their impatient incredulity, and a third time Jesus repels them with an allusion to the great "sign" of his resurrection.ᵐ

As the Pentecost draws near, he again retires to the utmost borders of the land. He crosses back to Bethsaida, where a blind man is restored to sight, with the same strict injunctions of concealment.ⁿ He then passes

---

ʰ This may be assigned to the period between the Passover and the Pentecost.
ⁱ Matt. xv. 29–31; Mark vii. 31–37.
ᵏ Matt. xv. 32–39; Mark viii. 1–9.
ᵐ Mart. xvi. 1–12; Mark viii. 11–21.
ⁿ Mark viii. 22–26.

to the neighbourhood of Cæsarea Philippi, at the extreme verge of the land, a modern town, recently built on the site of the older, now named Paneas, situated almost close to the fountains of the Jordan.[o]

Alone with his immediate disciples in this secluded region, he begins to unfold more distinctly, both his real character and his future fate, to their wondering ears. It is difficult to conceive the state of fluctuation and embarrassment in which the simple minds of the Apostles of Jesus must have been continually kept by what must have appeared the inexplicable, if not contradictory, conduct and language of their Master. At one moment he seemed entirely to lift the veil from his own character; the next, it fell again and left them in more than their former state of suspense. Now, all is clear, distinct, comprehensible; then again, dim, doubtful, mysterious. Here their hopes are elevated to the highest, and all their preconceived notions of the greatness of the Messiah seem ripening into reality; there, the strange foreboding of his humiliating fate, which He communicates with more than usual distinctness, thrills them with apprehension. Their own destiny is opened to their prospect, crossed with the same strangely mingling lights and shadows. At one time they are promised miraculous endowments, and seem justified in all their ambitious hopes of eminence and distinction in the approaching kingdom; at the next, they are warned that they must expect to share in the humiliations and afflictions of their Teacher. *Perplexity of the Apostles.*

Near Cæsarea Philippi Jesus questions his disciples as to the common view of his character. By some, it seems, he was supposed to be John the Bap- *Jesus near Cæsarea Philippi.*

---

[o] Mark viii. 27.

tist restored from the dead; by others, Elias, who was to reappear on earth, previous to the final revelation of the Messiah; by others, Jeremiah, who, according to a tradition to which we have before alluded, was to come to life: and when the ardent zeal of Peter recognises him under the most sacred title, which was universally considered as appropriated to the Messiah, "the Christ, the Son of the Living God," his homage is no longer declined; and the Apostle himself is commended in language so strong, that the pre-eminence of Peter over the rest of the twelve has been mainly supported by the words of Jesus, employed on this occasion. The transport of the Apostles at this open and distinct avowal of his character, although at present confined to the secret circle of his more immediate adherents, no doubt before long to be publicly proclaimed and asserted with irresistible power, is almost instantaneously checked. The bright expanding prospects change in a moment to the gloomy reverse, when Jesus proceeds to foretell to a greater number of his followers[p] his approaching lamentable fate, the hostility of all the rulers of the nation, his death, and that which was probably the least intelligible part of the whole prediction—his resurrection.[q] The highly excited Peter cannot endure the sudden and unexpected reverse; he betrays his reluctance to believe that the Messiah, whom he had now, he supposed, full authority to array in the highest temporal splendour which his imagination could suggest, could possibly apprehend so degrading a doom. Jesus not only represses the ardour of the Apostle, but enters at some length into the earthly dangers to which his disciples

---

[p] Mark viii. 34.
[q] Matt. xvi. 21-28; Mark viii. 31, ix. 1; Luke ix. 18-27.

would be exposed, and the unworldly nature of Christian reward. They listened, but how far they comprehended these sublime truths must be conjectured from their subsequent conduct.

It was to minds thus preoccupied, on the one hand full of unrepressed hopes of the instantaneous revelation of the Messiah in all his temporal greatness, on the other embarrassed with the apparently irreconcileable predictions of the humiliation of their Master, that the extraordinary scene of the Transfiguration was presented.[r] Whatever explanation we adopt of this emblematic vision, its purport and its effect upon the minds of the three disciples who beheld it, remain the same.[s] Its significant sights and sounds manifestly announced the equality, the superiority of Jesus to the founder, and to him who may almost be called the restorer of the Theocracy, to Moses the lawgiver, and Elias the representative of the prophets. These holy personages had, as it were, seemed to pay homage to Jesus; they had vanished, and He alone had remained. The appearance of Moses and Elias at the time of the Messiah, was strictly in accordance with the general tradition;[t] and when in his astonishment Peter proposes to make there three of those huts or cabins of boughs,

The Transfiguration.

---

[r] Tradition has assigned this scene to Mount Tabor, probably for no better reason than because Tabor is the best known and most conspicuous height in the whole of Galilee. The order of the narrative points most distinctly to the neighbourhood of Cæsarea Philippi, and the Mons Paneus is a much more probable situation. Dr. Robinson has adduced a conclusive argument against Mount Tabor. The summit of that eminence was then, and for some time after, occupied by a considerable fortified town. iii. 221.

[s] Matt. xvii. 1-21; Mark ix. 2-29; Luke ix. 28-42.

[t] Dixit sanctus benedictus Moai, sicut vitam tuam dedisti pro Israele in hoc seculo, sic tempore futuro, tempore Messiæ, quando mittam ad eos Eliam prophetam vos duo venietis simul. Debar. Rab. 293. Compare Lightfoot, Schoetgen, and Eisenmenger, in loco.

which the Jews were accustomed to run up as temporary dwellings at the time of the Feast of the Tabernacles, he seems to have supposed that the spirits of the lawgiver and the prophet were to make their permanent residence with the Messiah, and that this mountain was to be, as it were, another sacred place, a second Sinai, from which the new kingdom was to commence its dominion, and issue its mandates.

The other circumstances of the transaction, the height on which they stood, their own half-waking state, the sounds from heaven (whether articulate voices or thunder, which appeared to give the divine assent to their own preconceived notions of the Messiah), the wonderful change in the appearance of Jesus, the glittering cloud which seemed to absorb the two spirits, and leave Jesus alone upon the mountain,—all the incidents of this majestic and mysterious scene, whether presented as dreams before their sleeping, or as visions before their waking senses, tended to elevate still higher their already exalted notions of their Master. Again, however, they appear to have been doomed to hear a confirmation of that, which, if their reluctant minds had not refused to entertain the humiliating thought, would have depressed them to utter despondency. After healing the dæmoniac, whom they had in vain attempted to exorcise, the assurance of his approaching death is again renewed, and in the clearest language, by their Master.^a

From the distant and the solitary scenes where these transactions had taken place, Jesus now returns to the populous district about Capernaum. On his entrance into the city, the customary payment of half a shekel for the maintenance of the Temple, a

---

^a Matt. xvii. 22, 23; Mark ix. 30-32; Luke ix. 44, 45.

CONTENTION OF THE APOSTLES.

capitation tax which was levied on every Jew, in every quarter of the world, is demanded of Jesus.[x] How then will He act, who but now declared himself to his disciples as the Messiah, the Son of God? Will he claim his privilege of exemption as the Messiah? Will the Son of God contribute to the maintenance of the Temple of the Father? Or will the long-expected public declaration at length take place? Will the claim of immunity virtually confirm his claim to the privileges of his descent? He again reverts to his former cautious habit of never unnecessarily offending the prejudices of the people; he complies with the demand, and the money is miraculously supplied.

But on the minds of the Apostles the recent scenes are still working with unallayed excitement. The dark, the melancholy language of their Master appears to pass away and leave no impression upon their minds; while every circumstance which animates or exalts, is treasured with the utmost care; and in a short time, on their road to Capernaum, they are fiercely disputing among themselves their relative rank in the instantaneously expected kingdom of the Messiah.[y] The beauty of the significant action by which Jesus repressed the rising emotions of their pride, is heightened by considering it in relation to the immediate circumstances.[z] Even now, at this crisis of their exaltation,

Contention of the Apostles.

Jesus commends a child to the imitation of the Apostles.

---

[x] Matt. xvii. 24-28.

[y] It is observable that the ambitious disputes of the disciples concerning primacy or preference, usually follow the mention of Christ's death and resurrection. Luke ix. 44-46; Matt. xx. 18-20; Luke xxii. 22-24. They had so strong a prepossession that the resurrection of Christ (which they no doubt understood in a purely Jewish sense; compare Mark ix. 10) should introduce the earthly kingdom of the Messiah, that no declaration of our Lord could remove it from their minds: they always " understood not what was spoken." Lightfoot, in loco.

[z] Matt. xviii. 1-6; Mark ix. 33-37.

He takes a child, places it in the midst of them, and declares, that only those in such a state of innocence and docility, are qualified to become members of the new community. Over such humble and blameless beings, over children, and over men of child-like dispositions, the vigilant providence of God would watch with unsleeping care, and those who injured them would be exposed to his strong displeasure.[a] The narrow jealousy of the Apostles, which would have prohibited a stranger from making use of the name of Jesus for the purpose of exorcism, was rebuked in the same spirit: all who would embrace the cause of Christ, were to be encouraged rather than discountenanced. Some of the most striking sentences, and one parable which illustrates in the most vivid manner the extent of Christian forgiveness and mutual forbearance, close, as it were, this period of the Saviour's life, by instilling into the minds of his followers, as the time of the final collision with his adversaries approaches, the milder and more benignant tenets of the evangelic religion.

The Passover had come, and Jesus had remained in the obscure borders of the land; the Pentecost had passed away, and the expected public assumption of the title and functions of the Messiah had not yet been made. The autumnal Feast of Tabernacles[b] is at hand. His incredulous brethren again assemble around him, and even the impatient disciples can no longer endure the suspense: they urge him with almost imperious importunity to cast off at length his prudential, his mysterious reserve; at least to

Feast of Tabernacles.

---

[a] Matt. xviii. 6–10; Mark ix. 37.
[b] On the fifteenth day of the seventh month. Deut. xxiii. 39–43. About the end of our September, or the beginning of October.

vindicate the faith of his followers, and to justify the zeal of his partisans, by displaying those works, which he seemed so studiously to conceal among the obscure towns of Galilee, in the crowded metropolis of the nation at some great period of national assemblage.[c] In order to prevent any indiscreet proclamation of his approach, or any procession of his followers through the country, and probably lest the rulers should have time to organise their hostile measures, Jesus disguises under ambiguous language his intention of going up to Jerusalem; he permits his brethren, who suppose that he is still in Galilee, to set forward without him. Still, however, his movements are the subject of anxious inquiry among the assembling multitudes in the capital; and many secret and half-stifled murmurs among the Galileans, some exalting his virtues, others representing him as a dangerous disturber of the public peace, keep up the general curiosity about his character and designs.[d] On a sudden, in the midst of the festival, he appears in the Temple, and takes his station as a public teacher. The rulers seem to have been entirely off their guard; and the multitude are perplexed by the bold and as yet uninterrupted publicity, with which a man, whom the Sanhedrin were well known to have denounced as guilty of a capital offence, entered the court of the Temple, and calmly pursued his office of instructing the people. The fact that he had taken on himself that office was of itself unprecedented and surprising to many. As has been observed before, he belonged to no school, he had been bred at the feet of none of the recognised and celebrated teachers; yet he assumed superiority to all, and

Jesus in the Temple at Jerusalem.

---

[c] John vii. 2, to viii. 59. [d] John vii. 11-13.

arraigned the whole of the wise men of vain glory rather than of sincere piety. His own doctrine was from a higher source, and possessed more undeniable authority. He even boldly anticipated the charge, which he knew would be renewed against him, his violation of the Sabbath by his works of mercy. He accused his adversaries of conspiring against his life; a charge which seems to have excited indignation as well as astonishment.* The suspense and agitation of the assemblage are described with a few rapid, but singularly expressive, touches. It was part of the vague popular belief, that the Messiah would appear in some strange, sudden, and surprising manner. The circumstances of his coming were thus left to the imagination of each to fill up, according to his own notions of that which was striking and magnificent. But the extraordinary incidents which attended the birth of Jesus were forgotten, or had never been generally known; his origin and extraction were supposed to be ascertained; he appeared but as the legitimate descendant of a humble Galilean family; his acknowledged brethren were ordinary and undistinguished men. "We know this man whence he is; but when Christ cometh no man knoweth whence he is." His mysterious allusions to his higher descent were heard with mingled feelings of indignation and awe. On the multitude his wonderful works had made a favourable impression, which was not a little increased by the inactivity and hesitation of the rulers. The Sanhedrin, in which the Pharisaic party still predominated, were evidently unprepared, and had concerted no measures either to counteract his progress in the public mind, or to secure

---

* John vii. 19-24.

his person. Their authority in such a case was probably, in the absence of the Roman prefect, or without the concurrence of the commander of the Roman guard in the Antonia, by no means clearly ascertained. With every desire, therefore, for his apprehension, they at first respected his person, and their non-interference was mistaken for connivance at, if not as a sanction for his proceedings. They determine at length on stronger measures; their officers are sent out to arrest the offender, but seem to have been overawed by the tranquil dignity and commanding language of Jesus, and were perhaps in some degree controlled by the manifest favour of the people.[f]

On the great day of the feast the agitation of the assembly, as well as the perplexity of the Sanhedrin, is at its height. Jesus still appears publicly; he makes a striking allusion to the ceremonial of the day. Water was drawn from the hallowed fountain of Siloah, and borne into the Temple with the sound of the trumpet and with great rejoicing. "Who," say the Rabbins, "hath not seen the rejoicing on the drawing of this water, hath seen no rejoicing at all." They sang in the procession, "With joy shall they draw water from the wells of salvation."[g] In the midst of this tumult, Jesus, according to his custom, calmly diverts the attention to the great moral end of his own teaching, and in allusion to the rite, declares that from himself are to flow the real living waters of salvation. The ceremony almost appears to have been arrested in its progress; and open discussions of his claims to be considered as the Messiah divide the wondering multitude. The Sanhedrin find that they cannot depend on their own officers, whom

[f] John vii. 32.   [g] John vii. 32-39; Lightfoot, in loco.

they accuse of surrendering themselves to the popular deception, in favour of one condemned by the rulers of the nation. Even within their council, Nicodemus, the secret proselyte of Jesus, ventures to interfere in his behalf; and though, with the utmost caution, he appeals to the law, and asserts the injustice of condemning Jesus without a hearing (he seems to have desired that Jesus might be admitted publicly to plead his own cause before the Sanhedrin), he is accused by the more violent of leaning to the Galilean party—the party which bore its own condemnation in the simple fact of adhering to a Galilean prophet. The council dispersed without coming to any decision.

On the next day (for the former transactions had taken place in the earlier part of the week), the last, the most crowded and solemn day of the festival, a more insidious attempt is made, whether from a premeditated or fortuitous circumstance, to undermine the growing popularity of Jesus; an attempt to make him assume a judicial authority in the case of a woman taken in the act of adultery. Such an act would probably have been resisted by the whole Sanhedrin as an invasion of their province; and as it appeared that he must acquit or condemn the criminal, in either case he would give an advantage to his adversaries. If he inclined to severity, they might be able, notwithstanding the general benevolence of his character, to contrast their own leniency in the administration of the law (this was the characteristic of the Pharisaic party, which distinguished them from the Sadducees, and of this the Rabbinical writings furnish many curious illustrations) with the rigour of the new teacher, and thus to conciliate the naturally compassionate feelings of the people, which would have been

Woman taken in adultery.

shocked by the unusual spectacle of a woman suffering death, or even condemned to capital punishment, for such an offence. If, on the other hand, he acquitted her, he abrogated the express letter of the Mosaic statute; and the multitude might be inflamed by this new evidence of that which the ruling party had constantly endeavoured to instil into their minds, the hostility of Jesus to the Law of their forefathers, and his secret design of abolishing the long-reverenced and heaven-enacted code.[b] Nothing can equal, if the expression may be ventured, the address of Jesus, in extricating himself from this difficulty; his turning the current of popular odium, or even contempt, upon his assailants; the manner in which, by summoning them to execute the law, he extorts a tacit confession of their own loose morals,—" He that is without sin among you, let him first cast a stone at her" (this being the office of the chief accuser),—and finally shows mercy to the accused, without in the least invalidating the decision of the Law against the crime, yet not without the most gentle and effective moral admonition.

After this discomfiture of his opponents, Jesus appears to have been permitted to pursue his course of teaching undisturbed, until new circumstances occurred to inflame the resentment of his enemies. He had taken his station in a part of the Temple court called the Treasury. His language became more mysterious, yet at the same time more authoritative—more full of those allusions to his character as the Messiah, to his divine descent, and at length to his pre-existence.

Jesus teaches in the Temple.

---

[b] Grotius has a different view:— Ut eum accusarent aut apud Romanos imminutæ majestatis, aut apud populum imminutæ libertatis. That they might accuse him to the Romans of encroaching on their authority, or to the people of surrendering their rights and independence.

The former of these were in some degree familiar to the popular conception; the latter, though it entered into the higher notion of the Messiah, which was prevalent among those who entertained the loftiest views of his character, nevertheless, from the manner in which it was expressed, jarred with the harshest discord upon the popular ear. They listened with patience to Jesus while He proclaimed himself the light of the world: though they questioned his right to assume the title of "Son of the Heavenly Father" without further witness than He had already produced, they yet permitted him to proceed in his discourse: they did not interrupt him when He still further alluded, in dark and ambiguous terms, to his own fate: when He declared that God was with him, and that his doctrines were pleasing to the Almighty Father, a still more favourable impression was made, and many openly espoused his belief; but when He touched on their rights and privileges as descendants of Abraham, the subject on which above all they were most jealous and sensitive, the collision became inevitable. He spoke of their freedom, the moral freedom from the slavery of their own passions, to which they were to be exalted by the revelation of the truth; but freedom was a word which to them only bore another sense. They broke in at once with indignant denial that the race of Abraham, although the Roman troops were guarding their Temple, had ever forfeited their national independence.[1] He spoke as if the legitimacy of their descent from Abraham depended not on their hereditary genealogy, but on the moral evidence of their similarity in virtue to their great forefather. The good, the pious, the gentle Abraham

---

[1] John viii. 33.

was not the father of those who were meditating the murder of an innocent man. If their fierce and sanguinary disposition disqualified them from being the children of Abraham, how much more from being, as they boasted, the adopted children of God! The spirit of evil, in whose darkest and most bloody temper they were ready to act, was rather the parent of men with dispositions so diabolic.[k] At this their wrath bursts forth in more unrestrained vehemence; the worst and most bitter appellations by which a Jew could express his hatred, are heaped on Jesus; he is called a Samaritan, and declared to be under dæmoniac possession. But when Jesus proceeds to assert his title to the Messiahship, by proclaiming that Abraham had received some intimation of the future great religious revolution to be effected by him; when he who was " not fifty years old " (that is, not arrived at that period when the Jews, who assumed the public offices at thirty, were released from them on account of their age) declared that he had existed before Abraham; when He thus placed himself not merely on an equality with, but asserted his immeasurable superiority to, the great father of their race; when He uttered the awful and significant words which identified him, as it were, with Jehovah, the great self-existent Deity, "Before Abraham was, I am," they immediately rushed forward to crush without trial, without further hearing, him whom they considered the self-convicted blasphemer. As there was always some work of building or repair going on within the Temple, which was not considered to be finished till many years after, these instruments for the fulfilment of the legal punishment were immediately at

---

[k] John viii. 44.

hand; and Jesus only escaped from being stoned on the spot by passing (we know not how), during the wild and frantic tumult, through the midst of his assailants, and withdrawing from the court of the Temple.

But even in this exigency he pauses at no great distance to perform an act of mercy.[m] There was a man, notoriously blind from his birth, who seems to have taken his accustomed station in some way leading to the Temple. Some of the disciples of Jesus had accompanied Him, and perhaps, as it were, covered his retreat from his furious assailants; and by this time, probably, being safe from pursuit, they

Healing the blind man.

---

[m] I hesitate at the arrangement of no passage in the whole narrative more than this history of the blind man. Many harmonists have placed it during the visit of Jesus to Jerusalem, at the Feast of Dedication. The connexion in the original, however, seems more natural, as a continuation of the preceding incident; yet at first sight it seems extremely improbable that Jesus should have time during his hurried escape to work this miracle; and still more that he should again encounter his enraged adversaries without dangerous or fatal consequences. We may, however, suppose that this incident took place without the Temple, probably in the street leading down from the Temple to the Valley of Kidron, and to Bethany, where Jesus spent the night. The attempt to stone him was an outburst of popular tumult: it is clear that he had been guilty of no offence, legally capital, or it would have been urged against him at his last trial, since witnesses could not have been wanting to his words; and it seems quite as clear that, however they might have been glad to have availed themselves of any such ebullition of popular violence, as a court, the Sanhedrin, divided and in awe of the Roman power, was constrained to proceed with regularity and according to the strict letter of the law. Macknight would place the cure immediately after the escape from the Temple, the recognition of the man, and the subsequent proceedings, during the visit at the Dedication. But in fact the popular feeling seems to have been in a perpetual state of fluctuation. At one instant violent indignation was inflamed by the language of Jesus; at the next, some one of the Saviour's extraordinary works seems to have caused as strong a sensation, at least with a considerable party, in his favour.

stopped near the place where the blind man stood. The whole history of the cure of this blind man is remarkable, as singularly illustrative of Jewish feeling and opinion, and on account both of the critical juncture at which it took place, and the strict judicial investigation which it seems to have undergone before the hostile Sanhedrin. The common popular belief ascribed every malady or affliction to some sin, of which it was the direct and providential punishment—a notion, as we have before hinted, of all others, the most likely to harden the bigoted heart to indifference, or even contempt and abhorrence of the heaven-visited, and therefore heaven-branded, sufferer. This notion, which however was so overpowered by the strong spirit of nationalism as to obtain for the Jews in foreign countries the admiration of the heathen for their mutual compassion towards each other, while they had no kindly feeling for strangers, no doubt, from the language of Jesus on many occasions, exercised a most pernicious influence on the general character in their native land, where the lessons of Christian kindliness and humanity appear to have been as deeply needed as they were unacceptable. But how was this notion of the penal nature of all suffering to be reconciled with the fact of a man being born subject to one of the most grievous afflictions of our nature—the want of sight? They were thus thrown back upon those other singular notions which prevailed among the Jews of that period —either his fathers or himself must have sinned. Was it, then, a malady inherited from the guilt of his parents? or was the soul, having sinned in a preexistent state, now expiating its former offences in the present form of being? This notion, embraced by Plato in the West, was more likely to have been derived by the Jews from the East,[a] where it may be regularly traced from India through the different Oriental religions. Jesus at once corrected this inveterate error, and having anointed the eyes of the blind man with clay, sent him to wash in the celebrated pool of Siloam, at no great distance from the Street of the Temple. The return of the blind man, restored to sight, excited so much astonishment, that the bystanders began to dispute whether he was really the same who had been so long familiarly known. The man set their doubts at rest by declaring himself to be the same. The Sanhedrin, now so actively watching the actions of Jesus, and indeed inflamed to the utmost resentment, had no course but, if possible, to invalidate the effect of such a miracle on the public mind; they hoped either to detect some collusion between the parties, or to throw suspicion on the whole transaction: at all events the case was so public, that they could not avoid bringing it under the cognisance of their tribunal. The man was summoned, and, as it happened to have been the Sabbath,[b] the stronger Pharisaic party were in hopes of getting rid of the question altogether by the immediate decision, that a man guilty of a violation of the Law could not act under the sanction of God. But a considerable party in the Sanhedrin were still either too prudent, too just, or too much impressed by the evidence of the case, to concur in so summary a sentence.

---

[a] It may be traced in the Egypto-Jewish book of the Wisdom of Solomon, viii. 19, 20. The Pharisees' notion of the transmigration of souls may be found in Josephus, Ant. xviii. 1.

[b] It is a curious coincidence that anointing a blind man's eyes on the Sabbath is expressly forbidden in the Jewish traditional law. Kuinoel, in loc. According to Grotius, opening the eyes of the blind was an acknowledged sign of the Messiah. Midrash in Psalm cxlvi. 8, Isai. xlii. 7; it was a miracle never known to be wrought by Moses or by any other prophet.

This decision of the council appears to have led to a more close investigation of the whole transaction. The first object appears to have been, by questioning the man himself, to implicate him as an adherent of Jesus, and so to throw discredit upon his testimony. The man, either from caution or ignorance of the character assumed by Jesus, merely replied that he believed him to be a prophet. Baffled on this point, the next step of the Pharisaic party is to inquire into the reality of the malady and the cure. The parents of the blind man are examined; their deposition simply affirms the fact of their son having been born blind, and having received his sight; for it was now notorious that the Sanhedrin had threatened all the partisans of Jesus with the terrible sentence of excommunication; and the timid parents, trembling before this awful tribunal, refer the judges to their son for all further information on this perilous question.

The further proceedings of the Sanhedrin are still more remarkable: unable to refute the fact of the miraculous cure, they endeavour, nevertheless, to withhold from Jesus all claim upon the gratitude of him whom he had relieved, and all participation in the power with which the instantaneous cure was wrought. The man is exhorted to give praise for the blessing to God alone, and to abandon the cause of Jesus of Nazareth, whom they authoritatively denounce as a sinner. He rejoins, with straightforward simplicity, that he merely deposes to the fact of his own blindness, and to his having received his sight: on such high questions as the character of Jesus, he presumes not at first to dispute with the great legal tribunal, with the chosen wisdom of the nation. Wearied, however, at length with their pertinacious examination, the man

seems to discover the vantage ground on which he
stands; the altercation becomes more spirited on his
part, more full of passionate violence on theirs. He
declares that he has already again and again repeated
the circumstances of the transaction, and that it is in
vain for them to question him further, unless they are
determined, if the truth of the miracle should be
established, to acknowledge the divine mission of Jesus.
This seems to have been the object at which the more
violent party in the Sanhedrin aimed; so far to throw
him off his guard, as to make him avow himself the
partisan of Jesus, and by this means to shake his whole
testimony. On the instant they begin to revile him, to
appeal to the popular clamour, to declare him a secret
adherent of Jesus, while they were the steadfast disciples
of Moses. God was acknowledged to have spoken by
Moses, and to compare Jesus with him was inexpiable
impiety—Jesus, of whose origin they professed themselves ignorant. The man rejoins in still bolder terms,
"Why, herein is a marvellous thing, that ye know not
from whence he is, but yet he hath opened mine eyes."
He continues in the same strain openly to assert his
conviction that no man, unless commissioned by God,
could work such wonders. Their whole history, abound-
ing as it did with extraordinary events, displayed
nothing more wonderful than that which had so recently
taken place in his person. This daring and disrespectful
language excites the utmost indignation in the whole
assembly. They revert to the popular opinion, that
the blindness with which the man was born, was a
proof of his having been accursed of God. "Thou wast
altogether born in sin, and dost thou teach us?" God
marked thy very birth, thy very cradle, with the
indelible sign of his displeasure; and therefore the

testimony of one branded by the wrath of Heaven can be of no value. Forgetful that even on their own principle, if, by being born blind, the man was manifestly an object of the divine anger, his gaining his sight was an evidence equally unanswerable of the divine favour. But while they traced the hand of God in the curse, they refused to trace it in the blessing; to close the eyes was a proof of divine power, but to open them none whatever. The fearless conduct, however, of the man appears to have united the divided council; the formal and terrible sentence of excommunication was pronounced, probably for the first time, against any adherent of Jesus. The Evangelist concludes the narrative, as if to show that the man was not as yet a declared disciple of Christ, with a second interview between the blind man and Jesus, in which Jesus openly accepted the title of the Messiah, the Son of God, and received the homage of the now avowed adherent. Nor did Jesus discontinue his teaching on account of this declared interposition of the Sanhedrin; his manifest superiority throughout this transaction rather appears to have caused a new schism in the council, which secured him from any violent measures on their part, until the termination of the festival.

Another collision takes place with some of the Pharisaic party, with whom he now seems scarcely to keep any measure: he openly denounces them as misleading the people, and declares himself the "one true Shepherd." Whither Jesus retreated after this conflict with the ruling powers, we have no distinct information—most probably however into Galilee;[9] nor

---

[9] From this period the difficulty of arranging a consistent chronological narrative out of the separate relations of the Evangelists, increases to the

is it possible with certainty to assign those events, which filled up the period between the autumnal Feast of Tabernacles and that of the Dedication of the Temple, which took place in the winter.

Now, however, Jesus appears more distinctly to have avowed his determination not to remain in his more concealed and private character in Galilee: but when the occasion should demand, when, at the approaching Passover, the whole nation should be assembled in the metropolis, He would confront them, and at length bring his acceptance or rejection to a crisis.[q] He now, at times at least, assumes greater state; messengers are sent before him to proclaim his arrival in the different towns and villages; and as the Feast of Dedication draws near, He approaches the borders of Samaria, and sends forward some of his followers into a neighbouring village, to announce his approach.[r] Whether the Samaritans may have entertained some hopes, from the rumour of his former proceedings in their country, that, persecuted by the Jews, and avowedly opposed to the leading parties in Jerusalem, the Lord might espouse their party in the national quarrel, and were therefore instigated by disappointment as well as jealousy; or whether it was merely an

Near Samaria.

---

greatest degree. Mr. Greswell, to establish his system, is actually obliged to make Jesus, when the Samaritans refuse to receive him because "his face was as though he would go to Jerusalem," to be travelling absolutely in the opposite direction. He likewise, in my opinion, on quite unsatisfactory grounds, endeavours to prove that the "village of Martha and Mary was not Bethany." Any arrangement which places (Luke x. 38-42) the scene in the house of Mary and Martha, *after* the raising of Lazarus, appears highly improbable.

[q] By taking the expression of St. Luke, "he stedfastly set his face to go to Jerusalem," in this more general sense, many difficulties, if not avoided, are considerably diminished.

[r] Luke ix. 51-56.

accidental outburst of the old irreconcileable feud, the inhospitable village refused to receive him.* The disciples were now elate with the expectation of the approaching crisis; on their minds all the dispiriting predictions of the fate of their Master passed away without the least impression; they were indignant that their triumphant procession should be arrested; and with these more immediate and peculiar motives mingled, no doubt, the implacable spirit of national hostility. They thought that the hour of vengeance was now come; that even their gentle Master would rescnt on these deadliest foes of the race of Israel, this deliberate insult on his dignity; that, as He had in some respects resembled the ancient prophets, He would now not hesitate to assume that fiercer and more terrific majesty, with which, according to their ancient histories, these holy men had at times been avenged; they entreated their Master to call down fire from heaven to consume the village. Jesus simply replied by a sentence, which at once established the incalculable difference between his own religion and that which it was to succeed. This sentence, most truly sublime and most characteristic of the evangelic religion, ever since the establishment of Christianity has been struggling to maintain its authority against the still-reviving Judaism, which, inseparable it would seem from unci-

---

* The attendance of the Jews at the Feast of the Dedication, a solemnity of more recent institution, was not unlikely to be still more obnoxious to the possessors of the rival temple than the other great national feasts. This consideration, in the want of more decisive grounds, may be some argument for placing this event at the present period. I find that Doddridge had before suggested this allusion. The inhabitants of Ginæa (Josephus, Ant. xx. ch. 6) fell on certain Galilæans proceeding to Jerusalem for one of the feasts, and slew many of them.

vilised and unchristian man, has constantly endeavoured to array the Deity, rather in his attributes of destructive power than of preserving mercy: "The Son of Man is not come to destroy men's lives, but to save them." So speaking He left the inhospitable Samaritans unharmed, and calmly passed to another village.

It appears to me probable that He here left the direct road to the metropolis through Samaria, and turned aside to the district about Scythopolis and the valley of the Jordan, and most likely crossed into Peræa.[1] From hence, if not before, He sent out his messengers with greater regularity,[2] and, it might seem, to keep up some resemblance with the established institutions of the nation, He chose the number of Seventy, a number already sanctified in the notions of the people, as that of the great Sanhedrin of the nation, who deduced their own origin and authority from the Council of Seventy, established by Moses in the wilderness. The Seventy after a short absence returned and made a favourable report of the influence which they had obtained over the people.[3] The language of Jesus, both in his charge to his disciples and in his observations on the report of their success, appears to indicate the still approaching crisis; it would seem that even the towns in which He had wrought his mightiest works, Chorazin, Bethsaida, and Capernaum, at least the general mass of the people, and the influential rulers, now had declared against him. They are condemned in terms of unusual severity for their blindness; yet among the meek and humble He had a still increasing

---

[1] After the visit to Jerusalem at the Feast of the Dedication, he went again (John x. 40) into the country beyond Jordan; he must therefore have been there before the Feast.
[2] Luke x. 1-16.
[3] Ibid. 17-20.

hold—and the days were now at hand, which the disciples were permitted to behold, and for which the wise and good for many ages had been looking forward with still baffled hopes.[7]

It was during the absence of the Seventy, or immediately after their return, that Jesus, who perhaps had visited in the interval many towns and villages both of Galilee and Peræa, which his central position near the Jordan commanded, descended to the winter Festival of the Dedication.[8] Once it is clear that He drew near to Jerusalem, at least as near as the village of Bethany; and though not insensible to the difficulties of this view, I cannot but think that this village, about two miles' distance from Jerusalem, and the house of the relations of Lazarus, was the place where He was concealed during both his two later unexpected and secret visits to the metropolis, and where He in general passed the nights during the week of the last Passover.[9] His appearance

Feast of Dedication. Jesus again in Jerusalem.

---

[7] Luke x. 24. The parable of the Good Samaritan may gain in impressiveness if considered in connexion with the recent transactions in Samaria, and as perhaps delivered during the journey to Jerusalem, near the place where the scene is laid—the wild and dangerous country between Jericho and Jerusalem.

[8] This feast was instituted by Judas Maccabæus, 1 Macc. 4, 5. It was kept on the 25th of the month Cisleu, answering to our 15th of December. The houses were illuminated at night during the whole period of the feast, which lasted eight days. John x. 22-39.

[9] In connecting Luke x. 38-42 with John x. 22-39, there is the obvious difficulty of the former Evangelist mentioning the comparatively unimportant circumstance which he relates, and being entirely silent about the latter. But this objection is common to all harmonies of the Gospels. The silence of the three former Evangelists concerning the events in Jerusalem is equally remarkable, under every system, whether, according to Bishop Marsh and the generality of the great German scholars, we suppose the Evangelists to have compiled from a common document, or adhere to any of the older theories, that each wrote either entirely independently or as supplementary to the preceding Evangelists.

at this festival seems to have been, like the former, sudden and unlooked-for. The multitude probably at this time was not so great, both on account of the season, and because the festival was kept in other places besides Jerusalem,[b] though of course with the greatest splendour and concourse in the Temple itself. Jesus was seen walking in one of the porticoes or arcades which surrounded the outer court of the Temple, that to the east, which from its greater splendour, being formed of a triple instead of a double row of columns, was called by the name of Solomon's. The leading Jews, whether unprepared for more violent measures, or with some insidious design, now address him, seemingly neither in a hostile nor unfriendly tone. It almost appears, that having before attempted force, they are now inclined to try the milder course of persuasion; their language sounds like the expostulation of impatience. Why, they inquire, does He thus continue to keep up this strange excitement? Why thus persist in endangering the public peace? Why does He not avow himself at once? Why does He not distinctly assert himself to be the Christ, and by some signal, some public, some indisputable, evidence of his being the Messiah, at once set at rest the doubts, and compose the agitation of the troubled nation? The answer of Jesus is an appeal to the wonderful works which he had already wrought; but this evidence the Jews, in their present state and disposition of mind, were morally incapable of appreciating. He had already avowed himself, but in language unintelligible to their ears; a few had heard him, a few would receive the reward of their obedience, and those few were, in the simple

---

[b] Lightfoot, in loco.

phrase, the sheep who heard his voice. But as he proceeded, his language assumed a higher, a more mysterious, tone. He spoke of his unity with the great Father of the worlds. "I and my Father are one."[c] However understood, his words sounded to the Jewish ears so like direct blasphemy, as again to justify on the spot the summary punishment of the Law. Without further trial they prepared to stone him where he stood. Jesus arrested their fury on the instant by a calm appeal to the manifest moral goodness, as well as the physical power, of the Deity displayed in his works. The Jews in plain terms accused him of blasphemously ascribing to himself the title of God. He replied by reference to their sacred books, in which they could not deny that the divine name was sometimes ascribed to beings of an inferior rank; how much less, therefore, ought they to be indignant at that sacred name being assumed by him, in whom the great attributes of divinity, both the power and the goodness, had thus manifestly appeared! His wonderful works showed the intercommunion of nature, in this respect, between himself and the Almighty. This explanation, far beyond their moral perceptions, only excited a new burst of fury, which Jesus eluded, and, retiring again from the capital, returned to the district beyond the Jordan.

The three months which elapsed between the Feast of Dedication and the Passover[d] were no doubt occupied in excursions, if not in regular progresses, through the different districts of the Holy Land, on both sides of the river, which his central position, near one of the most cele-

Period between the Feast of Dedication and the Passover.

[c] John x. 20.
[d] Luke xi. xii. xiii. to verse 30; also to xviii. 34; Matt. xix. xx. to verse 28; Mark x. 1-31.

brated fords, was extremely well suited to command. Wherever he went, multitudes assembled around him; and at one time the government of Herod was seized with alarm, and Jesus received information that his life was in danger, and that he might apprehend the same fate which had befallen John the Baptist if he remained in Galilee or Perœa, both which districts were within the dominions of Herod. It is remarkable that this intelligence came from some of the Pharisaic party,[*] whether suborned by Herod, thus peacefully, and without incurring any further unpopularity, to rid his dominions of one who might become either the designing or the innocent cause of tumult and confusion (the reflection of Jesus on the crafty character of Herod[f] may confirm the notion that the Pharisees were acting under his insidious direction), or whether the Pharisaic party were of themselves desirous to force Jesus, before the Passover arrived, into the province of Judæa, where the Roman government might either, of itself, be disposed to act with decision, or might grant permission to the Sanhedrin to interpose its authority with the utmost rigour. But it was no doubt in this quarter that he received intelligence of a very different nature, that led to one of his preternatural works, which of itself was the most extraordinary, and evidently made the deepest impression upon the public mind.[g] The

---

[*] Luke xiii. 31-35.

[f] Wetstein has struck out the character of Herod with great strength and truth:—"Hic, ut plerique ejus temporis principes et præsides, morex ad exemplum Tiberii imperatoris, qui nullam ex virtutibus suis magis quam dissimulationem diligebat, composuit; tum autem erat annos vulpes, cum jam triginta annos principatum gessisset, et diversissimas personas egisset, personam servi apud Tiberium, domini apud Galilæam, amici Sejano, Artabano, fratribus suis Archelao, Philippo, Herodi alteri, quorum studia erant diversissima, et inter se et a studiis Herodis ipsius." In loc.

[g] John xi. 1-16.

raising of Lazarus may be considered the proximate cause of the general conspiracy for his death, by throwing the popular feeling more decidedly on his side, and thereby deepening the fierce animosity of the rulers, who now saw that they had no alternative but to crush him at once, or to admit his triumph.

We have supposed that it was at the house of Lazarus, or of his relatives, in the village of Bethany, that Jesus had passed the nights during his recent visits to Jerusalem. At some distance from the metropolis he receives information of the dangerous illness of that faithful adherent, whom he seems to have honoured with peculiar attachment. He at first assures his followers in ambiguous language of the favourable termination of the disorder; and after two days' delay, notwithstanding the remonstrances of his disciples, who feared that he was precipitately rushing, as it were, into the toils of his enemies, and who resolve to accompany him, though in acknowledged apprehension that his death was inevitable, Jesus first informs his disciples of the actual death of Lazarus, yet, nevertheless, persists in his determination of visiting Bethany. On his arrival at Bethany the dead man, who according to Jewish usage had no doubt been immediately buried, had been four days in the sepulchre. The house was full of Jews, who had come to console, according to their custom, the afflicted relatives; and the characters assigned in other parts of the history to the two sisters, are strikingly exemplified in their conduct on this mournful occasion. The more active Martha hastens to meet Jesus, laments his absence at the time of her brother's death, and, on his declaration of the resurrection of her brother, reverts only to the general resurrection of mankind, a truth embodied in a

Raising of Lazarus.

certain sense in the Jewish creed. So far Christ answers in language which intimates his own close connexion with that resurrection of mankind. The gentler Mary falls at the feet of Jesus, and with many tears expresses the same confidence in his power, had he been present, of averting her brother's death. So deep, however, is their reverence, that neither of them ventures the slightest word of expostulation at his delay; nor does either appear to have entertained the least hope of further relief. The tears of Jesus himself (for *Jesus wept*) appear to confirm the notion that the case is utterly desperate; and some of the Jews, in a less kindly spirit, begin to murmur at his apparent neglect of a friend, to whom, nevertheless, he appears so tenderly attached. It might seem that it was in the presence of some of these persons, by no means well disposed to his cause, that Jesus proceeded to the sepulchre, summoned the dead body to arise, and was obeyed.

The intelligence of this inconceivable event spread with the utmost rapidity to Jerusalem. The Sanhedrin was instantly summoned, and a solemn debate commenced, finally to decide on their future proceedings towards Jesus. It had now become evident that his progress in the popular belief must be at once arrested, or the power of the Sanhedrin, the influence of the Pharisaic party, was lost for ever. With this may have mingled, in minds entirely ignorant of the real nature of the new religion, an honest and conscientious, though blind, dread of some tumult or insurrection taking place, which would give the Romans an excuse for wresting away the lingering semblance of national independence, to which they adhered with such passionate attachment. The high priesthood was now filled by Caiaphas, the son-in-law of Annas or Ananus; for the Roman governors, as has been said, since the expulsion of Archelaus, either in the capricious or venal wantonness of power, or from jealousy of his authority, had perpetually deposed and reappointed this chief civil and religious magistrate of the nation. Caiaphas threw the weight of his official influence into the scale of the more decided and violent party; and endeavoured, as it were, to give an appearance of patriotism to the meditated crime, by declaring the expediency of sacrificing one life, even though innocent, for the welfare of the whole nation.[h] His language was afterwards treasured in the memory of the Christians, as inadvertently prophetic of the more extensive benefits derived to mankind by the death of their Master. The death of Jesus was deliberately decreed; but Jesus for the present avoided the gathering storm, withdrew from the neighbourhood of the metropolis, and retired to Ephraim, on the border of Judæa, near the wild and mountainous region which divided Judæa from Samaria.[i]

[h] John xi. 47-53. [i] John xi. 54.

CHAPTER VII.

The last Passover.—The Crucifixion.

Last Passover.

THE Passover rapidly approached; the roads from all quarters were already crowded with the assembling worshippers. It is difficult for those who are ignorant of the extraordinary power which local religious reverence holds over Southern and Asiatic nations, to imagine the state of Judæa and of Jerusalem at the time of this great periodical festival.* The rolling onward of countless and gathering masses of population to some of the temples in India; the caravans from all quarters of the Eastern world, which assemble at Mecca during the Holy Season; the multitudes which formerly flowed to Loreto or Rome at the great ceremonies, when the Roman Catholic religion held its unenfeebled sway over the mind of Europe—do not surpass, perhaps scarcely equal, the sudden, simultaneous confluence, not of the population of a single city, but of the whole Jewish nation, towards the capital of Judæa at the time of the Passover. Dispersed as they were throughout the world, it was not only the great mass of the inhabitants of Palestine, but many foreign Jews who thronged from every quarter—from Babylonia, from Arabia, from Egypt,

---

* Μύριοι ἀπὸ μυρίων ὅσων πόλεων, οἱ μὲν διὰ γῆς, οἱ δὲ διὰ θαλάττης, ἐξ ἀνατολῆς καὶ δύσεως, καὶ ἄρκτου καὶ μεσημβρίας, καθ᾽ ἑκάστην ἑορτὴν εἰς τὸ ἱερὸν καταίρουσιν. Philo, de Monarch. 821.

from Asia Minor and Greece, from Italy, probably even from Gaul and Spain. Some notion of the density and vastness of the multitude may be formed from the calculation of Josephus, who, having ascertained the number of paschal lambs sacrificed on one of these solemn occasions, which amounted to 256,500,[b] and assigning the ordinary number to a company who could partake of the same victim, estimated the total number of the pilgrims and residents in Jerusalem at 2,700,000. Through all this concourse of the whole Jewish race, animated more or less profoundly, according to their peculiar temperament, with the same national and religious feelings, rumours about the appearance, the conduct, the pretensions, the language of Jesus, could not but have spread abroad, and be communicated with unchecked rapidity. The utmost anxiety prevails throughout the whole crowded city and its neighbourhood, to ascertain whether this new prophet—this more, perhaps, than prophet—will, as it were, confront at this solemn period the assembled nation; or, as on the last occasion, remain concealed in the remote parts of the country. The Sanhedrin are on their guard, and strict injunctions are issued that they may receive the earliest intelligence of his approach, in order that they may arrest him before He has attempted to make any impression on the multitude.[c]

Already Jesus had either crossed the Jordan, or

---

[b] Or, according to Mr. Greswell's reading, 266,500. I must confess that my general scepticism as to the numbers in the Jewish history extends to this calculation.

The number and the space, embracing within that space all the adjacent villages, compared together, seem to me altogether irreconcileable with reason and probability. Still I doubt not the fact of an uncalculated and incalculable concourse.

[c] John xi. 55, 57.

descended from the hill country to the north. He had passed through Jericho, where he had been recognised by two blind men as the Son of David, the title of the Messiah probably the most prevalent among the common people; and instead of disclaiming the homage, he had rewarded the avowal by the restoration of their sight to the suppliants.[d]

Zaccheus. On his way from Jericho to Jerusalem, but much nearer to the metropolis, He was hospitably received in the house of a wealthy publican named Zaccheus, who had been so impressed with the report of his extraordinary character, that, being of small stature, he had climbed a tree by the road-side to see him pass by; and had evinced the sincerity of his belief in the just and generous principles of the new faith, both by giving up at once half of his property to the poor, and offering the amplest restitution to those whom he might have oppressed in the exercise of his function as a publican.[e] The noblest homage to the power of the new faith! It is probable that Jesus passed the night, perhaps the whole of the Sabbath, in the house of Zaccheus, and set forth, on the first day of the week, through the villages of Bethphage and Bethany to Jerusalem.

Let us, however, before we trace his progress, pause to ascertain, if possible, the actual state of feeling at this precise period, among the different ranks and orders of the Jews.

Jesus of Nazareth had now, for three years, assumed the character of a public teacher; his wonderful works were generally acknowledged; all no doubt considered him as an extraordinary being; but whether he was the

---

[d] Matt. xx. 30; Mark x. 46; Luke xviii. 35.   [e] Luke xix. 1-10.

Messiah still, as it were, hung in the balance. His language, plain enough to those who could comprehend the real superiority, the real *divinity* of his character, was necessarily dark and ambiguous to those who were insensible to the moral and spiritual beauty of his words and actions. Few, perhaps, beyond his more immediate followers, looked upon him with implicit faith; many with doubt, even with hope; perhaps still greater numbers, comprising the more turbulent of the lower class, and almost all the higher and more influential, with incredulity, if not with undisguised animosity. For, though thus for three years He had kept the public mind in suspense as to his being the promised Redeemer, of those circumstances to which the popular passions had looked forward as the only certain signs of the Messiah's coming; those, which among the mass of the community were considered inseparable from the commencement of the kingdom of heaven—the terrific, the awful, the national, not one had come to pass. The deliverance of the nation from the Roman yoke seemed as remote as ever; the governor had made but a short time, perhaps a year, before, a terrible assertion of his supremacy, by defiling the Temple itself with the blood of the rebellious or unoffending Galileans. The Sanhedrin, imperious during his absence, quailed and submitted whenever the tribunal of Pilate was erected in the metropolis. The publicans, those unwelcome remembrancers of the subjugation of the country, were still abroad in every town and village, levying the hateful tribute; and instead of joining in the popular clamour against these agents of a foreign rule, or even reprobating their extortions, Jesus had treated them with his accustomed equable gentleness; he had entered familiarly into their houses; one of his constant followers, one of his chosen twelve, was of this proscribed and odious profession.

Thus, then, the fierce and violent, the avowed or the secret partisans of the Galilean Judas, and all who, without having enrolled themselves in his sect, inclined to the same opinions, if not already inflamed against Jesus, were at least ready to take fire, on the instant that his success might appear to endanger their schemes and visions of independence: and their fanaticism once inflamed, no considerations of humanity or justice would arrest its course or assuage its violence. To every sect Jesus had been equally uncompromising. To the Pharisees he had always proclaimed the most undisguised opposition; and if his language rises from its gentle and persuasive, though authoritative tone, it is ever in inveighing against the hypocrisy, the avarice, the secret vices of this class, whose dominion over the public mind it was necessary to shake with a strong hand; all communion with whose peculiar opinions it was incumbent on the Teacher of purer virtue to disclaim in the most unmeasured terms.[f] But this hostility to the Pharisaic party was likely to operate unfavourably to the cause of Jesus, not only with the party itself, but with the great mass of the lower orders. If there be in man a natural love of independence both in thought and action, there is among the vulgar, especially in a nation so superstitious as the Jews, a reverence, even a passionate attachment to religious tyranny. The bondage in which the minute observances of the traditionists, more like those of the Brahminical Indians than the free and more generous institutes of their Lawgiver, had fettered

---

[f] Luke xi. 39-54.

the whole life of the Jew, was nevertheless a source of satisfaction and pride; and the offer of deliverance from this inveterate slavery would be received by most with unthankfulness or suspicion. Nor can any teacher of religion, however he may appeal to the better feelings and to the reason, without endangering his influence over the common people, permit himself to be outdone in that austerity which they ever consider the sole test of fervour and sincerity. Even those less en- *The Lawyers.* slaved to the traditional observances, the Lawyers (perhaps the religious ancestors of the Karaites[f]), who adhered more closely, and confined their precepts, to the sacred books, must have trembled and recoiled at the manner in which Jesus assumed an authority above that of Moses or the Prophets. *The Sadducees.* With the Sadducees Jesus had come less frequently into collision: it is probable that this sect prevailed chiefly among the aristocracy of the larger cities and of the metropolis, while Jesus in general mingled with the lower orders; and the Sadducees were less regular attendants in the synagogues and schools, where he was wont to deliver his instructions. They, in all likelihood, were less possessed than the rest of the nation with the expectation of the Messiah; at all events they rejected as innovations not merely the Babylonian notions about the angels and the resurrection, which prevailed in the rest of the community, but altogether disclaimed these doctrines, and professed themselves adherents of the original simple Mosaic Theocracy. Hence, though on one or two occasions

---

[f] The Karaites among the later Jews were the Protestants of Judaism (see Hist. of Jews); it is probable that a party of this nature existed much earlier, though by no means numerous or influential.

they appear to have joined in the general confederacy to arrest his progress, the Sadducees for the most part would look on with contemptuous indifference; and although the declaration of eternal life mingled with the whole system of the teaching of Jesus, yet it was not till his Resurrection had become the leading article of the new faith—till Christianity was thus, as it were, committed in irreconcileable hostility with the main principle of their creed—that their opposition took a more active turn, and from the accidental increase of their weight in the Sanhedrin, came into perpetual and terrible collision with the Apostles. The only point of union which the Sadducaic party would possess with the Pharisees would be the most extreme jealousy of the abrogation of the Law, the exclusive feeling of its superior sanctity, wisdom, and irrepealable authority: on this point the spirit of nationality would draw together these two conflicting parties, who would vie with each other in the patriotic, the religious vigilance with which they would seize on any expression of Jesus which might imply the abrogation of the divinely inspired institutes of Moses, or even any material innovation on their strict letter. But, besides the general suspicion that Jesus was assuming an authority above, in some cases contrary to, the Law, there were other trifling circumstances which threw doubts on that genuine and uncontaminated Judaism, which the nation in general would have imperiously demanded from their Messiah. There seems to have been some apprehension, as we have before stated, of his abandoning his ungrateful countrymen, and taking refuge among a foreign race; and his conduct towards the Samaritans was directly contrary to the strongest Jewish prejudices. On more than one occasion, even if his remarkable conduct and language during his first journey through Samaria had not transpired, He had avowedly discountenanced that implacable national hatred, which no one can ever attempt to allay without diverting it, as it were, on his own head. He had adduced the example of a Samaritan as the only one of the ten lepers [b] who showed either gratitude to his benefactor, or piety to God; and in the exquisite apologue of the Good Samaritan, he had placed the Priest and the Levite in a most unfavourable light, as contrasted with the descendant of that hated race.

Yet there could be no doubt that He had already avowed himself to be the Messiah: his harbinger, the Baptist, had proclaimed the rapid, the instantaneous approach of the kingdom of Christ. Of that kingdom Jesus himself had spoken as commencing, as having already commenced; but where were the outward, the visible, the undeniable signs of sovereignty? He had permitted himself, both in private and in public, to be saluted as the Son of David, an expression which was equivalent to a claim to the hereditary throne of David: but still to the common eye he appeared the same lowly and unroyal being, as when he first set forth as a teacher through the villages of Galilee. As to the nature of this kingdom, even to his closest followers, his language was most perplexing and contradictory. An unworldly kingdom, a moral dominion, a purely religious community, held together only by the bond of common faith, was so unlike the former intimate union of civil and religious polity—so diametrically opposite to the first principles of their Theocracy—as to be utterly unintelligible. The real nature and design of the new religion seemed altogether

Jesus the Messiah.

---

[b] Luke xvii. 18.

beyond their comprehension; and it is most remarkable to trace it, as it slowly dawned on the minds of the Apostles themselves, and gradually, after the death of Jesus, extended its horizon till it comprehended all mankind within its expanding view. To be in the highest sense the religious ancestors of mankind; to be the authors, or at least the agents, in the greatest moral revolution which has taken place in the world; to obtain an influence over the human mind, as much more extensive than that which had been violently obtained by the arms of Rome, as it was more conducive to the happiness of the human race; to be the teachers and disseminators of doctrines, opinions, sentiments, which, slowly incorporating themselves, as it were, with the intimate essence of man's moral being, were to work a gradual but total change—a change which, as to the temporal as well as the eternal destiny of our race, to those who look forward to the simultaneous progress of human civilisation and the genuine religion of Jesus, is yet far from complete—all this was too high, too remote, too mysterious, for the narrow vision of the Jewish people. They, as a nation, were better prepared indeed, by already possessing the rudiments of the new faith, for becoming the willing agents in this divine work. On the other hand they were, in some respects, disqualified by that very distinction, which, by keeping them in rigid seclusion from the rest of mankind, had rendered them, as it were, the faithful depositaries of the great principle of religion, the Unity of God. The peculiar privilege, with which they had been entrusted for the benefit of mankind, had become, as it were, their exclusive property: nor were they willing, indiscriminately, to communicate to others this their own distinctive prerogative.

Those, for such doubtless there were, who pierced, though dimly, through the veil—the more reasoning, the more advanced, the more philosophical—were little likely to espouse the cause of Jesus with vigour and resolution. Persons of this character are usually too calm, dispassionate, and speculative, to be the active and zealous instruments in a great religious revolution. It is probable that most of this class were either far gone in Oriental mysticism, or in some instances in the colder philosophy of the Greeks. For these Jesus was as much too plain and popular, as he was too gentle and peaceable for the turbulent. He was scarcely more congenial to the severe and ascetic practices of the Essene, than to the fiercer followers of the Galilean Judas. Though the Essene might admire the exquisite purity of his moral teaching and the uncompromising firmness with which he repressed the vices of all ranks and parties; however he might be prepared for the abrogation of the ceremonial law, and the substitution of the religion of the heart for that of the prevalent outward forms, on his side he was too closely bound by his own monastic rules: his whole existence was recluse and contemplative. His religion was altogether unfitted for aggression, so that, however apparently it might coincide with Christianity in some material points, in fact its vital system was repugnant to that of the new faith. Though, after strict investigation, the Essene would admit the numerous candidates who aspired to unite themselves with his cœnobitic society, in which no one, according to Pliny's expression, was born but which was always full, he would never seek proselytes, or use any active means for disseminating his principles; and it is worthy of remark, that almost the only quarter of Palestine which Jesus

The Essenes.

does not appear to have visited, is the district near the Dead Sea, where the agricultural settlements of the Essenes were chiefly situated.

While the mass of the community were hostile to Jesus, from his deficiency in the more imposing, the warlike, the destructive signs of the Messiah's power and glory; from his opposition to the genius and principles of the prevailing sects; from his want of nationality, both as regarded the civil independence and the exclusive religious superiority of the race of Abraham; and from their own general incapacity for comprehending the moral sublimity of his teaching; additional, and not less influential, motives, conspired to inflame the animosity of the Rulers. Independent of the dread of innovation, inseparable from established governments, they could not but discern the utter incompatibility of their own rule with that of an unworldly Messiah. They must abdicate at once, if not their civil office as magistrates, unquestionably their sovereignty over the public mind; retract much which they had been teaching on the authority of their fathers, the Wise men; and submit, with the lowest and most ignorant, to be the humble scholars of the new Teacher.

<small>The Rulers.</small>

With all this mingled, no doubt, a real apprehension of offending the Roman power. The Rulers could not but discern on how precarious a foundation rested not only the feeble shadow of national independence, but even the national existence. A single mandate from the Emperor, not unlikely to be precipitately advised and relentlessly carried into execution, on the least appearance of tumult, by a governor of so decided a character as Pontius Pilate, might annihilate at once all that remained of their civil, and even of their religious, constitution. If we look forward we find that, during the whole of the period which precedes the last Jewish war, the ruling authorities of the nation pursued the same cautious policy. They were driven into the insurrection, not by their own deliberate determination, but by the uncontrollable fanaticism of the populace. To every overture of peace they lent a willing ear; and their hopes of an honourable capitulation, by which the city might be spared the horrors of a storm, and the Temple be secured from desecration, did not expire till their party was thinned by the remorseless sword of the Idumean and the Assassin, and the Temple had become the stronghold of one of the contending factions. Religious fears might seem to countenance this trembling apprehension of the Roman power, for there is strong ground, both in Josephus and the Talmudic writings, for believing that the current interpretation of the prophecies of Daniel designated the Romans as the predestined destroyers of the Theocracy.[1] And however the more enthusiastic might look upon this only as one of the inevitable calamities which were to precede the appearance and final triumph of the Messiah, the less fervid faith of the older and more commanding party was far more profoundly impressed with the dread of the impending ruin, than elated with the remoter hope of final restoration. The advice of Caiaphas, therefore, to sacrifice even an innocent man for the safety of the

---

[1] It is probable that in the allusion of Jesus to the "abomination of desolation," the phrase was already applied by the popular apprehensions to some impending destruction by the Romans. Τὸν αὐτὸν τρόπον Δανίηλος καὶ περὶ τῆς Ῥωμαίων ἡγεμονίας ἀνέγραψε, καὶ ὅτι ὑπ' αὐτῶν ἐρημωθήσεται. Ant. x. 2, 7, and in the Bell. Jud. iv. 6, 3, the προφήτεια κατὰ τῆς πατρίδος, referred to this interpretation of the verse of the prophet. Compare Babyl. Talm. Gemara, Masseck Nadr, c. 5, Masseck Sanhedrin, c. 11, Jerusalem Talmud, Masseck Kelaim. c. 9. Bertholdt on Daniel, p. 585. See likewise Jortin's Eccl. Hist. L. 69.

state, would appear to them both sound and reasonable policy.

<small>Demeanour of Jesus.</small> We must imagine this suspense, this agitation of the crowded city, or we shall be unable fully to enter into the beauty of the calm and unostentatious dignity with which Jesus pursues his course through the midst of this terrific tumult. He preserves the same equable composure in the triumphant procession into the Temple and in the Hall of Pilate. Everything indicates his tranquil conviction of his inevitable death; He foretells it with all its afflicting circumstances to his disciples, incredulous almost to the last to this alone of their Master's declarations. At every step He feels himself more inextricably within the toils; yet He moves onwards with the self-command of a willing sacrifice, constantly dwelling with a profound, though chastened, melancholy on his approaching fate, and intimating that his death was necessary, in order to secure indescribable benefits for his faithful followers and for mankind. Yet there is no needless exasperation of his enemies; He observes the utmost prudence, though He seems so fully aware that his prudence can be of no avail; He never passes the night within the city; and it is only by the treachery of one of his followers that the Sanhedrin at length make themselves masters of his person.

The Son of Man had now arrived at Bethany, and we must endeavour to trace his future proceedings in a consecutive course.[k] But if it has been difficult to dispose the events of the life of Jesus, in the order of time, this difficulty increases as we approach its termination. However embarrassing this fact to those who require something more than his-

<small>Difficulty of chronological arrangement.</small>

---

[k] Matt. xxi. 1; Mark xi. 1; Luke xix. 28; John xii. 1.

torical credibility in the evangelical narratives, to those who are content with a lower and more rational view of their authority, it throws not the least suspicion on their truth. It might almost seem, at the present period, that the Evangelists, confounded as it were, and stunned with the deep sense of the importance of the crisis, however they might remember the facts, had in some degree perplexed and confused their regular order.

At Bethany the Lord took up his abode in the house of Simon, who had been a leper, and, it is not improbably conjectured, had been healed by the wonderful power of Jesus.[a] Simon was, in all likelihood, closely connected, though the degree of relationship is not intimated, with the family of Lazarus, for Lazarus was present at the feast, and it was conducted by Martha his sister. The fervent devotion of their sister Mary had been already indicated on two occasions; and this passionate zeal, now heightened by gratitude for the recent restoration of her brother to life, evinced itself in her breaking an alabaster box of very costly perfume, and anointing the Saviour's head,[b] according, as we have seen on a former occasion, to a usage not uncommon in Oriental banquets. It is possible that vague thoughts of the royal character, which she expected that Jesus was about to assume, might mingle with those purer feelings which led her to pay this prodigal homage to his person. The mercenary character of Judas now begins to be developed. Judas had been appointed a kind of treasurer, and entrusted with the care of the common purse, from which the scanty necessities of

---

[a] Matt. xxvi. 1-13; Mark xiv. 3-9; John xii. 1-11. (I follow St. John's narrative in placing this incident at the present period.)

[b] See Psalm xxv. 5. Horat. Carm. ii. 11, 16. Martial, iii. 12, 4.

the humble and temperate society had been defrayed, and the rest reserved for distribution among the poor. Some others of the disciples had been seized with astonishment at this unusual and seemingly unnecessary waste of so valuable a commodity: but Judas broke out into open remonstrance, and, concealing his own avarice under the veil of charity for the poor, protested against the wanton prodigality. Jesus contented himself with praising the pious and affectionate devotion of the woman, and, reverting to his usual tone of calm melancholy, declared that unknowingly she had performed a more pious office, the anointing his body for his burial.

The intelligence of the arrival of Jesus at Bethany spread rapidly to the city, from which it was not quite two miles distant. Multitudes thronged forth to behold him: nor was Jesus the only object of interest, for the fame of the resurrection of Lazarus was widely disseminated, and the strangers in Jerusalem were scarcely less anxious to behold a man who had undergone a fate so unprecedented.

Jesus enters Jerusalem in triumph

Lazarus, thus an object of intense interest to the people,° became one of no less jealousy to the ruling authorities, the enemies of Jesus. His death was likewise decreed, and the magistracy only awaited a favourable opportunity for the execution of their edicts. But the Sanhedrin is at first obliged to remain in overawed and trembling inactivity. The popular sentiment is so decidedly in favour of Jesus of Nazareth, that they dare not venture to oppose his open, his public, his tri-

---

° John xii. 9-11. *But the Chief Priests consulted that they might put Lazarus also to death; because that by reason of him many of the Jews went away, and believed on Jesus.*

umphant procession into the city, or his entrance amid
the applauses of the wondering multitude into the
Temple itself. On the morning of the second day of
the week,[p] Jesus is seen, in the face of day, Monday,
approaching one of the gates of the city which Nisan 2, March.
looked towards Mount Olivet.[q] In avowed conformity
to a celebrated prophecy of Zechariah, he appears
riding on the yet unbroken colt of an ass; the procession of his followers, as he descends the side of the
Mount of Olives, escort him with royal honours, and
with acclamations expressive of the title of the Messiah,
towards the city: many of them had been witnesses of
the resurrection of Lazarus, and no doubt proclaimed, as
they advanced, this extraordinary instance of power.
They are met[r] by another band advancing from the
city, who receive him with the same homage, strew
branches of palm and even their garments in his way;
and the Sanhedrin could not but hear within the courts
of the Temple, the appalling proclamation, "Hosannah!
Blessed is the King of Israel, that cometh in the name
of the Lord." Some of the Pharisees, who had mingled
with the multitude, remonstrate with Jesus, and command him to silence what to their ears sounded like the
profane, the impious adulation of his partisans. Uninterrupted, and only answering that *if these were silent, the
stones on which He trod would bear witness*, Jesus still
advances; the acclamations become yet louder; He is
hailed as the Son of David, the rightful heir of David's
kingdom; and the desponding Pharisees, alarmed at the
complete mastery over the public mind which He appears
to possess, withdraw for the present their fruitless oppo-

---

[p] John xii. 12.
[q] Matt. xxi. 1-10; Mark xi. 1-10;   [r] Luke xix. 29-40; John xii. 12-19.
[r] John xii. 18.

sition. On the declivity of the hill he pauses to behold the city at his feet, and something of that emotion, which afterwards is expressed with much greater fulness, betrays itself in a few brief and emphatic sentences, expressive of the future miserable destiny of the devoted Jerusalem.[a]

The whole crowded city is excited by this increasing tumult. Anxious inquiries about the cause, and the intelligence that it is the entrance of Jesus of Nazareth into the city, still heighten the universal suspense.[b] And even in the Temple itself, where perhaps the religion of the place, or the expectation of some public declamation, or perhaps of some immediate sign of his power, had caused a temporary silence among his older followers, the children prolong the acclamations.[c] Then, too, as the sick, the infirm, the afflicted with different maladies, are brought to him to be healed, and are restored at once to health or to the use of their faculties, at every instance of the power and goodness of Jesus the same uncontrolled acclamations from the younger part of the multitude are renewed with increasing fervour.

Those of the Sanhedrin who are present, though they do not attempt at this immediate juncture to stem the torrent, venture to remonstrate against the disrespect to the sanctity of the Temple, and demand of Jesus to silence what to their feelings sounded like profane violation of the sacred edifice. Jesus replies, as usual, with an apt quotation from the sacred writings, which declared that even the voices of children and infants might be raised, without reproof, in praise and thanksgiving to God.

---

[a] Luke xix. 41-44.   [b] Matt. xxi. 10, 11.   [c] Ibid. 15.

Among the multitudes of Jews who assembled at the Passover, there were usually many proselytes who were called Greeks[a] (a term in Jewish language of as wide signification as that of Barbarians with the Greeks, and including all who were not of Jewish descent). *The Greeks.* Some of this class, carried away by the general enthusiasm towards Jesus, expressed an anxious desire to be admitted to his presence. It is not improbable that these proselytes might be permitted to advance no farther than the division in the outer Court of the Gentiles, where certain palisades were erected, with inscriptions in various languages, prohibiting the entrance of all foreigners; or even if they were allowed to pass this barrier, they may have been excluded from the Court of Israel, into which Jesus may have passed. By the intervention of two of the Apostles, their desire is made known to Jesus; who, perhaps as he passes back through the outward Court, permits them to approach. No doubt as these proselytes shared in the general excitement towards the person of Jesus, so they shared in the general expectation of the immediate, the instantaneous commencement of the splendour, the happiness of the Messiah's kingdom. To their surprise, either in answer to or anticipating their declaration to this effect, instead of enlarging on the glory of that great event, the somewhat ambiguous language of Jesus dwells, at first, on his approaching fate, on the severe trial which awaits the devotion of his followers; yet on the necessity of this humiliation, this dissolution, to his final glory, and to the triumph of his beneficent religion. It rises at length into a devotional address to the Father, to bring immediately to accomplishment all his promises, for the glori-

---

[a] John xii. 20, 43.

fication of the Messiah. As he was yet speaking, a rolling sound was heard in the heavens, which the unbelieving part of the multitude heard only as an accidental burst of thunder: to others, however, it seemed an audible, a distinct, or, according to those who adhere to the strict letter, the articulate voice[y] of an angel, proclaiming the divine sanction to the presage of his future glory. Jesus continues his discourse in a tone of profounder mystery, yet evidently declaring the immediate discomfiture of the "Prince of this world," the adversary of the Jewish people and of the human race, his own departure from the world, and the important consequences which were to ensue from that departure. After his death, his religion was to be more attractive than during his life. "I, if I be lifted up from the earth, will draw all men unto me." Among the characteristics of the Messiah which were deeply rooted in the general belief, was the eternity of his reign; once revealed, he was revealed for ever; once established in their glorious, their paradisiacal state, the people of God, the subjects of the kingdom, were to be liable to no change, no vicissitude. The allusions of Jesus to his departure, clashing with this notion of his perpetual presence, heightened their embarrassment; and, leaving them in this state of mysterious suspense, he withdrew unperceived from the multitude, and retired again with his own chosen disciples to the village of Bethany.

The second morning Jesus returned to Jerusalem. A fig-tree stood by the wayside, of that kind well known in Palestine, which during a mild

Cursing the barren fig-tree.

---

[y] Kuinoel, in loco. Some revert to the Jewish superstition of the Bath-Kol, or audible voice from heaven; but the more rational of the Jews interpret this Bath-Kol as an impression upon the mind, rather than on the outward senses.

winter preserve their leaves, and with the early spring put forth and ripen their fruit.¹ Jesus approached the tree to pluck the fruit; but finding that it bore none, condemned it to perpetual barrenness.

This transaction is remarkable, as almost the only instance in which Jesus adopted that symbolic mode of teaching by action, rather than by language, so peculiar to the East, and so frequently exemplified in the earlier books, especially of the Prophets. For it is difficult to conceive any reason either for the incident itself, or for its admission into the evangelic narrative at a period so important, unless it was believed to convey some profounder meaning. The close moral analogy, the accordance with the common phraseology between the barren tree, disqualified by its hardened and sapless state from bearing its natural produce, and the Jewish nation, equally incapable of bearing the fruits of Christian goodness, formed a most expressive, and, as it were, living apologue.

On this day, Jesus renews the remarkable scene which had taken place at the first Passover. The *Second day in* customary traffic, the tumult and confusion, *Jerusalem.* which his authority had restrained for a short time, had been renewed in the courts of the Temple; and Jesus again expelled the traders from the holy precincts, and, to secure the silence and the sanctity of the whole enclosure, prohibited the carrying any vessel through the Temple courts.ᵃ Through the whole of this day the

---

¹ There are three kinds of figs in Palestine: 1, the early fig, which blossoms in March, and ripens its fruit in June; 2, the Kermus, which shows its fruit in June, and ripens in August; and, 3, the kind in question. See Kuinoel, in loco. Pliny, H. N. xvi. 27. Theophr. 3, 8. Shaw's Travels. Matt. xxi. 18, 19; Mark xi. 12, 14.

ᵃ Matt. xxi. 12, 13; Luke xix. 45, 46; Mark xi. 15, 17.

Sanhedrin, as it were, rested on their arms; they found, with still increasing apprehension, that every hour the multitude crowded with more and more anxious interest around the Prophet of Nazareth; his authority over the Temple courts seems to have been admitted without resistance; and probably the assertion of the violated dignity of the Temple was a point on which the devotional feelings would have been so strongly in favour of the Reformer, that it would have been highly dangerous and unwise for the magistrates to risk even the appearance of opposition or of dissatisfaction.

The third day. The third morning arrived. As Jesus passed to the Temple, the fig-tree, the symbol of the Jewish nation, stood utterly withered and dried up. But, as it were, to prevent the obvious inference from the immediate fulfilment of his malediction—almost the only destructive act during his whole public career, and that on a tree by the wayside, the common property— Jesus mingles with his promise of power to his Apostles to perform acts as extraordinary, the strictest injunctions to the milder spirit inculcated by his precept and his example. Their prayers were to be for the pardon, not for the providential destruction, of their enemies.

Deputation from the rulers. The Sanhedrin had now determined on the necessity of making an effort to discredit Jesus with the more and more admiring multitude. A deputation arrives to demand by what authority He had taken up his station, and was daily teaching in the Temple, had expelled the traders, and, in short, had usurped a complete superiority over the accredited and established instructors of the people?[b] The self-command and promptitude of Jesus caught them, as it were, in their

---

[b] Matt. xxi. 23-27; Mark xi. 27-34; Luke xx. 1-8.

own toils, and reduced them to the utmost embarrassment. The claim of the Baptist to the prophetic character had been generally admitted, and even passionately asserted; his death had, no doubt, still further endeared him to all who detested the Herodian rule, or who admired the uncompromising boldness with which he had condemned iniquity even upon the throne. The popular feeling would have resented an impeachment on his prophetic dignity. When, therefore, Jesus demanded their judgement as to the Baptism of John, they had but the alternative of acknowledging its divine sanction, and so tacitly condemning themselves for not having submitted to his authority, and even for not admitting his testimony in favour of Jesus; or of exposing themselves, by denying it, to popular insult and fury. The self-degrading confession of their ignorance placed Jesus immediately on the vantage ground, and at once annulled their right to question or to decide upon the authority of his mission—that right which was considered to be vested in the Sanhedrin. They were condemned to listen to language still more humiliating. In two striking parables, that of the Lord of the Vineyard, and of the Marriage Feast,[c] Jesus not obscurely intimated the rejection of those labourers who had been first summoned to the work of God; of those guests who had been first invited to the nuptial banquet; and the substitution of meaner and most unexpected guests or subjects in their place.

The fourth day[d] arrived; and once more Jesus ap-

---

[c] Matt. xxi. 28 to xxii. 14; Mark xii. 1-12; Luke xx. 9-18.

[d] There is considerable difficulty in ascertaining the events of the Wednesday. It does not appear altogether probable that Jesus should have remained at Bethany in perfect inactivity or seclusion during the whole of this important day: either, therefore, as some suppose, the triumphant entry

peared in the Temple with a still increasing concourse of followers. No unfavourable impression had yet been made on the popular mind by his adversaries; his career is yet unchecked; his authority unshaken.

<small>The fourth day.</small>

His enemies are now fully aware of their own desperate position. The apprehension of the progress of Jesus unites the most discordant parties into one formidable conspiracy; the Pharisaic, the Sadducaic, and the Herodian factions agree to make common cause against the common enemy: the two national sects, the Traditionists and the Anti-traditionists, no longer hesitate to accept the aid of the foreign or Herodian faction.[e] Some suppose the Herodians to have been the officers and attendants on the court of Herod, then present at Jerusalem; but the appellation more probably includes all those who, estranged from the more inveterate Judaism of the nation, and having, in some degree, adopted Grecian habits and opinions, considered the peace of the country best secured by the government of the descendants of Herod, with the sanction and under the protection of Rome.[f] They were the foreign faction, and as such, in general, in direct opposition to the Pharisaic, or national party. But the

<small>The Herodians.</small>

---

into Jerusalem took place on the Monday, not on the Sunday, according to the common tradition of the Church; or, as here stated, the collision with his various adversaries spread over the succeeding day.

[e] Matt. xxii. 15-22; Mark xii. 13-17; Luke xxi. 19-26.

[f] Of all notions on the much-contested point of the Herodians, the most improbable is that which identifies them with the followers of the Galilean Judas. The whole policy of the Herodian family was in diametrical hostility to those opinions. They maintained their power by foreign influence, and, with the elder Herod, had systematically attempted to soften the implacable hostility of the nation by the introduction of Grecian manners. Their object accordingly was, to convict Jesus of the Galilean opinions, which they themselves held in the utmost detestation.

success of Jesus, however at present it threatened more immediately the ruling authorities in Jerusalem, could not but endanger the Galilean government of Herod. The object, therefore, was to implicate Jesus with the faction, or at least to tempt him into acknowledging opinions similar to those of the Galilean demagogue—a scheme the more likely to work on the jealousy of the Roman government, if it was at the last Passover that the apprehension of tumult among the Galilean strangers had justified, or appeared to justify, the massacre perpetrated by Pilate. The plot was laid with great subtlety; for either way Jesus, it appeared, must commit himself. The great test of the Galilean opinion was, the lawfulness of tribute to a foreign power; which Judas had boldly declared to be not merely a base compromise of the national independence, but an impious infringement on the first principles of their theocracy. But the independence, if not the universal dominion, of the Jews was inseparably bound up with the popular belief in the Messiah. Jesus, then, would either, on the question of the lawfulness of tribute to Cæsar, confirm the bolder doctrines of the Galilean, and so convict himself, before the Romans, as one of that dangerous faction; or he would admit its legality, and so annul at once all his claims to the character of the Messiah. Not in the least thrown off his guard by the artful courtesy, or rather the adulation of their address, Jesus appeals to the current coin of the country, which, bearing the impress of the Roman Emperor, was in itself a recognition of Roman supremacy.[f]

---

[f] The latter part of the sentence, "Render therefore unto Cæsar the things that are Cæsar's, and to God the things that are God's," refers, in all probability, to the payment of the Temple tribute, which was only received in the coin of the country. Hence, as before observed, the money-changers in the Temple. Matt. xxii. 21-33; Mark xii. 18-27; Luke xx. 27-36.

The Herodian or political party thus discomfited, the Sadducees advanced to the encounter. Nothing can appear more captious or frivolous than their question with regard to the future possession of a wife in another state of being, who had been successively married to seven brothers, according to the Levirate law. But, perhaps, considered in reference to the opinions of the time, it will seem less extraordinary. The Sadducees, no doubt, had heard that the resurrection, and the life to come, had formed an essential tenet in the teaching of Jesus. They concluded that his notions on these subjects were those generally prevalent among the people. But, if the later Rabbinical notions of the happiness of the renewed state of existence were current, or even known in their general outline, nothing could be more gross or unspiritual:[b] if less voluptuous, they were certainly not less strange and unreasonable than those which perhaps were derived from the same source—the Paradise of Mohammed. The Sadducees were accustomed to contend with these disputants, whose paradisiacal state, to be established by the Messiah, after the resurrection, was but the completion of those temporal promises in the book of Deuteronomy, a perpetuity of plenty, fertility, and earthly enjoyment.[i] The answer of Jesus, while it declares the certainty of another state of existence, carefully purifies it from all these corporeal and earthly images; and assimilates man, in another

---

[b] It is decided, in the Sohar on Genesis, fol. 24, col. 96, "that woman, who has married two husbands in this world, is restored to the first in the world to come." Schoetgen, in loco.

Josephus, in his address to his countrymen, mingles up into one splendid picture the Metempsychosis and the Elysium of the Greeks. In Schoetgen, in loco, may be found extracts from the Talmud, of a purer character, and more resembling the language of our Lord.

state of existence, to a higher order of beings. And in his concluding inference from the passage in Exodus, in which God is described as the God of Abraham, Isaac, and Jacob, the allusion may perhaps be still kept up. The temporal and corporeal resurrection, according to the common Pharisaic belief, was to take place only after the coming of the Messiah; yet their reverence for the fathers of the race, their holy ancestors, would scarcely allow even the Sadducee to suppose their total extinction. The actual, the pure beatitude of the Patriarchs, was probably an admitted point; if not formally decided by their teachers, implicitly received, and fervently embraced by the religious feelings of the whole people. But if, according to the Sadducaic principle, the soul did not exist independent of the body, even Abraham, Isaac, and Jacob had shared the common fate, the favour of God had ceased with their earthly dissolution; nor in the time of Moses could He be justly described as the God of those who in death had sunk into utter annihilation.

Although now engaged in a common cause, the hostility of the Pharisaic party to the Sadducees could not but derive gratification from their public discomfiture. One Scribe of their sect is so struck by the superiority of Jesus, that, though still with something of an insidious design, he demands in what manner he should rank the commandments, which in popular belief were probably of equal dignity and importance.[k] But when Jesus comprises the whole of religion under the simple precepts of the love of God and the love of man, the Scribe is so struck with the sublimity of the

---

[k] Matt. xxii. 34-40; Mark xii. 28-40; Luke xx. 39, 40.

language, that he does not hesitate openly to espouse his doctrines.

Paralysed by this desertion, and warned by the discomfiture of the two parties which had preceded them in dispute with Jesus, the Pharisees appear to have stood wavering and uncertain how to speak or act. Jesus seizes the opportunity of still further weakening their authority with the assembled multitude; and, in his turn, addresses an embarrassing question as to the descent of the Messiah.[m] The Messiah, according to the universal belief, would be the heir and representative of David: Jesus, by a reference to the Second Psalm, which was generally considered prophetic of the Redeemer, forces them to confess that, even according to their own authority, the kingdom of the Messiah was to be of far higher dignity, far wider extent, and administered by a more exalted sovereign than David, for even David himself, by their own admission, had called him his Lord.

The Pharisees

The Pharisees withdrew in mortified silence, and for that time abandoned all hope of betraying him into any incautious or unpopular denial by their captious questions. But they withdrew unmoved by the wisdom, unattracted by the beauty, unsubdued by the authority of Jesus.

After some delay, during which took place the beautiful incident of his approving the charity of the poor widow,[n] who cast her mite into the treasury of the Temple, he addressed the wondering multitude ("for the common people heard him gladly"[o]) in a grave and

---

[m] Matt. xxii. 41-46; Mark xii. 35-37; Luke xx. 39-44.

[n] Mark xii. 41-44; Luke xxi. 1-4.

[o] "And the common people heard him gladly."—Mark xii. 37.

solemn denunciation against the tyranny, the hypocrisy, the bigoted attachment to the most minute observances, and at the same time the total blindness to the spirit of religion, which actuated that great predominant party. He declared them possessed by the same proud and inhuman spirit, which had perpetually bedewed the city with the blood of the Prophets.[p] Jerusalem had thus for ever rejected the mercy of God.

This appalling condemnation was, as it were, the final declaration of war against the prevailing religion; it declared that the new doctrines could not harmonise with minds so inveterately wedded to their own narrow bigotry. But even yet the people were not altogether estranged from Jesus, and in that class in which the Pharisaic interest had hitherto despotically ruled, it appeared as it were trembling for its existence.

And now everything indicated the approaching, the immediate crisis. Although the populace were so decidedly, up to the present instant, in his favour—though many of the ruling party were only withholden by the dread of that awful sentence of excommunication, which inflicted civil, almost religious death,[q] from avowing themselves his disciples — yet Jesus never entered the Temple again. The next time he appeared before the people was as a prisoner, as a condemned malefactor. As he left the Temple, a casual expression of admiration from some of his followers, at the magnificence and solidity of the building and the immense size of the stones of which it was formed, called forth a prediction of its impending ruin; which was expanded, to four of his Apostles, into a more detailed and

The crisis in the fate of Jesus.

---

[p] Matt. xxiii.; Mark xii. 38-40; Luke xi. 45-47. [q] See Hist. of the Jews, vol. ii. p. 465.

circumstantial description of its appalling fate, as he sat, during the evening, upon the Mount of Olives.*

It is impossible to conceive a spectacle of greater natural or moral sublimity than the Saviour seated on the slope of the Mount of Olives, and thus looking down, almost for the last time, on the Temple and city of Jerusalem, crowded as it then was with near three millions of worshippers. It was evening, and the whole irregular outline of the city, rising from the deep glens, which encircled it on all sides, might be distinctly traced. The sun, the significant emblem of the great Fountain of moral light, to which Jesus and his faith had been perpetually compared, may be imagined sinking behind the western hills, while its last rays might linger on the broad and massy fortifications on Mount Sion, on the stately palace of Herod, on the square tower, the Antonia, at the corner of the Temple, and on the roof of the Temple, fretted all over with golden spikes, which glittered like fire; while below, the colonnades and lofty gates would cast their broad shadows over the courts, and afford that striking contrast between vast masses of gloom and gleams of the richest light, which only an evening scene, like the present, can display. Nor, indeed (even without the sacred and solemn associations connected with the Holy City), would it be easy to conceive any natural situation in the world of more impressive grandeur, or likely to be seen with greater advantage under the influence of such accessaries, than that of Jerusalem, seated, as it was, upon hills of irregular height, intersected by bold ravines, and with still loftier mountains in the distance; itself formed,

---

* Matt. xxiv. xxv.; Mark xiii.; Luke xxi. 5-38.

in its most conspicuous parts, of gorgeous ranges of Eastern architecture, in all its lightness, luxuriance, and variety. The effect may have been heightened by the rising of the slow volumes of smoke from the evening sacrifices, while even at the distance of the slope of Mount Olivet the silence may have been faintly broken by the hymns of the worshippers.

Yet the fall of that splendid edifice was inevitable; the total demolition of all those magnificent and time-hallowed structures might not be averted. It was necessary to the complete development of the designs of Almighty Providence for the welfare of mankind in the promulgation of Christianity. Independent of all other reasons, the destruction certainly of the Temple, and if not of the city, at least of the city as the centre and metropolis of a people, the only true and exclusive worshippers of the one Almighty Creator, seemed essential to the progress of the new faith. The universal and comprehensive religion to be promulgated by Christ and his Apostles, was grounded on the abrogation of all local claims to peculiar sanctity, of all distinctions of one nation above another as possessing any especial privilege in the knowledge or favour of the Deity. The time was come when "neither in Jerusalem nor on the mountain of Gerizim," was the great Universal Spirit to be worshipped with circumscribed, or local homage. As long, however, as the Temple on Mount Moriah remained, hallowed by the reverence of ages, sanctified, according to the general belief, for perpetuity, by the especial command of God as his peculiar dwelling-place; so long, among the Jews at least, and even among other nations, the true principle of Christian worship might be counteracted by the notion of the inalienable sanctity of this one place.

Necessity for the destruction of the Temple at Jerusalem.

Judaism would scarcely be entirely annulled, so long as the Temple rose in its original majesty and veneration.

Jesus contemplates with sadness the future ruin of Jerusalem. Yet, notwithstanding this absolute necessity for its destruction, notwithstanding that it thus stood, as it were, in the way of the progress of human advancement and salvation, the Son of Man does not contemplate its ruin without emotion. And in all the superhuman beauty of the character of Jesus, nothing is more affecting and impressive than the profound melancholy with which He foretells the future desolation of the city, which, before two days were passed, was to reek with his own blood. Nor should we do justice to this most remarkable incident in his life, if we should consider it merely as a sudden emotion of compassion, as the natural sensation of sadness at the decay or dissolution of that which has long worn the aspect of human grandeur. It seems rather a wise and far-sighted consideration, not merely of the approaching guilt and future penal doom of the city, but of the remoter moral causes, which, by forming the national character, influenced the national destiny; the long train of events, the wonderful combination of circumstances, which had gradually wrought the Jewish people to that sterner frame of mind, too soon to display itself with such barbarous, such fatal ferocity. Jesus might seem not merely to know what was in man, but how it entered into man's heart and mind. His was divine charity, enlightened by infinite wisdom.

In fact, there was an intimate moral connexion between the murder of Jesus and the doom of the Jewish city. It was the same national temperament, the same characteristic disposition of the people, which now morally disqualified them "from knowing," in the language of Christ, "the things which belonged unto their peace," which forty years afterwards committed them in their deadly and ruinous struggle with the masters of the world. Christianity alone could have sub- *The ruin of the Jews the* dued or mitigated that stubborn fanaticism, *consequence of their cha-* which drove them at length to their desperate *racter.* collision with the arms of Rome. As Christians, the Jewish people might have subsided into peaceful subjects of the universal empire. They might have lived, as the Christians did, with the high and inalienable consolations of faith and hope under the heaviest oppressions; and calmly awaited the time when their holier and more beneficent ambition might be gratified by the submission of the lords of the world to the religious dominion founded by Christ and his Apostles. They would have slowly won that victory by the patient heroism of martyrdom and the steady perseverance in the dissemination of their faith, which it was madness to hope that they could ever obtain by force of arms. As Jews, they were almost sure, sooner or later, to provoke the implacable vengeance of their foreign sovereigns. The same vision of worldly dominion, the same obstinate expectation of a temporal Deliverer, which made them unable to comprehend the nature of the redemption to be wrought by the presence, and the kingdom to be established by the power, of Christ, continued to the end to mingle with their wild and frantic resistance.

In the rejection and murder of Jesus, the Rulers, as their interests and authority were more imme- *Immediate causes of the* diately endangered, were more deeply impli- *rejection of Jesus by the* cated than the people; but unless the mass of *Jews.* the people had been blinded by these false notions of the Messiah, they would not have demanded, or at least, with the general voice, assented to the sacrifice of Jesus.

The progress of Jesus at the present period in the public estimation, his transient popularity, arose from the enforced admiration of his commanding demeanour, the notoriety of his wonderful works, perhaps, for such language is always acceptable to the common ear, from his bold animadversions on the existing authorities; but it was no doubt supported in the mass of the populace by a hope, that even yet He would conform to the popular views of the Messiah's character. Their present brief access of faith would not have stood long against the continued disappointment of that hope: and it was no doubt by working on the reaction of this powerful feeling, that the Sanhedrin were able so suddenly, and, it almost appears, so entirely, to change the prevailing sentiment. Whatever the proverbial versatility of the popular mind, there must have been some chord strung to the most sensitive pitch, the slightest touch of which would vibrate through the whole frame of society, and madden at least a commanding majority to their blind concurrence in this revolting iniquity. Thus in the Jewish nation, but more especially in the prime movers, the Rulers and the heads of the Pharisaic party, the murder of Jesus was an act of unmitigated cruelty, but, as we have said, it arose out of the generally fierce and bigoted spirit, which morally incapacitated the whole people from discerning the evidence of his mission from heaven, in his acts of divine goodness as well as of divine power. It was an act of religious fanaticism; they thought, in the language of Jesus himself, that they were "doing God service" when they slew the Master, as much as afterwards when they persecuted his followers.

When however the last, and, as far as the existence of the nation, the most fatal display of this fanaticism took place, it was accidentally allied with nobler motives, with generous impatience of oppression, and the patriotic desire of national independence. However desperate and frantic the struggle against such irresistible power, the unprecedented tyranny of the later Roman procurators, Felix, Albinus, and Florus, might almost have justified the prudence of manly and resolute insurrection. Yet in its spirit and origin it was the same; and it is well known that even to the last, during the most sanguinary and licentious tumults in the Temple as well as the city, they never entirely lost sight of a deliverance from Heaven: God, they yet thought, would interpose in behalf of his chosen people. In short, the same moral state of the people (for the Rulers for obvious reasons were less forward in the resistance to the Romans), the same temperament and disposition now led them to reject Jesus and demand the release of Barabbas, which, forty years later, provoked the unrelenting vengeance of Titus, and deluged their streets with the blood of their own citizens. Even after the death of Jesus, this spirit might have been allayed, but only by a complete abandonment of all the motives which led to his crucifixion—by the general reception of Christianity in all its meekness, humility, and purity—by the tardy substitution of the hope of a moral, for that of temporal dominion. This unhappily was not the case: but it belongs to Jewish history to relate how the circumstances of the times, instead of assuaging or subduing, exasperated the people into madness; instead of predisposing to Christianity, confirmed the inveterate Judaism, and led at length to the accomplishment of their anticipated doom.

Altogether, then, it is evident, that it was this brooding hope of sovereignty, at least of political independence, moulded up with religious enthusiasm, and lurking, as it were, in the very heart's core of the people, which rendered it impossible that the pure, the gentle, the humane, the unworldly and comprehensive doctrines of Jesus should be generally received, or his character appreciated, by a nation in that temper of mind; and the nation who could thus incur the guilt of his death, was prepared to precipitate itself to such a fate as at length it suffered.

Hence political sagacity might, perhaps, have anticipated the crisis, which could only be averted, by that which was morally impossible, the simultaneous conversion of the whole people to Christianity. Yet the distinctness, the minuteness, the circumstantial accuracy, with which the prophetic outline of the siege and fall of Jerusalem is drawn, bear, perhaps, greater evidence of more than human foreknowledge, than any other in the sacred volume: and in fact this profound and far-sighted wisdom, this anticipation of the remote political consequences of the reception or rejection of his doctrines, supposing Jesus but an ordinary human being, would be scarcely less extraordinary than prophecy itself.

Distinctness with which Jesus prophesied the fall of Jerusalem.

Still though determined, at all hazards, to suppress the growing party of Jesus, the Sanhedrin were greatly embarrassed as to their course of proceeding. Jesus invariably passed the night without the walls, and only appeared during the daytime, though with the utmost publicity, in the Temple. His seizure in the Temple, especially during the festival, would almost inevitably lead to tumult, and (since it was yet doubtful on which side the populace would array themselves) tumult as inevitably to the prompt interference of the Roman authority. The Procurator, on the slightest indication of disturbance, without in-

Embarrassment of the Sanhedrin.

quiring into the guilt or innocence of either party, might coerce both with equal severity; or, even without further examination, let loose the guard, always mounted in the gallery which connected the fortress of Antonia with the north-western corner of the Temple, to mow down both the conflicting parties in indiscriminate havoc. He might thus mingle the blood of all present, as he had done that of the Galileans, with the sacrificial offerings. To discover then where Jesus might be arrested without commotion or resistance from his followers, so reasonably to be apprehended, the treachery of one of his more immediate disciples was absolutely necessary; yet this was an event, considering the commanding influence possessed by Jesus over his followers, rather to be desired than expected.

On a sudden, however, appeared within their court one of the chosen Twelve, with a voluntary offer of assisting them in the apprehension of his Master.* Much ingenuity has been displayed by some recent writers in attempting to palliate, or rather to account for, this extraordinary conduct of Judas; but the language in which Jesus spoke of the crime, appears to confirm the common opinion of its enormity. It has been suggested, either that Judas might expect Jesus to put forth his power, even after his apprehension, to elude or to escape from his enemies; and thus his avarice might calculate on securing the reward without being an accomplice in absolute murder, thus at once betraying his Master and defrauding his employers. According to others still higher motives may have mingled with his love of gain: he may have supposed, that by thus involving Jesus in diffi-

<small>*Treachery and*</small>

<small>*Motives of Judas.*</small>

---

* Matt. xxvi. 14-16; Mark xiv. 10, 11; Luke xxii. 2-6.

culties otherwise inextricable, he would leave him only the alternative of declaring himself openly and authoritatively to be the Messiah, and so force him to the tardy accomplishment of the ambitious visions of his partisans. It is possible that the traitor may not have contemplated, or may not have permitted himself clearly to contemplate, the ultimate consequences of his crime: he may have indulged the vague hope, that if Jesus were really the Messiah, he bore, if we may venture the expression, "a charmed life," and was safe in his inherent immortality (a notion in all likelihood inseparable from that of the Deliverer) from the malice of his enemies. If He were not, the crime of his betrayal would not be of very great importance. There were other motives which would concur with the avarice of Judas: the rebuke which he had received when he expostulated about the waste of the ointment, if it had not excited any feeling of exasperation against his Master, at least showed that his character was fully understood by the Saviour. He must have felt himself out of his element among the more honest and sincere disciples; nor can he have been actuated by any real or profound veneration for the exquisite perfection of a character so opposite to his own. And thus insincere and doubting, he may have shrunk from the approaching crisis, and as he would seize any means of extricating himself from that cause which had now become so full of danger, his covetousness would direct him to those means which would at once secure his own personal safety, and obtain the price, the thirty pieces of silver,[1] set by public proclamation on the head of Jesus.

---

[1] The thirty pieces of silver (shekels) are estimated at 3*l*. 10*s*. 8*d*. of our present money. It was the sum named in the Law (Exod. xxi. 32) as the value of the life of a slave; and it has been supposed that the Sanhedrin were

Nor is the desperate access of remorse, which led to the public restitution of the reward, and to the suicide of the traitor, irreconcileable with the unmitigated heinousness of the treachery. Men coolly meditate a crime, of which the actual perpetration overwhelms them with horror. The general detestation, of which, no doubt, Judas could not but be conscious, not merely among his former companions, the followers of Jesus, but even among the multitude; the supercilious coldness of the Sanhedrin, who, having employed him as their instrument, treat his recantation with the most contemptuous indifference, might overstrain the firmest, and work upon the basest mind: and even the unexampled sufferings and tranquil endurance of Jesus, however the betrayer may have calmly surveyed them when distant, and softened and subdued by his imagination, when present to his mind in their fearful reality, forced by the busy tongue of rumour upon his ears, perhaps not concealed from his sight, might drive him to desperation, little short of insanity.[a]

It was on the last evening[z] but one before the death of Jesus that the fatal compact was made: the next day, the last of his life, Jesus determines

The Passover.

---

desirous of showing their contempt for Jesus by the mean price that they offered for his head.

Perhaps, when we are embarrassed at the smallness of the sum covenanted for and received by Judas, we are imperceptibly influenced by our own sense of the incalculable importance of those consequences which arose out of the treachery of Judas. The service which he performed for this sum was, after all, no more than giving information as to the time and place in which Jesus might be seized among a few disciples without fear of popular tumult, conducting their officers to the spot where he might be found, and designating his person when they arrived at that spot.

[a] Matt. xxvi. 17-29; Mark xiv. 12-25; Luke xii. 36; John xiii. to end of xvii.

[z] "After two days was the Passover," in Jewish phraseology implies on the second day after.

on returning to the city to celebrate the Feast of the Passover: his disciples are sent to occupy a room prepared for the purpose.' His conduct and language before and during the whole repast clearly indicate his preparation for inevitable death.' His washing the feet of the disciples, his prediction of his betrayal, his intimation to Judas that he is fully aware of his design, his quiet dismissal of the traitor from the assembly, his institution of the second characteristic ordinance of the new religion, his allusions in that rite to the breaking of his body, and the pouring forth of his blood, his prediction of the denial of Peter, his final address to his followers, and his prayer before he left the chamber, are all deeply impregnated with the solemn melancholy, yet calm and unalterable composure, with which He looks forward to all the terrible details of his approaching, his almost immediate, sufferings. To his followers He makes, as it were, the valedictory promise, that his religion would not expire at his death, that his place would be filled by a mysterious

<small>The Last Supper.</small>

' All houses, according to Josephus, were freely open to strangers during the Passover; no payment was received for lodging. The Talmudic writings confirm this:—"The master of the family received the skins of sacrifices. It is a custom that a man leave his earthen jug, and also the skin of his sacrifice, to his host." The Gloss. The inhabitants did not let out their houses at a price to them that came up to the feasts, but granted them to them gratis. Lightfoot, vol. ii. p. 44.

' Of all difficulties, that concerning which we arrive at the least satisfactory conclusion is the apparent anticipation of the Passover by Christ. The fact is clear that Jesus celebrated the Passover on the Thursday, the leading Jews on the Friday; the historical evidence of this in the Gospels is unanswerable, independent of all theological reasoning. The reason of this difference is and must, I conceive, remain undecided. Whether it was an act of supreme authority assumed by Jesus, whether there was any schism about the right day, whether that schism was between the Pharisaic and Anti-Pharisaic party, or between the Jews and Galileans, all is purely conjectural.

Comforter, who was to teach, to guide, to console—the promise of the Holy Ghost, which was to be great Principle, and to the end the Life of Christianity.

This calm assurance of approaching death in Jesus is the more striking when contrasted with the inveterately Jewish notions of the Messiah's kingdom, which even yet possess the minds of the Apostles. They are now fiercely contesting[a] for their superiority in that earthly dominion, which even yet they suppose on the eve of its commencement. Nor does Jesus at this time altogether correct these erroneous notions, but in some degree falls into the prevailing language, to assure them of the distinguished reward which awaited his more faithful disciples. After inculcating the utmost humility by an allusion to the lowly fraternal service which He had just before performed in washing their feet, He describes the happiness and glory which they are at length to attain, by the strong, and no doubt familiar, imagery, of their being seated on twelve thrones, judging the twelve tribes of Israel.

The festival was closed according to the usage with the second part of the Hallel,[b] the Psalms, from the 113th to the 118th inclusive, of which the former were customarily sung at the commencement, the latter at the end, of the paschal supper. Jesus with his disciples again departed from the room in the city[c] where the feast had been held, probably down the Street of the Temple, till they came to the valley: they crossed the brook of Kidron, and began to ascend the slope of the Mount of Olives. Within the city no open space was

---

[a] Luke xxii. 24-30.
[b] Buxtorf, Lex Talmudica, p. 613. Lightfoot, in loco.
[c] Matt. xxvi. 30-56; Mark xiv. 32-52; Luke xxii. 89-53; John xviii. 1.

left for gardens;[d] but the whole neighbourhood of Jerusalem was laid out in inclosures for the convenience and enjoyment of the inhabitants. The historian of the war relates, not without feelings of poignant sorrow, the havoc made among these peaceful retreats by the devastating approaches of the Roman army.[e] Jesus turned aside into one of these inclosures,[f] which, it would seem from the subsequent history, was a place of customary retreat, well known to his immediate followers. The early hours of the night were passed by him in retired and devotional meditation, while the weary disciples are overpowered by involuntary slumber. Thrice Jesus returns to them, and each time He finds them sleeping. But to him it was no hour of quiet or repose. In the solitary garden of Gethsemane, Jesus, who in public, though confronting danger and suffering neither with stoical indifference, nor with the effort of a strong mind working itself up to the highest moral courage, but with a settled dignity, a calm and natural superiority, now, as it were, endured the last struggle of human nature. The whole scene of his approaching trial, his inevitable death, is present to his mind, and for an instant He prays to the Almighty Father to release him from the task, which, although of such importance to the welfare of mankind, is to be accomplished by such fearful means. The next instant, however, the momentary weakness is subdued, and though the agony is so severe that the sweat falls like large drops of blood to the ground, he resigns himself

---

[d] Lightfoot's derivations of some of the places on Mount Olivet are curious:— Beth-hana, the place of dates; Beth-phage, the place of green figs; Geth-semane, the place of oil presses.

[e] Hist. of the Jews, II. 324.

[f] Matt. xxvi. 36-46; Mark xiv. 32-42; Luke xxii. 41-48; John xviii. 1.

at once to the will of God. Nothing can heighten the terrors of the coming scene so much, as its effect, in anticipation, on the mind of Jesus himself.

The devotions of Jesus and the slumbers of his followers, as midnight approached, were rudely interrupted. Jesus had rejoined his, now awakened, disciples for the last time; he had commanded them to rise, and be prepared for the terrible event. Still, no doubt, incredulous of the sad predictions of their Master—still supposing that his unbounded power would secure him from any attempt of his enemies, they beheld the garden filled with armed men, and gleaming with lamps and torches. Judas advances and makes the signal which had been agreed on, saluting his Master with the customary mark of respect, a kiss on the cheek, for which he receives the calm but severe rebuke of Jesus for thus treacherously abusing this mark of familiarity and attachment: "Judas, betrayest thou the Son of Man with a kiss?"[1] The tranquil dignity of Jesus overawed the soldiers who first approached; they were most likely ignorant of the service on which they were employed; and when Jesus announces himself as the object of their search, they shrink back in astonishment, and fall to the earth. Jesus, however, covenanting only for the safe dismissal of his followers, readily surrenders himself to the guard. The fiery indignation of Peter, who had drawn his sword, and endeavoured, at least by his example, to incite the few adherents of Jesus to resistance, is repressed by the command of his Master: his peaceful religion disclaims all alliance with the acts or the weapons of the violent.

---

[1] Matt. xxvi. 47-56; Mark xiv. 43-50; Luke xxii. 47-53; John xviii. 2-11.

The man[b] whose ear had been struck off, was instantaneously healed; and Jesus, with no more than a brief and calm remonstrance against this ignominious treatment, against this arrestation, not in the face of day, in the public Temple, but at night, by men with arms in their hands, as though He had been a robber, allows himself to be led back, without resistance, into the city. His panic-stricken followers disperse on all sides, and Jesus is left, forsaken and alone, amid his mortal enemies.

Jesus led prisoner to the city.

The caprice, the jealousy, or the prudence, of the Roman government, as has been before observed, had in no point so frequently violated the feelings of the subject nation, as in the deposition of the High Priest, and the appointment of a successor to the office, in whom they might hope to place more implicit confidence. The stubbornness of the people, revolted by this wanton insult, persisted in honouring with the title those whom they could not maintain in the post of authority; all who had borne the office retained, in common language, the appellation of High Priest, if indeed the appellation was not still more loosely applied. Probably the most influential man in Jerusalem at this time was Annas, or Ananus, four of whose sons in turn either had been, or were subsequently, elevated to that high dignity now filled by his son-in-law, Caiaphas.

The High Priest.

The house of Annas was the first place[i] to which Jesus was led, either that the guard might receive further instructions, or perhaps as the

House of Annas.

---

[b] It is a curious observation of Sembler, that St. John alone gives the name of the servant of the High Priest, Malchus; and John, it appears, was known to some of the household of the chief magistrate.

[i] John xviii. 12-14.

place of the greatest security, while the Sanhedrin was hastily summoned to meet at that untimely hour, towards midnight or soon after, in the house of Caiaphas. Before the houses of the more wealthy in the East, or rather within the outer porch, there is usually a large square open court, in which public business is transacted, particularly by those who fill official stations. Into such a court, before the palace of Caiaphas, Jesus was led by the soldiers, and Peter, following unnoticed amid the throng, lingered before the porch until John, who happened to be familiarly known to some of the High Priest's servants, obtained permission for his entrance.[k]

The first process seems to have been a private examination,[m] perhaps while the rest of the Sanhedrin were assembling, before the High Priest. *First Interrogatory.* He demanded of Jesus the nature of his doctrines, and the character of his disciples. Jesus appealed to the publicity of his teaching, and referred him to his hearers for an account of the tenets which He had advanced. He had no secret doctrines, either of tumult or sedition; He had ever spoken "in public, in the synagogue, or in the Temple."

And now the fearful scene of personal insult and violence began. An officer of the High Priest, enraged at the calm composure with which Jesus answered the interrogatory, struck him on the mouth (beating on the mouth, sometimes with the hand, more often with a thong of leather or a slipper, is still a common act of violence in the East).[n] He bore the insult with the same equable placidity:—"If I have spoken evil, bear

---

[k] John xviii. 15-19.
[m] Matt. xxvi. 57; Mark xiv. 55-64; Luke xxii. 54.
[n] John xviii. 20-24.

witness of the evil; but if well, why smitest thou me?"

The more formal arraignment began:[*] and, however hurried and tumultuous the meeting, the Sanhedrin, either desirous that their proceedings should be conducted with regularity, or, more likely, strictly fettered by the established rules of their court, perhaps by no means unanimous in their sentiments, were, after all, in the utmost embarrassment how to obtain a legal capital conviction. Witnesses were summoned, but the immutable principles of the Law, and the invariable practice of the tribunal, required, in every case of life and death, the agreement of two witnesses on some specific charge. Many were at hand, suborned by the enemies of Jesus, and hesitating at no falsehood; but their testimony was so confused, or bore so little on any capital charge, that the court was still further perplexed. At length two witnesses deposed to the misapprehended speech of Jesus, at his first visit to Jerusalem, relating to the destruction of the Temple. But even these depositions were so contradictory, that it was scarcely possible to venture on a conviction upon such loose and incoherent statements. Jesus, in the mean time, preserved a tranquil and total silence. He neither interrupted nor questioned the witnesses; He did not condescend to place himself upon his defence. Nothing, therefore, remained[p] but to question the pri-

Second more public interrogatory.

---

[*] Matt. xxvi. 59-66; Mark xiv. 55-64; Luke xxii. 66-71; John xviii. 19-24.

[p] Some have supposed that there were two examinations in different places before the Sanhedrin—one more private in the house of Caiaphas, another more public, in the Gazith, the chamber in the Temple where the Sanhedrin usually sat. But the account of St. John, the most particular of the whole, says expressly (xviii. 28), that He was carried directly from the house of Caiaphas to the Prætorium of Pilate.

soner, and, if possible, to betray him into criminating himself. The High Priest, rising to give greater energy to his address, and adjuring him in the most solemn manner, in the name of God, to answer the truth, demands whether He is indeed the Messiah, the Christ, the Son of the Living God. Jesus at once answers in the affirmative, and adds a distinct allusion to the prediction of Daniel,[q] then universally admitted to refer to the reign of the Messiah. His words may be thus paraphrased:—" Ye shall know me for that mighty King described by the prophet; ye shall know me when my great, eternal, and imperishable kingdom shall be established on the ruins of your Theocracy." *Jesus acknowledges himself the Messiah*

The secret joy of the High Priest, though perhaps his devout horror was not altogether insincere, was disguised by the tone and gesture of religious indignation which he assumed. He rent his clothes; an act considered indecorous, almost indecent, in the High Priest, unless justified by an outrage against the established religion so flagrant and offensive as this declaration of Jesus.[r] He pronounced that speech (strangely indeed did its lofty tone contrast with the appearance of the prisoner) to be direct and treasonable blasphemy. The whole court, either sharing in the indignation, or hurried away by the vehement gesture *Conduct of the High Priest.*

---

[q] The allusion to this prophecy (Dan. vii. 13, 14) is manifest.

[r] They who judge a blasphemer, first bid the witness to speak out plainly what he hath heard; and when he speaks it, the judges, standing on their feet, rend their garments, and do not sew them up again. Sanhed. i. 7, 10, and Babyl. Gemar. in loc.

The High Priest was forbidden to rend his garments in the case of private mourning for the dead. Lev. x. 6, xxi. 10. In the time of public calamity he did. 1 Mac. xi. 71; Joseph. B. J. ii. 26, 27.

and commanding influence of the High Priest, hastily passed the fatal sentence, and declared Jesus guilty of the capital crime.

The insolent soldiery (as the Saviour was withdrawn from the court) had now full licence, and perhaps more than the licence, of their superiors to indulge the brutality of their own dispositions. They began to spit on his face—in the East the most degrading insult; they blindfolded him, and struck him with the palms of their hands, and, in their miserable merriment, commanded him to display his prophetic knowledge by detecting the hand that was raised against him.[a]

Jesus insulted by the soldiery.

The dismay, the despair, which had seized upon his adherents, is most strongly exemplified by the denial of Peter. The zealous disciple, after he had obtained admittance into the hall, stood warming himself, in the cool of the dawning morning, probably by a kind of brazier.[b] He was first accosted by a female servant, who charged him with being an accomplice of the prisoner: Peter denied the charge with vehemence, and retired to the portico or porch in front of the palace. A second time, another female renewed the accusation: with still more angry protestations Peter disclaimed all connexion with his Master; and once, but unregarded, the cock crew. An hour afterwards, probably about this time, after the formal condemnation, the charge was renewed by a relation of the man whose ear he had cut off. His harsh Galilean pronunciation had betrayed him as coming from that

Denial of Peter.

---

[a] Matt. xxvi. 67, 68; Mark xiv. 65; Luke xxii. 63-65.   xiv. 54, 66, 72; Luke xxii. 54-62; John xviii. 15, 16.
[b] Matt. xxvi. 58, 69, 75, Mark

province; but Peter now resolutely confirmed his denial with an oath. It was the usual time of the second cockcrowing, and again it was distinctly heard. Jesus, who was probably at that time in the outer hall or porch in the midst of the insulting soldiery, turned his face towards Peter, who, overwhelmed with shame and distress, hastily retreated from the sight of his deserted Master, and wept the bitter tears of self-reproach and humiliation.

But, although the Sanhedrin had thus passed their sentence, there remained a serious obstacle before it could be carried into execution. On the contested point, whether the Jews, under the Roman government, possessed the power of life and death,[a] it is not easy to state the question with brevity and distinctness. Notwithstanding the apparently clear and distinct recognition of the Sanhedrin, that they had not authority to put any man to death;[b] notwithstanding the remarkable concurrence of Rabbinical tradition with this declaration, which asserts that the nation had been deprived of the power of life and death forty years before the destruction of the city,[f] many of the most learned writers, some indeed of the ablest of the Fathers,[s] from arguments arising out of the

<small>Question of the right of the Sanhedrin to inflict capital punishment.</small>

---

[a] The question is discussed in all the commentators. See Lardner, Credib. L 2; Basnage, B. v. c. 2; Biscoe on the Acts, c. 6; note to Law's Theory, 147; but above all Krebs, Observat. in Nov. Test., 64-155; Rosenmüller and Kuinoel, in loc.

[b] John xviii. 31.

[f] Traditio est quadraginta annos ante excidium templi, ablatum fuisse jus vitæ et mortis. Hieros. Sanhed. fol. 18, 1. Ib. fol. 242: Quadraginta annis ante vastatum templum, ablata sunt judicia capitalia ab Israele. There is, however, some doubt about the reading and translation of this passage. Wagenseil reads four for forty. Selden (De Syn.) insists that the judgements were not taken away, but interrupted and disused.

[s] Among the ancients, Chrysostom and Augustine; among the moderns, Lightfoot, Lardner, Kiebs,

practice of Roman provincial jurisprudence, and from later facts in the Evangelic history and that of the Jews, have supposed, that even if, as is doubtful, they were deprived of this power in civil, they retained it in religious cases. Some have added, that even in the latter, the ratification of the sentence by the Roman governor, or the permission to carry it into execution, was necessary. According to this view, the object of the Sanhedrin was to bring the case before Pilate as a civil charge; since the assumption of a royal title and authority implied a design to cast off the Roman yoke. Or, if they retained the right of capital punishment in religious cases, it was contrary to usage, in the proceedings of the Sanhedrin, as sacred as law itself, to order an execution on the day of preparation for the Passover.* As then they dared not violate that usage, and as delay was in every way dangerous, either from the fickleness of the people, who, having been momentarily wrought up to a pitch of deadly animosity against Jesus, might again, by some act of power or goodness on his part, be carried away back to his side, or, in case of tumult, from the unsolicited intervention of the Romans, their plainest course was to obtain, if possible, the immediate support and assistance of the government.

<small>Real relation of the Sanhedrin to the government.</small> In my own opinion, formed upon the study of the cotemporary Jewish history, the power of the Sanhedrin, at this period of political change and confusion, on this, as well as on other points, was altogether undefined. Under the Asmonean

---

Rosenmüller, Kuinoel. The best disquisition on that side of the question appears to me that of Krebs; on the other, that of Basnage.

* Cyril and Augustine, with whom Kuinoel is inclined to agree, interpret the words of St. John, "It is not lawful for us to put any man to death," by subjoining "on the day of the Passover."

princes, the sovereign, uniting the civil and religious
supremacy, the High-Priesthood with the royal power,
exercised, with the Sanhedrin as his council, the highest
political and civil jurisdiction. Herod, whose authority
depended on the protection of Rome, and was maintained by his wealth, and in part by foreign mercenaries,
although he might leave to the Sanhedrin, as the supreme tribunal, the judicial power, and in ordinary
religious cases might admit their unlimited jurisdiction,
yet no doubt watched and controlled their proceedings
with the jealousy of an Asiatic despot, and practically,
if not formally, subjected all their decrees to his re-
vision: at least he would not have permitted any
encroachment on his own supreme authority. In fact,
according to the general tradition of the Jews, he at
one time put the whole Sanhedrin to death: and since,
as his life advanced, his tyranny became more watchful
and suspicious, he was more likely to diminish than
increase the powers of the national tribunal. In the
short interval of little more than thirty years which
had elapsed since the death of Herod, nearly ten had
been occupied by the reign of Archelaus. On his deposal, the Sanhedrin had probably extended or resumed
its original functions, but still the supreme civil authority
rested in the Roman Procurator. All the commotions
excited by the turbulent adventurers who infested the
country, or by Judas the Galilean and his adherents,
would fall under the cognisance of the civil governor,
and were repressed by his direct interference. Nor can
capital religious offences have been of frequent occurrence, since it is evident that the rigour of the Mosaic
Law had been greatly relaxed, partly by the feebleness
of the judicial power, partly by the tendency of the age,
which ran in a counter direction to those acts of idolatry

against which the Mosaic statutes were chiefly framed, and left few crimes obnoxious to the extreme penalty. Nor until the existence of their polity and religion was threatened, first by the progress of Christ, and afterwards of his religion, would they have cared to be armed with an authority, which it was rarely, if ever, necessary or expedient to put forth in its full force.[b]

<small>That of Jesus a new and unprecedented case.</small> This, then, may have been, strictly speaking, a new case, the first which had occurred since the reduction of Judæa to a Roman province. The Sanhedrin, from whom all jurisdiction in political cases was withdrawn, and who had no recent precedent for the infliction of capital punishment on any religious charge, might think it more prudent (particularly during this hurried and tumultuous proceeding, which commenced at midnight, and must be despatched with the least possible delay) at once to disclaim an authority which, however the Roman governor seemed <small>Motives of the rulers in disclaiming their power.</small> to attribute it to them, he might at last prevent their carrying into execution. All the other motives then operating on their minds would concur in favour of this course of proceeding:—their

---

[b] It may be worth observing, that not merely were the Pharisaic and Sadducaic parties at issue on the great question of the expediency of the severe administration of the law, which implied frequency of capital punishment; the latter party being notoriously sanguinary in the execution of public justice; but even in the Pharisaic party one school, that of Hillel, was accused (Jost, Geschichte der Israeliter), by the rival school of Shammai, of dangerous lenity in the administration of the law, and of culpable unwillingness to inflict the punishment of death.

The authority of them (says Lightfoot, from the Rabbins) was not taken away by the Romans, but rather relinquished by themselves. The slothfulness of the council destroyed its own authority. Hear it justly upbraided in this matter:—The council which puts one to death in seven years is called "destructive." R. Lazar ben Azariah said: "which puts one to death in seventy years." Lightfoot, in loc.

mistrust of the people, who might attempt a rescue from their feeble and unrespected officers, and could only, if they should fall off to the other side, be controlled by the dread of the Roman military, and the reluctance to profane so sacred a day by a public execution, of which the odium would thus be cast on their foreign rulers. It was clearly their policy, at any cost, to secure the intervention of Pilate, as well to insure the destruction of their victim, as to shift the responsibility from their own head upon that of the Romans. They might, not unreasonably, suppose that Pilate, whose relentless disposition had been shown in a recent instance, would not hesitate, at once, and on their authority, on the first intimation of a dangerous and growing party, to act without further examination or inquiry; and without scruple, add one victim more to the robbers or turbulent insurgents who, it appears, were kept in prison, in order to be executed as a terrible example at that period of national concourse.

It would seem that while Jesus was sent in chains to the Prætorium of Pilate, whether in the Antonia, the fortress adjacent to the Temple, or *Jesus before Pilate.* in part of Herod's palace, which was connected with the mountain of the Temple by a bridge over the Tyropœon, the council adjourned to their usual place of assemblage, the chamber called Gazith, within the Temple. A deputation only accompanied the prisoner to explain and support the charge, and here probably it was, in the Gazith, that, in his agony of remorse, Judas *Remorse and* brought back the reward that he had received;* *death of Judas.* and when the assembly, to his confession of his crime in betraying the innocent blood, replied with cold and

---

* Matt. xxvii. 3-10.

contumelious unconcern, he cast down the money on the pavement, and rushed away to close his miserable life. Nor must the characteristic incident be omitted. The Sanhedrin, who had not hesitated to reward the basest treachery, probably out of the Temple funds, scruple to receive back, and to replace in the sacred Treasury, the price of blood. The sum, therefore, is set apart for the purchase of a field for the burial of strangers, long known by the name of Aceldama, the Field of Blood.[d] Such is ever the absurdity, as well as the heinousness, of crimes committed in the name of religion.

The first emotion of Pilate at this strange accusation from the great tribunal of the nation, however rumours of the name and influence of Jesus had, no doubt, reached his ears, must have been the utmost astonishment. To the Roman mind the Jewish character was ever an inexplicable problem. But if so when they were seen scattered about and mingled with the countless diversities of races of discordant habits, usages, and religions, which thronged to the metropolis of the world, or were dispersed through the principal cities of the empire; in their own country, where there was, as it were, a concentration of all their extraordinary national propensities, they must have appeared, and did appear, in still stronger opposition to the rest of mankind. To the loose manner in which religious belief hung on the greater part of the subjects of the Roman empire, their recluse and uncompromising attachment to the faith of their ancestors offered the most singular

Astonishment of Pilate.

---

[d] The sum appears extremely small for the purchase of a field, even should we adopt the very probable suggestion of Kuinoel (in loc.), that it was a field in which the fuller's earth had been worked out, and which was therefore entirely barren and unproductive. Matt. xxvii. 2-14; Mark xiv. 1-5; Luke xxiii. 1-6; John xviii. 28-38.

contrast. Everywhere else the temples were open, the rites free to the stranger by race or country, who rarely scrupled to do homage to the tutelar deity of the place. The Jewish Temple alone received indeed, but with a kind of jealous condescension, the offerings even of the Emperor. Throughout the rest of the world, religious enthusiasm might not be uncommon; here and there, and in individual cases, particularly in the East, the priests of some of the mystic religions at times excited a considerable body of followers, and drove them blindfold to the wildest acts of superstitious frenzy; but the sudden access of religious fervour was, in general, as transient as violent; the flame burned with rapid and irresistible fury, and went out of itself. The Jews stood alone (according to the language and opinion of the Roman world) as a nation of religious fanatics; and this fanaticism was a deep, a settled, a conscientious feeling, and formed, an essential and inseparable part, the groundwork of their rigid and unsocial character.

Yet even to one familiarised by a residence of several years with the Jewish nation, on the present occasion the conduct of the Sanhedrin must have appeared utterly unaccountable. This senate, or municipal body, had left to the Roman governor to discover the danger, and suppress the turbulence, of the robbers and insurgents against whom Pilate had taken such decisive measures. Now, however, they appear suddenly seized with an access of loyalty for the Roman authority and a trembling apprehension of the least invasion of the Roman title to supremacy. And against whom were they actuated by this unwonted caution, and burning with this unprecedented zeal? Against a man who, as far as Pilate could discover, was a harmless, peaceful, and benevolent enthusiast, who had persuaded many of the lower orders to believe in certain unintelligible doctrines, which seemed to have no relation to the government of the country, and were, as yet, no way connected with insurrectionary movements. In fact, Pilate could not but clearly see that they were jealous of the influence obtained by Jesus over the populace; but whether Jesus or the Sanhedrin governed the religious feelings and practices of the people, was a matter of perfect indifference to the Roman supremacy.

The vehemence with which they pressed the charge, and the charge itself, were equally inexplicable. When Pilate referred back, as it were, the judgement to themselves, and offered to leave Jesus to be punished by the existing law; while they shrank from that responsibility, and disclaimed, at least over such a case and at such a season, the power of life and death, they did not in the least relax the vehement earnestness of their prosecution. Jesus was accused of assuming the title of King of the Jews, and an intention of throwing off the Roman yoke. But, however little Pilate may have heard or understood his doctrines, the conduct and demeanour of Christ were so utterly at variance with such a charge; the only intelligible article in the accusation, his imputed prohibition of the payment of tribute, so unsupported by proof, as to bear no weight. This redoubted king had been seized by the emissaries of the Sanhedrin, perhaps Roman soldiers placed under their orders; had been conveyed without resistance through the city; his few adherents, mostly unarmed peasants, had fled at the instant of his capture; not the slightest tumultuary movement had taken place during his examination before the High Priest, and the popular feeling seemed rather at present incensed against him than inclined to take his part.

To the mind of Pilate, indeed, accustomed to the disconnexion of religion and morality, the more striking contradiction in the conduct of the Jewish rulers may not have appeared altogether so extraordinary. At the moment when they were violating the great eternal and immutable principles of all religion, and infringing on one of the positive commandments of their Law, by persecuting to death an innocent man, they were withholden by religious scruple from entering the dwelling of Pilate; they were endangering the success of their cause, lest this intercourse with the unclean stranger should exclude them from the worship of their God—a worship for which they contracted no disqualifying defilement by this deed of blood. The deputation stood *without* the hall of Pilate;[*] and not even their animosity against Jesus could induce them to depart from that superstitious usage, so as to lend the weight of their personal appearance to the solemn accusation, or, at all events, to deprive the hated object of their persecution of any advantage which He might receive from undergoing his examination without being confronted with his accusers. Pilate seems to have paid so much respect to their usages, *that he went out to receive their charge,* and to inquire the nature of the crime for which Jesus was denounced.

The simple question put to Jesus, on his first interrogatory before Pilate, was, whether He claimed the title of King of the Jews?[†] The answer of Jesus may be considered as an appeal to the justice and right feeling

_{The deputation refuse to enter the hall of Pilate from fear of legal defilement.}

---

[*] John xviii. 28.   [†] John xviii. 33-37.

of the Governor. "*Sayest thou this thing of thyself,* *or did others tell it thee of me?*" "As Roman Prefect, have you any cause for suspecting me of ambitious or insurrectionary designs? Do you entertain the least apprehension of my seditious demeanour? Or are you not rather adopting the suggestions of my enemies, and lending yourself to their unwarranted animosity?" Pilate disclaims all communion with the passions or the prejudices of the Jewish rulers. *Am I a Jew?* But Jesus had been brought before him, denounced as a dangerous disturber of the public peace, and the Roman Governor was officially bound to take cognisance of such a charge. In the rest of the defence of Christ, the only part intelligible to Pilate would be the unanswerable appeal to the peaceful conduct of his followers. When Jesus asserted that He was a king, yet evidently implied a moral or religious sense in his use of the term, Pilate might attribute a vague meaning to his language, from the Stoic axiom, "I am a king when I rule myself;" and thus give a sense to that which otherwise would have sounded in his ears like unintelligible mysticism. His perplexity, however, must have been greatly increased when Jesus, in this perilous hour, when his life trembled as it were on the balance, declared that the object of his birth and of his life was the establishment of "the truth." "To this end was I born, and for this cause came I into the world, that I should bear witness to the *truth.* Every one that is of the *truth* heareth my voice." That the peace of a nation or the life of an individual should be endangered on

---

Ad summum sapiens uno minor est Jove, dives Liber, honoratus, pulcher, Rex denique regum.—Hor. Epist. II. 1. 106.

Comp. Sat. l. 3. 125.
At pueri ludentes, rex eris, inquit, Si recte facies.—Epist. l. 1. 59.

account of the truth or falsehood of any system of speculative opinions, was so diametrically opposite to the general opinion and feeling of the Roman world, that Pilate, either in contemptuous mockery, or with the merciful design of showing the utter harmlessness and insignificance of such points, inquired what He meant by *truth*,—what *truth* had to do with the present question, with a question of life and death, with a capital charge brought by the national council before the supreme tribunal. Apparently despairing, on one side, of bringing him, whom he seems to have considered a blameless enthusiast, to his senses; on the other, unwilling to attach so much importance to what appeared to him in so different a light, he wished at once to put an end to the whole affair. He abruptly left Jesus, and *Pilate endeavours to save Jesus.* went out again to the Jewish deputation at the gate (now perhaps increased by a greater number of the Sanhedrin), and declared his conviction of the innocence of Jesus.

At this unexpected turn, the Sanhedrin burst into a furious clamour, reiterated their vague, per- *Clamours of the accusers.* haps contradictory, and to the ears of Pilate unintelligible or insignificant charges, and seemed determined to press the conviction with implacable animosity. Pilate turned to Jesus, who had been led out, to demand his answer to these charges. Jesus stood collected, but silent, and the astonishment of Pilate was still further heightened. The only accusation which seemed to bear any meaning, imputed to Jesus the raising tumultuous meetings of the people throughout the country, from Judæa to Galilee.[b] This incidental mention of Galilee, made perhaps with an invidious design of awakening in

---

[b] Luke xxiii. 5.

the mind of the Governor the remembrance of the turbulent character of that people, suggested to Pilate a course by which he might rid himself of the embarrassment and responsibility of this strange transaction. It has been conjectured, not without probability, that the massacre of Herod's subjects was the cause of the enmity that existed between the tetrarch and the Roman Governor. Pilate had now an opportunity at once to avoid an occurrence of the same nature, in which he had no desire to be implicated, and to make overtures of reconciliation to the native sovereign. He was indifferent about the fate of Jesus, provided he could shake off all actual concern in his death; or he might suppose that Herod, uninfected with the inexplicable enmity of the Chief Priests, might be inclined to protect his innocent subject.[1]

Jesus sent to Herod. The fame of Jesus had already excited the curiosity of Herod, but his curiosity was rather that which sought amusement or excitement from the powers of an extraordinary wonder-worker, than that which looked for information or improvement from a wise moral, or a divinely-commissioned religious teacher. The circumstances of the interview, which probably took place in the presence of the tetrarch and his courtiers, and into which none of the disciples of Jesus could find their way, are not related. The investigation was long; but Jesus maintained his usual unruffled silence, and at the close of the examination *Jesus sent back with insult.* He was sent back to Pilate. By the murder of John, Herod had incurred deep and lasting unpopularity; he might be unwilling to increase his character for cruelty by the same conduct towards

---

[1] Luke xxiii. 5-12.

Jesus, against whom, as he had not the same private reasons for requiring his support, he had not the same bitterness of personal animosity; nor was his sovereignty, as has before been observed, endangered in the same manner as that of the Chief Priests, by the progress of Jesus. Herod therefore might treat with derision what appeared to him a harmless assumption of royalty, and determine to effect, by contempt and contumely, that degradation of Jesus in the estimation of the people which his more cruel measures in the case of John had failed to accomplish. With his connivance, therefore, if not under his instructions, his soldiers (perhaps some of them, as those of his father had been —foreigners, Gaulish or Thracian barbarians) were permitted or encouraged in every kind of cruel and wanton insult. They clothed the Saviour, in mockery of his royal title, in a purple robe, and so escorted him back to Pilate, who, if he occupied part of the Herodion, not the Antonia, was close at hand, only in a different quarter of the same extensive palace.

The refusal of Herod to take cognisance of the charge renewed the embarrassment of Pilate, but a way yet seemed open to extricate himself from his difficulty. There was a custom that, in honour of the great festival, the Passover, a prisoner should be set at liberty at the request of the people.[k] The multitude had already become clamorous for their annual privilege. Among the half-robbers, half-insurgents, who had so long infested the province of Judæa and the whole of Palestine, there was a celebrated bandit, named Barabbas, who, probably in some insurrec-

Barabbas.

---

[k] Matt. xxvii. 15-20; Mark xv. 6-11; Luke xxiii. 13-19; John xviii. 39.

tionary tumult, had been guilty of murder. Of the extent of his crime we are ignorant; but Pilate, by selecting the worst case, that which the people could not but consider the most atrocious and offensive to the Roman Government, might desire to force them, as it were, to demand the release of Jesus. Barabbas had been undeniably guilty of those overt acts of insubordination, which they endeavoured to infer as necessary consequences of the teaching of Jesus.

Pilate came forth, therefore, to the outside of his Prætorium, and, having declared that neither himself nor Herod could discover any real guilt in the prisoner who had been brought before them, he appealed to them to choose between the condemned insurgent and murderer, and the blameless Prophet of Nazareth. The High Priests had now wrought the people to madness, and had most likely crowded the courts round Pilate's quarters with their most zealous and devoted partisans. The voice of the Governor was drowned with an instantaneous burst of acclamation, demanding the release of Barabbas. Pilate made yet another ineffectual attempt to save the life of the innocent man. He thought by some punishment, short of death, if not to awaken the compassion, to satisfy the animosity, of the people.[m] The person of Jesus was given up to the lictors, and scourging with rods, the common Roman punishment for minor offences, was inflicted with merciless severity.

<small>Jesus crowned with thorns and shewn to the people.</small> The soldiers platted a crown of thorns, or, as is thought, of some prickly plant, as it is scarcely conceivable that life could have endured if the temples had been deeply pierced by a circle of thorns.[n]

---

[m] Luke xxiii. 16; John xix. 1-5.
[n] It would seem, says Grotius, that the mockery was more intended than the pain. Some suppose the plant,

In this pitiable state Jesus was again led forth, bleeding from the scourge, his brow throbbing with the pointed crown; and dressed in the purple robe of mockery, to make the last vain appeal to the compassion, the humanity, of the people. The wild and furious cries of "Crucify him! Crucify him!" broke out on all sides. In vain Pilate commanded them to be the executioners of their own sentence, and reasserted his conviction of the innocence of Jesus. In vain he accompanied his assertion by the significant action of washing his hands in the public view, as if to show that he would contract no guilt or defilement from the blood of a blameless man.[e] He was answered by the awful imprecation, *The people demand his crucifixion.* "His blood be upon us, and upon our children." The deputies of the Sanhedrin pressed more earnestly the capital charge of blasphemy—"He had made himself the Son of God."[f] This inexplicable accusation still more shook the resolution of Pilate, who, perhaps at this instant, was further agitated by a message from his wife. Claudia Procula (the law which prohibited the wives of the provincial rulers from accompanying their husbands to the seat of their governments now having fallen into disuse) had been *Intercession of Pilate's wife.* permitted to reside with her husband Pilate in Palestine.[g] The stern justice of the Romans had guarded by this law against the baneful effects of female influence. In this instance, had Pilate listened to the

---

the nabk or nabka of the Arabians—with many small and sharp spikes—which would be painful, but not endanger life. Hasselquist's Travels.

[e] Matt. xxvii. 24, 25.
[f] John xix. 7.
[g] Matt. xxvii. 19-23. This law had fallen into neglect in the time of Augustus; during the reign of Tiberius it was openly infringed, and the motion of Cæcina in the Senate to put it more strictly in force produced no effect. Tac. Ann. iii. 33.

humaner counsels of his wife, from what a load of guilt would he have delivered his own conscience and his province! Aware of the proceedings, which had occupied Pilate during the whole night—perhaps in some way better acquainted with the character of Jesus, she had gone to rest; but her sleep, her morning slumbers, when visions were supposed to be more than ordinarily true, were disturbed by dreams of the innocence o Jesus, and the injustice and inhumanity to which her husband might lend his authority.

The prisoner was withdrawn into the guard-room, and Pilate endeavoured to obtain some explanation of the meaning of this new charge from Jesus himself. He made no answer; and Pilate appealed to his fears, reminding him that his life and death depended on the power of the Prefect. Jesus replied, that his life was only in the power of Divine Providence, by whose permission alone Pilate enjoyed a temporary authority.[r] But touched, it may seem, by the exertions of Pilate to save him, with all his accustomed gentleness he declares Pilate guiltless of his blood, in comparison with his betrayers and persecutors among his own countrymen. This speech still further moved Pilate in favour of Jesus. But the justice and the compassion of the Roman gave way at once before the fear of weakening his own interest, or endangering his own personal safety, with his imperial master. He made one effort more to work on the implacable people; he was answered with the same furious exclamations, and with menaces of more alarming import. They accused him of indifference to the stability of the imperial power:—"Thou art not Cæsar's friend:"[s] they threat-

---

[r] John xix. 8-11.   [s] John xix. 12.

ened to report his conduct, in thus allowing the title of royalty to be assumed with impunity, to the reigning Cæsar. That Cæsar was the dark and jealous Tiberius. Up to this period the Jewish nation, when they had complained of the tyranny of their native sovereigns, had ever obtained a favourable hearing at Rome. Even against Herod the Great, their charges had been received; they had been admitted to a public audience; and though their claim to national independence at the death of that sovereign had not been allowed, Archelaus had received his government with limited powers, and on the complaint of the people had been removed from his throne. In short, the influence of that attachment to the Cæsarean family,[1] which had obtained for the nation distinguished privileges from both Julius and Augustus, had not yet been effaced by that character of turbulence and insubordination which led to their final ruin.

In what manner such a charge of not being "Cæsar's friend" might be misrepresented or aggravated, it was impossible to conjecture; but the very strangeness of the accusation was likely to work on the gloomy and suspicious mind of Tiberius; and the frail tenure by which Pilate held his favour at Rome is shown by his ignominious recall and banishment some years after, *on the complaint of the Jewish people*; though not, it is true, for an act of indiscreet mercy, but one of unnecessary cruelty. The latent and suspended decision of his character reappeared in all its customary recklessness. The life of one man, however blameless, was not for an instant to be considered, when his own advancement, his personal safety, were in peril: his sterner nature

---

[1] Compare Hist. of the Jews, II. 46.

resumed the ascendant; he mounted the tribunal, which was erected on a tesselated pavement near the Prætorium,* and passed the solemn, the irrevocable sentence. It might almost seem that, in bitter mockery, Pilate for the last time demanded, "Shall I crucify your king?" "We have no king, but Cæsar," was the answer of the Chief Priests. Pilate yielded up the contest; the murderer was commanded to be set at liberty, the Just man surrendered to crucifixion.

<small>Condemnation of Jesus.</small>

The remorseless soldiery were at hand, and instigated, no doubt, by the influence, by the bribes, of the Sanhedrin, carried the sentence into effect with the most savage and wanton insults. They dressed him up in all the mock semblance of royalty (He had already the purple robe and the crown); a reed was now placed in his hand for a sceptre; they paid him their insulting homage; struck him with the palms of their hands; spat upon him; and then stripping him of his splendid attire, dressed him again in his own simple raiment, and led him out to death.²

<small>Insults of Jesus by the populace and soldiery.</small>

The place of execution was without the gates. This was the case in most towns; and in Jerusalem, which,

---

* I should not notice the strange mistake of the learned German, Hug, on this subject, if it had not been adopted by a clever writer in a popular journal. Hug has supposed the λιθόστρωτον (perhaps the tesselated) stone pavement on which Pilate's tribunal was erected, to be the same which was the scene of a remarkable incident mentioned by Josephus. During the siege of the Temple, a centurion, Julianus, charged on horseback, and forced his way into the inner court of the Temple, his horse stepped up on the pavement (λιθόστρωτον), and he fell. It is scarcely credible that any writer acquainted with Jewish antiquities, or the structure of the Temple, could suppose that the Roman Governor would raise his tribunal within the inviolable precincts of the inner court.

² Matt. xxvii. 27-30; Mark xv. 15-20.

according to tradition, always maintained a kind of resemblance to the camp in the wilderness,[v] as criminal punishments were forbidden to defile the sacred precincts, a field beyond the walls was set apart and desecrated for this unhallowed purpose.[s]

Hitherto I have been tempted into some detail, both by the desire of ascertaining the state of the public mind, and the motives of the different actors in this unparalleled transaction, and by the necessity of harmonising the various circumstances related in the four separate narratives. As we approach the appalling close, I tremble lest the colder process of explanation should deaden the solemn and harrowing impression of the scene, or weaken the contrast between the wild and tumultuous uproar of the triumphant enemies and executioners of the Son of Man, with the deep and unutterable misery of the few faithful adherents who still followed his footsteps: and, far above all, his own serene, his more than human, composure, the dignity of suffering, which casts so far into the shade every example of human heroism. Yet in the most trifling incidents there is so much life and reality, so remarkable an adherence to the usages of the time and to the state of public feeling, that I cannot but point out the most striking of these particulars. For, in fact,

Circumstances of the crucifixion.

---

[v] Numbers xv. 35; 1 Kings xxi. 13; Hebrews xiii. 12. Extra urbem, patibulum. Plautus. See Grotius.

[s] It is curious to trace on what uncertain grounds rest many of our established notions relating to incidents in the early history of our religion. No one scruples to speak in the popular language of "the Hill of Calvary;" yet there appears no evidence, which is not purely legendary, for the assertion that Calvary was on a hill. The notion arose from the fanciful interpretation of the word Golgotha (the Place of a Skull), which was thought to imply some resemblance in its form to a human skull; but it is far more probably derived from having been strewn with the remains of condemned malefactors.

there is no single circumstance, however minute, which does not add to the truth of the whole description, so as to stamp it (I have honestly endeavoured to consider it with the calmest impartiality) with an impression of credibility, of certainty, equal to, if not surpassing, every event in the history of man. The inability of Jesus (exhausted by a sleepless night, by the length of the trial, by insults and bodily pain, by the scourging and the blows) to bear his own cross (the constant practice of condemned criminals);[a] the seizure of a Cyrenian, from a province more numerously colonised by Jews than any other, except Egypt and Babylonia, as he was entering the city, and, perhaps, was known to be an adherent of Jesus, to bear the cross;[b] the customary deadening potion of wine and myrrh,[c] which was given to malefactors previous to their execution, but which Jesus, aware of its stupifying or intoxicating effect, and determined to preserve his firmness and self-command, but slightly touched with his lips; the title, the King[d] of the Jews, in three languages,[e] so strictly in accordance with the public usage of the time; the division and casting lots for his garments by the soldiers who executed him (those who suffered the ignominious punishment of the cross being exposed entirely naked, or with nothing more than was necessary for decency);[f]

---

[a] Hence the common term "furcifer." Patibulum ferat per urbem, deinde affigatur cruci. Plauti Frag.

[b] Mark xv. 21; Luke xxiii. 26.

[c] Matt. xxvii. 34; Mark xv. 24. The Rabbins say, wine with frankincense. This potion was given by the Jews out of compassion to criminals.

[d] Luke xxiii. 38; John xix. 19, 20.

[e] The inscriptions on the pallisades which divided the part of the Temple court which might be entered by the Gentiles from that which was open only to the Jews, were written, with the Roman sanction, in the three languages, Hebrew, Greek, and Latin.

[f] Matt. xxvii. 35; Mark xv. 24; Luke xxiii. 34; John xix. 23, 24. The Jewish modes of execution were by stoning, strangulation, and decapitation.

all these particulars, as well as the instrument of execution, the cross, are in strict unison with the well-known practice of Roman criminal jurisprudence. The execution of the two malefactors, one on each side of Jesus, is equally consonant with their ordinary administration of justice, particularly in this ill-fated province. Probably before, unquestionably at a later period, Jerusalem was doomed to behold the long line of crosses on which her sons were left by the relentless Roman authorities to struggle with slow and agonising death.

In other circumstances the Jewish national character is equally conspicuous. This appears even in the conduct of the malefactors. The fanatical Judaism of one, not improbably a follower, or infected with the doctrines of the Gaulonite, even in his last agony, has strength enough to insult the pretender to the name of a Messiah who yet has not the power to release himself and his fellow-sufferers from death. The other, of milder disposition, yet in death, inclines to believe in Jesus, and when he returns to assume his kingdom, would hope to share in its blessings. To him Jesus, speaking in the current, and therefore intelligible, language, promises an immediate reward; he is to pass at once from life to happiness—from the cross to Paradise.[e] Besides this, how striking the triumph of his enemies, as the Lord seemed to surrender himself without resistance to the growing pangs of death; the assembling, not only of the rude and ferocious populace, but of many of the most distinguished rank, the members of the Sanhedrin, to behold and to insult the last moments of their once redoubted, but now despised, adversary!

The two malefactors.

Spectators of the execution.

---

[e] Luke xxiii. 39-43.

And still every indication of approaching death seemed more and more to justify their rejection!—still no sign of the mighty, the all-powerful Messiah! Their taunting allusions to his royal title, to his misapprehended speech, which rankled in their hearts, about the demolition and rebuilding of the Temple;[a] to his power of healing others, and restoring life, a power in his own case so manifestly suspended or lost; the offer to acknowledge him as the Messiah, if he would come down from the cross in the face of day; the still more malignant reproach, that He, who had boasted of the peculiar favour of God, was now so visibly deserted and abandoned,—the Son of Man, as He called himself, is left to perish despised and disregarded by God; all this as strikingly accords with, and illustrates the state of, Jewish feeling, as do the former circumstances the Roman usages.

And amid the whole wild and tumultuous scene there are some quiet gleams of pure Christianity, which contrast with and relieve the general darkness and horror: not merely the superhuman patience, with which insult, and pain, and ignominy, are borne; not merely the serene self-command, which shows that the senses are not benumbed or deadened by the intensity of suffering; but the slight incidental touches of gentleness and humanity.[b] I cannot but indicate the answer to the afflicted women, who stood by the way weeping, as Jesus passed on to Calvary, and whom He commanded not "to weep for him," but for the deeper sorrows to which themselves or their children were devoted; the notice of the group of his own kindred

---

[a] Matt. xxvii. 39-40; Mark xv. 31, 32; Luke xxiii. 35.
[b] Luke xxiii. 27-31.

and followers who stood by the cross; his bequest of the support of his Virgin Mother to the beloved disciple;[k] above all, that most affecting exemplification of his own tenets, the prayer for the pardon of his enemies, the palliation of their crime from their ignorance of its real enormity,—"Father, forgive them, for they know not what they do."[m] Yet so little are the Evangelists studious of effect, that this incident of unrivalled moral sublimity, even in the whole life of Christ, is but briefly, we might almost say carelessly, noticed by St. Luke alone.

From the sixth hour (noonday), writes the Evangelist St. Matthew, there was darkness over all the land unto the ninth hour.[n] The whole earth (the term in the other Evangelists) is no doubt used according to Jewish phraseology, in which Palestine, the sacred land, was emphatically the earth. This supernatural gloom appears to resemble that terrific darkness which precedes an earthquake.

Preternatural darkness.

For these three hours Jesus had borne the excruciating anguish—his human nature begins to fail, and he complains of the burning thirst, the most painful but usual aggravation of such a death. A compassionate bystander filled a sponge with vinegar, fixed it on a long reed, and was about to lift it to his lips, when the dying Jesus uttered his last words, those of the Twenty-

---

[k] John xix. 25-27.
[m] Luke xxiii. 34.
[n] Matt. xxvii. 45-53; Mark xv. 33-38; Luke xxiii. 44, 45; John xix. 28-30.

Gibbon has said, and truly, as regards all well-informed and sober interpreters of the sacred writings, that "the celebrated passage of Phlegon is now wisely abandoned." It still maintains its ground, however, with writers of a certain class, notwithstanding that its irrelevancy has already been admitted by Origen, and its authority rejected by every writer who has the least pretensions to historical criticism.

second Psalm, in which, in the bitterness of his heart, David had complained of the manifest desertion of his God, who had yielded him up to his enemies—the phrase had perhaps been in common use in extreme distress—Eli, Eli, lama sabachthani?—My God, my God, why hast thou forsaken me?° The compassionate hand of the man, raising the vinegar, was arrested by others, who, a few perhaps in trembling curiosity, but more in bitter mockery, supposing that He called not on God (Eli) but on Elias, commanded him to wait and see, whether, even now, that great and certain sign of the Messiah, the appearance of Elijah, would at length take place.

Their barbarous triumph was uninterrupted; and He, who yet (his followers were not without some lingering hope, and the more superstitious of his enemies not without some trembling apprehension) might awaken to all his terrible and prevailing majesty, had now manifestly expired.ᴾ The Messiah, the imperishable, the eternal Messiah, had quietly yielded up the ghost.

Death of Jesus.

Even the dreadful earthquake ⁹ which followed, seemed to pass away without appalling the enemies of Jesus. The rending of the veil of the Temple from the top to the bottom, so strikingly significant of the approaching abolition of the local worship, would either be concealed by the priesthood, or attributed as a natural effect to the convulsion of the earth. The same convulsion would displace the stones which covered the ancient tombs, and lay open many of the innumerable rock-hewn

---

° Matt. xxvii. 46; Mark xv. 34-37; John xix. 28-30.
ᴾ Luke xxiii. 46.

⁹ Σεισμός is the ordinary word for an earthquake.

sepulchres which perforated the hills on every side of the city, and expose the dead to public view. To the awe-struck and depressed minds of the followers of Jesus, no doubt, were confined those visionary appearances of the spirits of their deceased brethren, which are obscurely intimated in the rapid narratives of the Evangelists.'

But these terrific appearances, which were altogether lost on the infatuated Jews, were not without effect on the less prejudiced Roman soldiery; they seemed to bear the testimony of Heaven to the innocence, to the divine commission, of the crucified Jesus. The centurion who guarded the spot, according to St. Luke, declared aloud his conviction that Jesus was "a just man;" according to St. Matthew, that He was "the Son of God."*

Burial of Jesus.

Secure now, by the visible marks of dissolution, by the piercing of his side, from which blood and water flowed out, that Jesus was actually dead; and still, even in their most irreligious acts of cruelty and wickedness, punctiliously religious (since it was a sin to leave the body of that blameless being on the cross during one day,' whom it had been no sin, but

---

' This is the probable and consistent view of Michaelis. Those who assert a supernatural eclipse of the sun rest on the most dubious and suspicious tradition; while those who look with jealousy on the introduction of natural causes, however so timed as in fact to be no less extraordinary than events altogether contrary to the course of nature, forget or despise the difficulty of accounting for the apparently slight sensation produced on the minds of the Jews, and the total silence of all other history. Compare the very sensible note of M. Guizot on the latter part of Gibbon's xvth chapter.

* Matt. xxvii. 54; Luke xxiii. 47. Lightfoot supposes that by intercourse with the Jews he may have learned their phraseology: Grotius, that he had a general impression that Jesus was a superior being.

' Deut. xxi. 23. The Jews usually buried executed criminals ignominiously, but at the request of a family would permit a regular burial. Lightfoot, from Babyl. San.

rather an act of the highest virtue, to murder the day before), the Sanhedrin gave their consent to a wealthy adherent of Jesus, Joseph, of the town of Arimathea, to bury the body. The sanction of Pilate was easily obtained: it was taken down from the cross, and consigned to the sepulchre prepared by Joseph for his own family, but in which no body had yet been laid.* The sepulchre was at no great distance from the place of execution; the customary rites were performed; the body was wrapped in fine linen and anointed with a mixture of costly spice and myrrh, with which the remains of those who were held in respect by their kindred were usually preserved. As the Sabbath was drawing on, the work was performed with the utmost despatch, and Jesus was laid to rest in the grave of his faithful adherent.

In that rock-hewn tomb might appear to be buried for ever both the fears of his enemies and the hopes of his followers. Though some rumours of his predictions concerning his resurrection had crept abroad, sufficient to awaken the caution of the Sanhedrin, and to cause them to seal the outward covering of the sepulchre, and, with the approbation of Pilate, to station a Roman guard upon the spot; yet, as far as the popular notion of the Messiah, nothing could be more entirely and absolutely destructive of their hopes than the patient submission of Jesus to insult, to degradation, to death. However, with some of milder nature, his exquisite sufferings might excite compassion; however the savage and implacable cruelty with which the Rulers urged his fate might appear revolting to the multitude, after their first access of religious indignation had passed away, and the recollection returned to

The religion apparently at an end.

---

* Matt. xxvii. 57-60; Mark xv. 42-47; Luke xxiii. 50-56; John xix. 38-42.

the gentle demeanour and beneficent acts of Jesus; yet the hope of REDEMPTION, whatever meaning they might attach to the term, whether deliverance from their enemies or the restoration of their theocratic government, had set in utter darkness. However vague or contradictory this notion among the different sects or classes, with the mass of the people, nothing less than an immediate instantaneous reappearance in some appalling or imposing form could have reinstated Jesus in his high place in the popular expectation. Without this, his career was finally closed, and He would pass away at once, as one of the brief wonders of the time, his temporary claims to respect or attachment refuted altogether by the shame, by the ignominy, of his death. His ostensible leading adherents were men of the humblest origin, and, as yet, of no distinguished ability; men from whom little danger could be apprehended, and who might safely be treated with contemptuous neglect. No attempt appears to have been made to secure a single person, or to prevent their peaceful retreat to their native Galilee. The whole religion centered in the person of Jesus, and in his death was apparently suppressed, crushed, extinguished for ever. After a few days, the Sanhedrin would dread nothing less than a new disturbance from the same quarter; and Pilate, as the whole affair had passed off without tumult, would soon suppress the remonstrances of his conscience at the sacrifice of an innocent life, since the public peace had been maintained, and no doubt his own popularity with the leading Jews considerably heightened, at so cheap a price. All then was at an end: yet, after the death of Christ, commences, strictly speaking, the history of Christianity.

BOOK II.

CHAPTER I.

The Resurrection, and first Promulgation of Christianity.

Christian doctrine of the immortality of the soul.

THE resurrection of Jesus is the basis of Christianity; it is the groundwork of the *Christian* doctrine of the immortality of the soul. Henceforward that great truth begins to assume a new character, and to obtain an influence over the political and social, as well as over the individual happiness of man, unknown in the former ages of the world.[a] It is no longer a feeble and uncertain instinct, nor a remote speculative opinion, obscured by the more pressing necessities and cares of the present life, but the universal predominant sentiment, constantly present to the thoughts, enwoven with the usages, and pervading the whole moral being of man. The dim and scattered rays, either of traditionary belief, of intuitive feeling, or of philosophic reasoning, were brought as it were to a focus, condensed and poured with an immeasurably stronger, an expanding, an all-permeating light upon the human soul.[b] Whatever its origin, whether in

---

[a] Our Saviour assumes the doctrine of another life, as the basis of his doctrines, because, in a certain sense, it was already the popular belief among the Jews; but it is very different with the Apostles, when they address the heathen, who formed far the largest part of the converts to Christianity.

[b] I have found some of these observations, and even expressions, anticipated by the striking remarks of Lessing: Und so ward Christus der erste zuverlässige praktische Lehrer der Unsterblichkeit der Seele. Der erste zuverlässige Lehrer. Zuverlässig durch seine Weissagungen, den in ihm erfüllt schienen: zuverlässig durch die Wunder die er verrichtete: zuverlässig durch

human nature, or the aspirations of high-thoughted individuals, propagated through their followers, or in former revelation, it received such an impulse, and was so deeply and universally moulded up with the popular mind in all orders, that from this period may be dated the true era of its dominion. If by no means new in its elementary principle, it was new in the degree and the extent to which it began to operate in the affairs of men.*

seine eigne Wiederbelebung nach einem Tode, durch den er seine Lehre versiegelt hatte. Der erste praktische Lehrer. Denn ein anders ist, die Unsterblichkeit der Seele, als eine philosophische Speculation, vermuthen, wünschen, glauben: ein anders seine Innern und aussern Handlungen darnach einrichten. Werke, x. p. 321.

* The most remarkable evidence of the extent to which German speculation has wandered away from the first principles of Christianity is this: that one of the most religious writers, the one who has endeavoured with the most earnest sincerity to reconnect religious belief with the philosophy of the times, has actually represented Christianity without, or almost without, the immortality of the soul; and this the ardent and eloquent translator of Plato! Copious and full on the moral regeneration effected by Christ in this world, with the loftiest sentiments of the emancipation of the human soul from the bondage of sin by the Gospel, Schleiermacher is silent, or almost silent, on the redemption from death. He beholds Christ distinctly as bringing life, only vaguely and remotely as bringing immortality, to light. I acknowledge that I mistrusted the extent of my own acquaintance with the writings of Schleiermacher and the accuracy with which I had read them (chiefly the Glaubenslehre and some of those sermons which were so highly admired at Berlin); but I have found my own conclusions confirmed by an author whom I cannot suspect to be unacquainted with the writings, or unjust to the character, of one for whom he entertains the most profound respect. So geschah es, dass dieser Glaubenslehre unter den Händen der Begriff des Heiles sich aus einem wesentlich jenseitigen in einem wesentlich diesseitigen verwandelte.... Hiermit ist nun aber die eigentliche Bedeutung des alten Glaubengrundsatzes in der that verloren gegangen. Wo die aussicht auf eine dereinstige, aus dem dann in Schauen umgewandten Glauben empurwachsende Seligkeit so, wie in Schleiermacher's eigener Darstellung in den Hintergrund tritt, so ganz nur als eine belläufige, in Bezug auf das Wie ganz und gar problematisch bleibende Folgerung, ja fast als ein hors d'œuvre hinzugebracht wird: da wird auch demjenigen Bewusstsein welches seine diesseitige Befriedigung in dem Glauben an Christus gewonnen hat, offenbar seine mächtigste, ja seine einzige Waffe gegen alle die ihm die Wahrheit solcher Befriedigung bestreiten, oder bezweifeln, aus den Händen gerissen. Weisse, Die Evangelische Geschichte, Band. II. p. 451.

The calm inquirer into the history of human nature, as displayed in the existing records of our race, if unhappily disinclined to receive the Christian faith as a divine revelation, must nevertheless behold in this point of time the crisis, and in this circumstance the governing principle, of the destinies of mankind during many centuries of their most active and fertile development. A new race of passions was introduced into the political arena, as well as into the individual heart, or rather the natural and universal passions were enlisted in the service of more absorbing and momentous interests. The fears and hopes by which man is governed took a wider range, embracing the future life in many respects with as much, or even stronger, energy and intenseness than the present. The stupendous dominion erected by the Church, the great characteristic feature of modern history, rested almost entirely on this basis; it ruled as possessing an inherent power over the destiny of the soul in a future world. It differed in this primary principle of its authority from the sacerdotal castes of antiquity. The latter rested their influence on hereditary claims to superiority over the rest of mankind; and though they dealt sometimes, more or less largely, in the terrors and hopes of another state of being, especially in defence of their own power and privileges, theirs was a kind of mixed aristocracy of birth and priestcraft. But if this new and irresistible power lent itself, in certain stages of society, to human ambition, and, as a stern and inflexible lictor, bowed down the whole mind of man to the fasces of a spiritual tyranny, it must be likewise contemplated in its far wider and more lasting, though perhaps less imposing character, as the parent of all which is purifying, ennobling, unselfish, in Christian civilisation; as a principle of every humanising virtue which philosophy must ever want; of self-sacrifice, to which the patriotism of antiquity shrinks into a narrow and national feeling: and as introducing a doctrine of equality as sublime as it is without danger to the necessary gradations which must exist in human society. Since the promulgation of Christianity, the immortality of the soul, and its inseparable consequence, future retribution, have not only been assumed by the legislator as the basis of all political institutions, but the general mind has been brought into such complete unison with the spirit of the laws so founded, that the individual repugnance to the principle has been constantly overborne by the general predominant sentiment. In some periods it has seemed to survive the religion on which it was founded. Wherever, at all events, it operates upon the individual or social mind, wherever it is even tacitly admitted and assented to by the prevalent feeling of mankind, it must be traced to the profound influence which Christianity has, at least at one time, exercised over the inner nature of man. This was the moral revolution which set into activity, before unprecedented, and endowed with vitality, till then unknown, this great ruling agent in the history of the world.[d]

Still, however, as though almost unconscious of the future effects of this event, the narratives of the Evangelists, as they approach this crisis in their own as well as in the destinies of man, preserve their serene and unimpassioned flow. Each follows his

---

[d] This primary blessing of Christianity seems to me too often lost sight of. Theology, even ordinary religion, has dwelt almost exclusively on other questions relating to salvation. But men required to be assured that they had immortal souls to be saved, before they became anxious how they were to be saved.

own course, with precisely that discrepancy which might be expected among inartificial writers relating the same event, without any mutual understanding or reference to each other's work, but all with the same equable and unexalted tone.

The Sabbath passed away without disturbance or commotion. The profound quiet which prevailed in the crowded capital of Judæa on the seventh day, at these times of rigid ceremonial observance, was unbroken by the partisans of Jesus. Yet even the Sabbath did not restrain the leading members of the Sanhedrin from taking the necessary precautions to guard the body of their victim; their hostile jealousy, as has been before observed, was more alive to the predictions of the resurrection than was the attachment of the disciples. To prevent any secret or tumultuous attempt of the followers to possess themselves of the remains of their Master, they caused a seal to be attached to the stone which formed the door to the sepulchral enclosure, and stationed the guard which was at their disposal, probably for the preservation of the public peace, in the garden around the tomb. The guard, being Roman, might exercise their military functions on the sacred day. The disciples were no doubt restrained by the sanctity of the Sabbath, as well as by their apprehensions of re-awakening the popular indignation, even from approaching the burial-place of their Master. The religion of the Sabbath day lulled alike the passions of the Rulers, the popular tumult, the fears and the sorrows of the disciples.

It was not till the early dawn of the following morning[*] that some of the women set out to pay the last melan-

---

[*] Matt. xxviii.; Mark xvi.; Luke xxiv.; John xx.

choly honours at the sepulchre. They had bought some of those precious drugs which were used for the preservation of the remains of the more opulent, on the evening of the crucifixion; and though the body had been anointed and wrapt in spices in the customary manner, previously to the burial, this further mark of respect was strictly according to usage. But this circumstance, thus casually mentioned, clearly shows that the women, at least, had no hope whatever of any change which could take place as to the body of Jesus.' The party of women consisted of Mary of Magdala, a town near the Lake of Tiberias; Mary, the wife of Alpheus, mother of James and Joses; Joanna, wife of Chuza, Herod's steward; and Salome, "the mother of Zebedee's children." They were all Galileans, and from the same neighbourhood; all faithful attendants on Jesus, and related to some of the leading disciples. They set out very early; and as perhaps they had to meet from different quarters, some not unlikely from Bethany, the sun was rising before they reached the garden. Before their arrival, the earthquake or atmos-

---

' In a prolusion of Griesbach, De fontibus unde Evangelistæ suas de resurrectione Domini narrationes hauserint, it is observed, that the Evangelists seem to have dwelt on those particular points in which they were personally concerned. This appears to furnish a very simple key to their apparent discrepancies. John, who received his first intelligence from Mary Magdalene, makes her the principal person in his narrative, while Matthew, who, with the rest of the disciples, derived his information from the other women, gives their relation, and omits the appearance of Jesus to the Magdalene. St. Mark gives a few additional minute particulars, but the narrative of St. Luke is altogether more vague and general. He blends together, as a later historian, studious of compression, the two separate transactions: he ascribes to the women collectively that communication of the intelligence to the assembled body of the Apostles which appears to have been made separately to two distinct parties; and disregarding the order of time, he after that reverts to the visit of St. Peter to the sepulchre.

pheric commotion* had taken place; the tomb had burst open; and the terrified guard had fled to the city. Of the sealing of the stone, and the placing of the guard, they appear to have been ignorant, as, in the most natural manner, they seem suddenly to remember the difficulty of removing the ponderous stone which closed the sepulchre, and which would require the strength of several men to raise it from its place. Sepulchres in the East, those at least belonging to men of rank and opulence, were formed of an outward small court or enclosure, the entrance to which was covered by a huge stone; and within were cells or chambers, often hewn in the solid rock, for the deposit of the dead. As the women drew near, they saw that the stone had been removed, and the first glance into the open sepulchre discovered that the body was no longer there. At this sight Mary Magdalene appears to have hurried back to the city, to give information to Peter and John. These disciples, it may be remembered, were the only two who followed Jesus to his trial; and it is likely that they were together in some part of the city, while the rest were scattered in different quarters, or perhaps had retired to Bethany. During the absence of Mary, the other women made a closer inspection; they entered the inner chamber, they saw the grave-clothes lying in an orderly manner, the bandage or covering of the head rolled up, and placed on one side;—this circumstance would appear incompatible with the haste of a surreptitious, or the carelessness of a violent, removal. To their minds thus highly excited, and bewildered with astonishment, with terror, and with grief, appeared, what

---

* Σεισμὸς, as before remarked, usually means an earthquake, but possibly may admit of a wider sense.

is described by the Evangelist as "a vision of angels." One or more beings in human form seated in the shadowy twilight within the sepulchre, and addressing them with human voices, told them that their Master had risen from the grave,—that he was to go before them into Galilee. They had departed to communicate these wonderful tidings to the other disciples, before the two summoned by Mary Magdalene arrived: of these the younger and more active, John, outran the older, Peter. But he only entered the outer chamber, from whence he could see the state in which the grave-clothes were lying; but before he entered the inner chamber, he awaited the arrival of his companion. Peter went in first, and afterwards John, who, as he states, not till then, believed that the body had been taken away, for, up to that time, the Apostles themselves had no thought or expectation of the resurrection.[b] These two Apostles returned home, leaving Mary Magdalene, who, probably wearied by her walk to the city and her return, had not come up with them till they had completed their search. The other women, meantime, had fled in haste, and in the silence of terror, through the hostile city; and until, later in the day, they found the Apostles assembled together, did not unburthen their hearts of this extraordinary secret. Mary Magdalene[i] was left alone; she had as yet seen and heard nothing; but on looking down into the sepulchre, she saw the same vision which had appeared to the others, and was in her turn addressed by the angels; and it seems

Arrival of Peter and John.

First appearance of Jesus to Mary Magdalene.

---

[b] John xx. 8, 9. For as yet they knew not the Scripture, that he should rise again from the dead.

[i] Mark xvi. 9-11; John xx. 11-18.

that her feelings were those of unmitigated sorrow. She stood near the sepulchre, weeping. To her Jesus then first appeared. So little was she prepared for his presence, that she at first mistook him for the person who had the charge of the garden. Her language is that of grief, because unfriendly hands have removed the body, and carried it away to some unknown place. Nor was it till He again addressed her, that she recognised his familiar form and voice.

The second[k] appearance of Jesus was to the other party of women, as they returned to the city, and, perhaps, separated to find out the different Apostles, to whom, when assembled, they related the whole of their adventure. In the mean time a third appearance[m] had taken place to two disciples who had made an excursion to Emmaus, a village between seven and eight miles from Jerusalem: a fourth to the Apostle Peter; this apparition is not noticed by the Evangelists; it rests on the authority of St. Paul.[n] The intelligence of the women had been received with the utmost incredulity by the assembled Apostles. The arrival of the two disciples from Emmaus, with their more particular relation of his conversing with them; his explaining the Scriptures; his breaking bread with them; made a deeper impression. Still mistrust seems to have predominated; and when Jesus appeared in the chamber, the doors of which had been closed from fear lest their meeting should be interrupted by the hostile Rulers, the first sensation was terror rather than joy. It was not

---

[k] Matt. xxviii. 9, 10.
[m] Mark xvi. 12, 13; Luke xxiv. 13-32.
[n] It does not appear possible that Peter could be one of the disciples near Emmaus. It would harmonize the accounts if we could suppose that St. Paul (1 Cor. xv. 5) originally dictated Κηφα, which was changed for the more familiar Κηφᾶς.

till Jesus conversed with them, and permitted them to ascertain by actual touch the identity of his body, that they yielded to emotions of gladness. Jesus appeared a second time, eight days after,[a] in the public assembly of the disciples, and condescended to remove the doubts of one Apostle, who had not been present at the former meeting, by permitting him to inspect and touch his wounds.

This incredulity of the Apostles, related with so much simplicity, is, on many accounts, most remarkable, considering the apparent distinctness with which Jesus appears to have predicted both his death and resurrection, and the rumour which put the Sanhedrin on their guard against any clandestine removal of the body. The key to this difficulty is to be sought in the opinions of the time. The notion of a resurrection was intimately connected with the coming of the Messiah, but that resurrection was of a character very different from the secret, the peaceful, the unimposing reappearance of Jesus after his death. It was an integral, an essential part of that splendid vision which represented the Messiah as summoning all the fathers of the chosen race from their graves to share in the glories of his kingdom.[b] Even after the Resurrection the bewildered Apostles inquire whether that kingdom, the only sovereignty of which they yet dreamed, was about to commence.[c] The death of Jesus, notwithstanding his care to prepare their minds for that appalling event, took them by surprise: they seem to have been stunned and confounded. It had shaken their faith by its utter incongruity with their preconceived

Incredulity of the Apostles: its cause.

---

[a] Mark xvi. 14-18; Luke xxiv. 36-49; John xx. 19-29.
[b] See Book I. ch. l. p. 78.   [c] Acts ii. 6. Compare Luke xxiv. 21.

notions, rather than confirmed it by its accordance with his own predictions; and in this perplexed and darkling state the resurrection came upon them not less strangely at issue with their conceptions of the manner in which the Messiah would return to the world. When Jesus had alluded with more or less prophetic distinctness to that event, their minds had, no doubt, reverted to their rooted opinions on the subject, and moulded up the plain sense of his words with some vague and confused interpretation framed out of their own traditions; the latter so far predominating, that their memory retained scarcely a vestige of the simpler truth, until it was forcibly reawakened by its complete fulfilment in the resurrection of their Lord.

Excepting among the immediate disciples, the intelligence of the resurrection remained, it is probable, a profound secret, or, at all events, little more than vague and feeble rumours would reach the ear of the Sanhedrin. For though Christ had taken the first step to reorganise his religion, by his solemn commission to the Apostles at his first appearance in their assembly, it was not till *Return of the Apostles to Galilee.* after the return to Galilee, more particularly during one interview near the Lake of Gennesareth, that he invested Peter, and with him the rest of the Apostles, with the pastoral charge over his new community. For, according to their custom, the Galilean Apostles had returned to their homes during the interval between the Passover and the Pentecost, and there, among the former scenes of his beneficent labours, on more than one occasion, the living Jesus had appeared, and conversed familiarly with them.*

---

* Matt. xxviii. 16-20; John xxi. 1-23. Mark, in his brief and summary account, omits the journey to Galilee. Luke (xxiv. 49) seems to intimate the

Forty days after the crucifixion, and ten before the Pentecost, the Apostles were again assembled at their usual place of resort, in the neighbourhood of Jerusalem, the village of Bethany. It was here, on the slope of the Mount of Olives, that, in the language of St. Luke, "he was parted from them;" "he was taken up, and a cloud received him out of their sight."[a]

Apostles in Judæa.

Ascension.

During the interval between the Ascension and the day of Pentecost, the Apostles of Jesus regularly performed their devotions in the Temple, but they may have been lost and unobserved among the thousands who either returned to Jerusalem for the second great annual festival, or, if from more remote parts, remained, as was

---

contrary, as if he had known nothing of this retreat. This verse, however, may be a kind of continuation of verse 47, and is not to be taken in this strict sense, so as positively to exclude an intermediate journey to Galilee.

[a] Neander has closed his Life of Christ with some forcible observations on the Ascension, to which it has been objected, that St. Luke alone, though in two places (Gosp. xxiv. 50, 51; Acts i. 9–11), mentions this extraordinary event: "How could the resurrection of Christ have been to the disciples the groundwork of their belief in everlasting life, if it had been again followed by his death? With the death of Christ the faith, especially in his resurrection and reappearance, must again, of necessity, have sunk away. Christ would again have appeared to them an ordinary man; their belief in him, as the Messiah, would have suffered a violent shock. How in this manner could that conviction of the exaltation of Christ have formed itself within them, which we find expressed in their writings with so much force and precision? Though the fact of his ascension, as visible to the senses, is witnessed expressly only by St. Luke, the language of St. John concerning his ascent to the Father, the declarations of all the Apostles concerning his exaltation to heaven [see especially the strong expression of St. Mark, xvi. 19.—H. M.], presuppose their conviction of his supernatural elevation from the earth, since the notion of his departure from this earthly life in the ordinary manner is thereby altogether excluded. Even if none of the apostolic writers had mentioned this visible and real fact, we might have safely inferred from all which they say of Christ, that in some form or other they presupposed a supernatural exaltation of Christ from this visible earthly world." Leben Jesu, p. 656.

customary, in the capital from the Passover to the Pentecost. The election of a new Apostle to fill the mysterious number of twelve, a number hallowed to Jewish feeling as that of the tribes of their ancestors, shows that they now looked upon themselves again as a permanent body, united by a federal principle, and destined for some ulterior purpose; and it is possible that they might look with eager hope to the feast of Pentecost, the celebration of the delivery of the Law on Mount Sinai;[1] the birthday as it were of the religious constitution of the Jews, as an epoch peculiarly suited for the reorganisation and reconstruction of the new kingdom of the Messiah.

<small>Election of a new Apostle.</small>

The Sanhedrin doubtless expected anything rather than the revival of the religion of Jesus. The guards, who had fled from the sepulchre, had been bribed to counteract any rumour of the Resurrection, by charging the disciples with the clandestine removal of the body. The city had been restored to peace, as if no extraordinary event had taken place. The Galileans, the followers of Jesus among the rest, had retired to their native province. In the popular estimation the claims of Jesus to the Messiahship were altogether extinguished by his death. The attempt to reinstate him, who had been condemned by the Sanhedrin and crucified by the Romans, in public reverence and belief as the promised Redeemer, might have appeared a proceeding so desperate as could not enter into the most enthusiastic mind. The character of the disciples of Jesus was as little calculated to awaken apprehension. The few richer or more influential persons who had been inclined to embrace his cause, even during his lifetime, had

---

[1] See the traditions on the subject in Meuschen, N. T., a Talmude Illustratum, p. 740.

maintained their obnoxious opinions in secret. The ostensible leaders were men of low birth, humble occupations, deficient education, and—no unimportant objection in the mind of the Jews—Galileans. Never indeed was sect so completely centred in the person of its founder: the whole rested on his personal authority, emanated from his personal teaching; and however it might be thought that some of his sayings might lie treasured in the minds of his blind and infatuated adherents; however they might refuse to abandon the hope that he would appear again, as the Messiah; all this delusion would gradually die away, from the want of any leader qualified to take up and maintain a cause so lost and hopeless. Great must have been their astonishment at the intelligence, that the religion of Jesus had reappeared, in a new, in a more attractive form; that on the feast day which next followed their total dispersion, those humble, ignorant, and despised Galileans were making converts by thousands, at the very gates, even perhaps within the precincts of the Temple. The more visible circumstances of the miracle which took place on the day of Pentecost, the descent of the Holy Ghost, under the appearance of fiery tongues, in the private assembly of the Christians, might not reach their ears; but they could not long remain ignorant of this strange and alarming fact, that these uneducated men, apparently reorganised, and acting with the most fearless freedom, were familiarly conversing with, and inculcating the belief in the resurrection of Jesus, on strangers from every quarter of the world, in all their various languages, or dialects.[a]

Reappearance of the religion of Jesus.

---

[a] Kuinoel (in loc. Act.) gives a lucid view of the various Rationalist and Anti-Rationalist Interpretations of this miracle. The most ingenious and probable is that (yet it is difficult to reconcile it with the language of the Acts)

The Jews whose families had been long domiciliated in the different provinces of the Roman and the Parthian dominions, gradually lost, or had never learned, the vernacular tongue of Palestine; they adopted the language of the surrounding people. The original sacred Hebrew was understood only by the learned. How far, on one side the Greek, on the other the Babylonian Chaldaic, which was nearly allied to the vernacular Aramaic, were admitted into the religious services of the synagogue, appears uncertain; but the different synagogues in Jerusalem were appropriated to the different races of Jews. Those from Alexandria, from Cyrene, the Libertines, descended from freed slaves at Rome, perhaps therefore speaking Latin, the Cilicians and Asiatics, had their separate places of assembly:[x] so, probably, those who came from more remote quarters, where Greek, the universal medium of communication in great part of the Roman empire, was less known, as in Arabia, Mesopotamia, and beyond the Euphrates.

The scene of this extraordinary incident must have been some place of general resort; yet, scarcely within the Temple, where, though there were many chambers

---

of Neander and Bunsen; they slightly differ. (See Christianity and Mankind, I. II.) Every way there are almost insurmountable difficulties. Taking the common notion, it is certainly remarkable that there is no mention of the use of this gift in early Christian history, or even, I believe, in tradition, for the purpose of conversion. In my youthful zeal I attempted to prove the contrary; my attempt, I confess, was a total failure. The mention of the gift of tongues in Corinth perplexes rather than elucidates the difficulty. It was obviously thought a very secondary gift, not the extraordinary endowment inferred from the passage in the Acts; and of all places in Greece, Corinth, though the resort of commercial strangers from different parts of the world, would be that in which this special gift would be least wanted for the extension of the religion.

[x] Acts vi.

set apart for instruction in the Law, and other devotional purposes, the Apostles were not likely to have obtained admittance to one of these, or to have been permitted to carry on their teaching without interruption. If conjecture might be hazarded, we should venture to place their house of assembly in one of the streets leading to the Temple; that, perhaps, which, descending the slope of the hill, led to the Mount of Olives, and to the village of Bethany. The time, the third hour, nine in the morning, was that of public prayer in the Temple. Multitudes, therefore, would throng all the avenues to the Temple, and would be arrested on their way by the extraordinary sight of Peter and his colleagues thus addressing the various classes in their different dialects; asserting openly the resurrection of Jesus; arraigning the injustice of his judicial murder; and re-establishing his claim to be received as the Messiah.

Disciples near the Temple. Gift of tongues.

These submissive, timid, and scattered followers of Jesus thus burst upon the public attention, suddenly invested with courage, endowed with commanding eloquence, in the very scene of their Master's cruel apprehension and execution, asserting his Messiahship, in a form as irreconcileable with their own preconceived notions as with those of the rest of the people; arraigning the Rulers, and, by implication, if not as yet in distinct words, the whole nation, of the most heinous act of impiety, as well as barbarity, the rejection of the Messiah; proclaiming the Resurrection, and defying investigation. The whole speech of Peter clashed with the strongest prejudices of those who had so short a time before given such fearful evidence of their animosity and remorselessness. It proclaimed that "the last days," the days of the

Speech of Peter.

Messiah, the days of prophecy and wonder, had already begun. It placed the Being whom but fifty days before they had seen helplessly expiring upon the cross, far above the pride, almost the idol of the nation, King David. The ashes of the king had long reposed in the tomb, which was before their eyes; but the tomb could not confine Jesus; death had no power over his remains. Nor was his Resurrection all: the crucified Jesus was now "on the right hand of God:" He had assumed that last, the highest distinction of the Messiah —the superhuman majesty; that intimate relation with the Deity, which, however vaguely and indistinctly shadowed out in the Jewish notion of the Messiah, was as it were the crowning glory, the ultimate height to which the devout hopes of the most strongly excited of the Jews followed up the promised Redeemer: "Therefore let all the house of Israel know assuredly, that God hath made that same Jesus, whom ye have crucified, both *Lord* and Christ."[f]

Three thousand declared converts were the result of this first appeal to the Jewish multitude. The religion thus reappeared, in a form new, complete, and more decidedly hostile to the prevailing creed and dominant sentiments of the nation. From this time the Christian community assumed its separate and organised existence, united by the federal rite of baptism; and the popular mind was deeply impressed by the preternatural powers exercised by its leading followers. Many of the converts threw their property, or part of it, into a common stock; now become necessary, as the teachers of Christianity had to take up their permanent residence in Jerusalem, at a distance from their homes and the scenes of their

---

[f] Acts ii. 36.

humble labours. The religion spread, of course, with the greatest rapidity among the lower orders. Assistance in their wants, and protection against the hostility, or at least the coldness and estrangement, of the powerful and opulent, were necessary to hold together the young society. Such was the general ardour, that many did not hesitate to sell their landed property, the tenure of which, however loosened by time, and by the successive changes in the political state of the country, probably, at this period of the Messiah's expected coming, assumed a new value. This, therefore, was no easy triumph over Jewish feeling. Yet nothing like an Essenian community of goods ever appears to have prevailed in the Christian Church; such a system, however favourable to the maintenance of certain usages or opinions within a narrow sphere, would have been fatal to the aggressive and comprehensive spirit of Christianity; the vital and conservative principle of a sect, it was inconsistent with an universal religion; and we cannot but admire the wisdom which avoided a precedent so attractive, as conducing to the immediate prosperity, yet so dangerous to the ultimate progress of the religion.*

The Sanhedrin at first stood aloof; whether from awe, or miscalculating contempt, or, it is possible, from internal dissension. It was not till they were assailed, as it were in the heart of their own territory—not till the miracle of healing the lame man near the Beautiful Gate of the Temple (this gate opened into the inner court of the Temple, and, from

---

* Mosheim appears to me to have proved this point conclusively. At a later period, every exhortation to alms-giving, and every sentence which alludes to distinctions of rich and poor in the Christian Churches, is decisive against the community of goods

the richness of its architecture, had received that name), and the public proclamation of the Resurrection, in the midst of the assembled worshippers, in the second recorded speech of Peter, had secured five thousand converts—that at length the authorities found it necessary to interfere, and to arrest, if possible, the rapid progress of the faith. The second speech of the Apostle[a] was in a somewhat more calm and conciliating tone than the former: it dwelt less on the crime of the crucifixion, than on the advantages of belief in Jesus as the Messiah. It did not shrink, indeed, from reasserting the guilt of the death of the Just One; yet it palliated the ignorance through which the people, and even the rulers, had rejected Jesus, and stained the city with his blood. It called upon them to repent of this national crime; and, as if even yet Peter himself was not disencumbered of that Jewish notion, it seemed to intimate the possibility of an immediate reappearance of Christ,[b] to fulfil to the Jewish people all that they hoped from this greater than Moses, this accomplisher of the sublime promise made to their father Abraham. To the Sanhedrin, the speech was, no doubt, but vaguely reported; but any speech delivered by such men, in such a place, and on such a subject, demanded their interference. Obtaining the assistance of the commander of the Roman guard, mounted, as has been said, in the gallery leading to the Antonia, they seized and imprisoned the Apostles. The

---

[a] Acts III. 12-26.
[b] Ib. 19, 20, 21: "The times of refreshing;" when "he shall send Jesus Christ, which before was preached unto you: whom the heaven must receive until the times of restitution of all things."

This restitution of all things, in the common Jewish belief, was to be almost simultaneous with or to follow very closely the appearance of the Messiah.

next morning they were brought up for examination. The boldness of the Apostles, who asserted their doctrines with calm resolution, avowed and enforced their belief in the resurrection and Messiahship of the crucified Jesus, as well as the presence of the man who had been healed, perplexed the council. After a private conference, they determined to try the effect of severe threatenings, and authoritatively commanded them to desist from disseminating their obnoxious opinions. The Apostles answered by an appeal to a higher power—"Whether it be right in the sight of God, to hearken unto you more than unto God, judge ye. For we cannot but speak the things which we have seen and heard."[c]

A remarkable revolution had taken place, either in the internal politics of the Sanhedrin, or in their prevailing sentiments towards Christianity. Up to the death of Jesus, the Pharisees were his chief opponents; against their authority he seemed chiefly to direct his rebukes; and, by their jealous animosity, he was watched, criminated, and at length put to death. Now, in their turn, the Sadducees[d] take the lead; either because the doctrine of the Resurrection struck more directly at the root of their system, or, otherwise, because their influence had gained a temporary ascendancy in the great council. But this predominance of the unpopular Saducean

Sadducees predominant in the Sanhedrin.

---

[c] Acts iv. 19, 20.
[d] Acts iv. 1. Annas is mentioned as the High Priest, and then Caiaphas, who it appears, from the Gospels, and from Josephus (Ant. xviii. 2, § 2, 4, § 3), was not deposed till a later period. The interpretation of Krebs (Observationes in N. T., e Josepho, p. 177) appears to me the best. Annas was the second High Priest, or deputy; but is named first, as the head of the family in which the High-priesthood was vested, being father-in-law to Caiaphas. The rest were the assessors of the High Priest.

party on the throne of the High Priest and in the council, if it increased their danger from the well-known severity with which that faction administered the law; on the other hand, it powerfully contributed to that reaction of popular favour, which again overawed the hostile Sanhedrin.* This triumph of the Apostles over their adversaries; this resolute determination to maintain their cause at all hazards (sanctioned, as it seemed, by the manifest approval of the Almighty); the rapid increase in their possessions, which enabled them to protect all the poorer classes who joined their ranks; the awful death of Ananias and Sapphira,† into the circumstances of which their enemies ventured no inquiry; the miracles of a gentler and more beneficent character, which they performed in public; the concourse from the neighbourhood of Jerusalem to partake in their powers of healing, and to hear their doctrines; the manifest superiority, in short, which Christianity was gaining over the established Judaism, determined the Sanhedrin, after a short time, to make another effort to suppress their growing power. The Apostles were seized, and cast ignominiously into the common prison. In the morning they were sought in vain: the doors were found closed, but the prisoners had disappeared; and the dismayed Sanhedrin received intelligence that they had taken up their customary station in the Temple. Even the Roman officer, despatched to secure their persons, found it necessary to act with caution and gentleness; for the multitude were ready to undertake their defence, even against

---

* "They let them go, finding nothing how they might punish them, because of the people: for all men glorified God for that which was done."—Acts iv. 21.

† Acts v.

the armed soldiery; and stones were always at hand in the neighbourhood or precincts of the Temple, for any tumultuary resistance. The Apostles, how- *Apostles before the Sanhedrin.* ever, peaceably obeyed the citation of the Sanhedrin; but the language of Peter was now even more bold and resolute than before: he openly proclaimed, in the face of the astonished council, the crucified Jesus to be the Prince and the Saviour, and asserted the inspiration of himself and his companions by the Spirit of God.[a]

The Sadducaic faction were wrought to the highest pitch of frenzy; they were eager to press the capital charge. But the Pharisaic party endeavoured, not without success, to mitigate the sentence. The perpetual rivalry of the two sects, and the general leniency of the Pharisaic administration of the law, may have concurred, with the moderation and judgment of the individual, to induce Gamaliel to interpose the weight of his own personal authority and that *Gamaliel.* of his party. Gamaliel does not appear, himself, to have been inclined to Christianity: he was most likely the same who is distinguished in Jewish tradition as president of the Sanhedrin (though the High Priest, being now present, would take the chief place), and as the master under whom St. Paul had studied the Law. The speech of Gamaliel, with singular address, confounded the new sect with those of two adventurers, Judas the Galilean, and Theudas, whose insurrections had excited great expectation, but gradually died away. With these affairs were left to take their course; against their pretensions God had decided by their failure: leave, then, to the same unerring Judge the present decision.

---

[a] Acts v. 32.

To this temporising policy the majority of the council assented; part probably considering that either the sect would, after all, die away, without establishing any permanent influence, or, like some of those parties mentioned by Gamaliel, run into wild excess, and so provoke the Roman Government to suppress them by force; others from mere party spirit, to counteract the power of the opposite faction; some from more humane principles and kindlier motives; others from perplexity; some, perhaps, from awe, which, though it had not yet led to belief, had led to hesitation; some from sincere piety; as, in fact, expecting that an event of such importance would be decided by some manifest interposition, or overruling influence at least, of the Almighty. The majority were anxious, from these different motives, to escape the perilous responsibility of decision. The less violent course was therefore followed; after the Apostles had suffered the milder punishment of scourging—a punishment inflicted with great frequency among the Jews, yet ignominious to the sufferer—the persecution, for the present, ceased: the Apostles again appeared in public; they attended in the Temple; but how long this period of security lasted, from the uncertain chronology of the early Christian history,[b] it

---

[b] There is no certain date in the Acts of the Apostles, except that of the death of Herod, A. D. 44, even if that is certain. Nothing can be more easy than to array against each other the names of the most learned authorities, who from the earliest days have laboured to build a durable edifice out of the insufficient materials in their power. Perhaps from Jerome to Dr. Burton and Mr. Greswell, no two systems agree. The passage in St. Paul, Gal. ii. 1, which might be expected to throw light on this difficult subject, involves it in still greater intricacy. In the first place, the reading, fourteen years, as Grotius and many others have shown, not without MS. authority, is by no means certain. Then, from whence is this period to be calculated?—from the conversion, with Pearson and many modern writers? or from the first visit of St. Paul to Jerusalem, with others? All is doubt-

is impossible to decide. Yet, as the jealousies which appear to have arisen in the infant community would require some time to mature and grow to a head, I should interpose two or three years between this collision with the authorities and the next, which first embrued the soil of Jerusalem with the blood of a Christian martyr. Nor would the peaceful policy adopted through the authority of Gamaliel have had a fair trial in a shorter period of time; it would scarcely have been overborne at once and immediately by the more violent party.

The first converts to Christianity were Jews,[1] but of two distinct classes:—1, the natives of Palestine, who spoke the Syrian dialect, and among whom perhaps were included the Jews from the East; 2, the Western Jews, who, having been settled in the different provinces of the Roman empire, generally spoke Greek. This class may likewise have comprehended proselytes to Judaism. Jealousies arose between these two parties. The Greeks complained that the distribution of the general charitable fund was conducted with partiality; that their "widows were neglected." The dispute led to the establishment of a new order in the community. The Apostles withdrew from the laborious, it might be the invidious, office; and seven disciples, from whose names we may conjecture that they were chosen from the Grecian party, were invested

<small>*Institution of Deacons.*</small>

<small>ful, contested, conjectural. The only plan, therefore, is to adopt, and uniformly adhere to, some one system. In fact the cardinal point of the whole calculation, the year of our Saviour's death, being as uncertain as the rest, I shall state that I assume that to have been A.D. 31. From thence I shall proceed to affix my dates according to my own view, without involving my readers in the inextricable labyrinth to which I am convinced that there is no certain or satisfactory clue. If I notice any arguments, they will be chiefly of a historical nature.

[1] Acts vi.</small>

by a solemn ceremony, the imposition of hands, as deacons or ministers, with the superintendence of the general funds.

It was in the synagogues of the foreign, the African and Asiatic Jews, that the success of Stephen, one of these deacons, excited the most violent hostility. The indignant people found that not even the priesthood was a security against this spreading apostasy: many of that order enrolled themselves among the disciples of Christ.[k] Whether the execution of this first martyr to Christianity was a legal or tumultuary proceeding,—whether it was a solemn act of the Sanhedrin, the supreme judicial as well as civil tribunal of the nation, or an outbreak of popular indignation and resentment,—the preliminary steps, at least, appear to have been conducted with regularity. He was formally arraigned before the Sanhedrin of blasphemy, as asserting the future destruction of the Temple, and the abrogation of the Law. This accusation, although the witnesses are said to have been false and suborned, seems to intimate that in those Hellenistic congregations Christianity had already assumed a bolder and more independent tone; that it had thrown aside some of the peculiar character which adhered to it in the other communities; that it already aspired to be an universal, not a national religion; and one destined to survive the local worship in Jerusalem and the abolition of the Mosaic institutes.[m] Whether inflamed by these popular topics of accusation, which struck at the vital principles of their religious influence,

A.D. 34.

---

[k] Acts vi. 7.

[m] Stephen has been called by some modern writers the forerunner of St. Paul. See Neander, Geschichte der Pflanzung der Christlichen Kirche, p. 41; a work which I had not the advantage of consulting when this part of the present volume was written.

or again taking alarm at the progress of Christianity, the Pharisaic party, which we found after the resurrection had lost their supremacy in the council, appear, from the active concurrence of Saul, and from the reawakened hostility of the multitude, over whom the Sadducees had no commanding influence, to have reunited themselves to the more violent enemies of the faith. The defence of Stephen recapitulated in bold language the chief points of the national history, the privileges and the crimes of the race of Israel, which gradually led to this final consummation of their impiety and guilt, the rejection of the Messiah, the murder of the Just One. It is evidently incomplete; it was interrupted by the fury of his opponents, who took fire at his arraigning them, not merely of the death of Jesus, but of this perpetual violation of the Law; "who have received the *law* by the disposition of angels, and have not kept it."[a] This charge struck directly at the Pharisaic party; the populace even under their control, either abandoned the Christians to their fate, or joined in the hasty and ruthless vengeance. The murmurs, the gestures of the indignant Sanhedrin, and of others, perhaps, who witnessed the trial, betrayed their impatience and indignation: they gnashed their teeth; and Stephen, breaking off, or unable to pursue his continuous discourse, in a kind of prophetic ecstasy declared that at that instant he beheld the Son of Man standing at the right hand of God. Whether legal or tumultuary, the execution of Stephen was conducted with so much attention to form, that he was first carried beyond the walls of the city;[c]

<small>Death of the protomartyr, A.D. 34.</small>

---

[a] Acts vii. 53.
[b] In one instance, it may be remembered, the multitude was so excited as to attempt to stone our Saviour within the precincts of the Temple.

the witnesses, whose office it was to cast the first stone,[p] put off their clothes, and perhaps observed the other forms peculiar to this mode of execution. He died as a true follower of Jesus, praying the divine mercy upon his barbarous persecutors; but neither the sight of his sufferings, nor the beauty of his dying words, allayed the excitement which had now united the conflicting parties of the Jews in their common league against Christianity. Yet the mere profession of Christianity did not necessarily involve any capital charge; or if it did, the Jews wanted power to carry the sentence of death into execution on a general scale. Though, therefore, they on this occasion had either deliberately ventured, or yielded to a violent impulse of fury, their vengeance in other cases was confined to those subordinate punishments which were left under their jurisdiction:—imprisonment; public scourging in the synagogue; and that which, of course, began to lose its terrors as soon as the Christians formed separate and independent communities, the once awful Excommunication.[q]

The martyrdom of Stephen led to the most important results, not merely as first revealing that great lesson which mankind has been so slow to learn, that religious

---

[p] Deut. xvii. 7.

[q] Michaelis, followed by Eichhorn, has argued, with considerable plausibility, that these violent measures would scarcely have been ventured by the Jews under the rigorous administration of Pilate. Vitellius, on the other hand, by whom Pilate was sent in disgrace to Rome, A. D. 36, visited Jerusalem, A. D. 37, was received with great honours, and seems to have treated the Jewish authorities with the utmost respect. On these grounds he places this persecution as late as the year 37. Yet the government of Pilate appears to have been capriciously, rather than systematically, severe. The immediate occasion of his recall was his tyrannical conduct to the Samaritans. It may have been his policy, while his administration was drawing to a close, to court the ruling authorities of the Jews.

persecution which stops short of extermination, always advances the cause which it endeavours to repress. It showed that Christian faith was stronger than death, the last resort of human cruelty. Thenceforth its triumph was secure. For every death, courageously, calmly, cheerfully endured, where it appalled one dastard into apostasy, made, or prepared the minds of a hundred proselytes. To the Jew, ready himself to lay down his life in defence of his Temple, this self-devotion, though an undeniable test of sincerity in the belief of facts of recent occurrence, was less extraordinary; to the heathen it showed a determined assurance of immortality, not less new, as an active and general principle, than attractive and ennobling.

The more immediate consequences of the persecution were no less favourable to the progress of Christianity. The Christians were driven out of Jerusalem, where the Apostles alone remained firm at their posts. Scattered through the whole region, if not beyond the precincts of Palestine, they bore with them the seed of the religion. The most important progress was made in Samaria; but the extent of their success in this region, and the opposition they encountered among this people, deeply tinged with Oriental opinion, will be related in another part of this work. Philip, one of the most active of the deacons, made another convert of rank and importance, an officer[r] who held the highest station and influence with Candace, the queen of the Ethiopians. The name of Candace[s] was the hereditary appellation of the

---

[r] The word "Eunuch" may be here used in its primary sense (cubicularius), without any allusion to its later meaning; as, according to the strict words of the law, a Jewish eunuch was disqualified from appearing at the public assemblies.

[s] Regnare fœminam Candacen, quod nomen multis jam annis ad reginas transiit. Plin. vi. 29. Conf. Strabo, xvii. p. 1175. Dion Cass. liv.

queens of Meroe, as Pharaoh of the older, and Ptolemy of the later Egyptian kings. The Jews had spread in great numbers to that region; and the return of a person of such influence, a declared convert to the new religion, can scarcely have been without consequences, of which, unhappily, we have no record.

But far the most important result of the death of Stephen, was its connexion with the conversion of St. Paul. To propagate Christianity in the enlightened West, where its most extensive, at least, most permanent, conquests were to be made; to emancipate it from the trammels of Judaism; a man was wanting of larger and more comprehensive views, of higher education, and more liberal accomplishments. Such an instrument for its momentous scheme of benevolence to the human race, Divine Providence found in Saul of Tarsus. Born in the Grecian and commercial town of Tarsus, where he had acquired no inconsiderable acquaintance with Grecian letters and philosophy; but brought up in the most celebrated school of Pharisaic learning, that of Gamaliel, for which purpose he had probably resided long in Jerusalem; having inherited, probably from the domiciliation of his family in Tarsus,[1] the valuable privilege of Roman citizenship; yet with his Judaism in no degree weakened by his Grecian culture,—Saul stood as it were on the confines of both regions, qualified beyond all men to develope a system which should unite Jew and Gentile under one more harmonious and comprehensive faith. The

---

[1] Compare Strabo's account of Tarsus. The natives of this city were remarkably addicted to philosophical studies; but in general travelled and settled in foreign countries: Οὗτοι αὐτοὶ οὗτοι μένουσιν αὐτόθι, ἀλλὰ καὶ τελειοῦνται ἐκδημοῦντες, καὶ τελεωθέντες ξενιτεύουσιν ἡδέως, κατέρχονται δ' ὀλίγοι.—Strabo, lib. xiv. p. 673.

zeal with which Saul urged on the subsequent persecution showed that the death of Stephen had made, as might have been expected, no influential impression upon a mind so capable, unless blinded by zeal, of appreciating its moral sublimity. The commission from the Sanhedrin, to bring in safe custody to Jerusalem such of the Jews of Damascus as had embraced Christianity, implies their unabated reliance on his fidelity. The national confidence which invested him in this important office, the unhesitating readiness with which he appears to have assumed it, in a man of his apparently severe integrity and unshaken sense of duty, imply, in all ordinary human estimation, that he had in no degree relaxed from that zeal which induced him to witness the execution of Stephen, if not with stern satisfaction, yet without commiseration. Even then, if the mind of Paul was in any degree prepared, by the noble manner in which Stephen had endured death, to yield to the miraculous interposition which occurred on the road to Damascus, nothing less than some occurrence of the most extraordinary and unprecedented character could have arrested so suddenly, and diverted so completely from its settled purpose, a mind of so much strength, and however of vivid imagination, to all appearance very superior to popular superstition. Saul set forth from Jerusalem, according to the narrative of the Acts, with his mind wrought up to the most violent animosity against these apostates from the faith of their ancestors.[a] He set forth, thus manifestly inveterate in his prejudices, unshaken in his ardent attachment to the religion of Moses, the immutability and perpetuity of which he considered it treasonable and impious to

---

[a] "Breathing threatenings and slaughter against the disciples of the Lord." Acts ix. 1-22.

question, with an austere and indignant sense of duty, fully authorised by the direct testimony of the Law, to exterminate all renegades from the severest Judaism. The ruling Jews must have heard with the utmost amazement, that the persecuting zealot who had voluntarily demanded the commission of the High Priest to repress the growing sect of the Christians, had arrived at Damascus, blinded for a time, humbled, and that his first step had been openly to join himself to that party which he had threatened to exterminate.

The Christians, far from welcoming so distinguished a proselyte, looked on him at first with natural mistrust and suspicion. And although at Damascus this jealousy was speedily allayed by the interposition of Ananias, a leading Christian, to whom his conversion had been revealed by a vision, at Jerusalem his former hostile violence had made so deep an impression, that, three years after his conversion, even the Apostles stood aloof, and with reluctance admitted a proselyte of such importance, yet whose conversion to them still appeared so highly improbable.

No event in Christian history, from this improbability, as well as its influence on the progress of the religion, would so demand, if the expression may be used, the divine intervention as the conversion of St. Paul. Paul was essentially necessary to the development of the Christian scheme. Neither the self-suggested workings of the imagination, even if coincident with some extraordinary but fortuitous atmospheric phenomena; nor any worldly notion of aggrandisement, as the head of a new and powerful sect; nor that more noble ambition, which might anticipate the moral and social blessings of Christianity, and, once conceived, would strike resolutely into the scheme for their advancement,—furnish even a plausible theory for the total change of such a man, at such a time, and under such circumstances. The minute investigation of this much-agitated question could scarcely be in its place in the present work; but to doubt, in whatever manner it took place, the divine mission of Paul, would be to discard all providential interposition in the design and propagation of Christianity.

Unquestionably it is remarkable how little encouragement Paul seems at first to have received from the party, to join which he had sacrificed all his popularity with his countrymen, the favour of the supreme magistracy, and a charge, if of a severe and cruel, yet of an important character; all, indeed, which hitherto appeared the ruling objects of his life. Instead of assuming at once, as his abilities and character might seem to command, a distinguished place in the new community into which he had been received; instead of being hailed, as renegades from the opposite faction usually are, by a weak and persecuted party, his early course is lost in obscurity. He passes several years in exile, as it were, from both parties; he emerges by slow degrees into eminence, and hardly wins his way into the reluctant confidence of the Christians; who, however they might at first be startled by the improbability of the fact, yet felt such reliance in the power of their Lord and Redeemer, as scarcely we should have conceived to be affected by lasting wonder at the conversion of any unbeliever.

Part of the three years which elapsed between the conversion of Paul and his first visit to Jerusalem were passed in Arabia.[1] The cause of this retirement into a

---

[1] The time of St. Paul's residence in Arabia is generally assumed to have been one whole year, and part of the preceding and the following. The ex-

foreign region, and the part of the extensive country, which was then called Arabia, in which he resided, are altogether unknown. It is possible, indeed, that he may have sought refuge from the Jews of Damascus, or employed himself in the conversion of the Jews who were scattered in great numbers in every part of Arabia.

Paul in Arabia. The frontiers of the Arabian king bordered closely on the territory of Damascus, and Paul may have retired but a short distance from that city. During this interval, Aretas, whose hostile intentions against Herod, the tetrarch of Galilee, the Prefect of Syria, Vitellius, had made preparations to repress, had the boldness to invade the Syrian prefecture, and to sieze the important city of Damascus. It is difficult to conceive this act of aggression to have been hazarded unless at some period of public confusion, such as took place at the death of Tiberius. According to Josephus, Vitellius, who had collected a great force to invest Petra, the capital of the Arabian king, on the first tidings of that event, instantly suspended his operations, and withdrew his troops into their winter quarters. At all events, at the close of these three years Damascus was in the power of Aretas. The Jews, who probably were under the authority of an ethnarch of their own people, obtained sufficient influence with the Arabian governor to carry into effect their designs against the life of Paul.[y] His sudden apostasy from their cause, his extraordinary powers, his ardent zeal, his unexampled success, had wrought their animosity to this deadly height; and Paul was with difficulty withdrawn from their fury by being let down from the walls in a

---

premises in the Epistle to the Galatians (I. 17, 18) appears to me by no means to require this arrangement.

[y] Acts ix. 23.

basket, the gates being carefully guarded by the command of the Arabian governor.

Among the most distinguished of the first converts was Barnabas, a native of Cyprus, who had contributed largely from his possessions in that island to the common fund, and whose commanding character and abilities gave him great influence. When Paul, after his escape from Damascus, arrived at Jerusalem, so imperfect appears to have been the correspondence between the more remote members of the Christian community (possibly from Damascus and its neighbourhood having been the seat of war, or because Paul had passed considerable part of the three years in almost total seclusion), at all events, such was the obscurity of the whole transaction, that no certain intelligence of so extraordinary an event as his conversion had reached the Apostolic body, or rather Peter and James, the only Apostles then resident in Jerusalem.[*] Barnabas alone espoused his cause, removed the timid suspicions of the Apostles, and Paul was admitted into the reluctant Christian community. As peculiarly skilled in the Greek language, his exertions to advance Christianity were particularly addressed to those of the Jews to whom Greek was vernacular. But a new conspiracy again endangering his life, he was carried away by the care of his friends to Cæsarea, and thence proceeded to his native city of Tarsus.[*]

About this time a more urgent and immediate danger than the progress of Christianity occupied the mind of the Jewish people. The very existence of their religion was threatened, for the frantic Caligula had issued orders to place his statue in the

<small>Persecution of the Jews by Caligula.</small>

---

[*] Acts ix. 26.   [*] Acts ix. 30.

Temple at Jerusalem. The historian of the Jews must relate the negotiations, the petitions, the artful and humane delays interposed by the prefect Petronius, and all the incidents which show how deeply and universally the nation was absorbed by this appalling subject.[b] It caused, no doubt, as it were a diversion in favour of the Christians; and the temporary peace enjoyed by the churches is attributed, with great probability, rather to the fears of the Jews for their own religious independence, than to the relaxation of their hostility against the Christians.[c]

This peace was undisturbed for about three years.[d] The Apostles pursued their office of disseminating the Gospel in every part of Judæa, until Herod Agrippa took possession of the hereditary dominions, which had been partly granted by the favour of Caligula, and were secured by the gratitude of Claudius. Herod Agrippa affected the splendour of his grandfather, the first Herod; but, unlike that monarch, he attempted to ingratiate himself with his subjects by the strictest profession of Judaism.[e] His power appears to have been as despotic as that of his ancestor; and, at the instigation, no doubt, of the leading Jews, he determined to take vigorous measures for the suppression of Christianity. James, the brother of St. John, was the first victim. He appears to have been summarily put to death by the military mandate of the king, without any process of the Jewish law.[f] The

A.D. 39-41.

Death of James.

---

[b] Joseph. Ant., xviii. 8. History of the Jews, ii. 145, 150.

[c] Benson (Hist. of First Planting of Christianity) and Lardner take this view.

[d] Acts ix. 31. From 39 to 41, the year of Caligula's death.

[e] Hist. of Jews, ii. 157, 160.

[f] Blasphemy was the only crime of which he could be accused, and stoning was the ordinary mode of execution for that offence. James was "cut off by the sword."

Jews rejoiced, no doubt, that the uncontrolled power of life and death was again restored to one who assumed the character of a national king. They were no longer restrained by the caprice, the justice, or the humanity of a Roman prefect, who might treat their intolerance with contempt or displeasure; and they were encouraged in the hope, that at the same great Festival, during which some years before they had extorted the death of Jesus from the reluctant Pilate, their new king would more readily lend himself to their revenge against his most active and powerful follower. Peter was cast into prison, perhaps with the intention of putting him to death before the departure of Herod from the capital. He was delivered from his bondage by supernatural intervention.[a] If the author of the Acts has preserved the order of time, two other of the most important adherents of Christianity ran considerable danger. The famine, predicted by Agabus at Antioch, commenced in Judæa, in the fourth year of Claudius, the last of Herod Agrippa. _{A.D. 44.} If, then, Barnabas and Paul proceeded to Jerusalem on their charitable mission to bear the contributions of the Christians in Antioch to their poorer brethren in Judæa,[b] they must have arrived there during the height of the persecution. Either they remained in concealment, or the extraordinary circumstances of the escape of Peter from prison so confounded the king and his advisers, notwithstanding their attempt to prove the connivance of the guards, to which the lives of the miserable men were sacrificed, that for a time the violence of the persecution was suspended, and those who would inevitably have been

---

[a] Acts xii. 1-23. [b] Acts xi. 30. History of the Jews.

its next victims, obtained, as it were, a temporary respite.

The death of Herod, during the same year, delivered the Christians from their determined enemy. In its terrific and repulsive circumstances they could not but behold the hand of their protecting God. In this respect alone differ the Jewish and the Christian historian, Josephus and the writer of the Acts. In the appalling suddenness of his seizure in the midst of his splendour and the impious adulations of his court, and in the loathsome nature of the disease, their accounts fully coincide.

CHAPTER II.

Christianity and Judaism.

CHRISTIANITY had now made rapid and extensive progress throughout the Jewish world. The death and resurrection of Jesus; the rise of a new religious community, which proclaimed the Son of Mary to be the Messiah, taking place on a scene so public as the metropolis, and at the period of the general concourse of the nation, must have been rumoured, more or less obscurely, in the most remote parts of the Roman Empire, and eastward as far as the extreme settlements of the Jews. If the religion may not have been actually embraced by any of those pilgrims from the more distant provinces who happened to be present during the great festivals, yet its seeds may have been already widely scattered. The dispersion of the community during the persecution after the death of Stephen, carried many zealous and ardent converts into the adjacent regions of Syria and the island of Cyprus. It had obtained a permanent establishment at Antioch, the chief city of Syria, where the community first received the distinctive appellation of Christians.

Christianity however, as yet, was but an expanded Judaism; it was preached by Jews; it was addressed to Jews. It was limited, national, exclusive. The race of Israel gradually recognising in Jesus of Nazareth the promised Messiah; superinducing, as it were, the exquisite purity of Evangelic morality upon the strict performance of the moral law; redeemed from the sins of their fathers and from their own by Christ; assured of the resurrection to eternal life; the children of Abraham were still, according to the general notion, to stand alone and separate from the rest of mankind, sole possessors of the divine favour, sole inheritors of God's everlasting promises. There can be no doubt that most Christians still looked for the speedy, if not the immediate, consummation of all things; the Messiah had as yet performed but part of his office; he was to come again, at no distant period, to accomplish all which was wanting to the established belief in his mission. His visible, his worldly kingdom was to commence; he had passed his ordeal of trial, of suffering, and of sacrifice; the same age, and the same people, were to behold him in his triumph, in his glory, and even, some self-deemed and self-named Christians would not hesitate to aver, in his revenge. At the head of his elect of Israel, he was to assume his dominion; and if his dominion was to be founded upon a still more rigid principle of exclusion than that of one favoured race, it entered not into the most remote expectation that it could be formed on a wider plan, unless, perhaps, in favour of the few who should previously have acknowledged the divine legislation of Moses, and sued for and obtained admission among the hereditary descendants of Abraham. Nothing is more remarkable than to see the horizon of the Apostles gradually receding, and, instead of resting on the borders of the Holy Land, comprehending at length the whole world; barrier after barrier falling down before the superior wisdom which was infused into their minds; first the proselytes of the Gate, the foreign

Gradual enlargement of the views of the Apostles

conformists to Judaism, and ere long the Gentiles themselves admitted within the pale; until Christianity stood forth, demanded the homage, and promised its rewards to the faith of the whole human race; proclaimed itself in language which the world had as yet never heard, the one, true, universal religion.

As an universal religion, aspiring to the complete moral conquest of the world, Christianity had to encounter three antagonists, Judaism, Paganism, and Orientalism. *Christianity an universal religion.* It is my design successively to exhibit the conflict with these opposing forces, its final triumph not without detriment to its own native purity and its divine simplicity, from the interworking of the yet unsubdued elements of the former systems into the Christian mind; until each, at successive periods, and in different parts of the world, formed a modification of Christianity equally removed from its unmingled and unsullied original: the Judæo-Christianity of Palestine, of which the Ebionites appear to have been the last representatives; the Platonic Christianity of Alexandria, as, at least at this early period, the new religion could coalesce only with the sublimer and more philosophical principles of Paganism; and, lastly, the Gnostic Christianity of the East.

With Judaism Christianity had to maintain a double conflict; one external, with the Judaism of the Temple, the Synagogue, the Sanhedrin; a contest of authority on one side, and the irrepressible spirit of moral and religious liberty on the other; of fierce intolerance against the stubborn endurance of conscientious faith; of relentless persecution against the calm and death-despising, and often death-seeking, heroism of martyrdom: *External conflict of Christianity with Judaism; and internal.* the other, more dangerous and destructive, the

Judaism of the infant Church; the old prejudices and opinions, which even Christianity could not altogether extirpate or correct in the earlier Jewish proselytes; the perpetual tendency to contract again the expanding circle; the enslavement of Christianity to the provisions of the Mosaic Law, and to the spirit of the antiquated religion of Palestine. Until the first steps were taken to throw open the new religion to mankind at large; until Christianity, it may be said without disparagement, from a Jewish sect assumed the dignity of an independent religion, even the external animosity of Judaism had not reached its height. But the successive admission of the proselytes of the Gate, and at length of the idolatrous Gentiles, into an equal participation in the privileges of the faith, showed that the breach was altogether irreparable. From that period the two systems stood in direct and irreconcileable opposition. To the eye of the Jew the Christian became, from a rebellious and heretical son, an irreclaimable apostate; and to the Christian the temporary designation of Jesus as the Messiah of the Jews, was merged in the more sublime title, the Redeemer of the world.

The same measures rendered the internal conflict with the lingering Judaism within the Church more violent and desperate. Its dying struggles, as it were, to maintain its ground, rent, for some time, the infant community with civil divisions. But the predominant influx of Gentile converts gradually obtained the ascendancy; Judaism slowly died out in the great body of the Church, and the Judæo-Christian sects in the East languished, and at length expired in obscurity.

Divine Providence had armed the religion of Christ with new powers adapted to the change in its situation and design, both for resistance against the more violent animosity, which was exasperated by its growing success, and for aggression upon the ignorance, the vice, and the misery, which it was to enlighten, to purify, or to mitigate. Independent of the supernatural powers occasionally displayed by the Apostles, the accession of two men so highly gifted with natural abilities, as well as with all the peculiar powers conferred on the first Apostles of Christianity, the enrolment of Barnabas and Paul in the Apostolic body, showed that for the comprehensive system about to be developed instruments were wanting of a different character from the humble and uninstructed peasants of Galilee. However extraordinary the change wrought in the minds of the earlier Apostles by the spirit of Christianity; however some of them, especially Peter and John, may have extended their labours beyond the precincts of Palestine, yet Paul appears to have exercised by far the greatest influence, not merely in the conversion of the Gentiles, but in emancipating the Christianity of the Jewish converts from the inveterate influence of their old religion.

Paul and Barnabas.

Yet the first step towards the more comprehensive system was made by Peter. Samaria, indeed, had already received the new religion to a great extent; an innovation upon Jewish prejudice, remarkable both in itself and its results. The most important circumstance in that transaction, the collision with Simon the magician, will be considered in a future chapter, that which describes the conflict of Christianity with Orientalism. The vision of Peter, which seemed by the Divine sanction to annul the distinction of meats, of itself threw down one of those barriers which separated the Jews from the rest

Difference between Jew and Gentile partially abrogated by Peter.

of mankind.[a] This sacred usage prohibited not merely all social intercourse, but all close or domestic communication with other races. But the figurative instruction which the Apostle inferred from this abrogation of all distinction between clean and unclean animals, was of still greater importance. The proselytes of the Gate, that is, those heathens who, without submitting to circumcision, or acknowledging the claims of the whole Law to their obedience, had embraced the main principles of Judaism, more particularly the Unity of God, were at once admitted into the Christian community.

Cornelius. Cornelius was, as it were, the representative of this class; his admission by the federal rite of baptism into the Christian community, the public sanction of the Almighty to this step by "the pouring out the gift of the Holy Ghost" upon the Gentiles, decided this part of the question.[b] Still the admission

---

[a] Acts x. 11 to 21.

[b] It is disputed whether Cornelius was, in fact, a proselyte of the Gate. (See, on one side, Lord Barrington's Works, vol. i. p. 128, and Benson's History of Christianity; on the other, Kuinoel, in loco.) He is called εὐσεβὴς and φοβούμενος τὸν Θεόν, the usual appellation of proselytes: he bestowed alms on the Jewish people; he observed the Jewish hours of prayer; he was evidently familiar with the Jewish belief in angels, and not unversed in the Jewish Scriptures. Yet, on the other hand, the objections are not without weight. The whole difficulty appears to arise from not considering how vaguely the term of "Proselyte at the Gate" must, from the nature of things, have been applied, and the different feelings entertained towards such converts by the different classes of the Jews. While the proselytes, properly so called,—those who were identified with the Jews by circumcision,—were a distinct and definite class; the Proselytes of the Gate must have comprehended all who made the least advances towards Judaism, from those who regularly attended on the services of the synagogue, and conformed in all respects, except circumcision, with the ceremonial law, down, through the countless shades of opinion, to those who merely admitted the first principle of Judaism,—the Unity of God,—were occasional attendants in the synagogue; and had only, as it were, ascended the first steps on the threshold of conversion. The more rigid Jews looked with jealousy even on the circumcised proselytes; the

into Christianity was *through Judaism*. It required all the influence of the Apostle, and his distinct asseveration that he acted by divine commission, to induce the Christians of Jerusalem to admit Gentiles imperfectly Judaised, and uninitiated by the national rite of circumcision into the race of Israel, to a participation in the kingdom of the Messiah.

To this subject I must, however, revert, when I attempt more fully to develope the internal conflict of Christianity with Judaism.

The conversion of Cornelius took place before the persecution of Herod Agrippa, down to which period this history has traced the external conflict maintained by Christianity against the dominant Judaism. On the death of Herod, his son Agrippa being a minor and educated at Rome, a Roman Prefect resumed the provincial government of Judæa. This Prefect ruled almost always with a stern, sometimes

_{State of Judæa.}

---

terms of admission were made as difficult and repulsive as possible; on the imperfect they looked with still greater suspicion, and were rather jealous of communicating their exclusive privileges, than eager to extend the influence of their opinions. But the more liberal must have acted on different principles: they must have encouraged the advances of incipient proselytes; the synagogues were open throughout the Roman Empire, and many who, like Horace, "went to scoff," may "have remained to pray." As, then, the Christian Apostles always commenced their labours in the synagogue of their countrymen, among all who might assemble there from regular habit, or accidental curiosity, they would address Heathen minds in every gradation of Jewish belief, from the proselyte who only wanted circumcision, to the Gentile who had only just begun to discover the superior reasonableness of the Jewish Theism. Hence the step from the conversion of imperfect proselytes to that of real Gentiles must have been imperceptible; or rather, even with the Gentile convert, that which was the first principle of Judaism, the belief in one God, was an indispensable preliminary to his admission of Christianity. The one great decisive change was from the decree of the Apostolic council (Acts xiv.), obviously intended for real, though imperfect proselytes, to the total abrogation of Judaism by the doctrines of St. Paul.

with an iron hand, and the gradually increasing turbulence of the province led to severity; severity with a profligate and tyrannical ruler degenerated into oppression; until the systematic cruelty of Florus maddened the nation into the last fatal insurrection. The Sanhedrin appear at no time to have possessed sufficient influence with the Prefect to be permitted to take violent measures against the Christians. With Cuspius Fadus, who had transferred the custody of the High Priest's robes into the Antonia, they were on no amicable terms. Tiberius Alexander, an apostate from Judaism, was little likely to lend himself to any acts of bigotry or persecution. During the prefecture of Cumanus, the massacre in the Temple, the sanguinary feuds between the Jews and Samaritans, occupied the public mind; it was a period of political disorder and confusion, which continued for a considerable time.

Procurator Judææ, A.D. 44.

A.D. 46.

A.D. 48.

The commencement of the administration of the whole province by the corrupt and dissolute Felix, the insurrection of Theudas, the reappearance of the sons of the Galilean Judas, the incursions of the predatory bands which rose in all quarters, would divert the attention of the ruler from a peaceful sect, who, to his apprehension, differed from their countrymen only in some harmless speculative opinions, and in their orderly and quiet conduct. If the Christians were thus secure in their peacefulness and obscurity from the hostility of the Roman rulers, the native Jewish authorities, gradually more and more in collision with their foreign masters, would not possess the power of conducting persecution to any extent. Instead of influencing the counsels of the Prefect, the High Priest was either a mere instrument, appointed by his caprice, or it

A.D. 50.

he aspired to independent authority, in direct opposition to his tyrannous master. The native authorities were, in fact, continually in collision with the foreign ruler; one, Ananias, had been sent in chains to Rome as accessary to the tumults which had arisen between the Jews and the Samaritans; his successor Jonathan, fell by the hand of an assassin, in the employ, or at least with the connivance, of the Roman governor. On his acquittal at Rome, Ananias returned to Jerusalem and reassumed the vacant pontificate; and it was during this period that Christianity, in the person of Paul, came again into conflict with the constituted authorities, as well as with the popular hostility. The prompt and decisive interference of the Roman guard; the protection and even the favour shown to Paul, directly it was discovered that he was not identified with any of the insurgent robbers; the adjournment of the cause to the tribunal of Felix at Cæsarea;—show how little weight or power was permitted either to the High Priest or the Sanhedrin, and the slight respect paid to the religious feelings of the people.

The details of this remarkable transaction will command our notice, in the order of time, when we have traced the proceedings of Paul and his fellow missionaries among the Jews beyond the borders of Palestine, and exhibited the conflict which they maintained with Judaism in foreign countries. The new opening, as it were, for the extension of Christianity, after the conversion of Cornelius, directed the attention of Barnabas to Saul, who, since his flight from Jerusalem, had remained in secure retirement at Tarsus. From thence he was summoned by Barnabas to Antioch.[c] Antioch, where

---

[c] Acts xi. 25.

the body of believers assumed the name of Christians, became, as it were, the head-quarters of the foreign operations of Christianity.[a] After the mission of Paul and Barnabas to Jerusalem during the famine (either about the time of, or soon after, the Herodian persecution), these two distinguished teachers of the Gospel were invested, with the Divine sanction, in the apostolic office.[b]

From this time St. Paul stands forth as the great central figure in the great unfolding Drama of the conversion of the world to Christianity. Of the chosen twelve, except Peter and John, some immediately, some after a certain time, are altogether lost to historic vision; they fade away into the dim page of legend. One indeed, James the brother of John, has been cruelly cut off by the hand of Herod. Three, at least two, survive in their writings—James the brother of the Lord (and there seems no valid reason for abandoning the popular belief) by common consent assumed a kind of headship of the Church in Jerusalem; it was he who presided in the councils, and, from his conformity to the Jewish Law, received the appellation of James the Just, whose death is to be hereafter recorded. St. Matthew lives in his Gospel; but where that Gospel was written, in what language originally, are questions to which no authoritative answer can be given. But it seems to me that it is undoubtedly Palestinian. It may have been written originally in Hebrew (Aramaic), for the Christians of Palestine and the East, or in Greek for more general and universal use; or possibly, as Josephus wrote his History, in both languages, both in Greek and Aramaic. But to my judgement, in the

---

[a] Acts xi. 26.   [b] Acts xiii. 2.

selection of facts, in imagery and in allusion, it has a native stamp—native, I mean, to the scene of our Lord's labours, and to the life of him whose calling was that of a publican in Judæa. Jude (Thadeus, Lebbeus) is known by his Epistle. This writing too, from its perpetual allusions to Jewish history and to Jewish tradition, must have been addressed to Christians of Jewish descent; it would have been unintelligible to Gentile Christians. Jude's sphere of action must therefore have been in Palestine or the East. Of those whose voices have not come down to us, we know historically nothing. The magnificent scheme of the partition of the world, each province of Asia, Europe, Africa, to its Apostolic Conqueror, their triumphal progress, each in his separate domain, the martyrdom of most in the scene of their labours, is a creation of later times, glaringly opposed to the quiet and practical modesty of the authentic Scripture. Even of Andrew in Achaia and in Scythia, of Thaddeus in Edessa, Matthew or Matthias in Æthiopia, of Thomas in Parthia and Southern India, of Bartholomew in Judea, there remain but vague, late, contradictory rumours, which hardly aspire to legends.

St. Peter himself recedes from view. After he had taken the first step to the more comprehensive Christianity, which would embrace the world, and know no distinction, "*Jew or Gentile, Greek or Barbarian, bond or free,*" he seems almost to relapse into that Judaism which was openly resisted at Antioch by St. Paul. His great sphere in Babylonia, and in those Churches of Asia to which his First Epistle is addressed, would afford ample scope for his holy activity among the brethren of the Circumcision, so widely dispersed.

St. John, if we may judge by internal evidence, became more distinctly Greek—Asiatic Greek. Tradition designates Ephesus as the seat of his more confined activity (most of these Asiatic Churches had already been founded by St. Paul), or of his contemplative quiescence, out of which grew the last Gospel, the crown and consummation of Christian faith, and the three Epistles, the most exquisite and perfect expression of Christian love. The Revelations, if, as I am disposed to believe, of St. John, belong to an earlier period of his life, before the destruction of Jerusalem.

St. Paul alone stands out in the fuller light of authoritative and documentary history. He is in all the great capital cities of the West, in all the great centres of civil, of commercial, and intellectual greatness, in Antioch, in Ephesus, in Athens, in Corinth, in Rome. He is among Barbarians at Lystra, in Galatia, in Melita. He is the one active ruling missionary of what we may call the foreign operations of the Christian Church.

But these foreign operations of the great Hebrew missionary or missionaries were at first altogether confined to the Jewish population, which was scattered throughout the whole of Syria and Asia Minor. On their arrival in a town which they had not visited before, they of course sought a hospitable reception among their countrymen; the first scene of their labours was the synagogue.[1] In the Island of Cyprus,

Cyprus.

the native country of Barnabas, a considerable part of the population must have been of Jewish descent.[2] Both at Salamis at the eastern, and at Paphos on the western, extremity, and, probably, in other

---

[1] Acts xiii. 4-12.

[2] History of the Jews, ii. 421. In the fatal insurrection during the reign of Hadrian, they are said to have massacred 240,000 of the Grecian inhabitants, and obtained temporary possession of the island.

places during their journey through the whole length of the island, they found flourishing communities of their countrymen. To the governor, a man of inquiring and philosophic mind,[b] the simple principles of Judaism could not be unknown; and, perhaps, the contrast between the chaste, and simple, and rational worship of the synagogue, and the proverbially sensual rites of Heathenism, for which Paphos was renowned, may have heightened his respect for, or increased his inclination to, the purer faith. The arrival of two new teachers among the Jews of the city could not but reach the ears of Sergius Paulus; the sensation they excited among their countrymen awoke his curiosity. He had already encouraged the familiar attendance of a Jewish wonder-worker, a man who probably misused some skill in natural science for purposes of fraud and gain. Bar-Jesus (the son of Jesus or Joshua) was probably less actuated, in his opposition to the Apostles, by Jewish bigotry, than by the apprehension of losing his influence with the governor. He saw, no doubt, in the Apostles, adventurers like himself. The miraculous blindness with which the magician was struck, convinced the governor of the superior claims of the Apostles; the beauty of the Christian doctrines filled him with astonishment; and the Roman proconsul, though not united by baptism to the Christian community, must, nevertheless, have added great weight, by his acknowledged support, to the cause of Christianity in Cyprus.[i]

[b] The remarkable accuracy of St. Luke in naming the governor, proconsul, has been frequently observed. The provincial governors appointed by the Emperors were called proprætors; those by the Senate, proconsuls. That of Cyprus was properly in the nomination of the Emperor, but Augustus transferred his right, as to Cyprus and Narbonese Gaul, to the Senate. Dion Cassius, l. liv. p. 523.

[i] Had he thus become altogether Christian, his baptism would assuredly have been mentioned by the sacred writer.

From Cyprus they crossed to the southern shore of Asia Minor, landed at Perga in Pamphylia, and passed through the chief cities of that region. In the more flourishing towns they found a considerable Jewish population, and the synagogue of the Jews appears to have been attended by great numbers of Gentiles, more or less disposed to embrace the tenets of Judaism. Everywhere the more rigid Jews met them with fierce and resentful opposition; but among the less bigoted of their countrymen, and this more unprejudiced class of proselytes, they made great progress. At the first considerable city in which they appeared, Antioch in Pisidia,[b] the address of St. Paul to the mingled congregation of Jews and Proselytes appears at some length. He dwelt on the prophesied Messiahship of Jesus, on the Resurrection, on the forgiveness of sins, unattainable by the Law, attainable through faith in Jesus. The opposition of the Jews seems to have been so general, and the favourable disposition of their Gentile hearers, proselytes, so decided, that the Apostles avowedly disclaimed all farther connexion with the more violent party, and united themselves to the Gentile believers. Either from the number or the influence of the Jews in this Antioch, the public interest in that dispute, instead of being confined within the synagogue, prevailed through the whole city; but the Jews had so much weight, especially with some of the women of rank, that they at length obtained the expulsion of the Apostles from the city by the ruling authorities. The Apostles shook off the dust from their feet, as renouncing all further connexion with the stern bigots, and went their way. At Iconium, to which city they retired, the opposition was still more

[b] Acts xiii. 14-52.

violent; the populace was excited; and here many of the Gentiles uniting with the Jews against them, they were constrained to fly for their lives into the barbarous district of Lycaonia. Lystra and Derbe appear to have been almost entirely Heathen towns. The remarkable collision of the Apostles with Paganism in the former of these places will hereafter be considered. To Lystra the hostility of the Jews pursued them, where, by some strange revulsion of popular feeling, Paul, a short time before worshipped as a god, was cast out of the city, half-dead. They proceeded to Derbe, and thence returned through the same cities to Antioch in Syria. The ordination of "elders,"* to preside over the Christian communities, implies their secession from the synagogues of their countrymen. In Jerusalem, from the multitude of synagogues, which belonged to the different races of foreign Jews, another might arise, or one of those usually occupied by the Galileans might pass into the separate possession of the Christians, without exciting much notice, particularly as great part of the public devotions of all classes were performed in the Temple, where the Christians were still regular attendants. Most likely the first distinct community which met in a chamber or place of assemblage of their own, the first "Church," was formed at Antioch. To the Heathen this would appear nothing more than the establishment of a new Jewish synagogue; an event, whenever their numbers were considerable, of common occurrence. To the Jew alone it assumed the appearance of a dangerous and formidable apostasy from the religion of his ancestors.

The barrier was now thrown down, but Judaism ral-

---

* Acts xiv. 23.

lied, as it were, for a last effort behind its ruins. It was now manifest that Christianity would no longer endure the rigid nationalism of the Jew, who demanded that every proselyte to his faith should be enrolled as a member of his race. Circumcision could no longer be maintained as the seal of conversion,[a] but still the total abrogation of the Mosaic Law, the extinction of all their privileges of descent, the substitution of a purely religious for a national community, to the Christianised Jew, appeared, as it were, a kind of treason against the religious majesty of their ancestors. A conference became necessary between the leaders of the Christian community to avert an inevitable collision, which might be fatal to the progress of the religion. Already the peace of the flourishing community at Antioch[b] had been disturbed by some of the more zealous converts from Jerusalem, who still asserted the indispensable necessity of circumcision. Paul and Barnabas proceeded as delegates from the community at Antioch; and what is called[c] the Council of Jerusalem, a full assembly of all the Apostles then present in the Metropolis, solemnly debated this great question. How far the earlier Apostles were themselves emancipated from the invete-

Margin notes: Jewish attachment to the Law. A.D. 48. — Council of Jerusalem. A.D. 48.

---

[a] The adherence, even of those Jews who might have been expected to be less bigoted to their institutions, to this distinctive rite of their religion, is illustrated by many curious particulars in the history. Two foreign princes, Aziz king of Emesa, and Polemo king of Cilicia, submitted to circumcision, an indispensable stipulation, in order to obtain in marriage, the former Drusilla, the latter Bernice, princesses of the Herodian family. On one occasion the alliance of some foreign troops was rejected, unless they would first qualify themselves in this manner for the distinction of associating with the Jews.

[b] Acts xv. 1.

[c] It is not absolutely certain whether James who presided in this assembly was either of the two Jameses included among the twelve Apostles, or a distinct person, a relative of Jesus. The latter opinion rests on the authority of Eusebius. I am inclined to "the brother of the Lord."

rate Judaism does not distinctly appear, but the situation of affairs required the most nicely-balanced judgment, united with the utmost moderation of temper. On one side a Pharisaic party had brought into Christianity a rigorous and passionate attachment to the Mosaic institutes, in their strictest and most minute provisions. On the other hand, beyond the borders of Palestine, far the greater number of converts had been formed from that intermediate class which stood between Heathenism and Judaism. There might seem, then, no alternative but to estrange one party by the abrogation of the Law, or the other by the strict enforcement of all its provisions. Each party might appeal to the Divine sanction. To the eternal, the irrepealable sanctity of the law, the God of their Fathers, according to the Jewish opinion, was solemnly pledged; while the vision of Peter, which authorised the admission of the Gentiles into Christianity—still more the success of Paul and Barnabas in proselyting the Heathen, accompanied by undeniable manifestations of Divine favour, seemed irresistible evidence of the Divine sanction to the abrogation of the law, as far as concerned the Gentile Proselytes. The influence of James effected a discreet and temperate compromise: Judaism as it were capitulated on honourable terms. The Christians were to be left to that freedom enjoyed by the Proselytes of the Gate, but they were enjoined to pay so much respect to those with whom they were associated in religious worship, as to abstain from those practices which were most offensive to their habits.[q] The partaking of the

---

[q] The reason assigned for these regulations appears to infer that as yet the Christians, in general, met in the same places of religious assemblage with the Jews; at least this view gives a clear and simple sense to a much contested passage. These provisions were necessary because the Mosaic Law was uni-

sacrificial feasts in the idolatrous Temples was so plainly repugnant to the first principles, either of the Jewish or the Christian Theism, as to be altogether irreconcileable with the professed opinions of a proselyte to either. The using things strangled, and blood, for food appears to have been the most revolting to Jewish feeling; and perhaps among the dietetic regulations of the Mosaic Law, none, in a southern climate, was more conducive to health. The last article in this celebrated decree was a moral prohibition, but, not improbably, directed more particularly against the dissolute rites of those Syrian and Asiatic religions, in which prostitution formed an essential part, and which prevailed to a great extent in the countries bordering upon Palestine.'

Second journey of Paul. A.D. 50.

The second journey* of Paul brought him more immediately into contact with Paganism. Though, no doubt, in every city there were resident Jews with whom he took up his abode, and his first public appearance was in the synagogue of his countrymen, yet he is now more frequently extending, as it were, his aggressive operations into the dominions of Heathenism. If he found hospitality, no doubt he encountered either violent or secret hostility from his brethren. Few circumstances, however, occur which be-

---

versally read and from immemorial usage in the synagogues. The direct violation of its most vital principles by any of those who joined in the common worship would be incongruous, and of course highly offensive to the more zealous Mosaists.

ʳ It should be remembered that as yet Christianity had only spread into countries where this religious flopoela chiefly prevailed, into Syria and Cyprus.

Of the first we may form a fair notion from Lucian's Treatise de Deâ Syriâ, and the Daphne of Antioch had no doubt already obtained its voluptuous celebrity; the latter, particularly Paphos, can require no illustration. Bentley's ingenious reading of Χοιρεία, swine's flesh, wants the indispensable authority of manuscripts.

ˢ Acts xvi. 1. to xviii. 22.

long more especially to the conflict between Judaism and Christianity.

Paul and Barnabas set out together on this more extensive journey: but on some dispute as to the companions who were to attend upon them, Barnabas turned aside with Mark to his native country of Cyprus; while Paul, accompanied by Silas, revisited those cities in Syria and Cilicia where they had already established Christian communities.

At Lystra, Paul showed his deference to Jewish opinion by permitting a useful disciple, named Timotheus, to be circumcised.[1] But this case was peculiar, as Timotheus, by his mother's side, was a Jew; and, though by a connexion with a man of Greek race, she had forfeited both for herself and her offspring the privileges of Jewish descent, the circumcision of the son might, in a great degree, remove the stigma which attached to his birth, and which would render him less acceptable among his Jewish brethren. Having left this region, the Apostle ranged northward, through Phrygia, Galatia, and Mysia; but, instead of continuing his course towards the shore of the Black Sea to Bithynia, admonished by a vision, he passed to Europe, and at Neapolis, in Macedonia,[2] landed the obscure and unregarded man to whom Europe, in Christianity, owes the great principle of her civilisation, the predominant element in her superiority over the more barbarous and unenlightened quarters of the world. At Philippi, the Jews, being few in number, appear only to have had a Proseucha, a smaller place of public worship, as usual, near the sea-side; at Thessalonica they were more numerous, and had a synagogue;[3] at Berea, they appear

---

[1] Acts xvi. 3.
[2] Acts xvi. 11, 12.
[3] Acts xvii. 1. Thessalonica is a city where the Jews have perhaps resided for a longer period, in considerable numbers, than in any other, at least

likewise to have formed a flourishing community; even at Athens the Jews had made many proselytes. Corinth, a new colony of settlers from all quarters, a central mercantile mart, through which passed a great part of the commerce between the East and West, offered a still more eligible residence for the Jews, who, no doubt, had already become traders to a considerable extent.[r] Their numbers had been lately increased by their expulsion from Rome, under the Emperor Claudius.[s] This edict is attributed by Suetonius to the tumults excited by the mutual hostility between the Jews and Christians. Christianity, therefore, must thus early have made considerable progress in Rome. The scenes of riot were, probably, either like those which took place in the Asiatic cities, where the Jews attempted to use violence against the Christians; or, as in Corinth itself, where the tribunal of the magistrate was disturbed by fierce, and to him unintelligible, disputes between, as

---

in Europe. When the Jews fled from Christian persecution to the milder oppression of the Turks, vast numbers settled at Thessalonica. Hist. Jews, iii. 338. Von Hammer states the present population of Thessalonica (Salonichi) at 16,000 Greeks; 12,000 Jews; and 50,000 Turks. Osmanische Geschichte, I. 442.

[r] Corinth, since its demolition by Mummius, had lain in ruins till the time of Julius Cæsar, who established a colony on its site. From the advantages of its situation, the connecting link, as it were, between Italy, the north of Greece, and Asia, it grew up rapidly to all its former wealth and splendour.

[s] The manner in which this event is related by the epigrammatic Biographer, even the mistakes in his account, are remarkably characteristic: "Judæos, Chresto duce, assidue tumultuantes Roma expulit." The confusion between the religion and its founder, and the substitution of the word Chrestos, a good man, which would bear an intelligible sense to a heathen, for Christos (the anointed), which would only convey a distinct notion to a Jew, illustrate the state of things. "Cum perperam Christianus pronuntiatur a vobis (nam nec nominis est certa notitia penes vos) de suavitate vel benignitate compositum est." Tert. Apolog. c. 3. "Sed exponenda hujus nominis ratio est propter ignorantium errorem, qui eum immutatâ literâ Chrestum solent dicere." Lact. Inst. 4. 7. 5.

be supposed, two Jewish factions. With two of the exiles, Aquila and Priscilla, Paul, as practising the same trade, that of tent-makers,[a] made a more intimate connexion, residing with them, and pursuing their craft in common.[b] At Corinth, possibly for the first time, the Christians openly seceded from the Jews, and obtained a separate school of public instruction; even the chief ruler of the synagogue, Crispus, became a convert. But the consequence of this secession was the more declared and open animosity of the Jewish party, which ended in an appeal to the public tribunal of the governor. The result of the trial before the judgment-seat of Gallio, the pro-consul of Achaia, appears to have been an ebullition of popular indignation in favour of the Christians, as another of the chief rulers of the synagogue, probably the prosecutor of the Christians, underwent the punishment of scourging before the tribunal.

From Corinth[c] Paul returned by sea to Cæsarea,[d] and from thence to Antioch.

---

[a] The Jews thought it right that every one, even the learned, should know some art or trade. "Sapientes plurimi artem aliquam fecerunt ne aliorum beneficentia indigerent." Maimonides. See Lightfoot, iii. 227.

[b] There was a coarse stuff called Cilicium, made of goats' hair, manufactured in the native country of Paul, and used for the purpose of portable tents, which it is ingeniously conjectured may have been the art practised by Paul.

[c] From Corinth, after he had been rejoined by Silas (Silvanus) and Timotheus, was most probably written the First Epistle to the Thessalonians. This epistle is full of allusions to his recent journey. On his arrival at Athens he had sent back Timotheus to ascertain the state of the infant Church. Subsequently it appears that the more Jewish opinion of the immediate reappearance of the Messiah to judgement had gained great ground in the community. It is slightly alluded to in the First Epistle, v. 2, 3. The second seems to have been written expressly to counteract this notion.

[d] I make no observation on the vow made at Cenchrea, as I follow the natural construction of the words. The Vulgate, St. Chrysostom, and many more commentators, attribute the vow, whatever it was, to Aquila, not to Paul.

There is great doubt as to the authenticity of the clause, verse 21

The third journey of St. Paul [*] belongs still more exclusively to the conflict of Christianity with Paganism. At Ephesus [†] alone, where he arrived after a circuit through Phrygia and Galatia, he encountered some wandering wonder-working sons of a certain Sceva, a Jew, who attempted to imitate the miraculous cures which he wrought. The failure of the exorcism, which they endeavoured to perform by the name of Jesus, and which only increased the violence of the lunatic, made a deep impression on the whole Jewish population. His circuit through Macedonia, Greece, back to Philippi, down the Ægean to Miletus, by Cos, Rhodes, Patara to Tyre, and thence to Cæsarea, brought him again near to Jerusalem, where he had determined to appear at the feast of Pentecost. Notwithstanding the remonstrances of his friends, and the prophetic denunciation of his imprisonment by a certain Agabus, he adhered to his resolution of confronting the whole hostile nation at their great concourse. For not the Jews alone, but perhaps the Jewish Christians likewise, in the head-quarters of Judaism, would confederate against this renegade, who not only asserted Jesus to be the Messiah, but had avowedly raised the uncircumcised Gentiles to the level of, if not to a superiority over, the descendant of Israel. Yet, of the real nature of St. Paul's Christianity, they were still singularly, though characteristically, ignorant; they could not yet persuade themselves that Christianity aspired to a total independence of Judaism. Their Temple was still, as it were, the vesti-

---

("I must by all means keep this feast that cometh in Jerusalem"). Those who suppose it to be genuine, explain the ἀναβὰς in the next verse, as going up to Jerusalem; but on the whole I am inclined to doubt any such visit.

[*] Acts xviii. 23, xxi. 6.
[†] Acts xviii. 24.

bule to the Divine favour; and, having no notion that the Gentile converts to Christianity would be altogether indifferent as to the local sanctity of any edifice, they appear to have apprehended an invasion, or, at least, a secret attempt to introduce the uncircumcised to the privilege of worship within the hallowed precincts.

The motive of Paul in visiting Jerusalem was probably to allay the jealousy of his countrymen; the period selected for his visit was, as it were, the birthday of the Law;[a] the solemnity which commemorated the divine enactment of that code, which every Jew considered of eternal and irreversible authority. Nor did he lay aside his customary prudence. He complied with the advice of his friends; and instead of appearing in the Temple as an ordinary worshipper, as if he would show his own personal reverence for the usages of his ancestors, he united himself to four persons who had taken upon them a vow, a deliberate acknowledgment not merely of respect for, but of zeal beyond, the Law.[b] His person, however, was too well known to the Asiatic Jews not to be recognised; a sudden outcry was raised against him— he was charged with having violated the sanctity of the holy precincts by introducing an uncircumcised stranger, Trophimus, an Ephesian, with whom he had been familiarly conversing in the city, within those pillars, or palisades, which, in the three predominant languages of the time, Hebrew, Greek, and Latin, forbade the advance of any who were not of pure Jewish descent. He was dragged out, no doubt, into the Court of the Gentiles, the doors closed, and but for the prompt

Paul in the Temple.

---

[a] The ceasing to attend at the Passover, after, in his own language, "the great Passover had been sacrificed," is a circumstance by no means unworthy of notice.

[b] Acts xxi. 17-26.

interference of the Roman guard, which was always mounted, particularly during the days of festival, he would have fallen a victim to the popular fury. For while the unconverted Jews would pursue his life with implacable indignation, he could, at best, expect no assistance from the Jewish Christians. The interposition of the Roman commander in Jerusalem was called forth, rather to suppress a dangerous riot, than to rescue an innocent victim from the tumultuous violence of the populace.

Apprehension of Paul

Lysias at first supposed Paul to be one of the insurgent chieftains who had disturbed the public peace during the whole administration of Felix. His fears identified him with a Jew of Egyptian birth, who, a short time before, had appeared on the Mount of Olives at the head of above 30,000 fanatic followers; and, though his partisans were scattered by the decisive measures of Felix, had contrived to make his escape.[1] The impression that his insurrection had made on the minds of the Romans, is shown by the terror of his reappearance, which seems to have haunted the mind of Lysias. The ease and purity with which Paul addressed him in Greek, as these insurgents probably communicated with their followers only in the dialect of the country; the commanding serenity of his demeanour; and the declaration that he was a citizen of an Asiatic town, not a native of Palestine, so far influenced Lysias in his favour, as to permit him to address the multitude. It was probably from the flight of steps which led from the outer court of the Temple up into the Antonia that Paul commenced his harangue. He spoke in the vernacular language of the country, and was heard in silence, as far as his account of his

---

[1] Hist. of Jews, ii. 171.

conversion to the new religion; but directly that he touched on the dangerous subject of the admission of the Gentiles to the privileges of Christianity, the popular frenzy broke out again with such violence as scarcely to be controlled by the Roman military. Paul was led away into the court of the fortress, and the commander, who probably understood nothing of his address, but only saw that instead of allaying, it increased the turbulence of the people (for, with the characteristic violence of an Asiatic mob, they are described as casting off their clothes, and throwing dust into the air), gave orders that he should suffer the usual punishment of scourging with rods, in order that he might be forced to confess the real origin of the disturbance. But this proceeding was arrested by Paul's claiming the privilege of a Roman citizen, whom it was treason against the majesty of the Roman people to expose to such indignity.[b] The soldiers, or lictors, engaged in scourging him recoiled in terror. The respect of Lysias himself for his prisoner rose to more than its former height; for, having himself purchased this valuable privilege at a high price, one who had inherited the same right appeared an important personage in his estimation.

The next morning the Sanhedrin was convened, and Paul was again brought into the Temple, to the Gazith, the chamber where the Sanhedrin held its judicial meetings. Ananias presided in the assembly as High Priest, an office which he possessed rather by usurpation than by legitimate authority. After the tu- <small>Paul before the Sanhedrin, etc.</small> mults between the Samaritans and the Jews, during the administration of Cumanus, Ananias had, as was before briefly stated, been sent as a prisoner to

---

[b] Acts xxii. 24-29.

Rome, to answer for the charges against his nation.[m] After two years he had been released by the interest of Agrippa, and allowed to return to Jerusalem. In the mean time the High Priesthood had been filled by Jonathan, who was murdered by assassins in the Temple, employed, or at least connived at, by the Governor.[o] Ananias appears to have resumed the vacant authority, until the appointment of Ismael, son of Fabi, by Agrippa.[o] Ananias was of the Sadducaic party, a man harsh, venal, and ambitious. Faction most probably ran very high in the national council. I am inclined to suppose, from the favourable expressions of Josephus, that the murdered Jonathan was of the Pharisaic sect; and his recent death, and the usurpation of the office by Ananias, would incline the Pharisaic faction to resist all measures proposed by their adversaries.

Of this state of things Paul seems to have been fully aware. He commenced with a solemn protestation of his innocence, which so excited the indignation of Ananias, that he commanded him to be struck over the mouth, a common punishment in the East for language which may displease those in power.[p] The answer of St. Paul to this arbitrary violation of the law (for by the Jewish course of justice no punishment could be inflicted without a formal sentence) was in a tone of vehement indignation,—" God shall smite thee, thou whited wall; for sittest thou to judge me after the law, and commandest me to be smitten contrary to the law?" Rebuked for thus disrespectfully answering the High Priest, Paul replied that he did not know that there was any one at that time lawfully exercising the

---

[m] Joseph. Ant. xx. 6. 2.
[n] Joseph. xx 8. 5.
[o] A. D. 56. Joseph. Ant. xx. 8. 8.
[p] Acts xxiii. 2, 3.

office of High Priest,[q] an office which he was bound, by the strict letter of the sacred writings, to treat with profound respect. He proceeded, without scruple, to avail himself of the dissensions of the Court; for by resting his defence on his belief in the Resurrection, he no doubt irritated more violently the Sadducaic party, but threw that of the Pharisees on his own side. The angry discussion was terminated by the interposition of the Roman commander, who again withdrew Paul into the citadel. Yet his life was not secure even there. The crime of assassination had become fearfully frequent in Jerusalem. Neither did the sanctity of the Temple protect the unsuspicious worshipper from the secret dagger, nor, as we have seen, did the majesty of the High Priest's office secure the first religious and civil magistrate of the nation from the same ignoble fate. A conspiracy was formed by some of these fanatic zealots against the life of Paul; but the plot being discovered by one of his relatives, a sister's son, he was sent under a strong guard to Cæsarea, the residence of the Roman provincial governor, the dissolute and tyrannical Felix.

The Sanhedrin pursued their hated adversary to the tribunal of the Governor, but with Felix they possessed no commanding influence. A hired orator, whom from his name we may conjecture to have been a Roman, employed perhaps according to the usage, which provided that all legal proceedings should be conducted in the Latin language, appeared as their advocate before the tribunal.[r] But the defence of Paul against the charge of sedition, of innovation,

Paul sent to Cæsarea— brought before Felix.

---

[q] "I wist not that there was a High Priest;" such appears to be the translation of this passage, suggested by Mr. Granwell, most agreeable to the sense.

[r] Acts xxiv. 1-26.

and the profanation of the Temple, was equally successful with Felix, who was well acquainted with the Jewish character, and by no means disposed to lend himself to their passions and animosities. The charge therefore was dismissed. Paul, though not set at liberty, was allowed free intercourse with his Christian brethren. Felix himself even condescended to hear, and heard not without emotion, the high moral doctrines of St. Paul, which were so much at variance with his unjust and adulterous life. But it was not so much the virtue as the rapacity of Felix which thus inclined him to look with favour upon the Apostle: knowing probably the profuse liberality of the Christians, and their zealous attachment to their teacher, he expected that the liberty of Paul would be purchased at any price he might demand. For the last two years therefore of the administration of Felix, Paul remained a prisoner; and Felix, at his departure, well aware that accusations were lodged against him by the representatives of the Jewish nation, endeavoured to propitiate their favour by leaving him still in custody.*

Paul is prisoner at Cæsarea.

---

* There is great chronological difficulty in arranging this part of the administration of Felix. But the difficulty arises, not so much in harmonising the narrative of the Acts with the historians of the period, as in reconciling Josephus with Tacitus. Taking the account of Josephus, it is impossible to compress all the events of that part of the administration of Felix, which he places after the accession of Nero, into a single year. Yet he states that, on the recall of Felix, he only escaped punishment for his crimes through the interest of his brother, Pallas. But, according to Tacitus, the influence of Pallas with Nero ceased in the second year of his reign: and he was deposed from all his offices. In the third he was indicted of læse majesté, and his acquittal was far from acceptable to the Emperor. In the fourth year his protectress Agrippina was discarded for Poppæa; in the next she was put to death. In the ninth of Nero's reign Pallas himself, though charged with no new crime, was poisoned. The question therefore is, whether, in any intermediate period, he could have regained, by any intrigue, sufficient influence to shield his brother from the prosecution of the Jews.

Nor had the Jews lost sight of this great object of animosity. Before the new Governor, Porcius Festus, a man of rigid justice, and less acquainted with the Jewish character, their charges were renewed with the utmost acrimony. On the first visit of Festus to Jerusalem, the High Priest demanded that Paul should be sent back for trial before the Sanhedrin; and though Festus refused the petition till he should himself have investigated the case at Cæsarea, on his return he proposed that Paul should undergo a public examination at Jerusalem in his own presence. The design of the Jews was to surprise and assassinate the prisoner, and Paul, probably informed of their secret intentions, persisted in his appeal to Cæsar. To this appeal from a Roman citizen, the Governor could not refuse his assent.

The younger Agrippa had now returned from Rome, where he had resided during his minority. He had succeeded to part only of his father's dominions; he was in possession of the Asmonean palace at Jerusalem, and had the right of appointing the High Priest, which he exercised apparently with all the capricious despotism of a Roman governor. He appeared in great pomp at Cæsarea, with his sister Bernice, on a visit to Festus. The Roman Governor seems to have consulted him, as a man of moderation and knowledge of the Jewish law, upon the case of Paul. The Apostle was summoned before him. The defence of Paul made a strong impression upon Agrippa, who, though not a convert, was probably from that time favourably disposed to Christianity. The appeal of Paul to the Emperor was irrevocable by an inferior authority; whether he would have preferred remaining in Judæa, after an acquittal from Festus, and perhaps under the protection of Agrippa, or whether to his own mind Rome offered a more noble and promising field for his Christian zeal, Paul, setting forth on his voyage, left probably for ever the land of his forefathers—that land beyond all others inhospitable to the religion of Christ—that land which Paul, perhaps almost alone of Jewish descent, had ceased to consider the one narrow portion of the habitable world, which the love of the Universal Father had sanctified as the chosen dwelling of his people, as the future seat of dominion, glory, and bliss.

Paul sent to Rome.

The great object of Jewish animosity had escaped the hostility of the Sanhedrin; but an opportunity soon occurred of wreaking their baffled vengeance on another victim, far less obnoxious to the general feelings even of the more bigoted among the Jews. The head of the Christian community in Jerusalem was James, whom Josephus himself, if the expression in that remarkable passage be genuine (which is difficult to believe), dignifies with the appellation of the brother of Jesus. On the death of Festus, and before the arrival of his successor Albinus, the High Priesthood was in the hands of Annas, or Ananus, the last of five sons of the former Annas, who had held that rank. Annas was the head of the Sadducaic party, and seized the opportunity of this suspension of the Roman authority to reassert the power of the Sanhedrin over life and death. Many persons, whom it is impossible not to suppose Christians, were executed by the legal punishment of stoning. Among these, the head of the community was the most exposed to the animosity of the Government, and therefore least likely to escape in their day of temporary power. The fact of the murder of St. James, at least of certain sup-

A.D. 62.

Martyrdom of James.

posed offenders against the law, whom it is difficult not to identify with the Christians,[1] rests on the authority of the Jewish historian:[2] in the details which are related on the still more questionable testimony of Hegesippus,[3] we feel that we are passing from the clear

[1] Connecting this narrative of Josephus, even without admitting the authenticity of the passage about St. James, with the proceedings against St. Paul as related in the Acts, it appears to me highly improbable that, if Ananus put any persons to death for crimes against religion, they should have been any other than Christians. Who but Christians would be obnoxious to capital punishment? and against whom, but them, would a legal conviction be obtained? Certainly not against the Pharisees, who went beyond the law, or the Zealots and followers of Judas the Galilean, whose fate would have excited little commiseration or regret among the moderate and peaceful part of the community. Lardner therefore appears to me in error, in admitting the persecutions of Ananus, but disconnecting them from the Christian history.

[2] Joseph. Ant. xx. 8. 1. See also Lardner's Jewish Testimonies, vol. iii. p. 342. 4to. edit.

[3] This narrative of Hegesippus has undergone the searching criticism of Scaliger in Chron. Euseb. and Le Clerc. Hist. Eccles. and Ars Critica; it has been feebly defended by Petavius, and zealously by Tillemont. Heinichen, the recent editor of Eusebius, seems desirous to trace some vestiges of truth. In these early forgeries it is interesting and important to ascertain not only the truth or falsehood of the traditions themselves, but the design and the authors of such pious frauds. This legend seems imagined in a spirit of Christian asceticism, endeavouring to conform itself to Jewish usage, of which, nevertheless, it betrays remarkable ignorance. It attributes to the Christian bishop the Nazaritish abstinence from the time of his birth, not only from wine, but, in the spirit of Buddhism, from every thing which had life; the self-denial of the luxury of anointment with oil, with a monkish abhorrence of ablutions—a practice positively commanded in the Law, and from which no Jew abstained. It gives him the power of entering the Holy Place at all times,—a practice utterly in opposition to the ritual principles of Judaism, as he could not have been of the race of Levi. It describes his kneeling till his knees were as hard as those of a camel—another indication of the growing spirit of monkery. I may add the injudicious introduction of the "Scribes and Pharisees," in language borrowed from the Gospel, as the authors of his fate; which, according to the more probable account of Josephus, and the change in the state of feeling in Jerusalem, was solely to be attributed to the Sadducees. The final improbability is the leading to the pinnacle of the Temple (a circumstance obviously borrowed from our Lord's temptation) a man who had been for

and pellucid air of the Apostolic history into the misty atmosphere of legend. I would willingly attempt to disentangle the more probable circumstances of this impressive story from the embellishments of later invention; but it happens that its more striking and picturesque incidents are precisely the least credible. After withdrawing every particular inconsistent either with the character or usages of the time, little remains but the simple facts that James was so highly esteemed in Jerusalem, as to have received the appellation of the Just (a title, it would seem, clearly of Jewish origin); that he perished during this short period of the sanguinary administration of Ananus, possibly was thrown down in a tumult from the precipitous walls of the Temple, where a more merciful persecutor put an end to his sufferings with a fuller's club; finally, that these cruel proceedings of Ananus were contemplated with abhorrence by the more moderate, probably by the whole Pharisaic party; his degradation from the supreme office was demanded, and hailed with satisfaction by the predominant sentiment of the people.

But the days of Jewish persecution were drawing to a close. Even religious animosity was subdued in the collision of still fiercer passions. A darker and more absorbing interest, the fate of the nation in the imminent, the inevitable conflict with the arms of Rome, occupied the Jewish mind in every quarter of the world. In Palestine it mingled personal

---

was the acknowledged head of the Christian community in Jerusalem, that he might publicly dissuade the people from believing in Christ; still further, his burial after such a death within the walls of the city, and close to the Temple: all these incongruities indicate a period at which Christianity had begun to degenerate into asceticism, and had been so long estranged from Judaism as to be ignorant of its real character and usages.

apprehensions, and either a trembling sense of the insecurity of life, or a desperate determination to risk life itself for liberty, with the more appalling anticipations of the national destiny, of the total extinction of the Heaven-ordained polity, the ruin of the city of Sion, and the Temple of God. To the ferocious and fanatical party, who gradually assumed the ascendancy, Christianity would be obnoxious, as secluding its peaceful followers from all participation in the hopes, the crimes, or what, in a worldly sense, might have been, not unjustly, considered the glories of the insurrection. Still, to whatever dangers or trials they were exposed, these were the desultory and casual attacks of individual hostility, rather than the systematic and determined persecution of one ruling party. Nor, perhaps, were the Christians looked upon with the same animosity as many of the more eminent and influential of the Jews, who vainly attempted to allay the wild ferment. A general tradition, preserved by Eusebius, intimates that the Christian community, especially forewarned by Providence, left Jerusalem before the formation of the siege, and took refuge in the town of Pella, in the Trans-Jordanic province. According to Josephus, the same course was pursued by most of the higher order, who could escape in time from the sword of the Zealot or the Idumean. Rabbinical tradition dates from the same period the flight of the Sanhedrin from the Capital: its first place of refuge, without the walls of Jerusalem, was Jafna (Jamnia), from whence it passed to other cities, until its final settlement in Tiberias.[y]

The Jewish war, the final desolation of the national polity, the destruction of the city, and the demolition

---

[y] Hist. of Jews, ii. 403.

of the Temple, were events which could not but
influence the progress of Christianity to a far greater
extent than by merely depriving the Jews of the power
to persecute under a legal form. While the
Christian beheld in all these unexampled
horrors the accomplishment of predictions
uttered by his Lord, the less infatuated among
the Jews could not be ignorant that such predictions
prevailed among the Christians. However the prudence of the latter might shrink from exasperating the
more violent party by the open promulgation of such
dispiriting and ill-omened auguries, they must have
transpired among those who were hesitating between
the two parties, and powerfully tended to throw that
fluctuating mass into the preponderating scale of Christianity. With some of the Jews, no doubt, the hope
of the coming of the Messiah must have expired with
the fall of the Temple. Not merely was the period of
time assigned, according to the general interpretation
of the prophecies, for the appearance of the Deliverer,
gone by, but their less stern and obstinate Judaism
must have begun to entertain apprehensions that the
visible rejection of the people intimated, not obscurely,
the withdrawal of the Divine favour. They would thus
be thrown back, as it were, upon Jesus of Nazareth as
the only possible Messiah, and listen to his claims with
greater inclination to believe. The alternative might
seem to be between Christ and the desperate abandonment, or the adjournment to an indefinite period, of all
their hopes of redemption. The hearts of many would
be softened by the experience of personal suffering, or
the sight of so many cases of individual misery.
Christianity, with its consolatory promises,
must have appeared the only refuge to those with

whom the wretchedness of their temporal condition seemed to invalidate their hopes of an hereditary claim to everlasting life as children of Abraham; where they despaired of a temporal, they would be more inclined to accept a spiritual and moral deliverance. At the same time the temporary advantage of the few converts, gained from such motives, would be counterbalanced by the more complete alienation of the Jewish mind from a race who not only apostatised from the religion of their fathers, but by no means repudiated the most intimate connexion with the race of Esau, for thus the dark hostility of the Jews began to denominate the Romans. By the absorption of this intermediate class, who had wavered between Christianity and Judaism, and who either melted into the mass of the Christian party, or yielded themselves to the desperate infatuation of Judaism, the breach between the Jew and the Christian became more wide and irreparable. The prouder and more obstinate Jew sternly wrapped himself up in his sullen isolation; his aversion from the rest of mankind, under the sense of galling oppression and of disappointed pride, settled into hard hostility. That which those of less fanatic Judaism found in Christianity, he sought in a stronger attachment to his own distinctive ceremonial; in a more passionate and deep-rooted conviction of his own prerogative, as of the elect people of God. He surrendered himself, a willing captive, to the new priestly dominion, that of the Rabbins, which enslaved his whole life to a system of minute ordinances; he rejoiced in the riveting and multiplying those bonds, which had been burst by Christianity, but which he wore as the badge of hopes still to be fulfilled, of glories which were at length to compensate for his present humiliation.

This more complete alienation between the Jew and the Christian tended to weaken that internal spirit of Judaism, which, nevertheless, was eradicated with the utmost difficulty, and indeed has perpetually revived within the bosom of Christianity under another name. Down to the destruction of Jerusalem, Palestine, or rather Jerusalem itself, was at once the centre and the source of this predominant influence. In foreign countries, as I shall presently explain, the irrepealable and eternal sanctity of the Mosaic Law was the repressive power which was continually struggling against the expansive force of Christianity. In Jerusalem this power was the Holiness of the Temple; and therefore, with the fall of the Temple, this strongest bond, with which the heart of the Jewish Christian was riveted to his old religion, at once burst asunder. To him the practice of his Lord and the Apostles had seemed to confirm the inalienable local sanctity of this "chosen dwelling" of God; and while it yet stood in all its undegraded splendour, to the Christian of Jerusalem it was almost impossible fully to admit the first principle of Christianity, that the Universal Father is worshipped in any part of his created universe with equal advantage. One mark by which the Jewish race was designated as the great religious caste of mankind, was thus for ever abolished. The synagogue had no reverential dignity, no old and sacred majesty to the mind of the convert, beyond his own equally humble and unimposing place of devotion. Hence, even before the destruction of the Temple, this feeling depended upon the peculiar circumstances of the individual convert.

Though even among the foreign Jews the respect for the Temple was maintained by traditionary reverence, though the impost for its maintenance was regularly levied and willingly paid by the race of Israel in every part of the Roman empire, and occasional visits to the capital at the periods of the great festivals revived in many the old sacred impressions, still, according to the universal principles of human nature, the more remote the residence, and the less frequent the impression of the Temple services upon the senses, the weaker became this first conservative principle of Jewish feeling.

But there remained another element of that exclusiveness, which was the primary principle of the existing Judaism; that exclusiveness which, limiting the Divine favour to a certain race, would scarcely believe that foreign branches could be engrafted into the parent stock, even though incorporated with it; and still obstinately resisted the notion that Gentiles, without becoming Jews, could share in the blessings of the promised Messiah; or, in their state of uncircumcision, or at least of insubordination to the Mosaic ordinances, become heirs of the kingdom of Heaven.

<small>Jewish attachment to the Law.</small>

What the Temple was to the inhabitant of Jerusalem, the Law was to the worshipper in the synagogue. As early, no doubt, as the present time, the book of the Law was the one great sacred object in every religious edifice of the Jews in all parts of the world. It was deposited in a kind of ark; it was placed in that part of the synagogue which represented the Holy of Holies; it was brought forth with solemn reverence by the "angel" of the assembly; it was heard as an "oracle of God" from the sanctuary. The whole Rabbinical supremacy rested on their privilege as interpreters of the Law; and tradition, though, in fact, it assumed a co-ordinate authority, yet veiled its preten-

<small>The Law.</small>

sions under the humbler character of an exposition, a supplementary comment, on the Heaven-enacted code. If we reascend, in our History, towards the period in which Christianity first opened its pale to the Gentiles, we shall find that this was the prevailing power by which the internal Judaism maintained its conflict with purer and more liberal Christianity within its own sphere. Even at Antioch, the Christian community had been in danger from this principle of separation; the Jewish converts, jealous of all encroachment upon the Law, had drawn off and insulated themselves from those of the Gentiles.* Peter withdrew within the narrower and more exclusive party; Barnabas alone, the companion and supporter of Paul, did not incline to the same course.* It required all the energy and resolution of Paul to resist the example and influence of the older Apostles. His public expostulation had the effect of allaying the discord at Antioch; and the temperate and conciliatory measures adopted in Jerusalem, to a certain degree reunited the conflicting parties. Still, in most places where Paul established a new community, immediately after his departure this same spirit of Judaism seems to have rallied, and attempted to re-establish the great exclusive principle, that Christianity was no more than Judaism, completed by the reception of Jesus as the Messiah. The universal religion of Christ was thus in perpetual danger of being contracted into a national and ritual worship. The eternal

---

* It is difficult to decide whether this dispute took place before or after the decree of the assembly in Jerusalem. Planck, in his Geschichte des Christenthums, places it before the decree, and on the whole this appears the most probable opinion. The event is noticed here as exemplifying the Judaising spirit rather than in strict chronological order.

* Acts xv.

Law of Moses was still to maintain its authority with all its cumbrous framework of observances; and the Gentile proselytes who were ready to submit to the faith of Christ, with its simple and exquisite morality, were likewise to submit to all the countless provisions, and, now in many respects, unmeaning and unintelligible regulations, of diet, dress, manners, and conduct.

This conflict may be traced most clearly in the Epistles of St. Paul, particularly in those to the remote communities in Galatia and in Rome. The former, written probably during the residence of the Apostle at Ephesus, was addressed to the Christians of Galatia, a district in the northern part of Asia Minor, occupied by a mingled population.[b] The descendants of the Gaulish invaders, from whom the region derived its name, retained to a late period vestiges of their original race, in the Celtic dialect, and probably great numbers of Jews had settled in these quarters. Paul had twice visited the country, and his Epistle was written at no long period after his second visit. But even in that short interval Judaism had revived its pretensions. The adversaries of Paul had even gone so far as to disclaim him as an Apostle of Christianity; and before he vindicates the essential independence of the new faith, and declares the Jewish Law to have been only a temporary institution,[c] designed, during a dark and barbarous period of human society, to keep alive the first prin-

The strength of the internal Judaism within the Church opposed by St. Paul.

---

[b] I decline the controversy concerning the place and time at which the different epistles were written; I shall give only the result, not the process of my investigations. This to the Galatians I suppose to have been written during St. Paul's first visit to Ephesus. (Acts xix.)

[c] Galat. iii. 19.

ciples of true religion, he has to assert his own divine appointment as a delegated teacher of Christianity.*

The Epistle to the Romans* enters with more full and elaborate argument into the same momentous question. The history of the Roman community is most remarkable. It grew up in silence, founded by some unknown teachers,' probably of those who were present in Jerusalem at the first publication of Christianity by the Apostles. During the reign of Claudius it had made so much progress as to excite open tumults and dissensions among the Jewish population of Rome; these animosities rose to such a height, that the attention of the government was aroused, and both parties expelled from the city. With some of these exiles, Aquila and Priscilla, St. Paul, as we have seen, formed an intimate connexion during his first visit to Corinth: from them he received information of the extraordinary progress of the faith in Rome. The Jews seem quietly to have crept back to their old quarters, when the rigour with which the Imperial Edict was at first executed, had insensibly relaxed; and from these persons, on their return to the capital, and most likely from other Roman Christians, who may have taken refuge in

---

* Galat. i. 1, 2.
* This epistle, there seems no doubt, was written from Corinth, during St. Paul's second residence in that city.

The foundation of the Church of Rome by either St. Peter or St. Paul is utterly irreconcileable with any reasonable view of the Apostolic history. Among Roman Catholic writers Count Stolberg abandons this point, and carries St. Peter to Rome for the first time at the commencement of Nero's reign. The account in the Acts seems to be so far absolutely conclusive. Many Protestants of the highest learning are as unwilling to reject the general tradition of St. Peter's residence in Rome. This question will recur on another occasion. As to St. Paul, the first chapter of this epistle is positive evidence, that the foundation of the Church in Rome was long previous to his visit to the western metropolis of the world.

Corinth,[a] or in other cities where Paul had founded Christian communities, the first, or at least the more perfect knowledge of the higher Christianity, taught by the Apostle of the Gentiles, would be conveyed to Rome. So complete indeed does he appear to consider the first establishment of Christianity in Rome, that he merely proposes to take that city in his way to a more remote region, that of Spain.[b] The manner in which he recounts, in the last chapter, the names of the more distinguished Roman converts, implies both that the community was numerous, and that the name of Paul was held in high estimation by its leading members. It is evident that Christianity had advanced already beyond the Jewish population, and the question of necessary conformity to the Mosaic Law was strongly agitated. It is therefore the main scope of this celebrated epistle to annul for ever this claim of the Mosaic Law to a perpetual authority, to show Christianity as a part of the providential design in the moral history of man, while Judaism was but a temporary institution, unequal to, as it was unintended for, the great end of revealing the immortality of mankind, altogether repealed by this more wide and universal system, which comprehends in its beneficent purposes of redemption the whole human race.

Closely allied with this main element of Judaism,

---

[a] It would appear probable that the greater part of the Christian community took refuge, with Aquila and Priscilla, in Corinth and the neighbouring port of Cenchrea.

[b] The views of Paul on so remote a province as Spain at so early a period of his journey, appear to justify the notion that there was a considerable Jewish population in that country. It is not impossible that many of the "Libertines" may have made their way from Sardinia. There is a curious tradition among the Spanish Jews, that they were resident in that country before the birth of our Saviour, and consequently had no concern in his death. See Hist. of Jews, II. p. 455.

which struggled so obstinately against the Christianity of St. Paul, was the notion of the approaching end of the world, the final consummation of all things in the second coming of the Messiah. It has been shown how essential and integral a part of the Jewish belief in the Messiah was this expectation of the ultimate completion of his mission in the dissolution of the world, and the restoration of a paradisiacal state, in which the descendants of Abraham were to receive their destined inheritance. To many of the Jewish believers the death and resurrection of Jesus were but (if the expression be warranted) the first acts of the great drama, which was hastening onward to its immediate close. They had bowed in mysterious wonder before the incongruity of the life and sufferings of Jesus with the preconceived appearance of the "Great One," but expected their present disappointment to be almost instantly compensated by the appalling grandeur of the second coming of Christ. If, besides their descent from Abraham, and their reverence for the Law of Moses, faith in Jesus as the Messiah was likewise necessary to secure their title to their peculiar inheritance, yet that faith was speedily to receive its reward; and the original Jewish conception of the Messiah, though put to this severe trial, though its completion was thus postponed, remained in full possession of the mind, and seemed to gather strength and depth of colouring from the constant state of high-wrought agitation in which it kept the whole moral being. This appears to have been the last Jewish illusion from which the minds of the Apostles themselves were disenchanted; and there can be no doubt both that many of the early Christians almost hourly expected the final dissolution of the world, and that this opinion awed many timid believers into the profession of Christianity, and kept them in trembling subjection to its authority. The ambiguous predictions of Christ himself, in which the destruction of the Jewish Polity, and the ruin of the city and Temple, were shadowed forth under images of more remote and universal import; the language of the Apostles, so liable to misinterpretation, that they were obliged publicly to correct the erroneous conclusions of their hearers,[1] seemed to countenance an opinion so disparaging to the real glory of Christianity, which was only to attain its object, after a slow contest of many centuries, perhaps of ages, with the evil of human nature. Wherever Christianity made its way into a mind deeply impregnated with Judaism, the moral character of the Messiah had still to maintain a strong contest with the temporal; and, though experience yearly showed that the commencement of this visible kingdom was but more remote, at least the first generation of Christians passed away, before the majority had attained to more sober expectations. And at every period of more than ordinary religious excitement, a millennial, or at least a reign partaking of a temporal character, has been announced as on the eve of its commencement; the Christian mind has retrograded towards that state of Jewish error which prevailed about the time of Christ's coming.[k]

---

[1] 2 Thessalonians ii. 1, 2. 2 Peter iii. 4, 8.

[k] Compare the strange Rabbinical notion of the fertility of the earth during the millennial reign of Christ, given by Irenæus as an actual prophecy of our Lord:—" Venient dies in quibus vineæ nascentur, singulæ decem millia palmitum habentes, et in unâ palmite decem millia brachiorum, et in uno vero brachio decem millia flagellorum, et in unoquoque flagello decem millia botrorum, et in unoquoque botro decem millia acinorum;" et unumquodque acinum expressum, dabit viginti quinque metretas vini; et cum apprehendet

As Christianity advanced in all other quarters of the world, its proselytes were in far larger proportion of Gentile than of Jewish descent. The Synagogue and the Church became more and more distinct, till they stood opposed in irreconcileable hostility. The Jews shrunk back into their stern seclusion, while the Christians were literally spreading in every quarter through the population of the empire. From this total suspension of intercourse, Judaism gradually died away within the Christian pale; time and experience corrected some of the more inveterate prejudices; new elements came into action. The Grecian philosophy, and at a later period influences still more adverse to that of Judaism, mingled with the prevailing Christianity. A kind of latent Judaism has, however, constantly lurked within the bosom of the Church. During the darker ages of Christianity, its sterner spirit harmonizing with the more barbarous state of the Christian mind, led to a frequent and injudicious appeal to the Old Testament. Practically the great principle of Judaism, that the Law, as emanating from Divine Wisdom, must be of eternal obligation, was admitted by conflicting parties; the books of Moses and the Gospel were appealed to as of equal authority; while the great characteristic of the old religion, its exclusiveness, its restriction of the divine blessings within a narrow and visible pale, was too much in accordance both with pride and superstition,

---

aliquis sanctorum botrum, alius clamabit,—Botrus ego melior sum, me sume, et per me Dominum benedic." These chapters of Irenæus show the danger to which pure and spiritual Christianity was exposed from this gross and carnal Judaising spirit. Irenæus (ch. 35.) positively denies that any of these images can be taken in an allegorical sense. De Harv. v. c. 33.

not to reassert its ancient dominion. The sacerdotal and the sectarian spirit had an equal tendency to draw a wider or a more narrow line of demarcation around that which, in Jewish language, they pronounced to be the "Israel" of God; and to substitute some other criterion of Christianity for that exquisite perfection of piety, that sublimity of virtue, in disposition, in thought, and in act, which was the one true test of Christian excellence.

In Palestine, as the external conflict with Judaism was longest and most violent, so the internal influence of the old religion was latest obliterated. But when this separation at length took place, it was even more complete and decided than in any other countries. In Jerusalem, the Christians were perhaps still called, and submitted to be called, Nazarenes, while the appellation which had been assumed at Antioch was their common designation in all other parts of the world. The Christian community of Jerusalem, which had taken refuge at Pella, bore with them their unabated reverence for the Law. But insensibly the power of that reverence decayed; and on the foundation of the new colony of Ælia, by the Emperor Hadrian, after the defeat of Barchochab, and the second total demolition of the city, the larger part having nominated a man of Gentile birth, Marcus, as their bishop, settled in the New City, and thus proclaimed their final and total separation from their Jewish ancestors.[m] For not only must they have disclaimed all Jewish connexion, to be permitted to take up their residence in the new colony, the very approach to which was watched by Roman outposts, and prohibited to every Jew under the

---

[m] Eusb., H. E. iv. 6. Hieronym., Epist. ad Hedybiam, Quæst. 8.

severest penalties, but even the old Jewish feelings must have been utterly extinct. For what Jew, even if he had passed under the image of a swine which was erected in mockery over the Bethlehem Gate, would not have shrunk in horror at beholding the Hill of Moriah polluted by a Pagan temple, and the worship of heathen deities profaning by their reeking incense, and their idolatrous sacrifices, the site of the Holy of Holies? The Christian, absorbed in deeper veneration for the soil which had been hallowed by his Redeemer's footsteps and was associated with his mysterious death and resurrection, was indifferent to the daily infringement of the Mosaic Law, which God himself had annulled by the substitution of the Christian faith, or to the desecration of the site of that Temple which God had visibly abandoned.

The rest of the Judæo-Christian community at Pella, and in its neighbourhood, sank into an obscure sect, distinguished by their obstinate rejection of the writings of St. Paul, and by their own Gospel, most probably the original Hebrew of St. Matthew. But the language, as well as the tenets of the Jews, were either proscribed by the Christians, as they still farther receded from Judaism, or fell into disuse;[a] and whatever writings they possessed, whether originals or copies in the vernacular dialect of Palestine, of the genuine Apostolic books, or compilations of their own, entirely perished, so that it is difficult, from the brief notices which are extant, to make out their real nature and character.

In Palestine, as elsewhere, the Jew and the Christian were no longer confounded with each other, but consti-

---

[a] Sulpicius Severus, H. E. Mosheim, de Reb. Christ. ante Constant. Le Clerc, Hist. Ecclesiastica.

tuted two totally different and implacably hostile races. The Roman government began to discriminate between them, as clearly appears from the permission to the Christians to reside in Hadrian's New City, on the site of Jerusalem, which was interdicted to the Jews. Mutual hatred was increased by mutual alienation; the Jew, who had lost the power of persecuting, lent himself as a willing instrument to the heathen persecutor against those whom he still considered as apostates from his religion. The less enlightened Christian added to the contempt of all the Roman world for the Jew a principle of deeper hostility. The language of Tertullian is that of triumph, rather than of commiseration for the degraded state of the Jew.° Strong jealousy of the pomp and power assumed by the Patriarch of Tiberias may be traced in the vivid description of Origen.ᵖ No sufferings could too profoundly debase, no pride could become those, who shared in the hereditary guilt of the crucifixion of Jesus.

° Dispersi, palabundi, et cœli et soli sui extorres vagantur per orbem, sine nomine, sine Deo rege, quibus nec advenarum jure terram patriam saltem vestigio salutare conceditor. Lib. cont. Judæos, 13.

ᵖ Origen, Epist. ad Africanum. Hist. of Jews, ii. 465.

CHAPTER III.

Christianity and Paganism.

Relationship between Judaism and Christianity.

THE conflict of Christianity with Judaism was a civil war; that with Paganism, the invasion and conquest of a foreign territory. In the former case it was the declared design of the innovation to perfect the established constitution on its primary principles; to expand the yet undeveloped system, according to the original views of the Divine Legislator; in the latter it contemplated the total subversion of the existing order of things, a reconstruction of the whole moral and religious being of mankind. With the Jew, the abolition of the Temple service, and the abrogation of the Mosaic Law, were indispensable to the perfect establishment of Christianity. The first was left to be accomplished by the frantic turbulence of the people, and the remorseless vengeance of Rome. Yet, after all, the Temple service maintained its more profound and indelible influence only over the Jew of Palestine; its hold upon the vast numbers which were settled in all parts of the world was that of remote, occasional, traditionary reverence. With the foreign Jew, the service of the synagogue was his religion; and the synagogue, without any violent change, was transformed into a Christian church. The same Almighty God, to whom it was primarily dedicated, maintained his place: and the sole difference was, that He was worshipped through the mediation of the crucified Jesus of Nazareth. With the Pagan, the whole of his religious observances fell under the unsparing proscription. Every one of the countless temples and shrines, and sacred groves, and hallowed fountains, were to be desecrated by the abhorrent feelings of those who looked back with shame and contempt upon their old idolatries. Every image, from the living work of Phidias or Praxiteles, to the rude and shapeless Hermes or Terminus, was to become an unmeaning mass of wood or stone. In every city, town, or even village, there was a contest to be maintained, not merely against the general system of Polytheism, but against the local and tutelary deity of the place. Every public spectacle, every procession, every civil or military duty, was a religious ceremonial. Though later, when Christianity was in the ascendant, it might expel the deities of Paganism from some of the splendid temples, and convert them to its own use; though insensibly many of the usages of the Heathen worship crept into the more gorgeous and imposing ceremonial of triumphant Christianity; though even many of the vulgar superstitions incorporated themselves with the sacred Christian associations, all this reaction was long subsequent to the permanent establishment of the new religion. At first all was rigid and uncompromising hostility; doubts were entertained by the more scrupulous whether meat exposed to public sale in the market, but which might have formed part of a sacrifice, would not be dangerously polluting to the Christian. The Apostle, though anxious to correct this sensitive scrupulousness, touches on the point with the utmost caution and delicacy.[*]

Direct opposition of Christianity to Paganism.

The private life of the Jew was already, in part at

---

[*] 1 Corinth. x. 25-31.

least, fettered by the minute and almost Brahminical observances with which the later Rabbins established their despotic authority over the mind. Still some of these usages harmonised with the spirit of Christianity; others were less invetenitely rooted in the feelings of the foreign Jew. The trembling apprehension of anything approaching to idolatry, the concentration of the heart's whole devotion upon the One Almighty God, prepared the soul for a Christian bias. The great struggle to Jewish feeling was the abandonment of circumcision, as the sign of his covenant with God. But this once over, baptism, the substituted ceremony, was perhaps already familiar to his mind; or, at least, emblematic ablutions were strictly in unison with the genius and the practice of his former religion. Some of the stricter Pharisaic distinctions were local and limited to Palestine, as, for instance, the payment of tithe; since the Temple tribute was the only national tax imposed by his religion on the foreign Jew. Their sectarian symbols, which in Palestine were publicly displayed upon their dress, were of course less frequent in foreign countries; and though worn in secret, might be dropped and abandoned by the convert to Christianity, without exciting observation. The whole life of the Heathen, whether of the philosopher who despised, or the vulgar who were indifferent to, the essential part of the religion, was pervaded by the spirit of Polytheism. It met him in every form, in every quarter, in every act and function of every day's business; not merely in the graver offices of the state, in the civil and military acts of public men; in the senate which commenced its deliberations with sacrifice; in the camp, the centre of which was a consecrated temple. The Pagan's domestic hearth was guarded by the Penates,

Universality of Paganism.

or by the ancestral gods of his family or tribe; by land he travelled under the protection of one tutelar divinity, by sea of another; the birth, the bridal, the funeral, had each its presiding deity; the very commonest household utensils and implements were cast in mythological forms; he could scarcely drink without being reminded of making a libation to the gods; and the language itself was impregnated with constant allusions to the popular religion.

However, as a religion, Polytheism might be undermined and shaken to the base, yet, as part of the existing order of things, its inert resistance would everywhere present a strong barrier against the invasion of a foreign faith. The priesthood of an effete religion, as long as the attack is conducted under the decent disguise of philosophical inquiry, or is only aimed at the moral or the speculative part of the faith; as long as the form, of which alone they are become the ministers, is permitted to subsist, go on calmly performing the usual ceremonial: neither their feelings nor their interests are actively alive to the veiled and insidious encroachments which are made upon the power and stability of their belief. In the Roman part of the Western world the religion was an integral part of the state. The greatest men of the last days of the Republic, the Ciceros and Cæsars, the Emperors themselves, aspired to fill the pontifical offices, and discharged their duties with grave solemnity, however their declared philosophical opinions were subversive of the whole system of Polytheism. Men might disbelieve, deny, even substitute foreign superstitions for the accustomed rites of their country, provided they did not commit any overt act of hostility, or publicly endeavour to bring the ceremonial into contempt. Such acts were not only impieties, they were treason against the majesty of Rome. In the Grecian cities, on the other hand, the interests and the feelings of the magistracy and the priesthood were less intimately connected; the former, those at least who held the higher authority, being Roman, the latter local or municipal. Though it was the province of the magistrate to protect the established religion, and it was sufficiently the same with his own to receive his regular worship, yet the strength with which he would resist, or the jealousy with which he would resent any dangerous innovation, would depend on the degree of influence possessed by the sacerdotal body, and the pride or enthusiasm which the people might feel for their local worship. Until, then, Christianity had made such progress as to produce a visible diminution in the attendance on the Pagan worship; until the temples were comparatively deserted, and the offerings less frequent, the opposition encountered by the Christian teacher, or the danger to which he would be exposed, would materially depend on the peculiar religious circumstances of each city.[L]

[L] In a former publication the author attempted to represent the manner in which the strength of Polytheism, and its complete incorporation with the public and private life of its votaries, might present itself to the mind of a Christian teacher on his first entrance into a heathen city. The passage has been quoted in Archbishop Whately's book on Rhetoric.

"Conceive then the Apostles of Jesus Christ, the tent-maker or the fisherman, entering as strangers into one of the splendid cities of Syria, Asia Minor, or Greece. Conceive them, I mean, as unendowed with miraculous powers, having adopted their itinerant system of teaching from human motives, and for human purposes alone. As they pass along to the remote and obscure quarter, where they expect to meet with precarious hospitality among their countrymen, they survey the strength of the established religion, which it is their avowed purpose to overthrow. Everywhere they behold temples, on which the utmost extravagance of expenditure has been lavished by succeeding generations; idols of the most exquisite workmanship, to which, even if the religious feeling of adoration is enfeebled, the

The narrative in the Acts, as far as it proceeds, is strikingly in accordance with this state of things. The people are strongly attached by national or local vanity. They meet processions in which the idle find perpetual occupation, the young excitement, the voluptuous a continual stimulant to their passions. They behold a priesthood numerous, sometimes wealthy; nor are these alone wedded by interest to the established faith; many of the trades, like those of the makers of silver shrines at Ephesus, are pledged to the support of that to which they owe their maintenance. They pass a magnificent theatre, on the splendour and success of which the popularity of the existing authorities mainly depends; and in which the serious exhibitions are essentially religious, the lighter as intimately connected with the indulgence of the baser passions. They behold another public building, where even worse feelings, the cruel and the sanguinary, are pampered by the animating contests of wild beasts and of gladiators, in which they themselves may shortly play a dreadful part,

Butcher'd to make a Roman holiday!

Show and spectacle are the characteristic enjoyments of a whole people, and every show and spectacle is either sacred to the religious feelings, or incentive to the lusts of the flesh; those feelings which must be entirely eradicated, those lusts which must be brought into total subjection to the law of Christ. They encounter likewise itinerant jugglers, diviners, magicians, who impose upon the credulous to excite the contempt of the enlightened; in the first case, dangerous rivals to those who should attempt to propagate a new faith by imposture and deception; in the latter, naturally tending to prejudice the mind against all miraculous pretensions whatever: here, like Elymas, endeavouring to outdo the signs and wonders of the Apostles, thereby throwing suspicion on all asserted supernatural agency, by the frequency and clumsiness of their delusions. They meet philosophers, frequently itinerant like themselves; or teachers of new religions, priests of Isis and Serapis, who have brought into equal discredit what might otherwise have appeared a proof of philanthropy, the performing laborious journeys at the sacrifice of personal ease and comfort, for the moral and religious improvement of mankind; or at least have so accustomed the public mind to similar pretensions, as to take away every attraction from their boldness or novelty. There are also the teachers of the different mysteries, which would engross all the anxiety of the inquisitive, perhaps excite, even if they did not satisfy, the hopes of the more pure and lofty-minded. Such must have been among the obstacles which must have forced themselves on the calmer moments of the most ardent; such the overpowering difficulties of which it would be impossible to overlook the importance, or elude the force; which required no sober calculation to estimate, no laborious inquiry to discover; which met and confronted them wherever they went, and which, either in desperate presumption, or deliberate

adventures of the Apostles in the different cities of Asia Minor and Greece are singularly characteristic of the population and the state of the existing Polytheism in each. It was not till it had extended beyond the borders of Palestine that Christianity came into direct collision with Paganism. The first Gentile convert admitted into the Christian community by St. Peter, Cornelius, if not a proselyte to Judaism, approached very nearly to it. He was neither polytheist nor philosopher; he was a worshipper of One Almighty Creator, and familiar, it might seem, with the Jewish belief in angelic appearances. Even beyond the Holy Land, Christianity did not immediately attempt to address the general mass of the Pagan community; its first collisions were casual and accidental; its operations commenced in the synagogue. A separate community was not invariably formed, or, if formed, appeared to the common observation only a new assemblage for Jewish worship; to which, if Heathen proselytes gathered in more than ordinary numbers, it was but the same thing on a larger, which had excited little jealousy on a smaller scale.

During the first journey of St. Paul, it is manifest that in Cyprus particularly, and in the towns of Asia Minor, the Jewish worship was an object of general respect: and Christianity appearing as

Christianity in Cyprus.

---

reliance on their own preternatural powers, they must have contemned and defied."—Bampton Lectures, p. 269, 273.

* The extent to which Jewish proselytism had been carried is a most intricate question. From the following passage, quoted from Seneca by St. Augustine, if genuine, it would seem

that it had made great progress:— "Cum interim usque eo sceleratissimae gentis consuetudo convaluit, ut per omnes terras jure recepta sit, victi victoribus leges dederunt." St. Augustine positively asserts that this sentence does not include the Christians. De Civit. Dei, vi. 11.

a modification of Jewish belief, shared in that deference which had been long paid to the national religion of the Jewish people. Sergius Paulus,[d] the governor of Cyprus, under the influence of the Jew Elymas, was already more than half, if not altogether, alienated from the religion of Rome. Barnabas and Paul appeared before him at his own desire; and their manifest superiority over his former teacher easily transformed him from an imperfect proselyte to Judaism into a convert to Christianity.

At Antioch in Pisidia there was a large class of proselytes to Judaism, who espoused the cause of the Christian teachers, and who probably formed the more considerable part of the Gentile hearers addressed by Paul on his rejection by the leading Jews of that city.

Antioch in Pisidia.

At Lystra,[e] in Lycaonia, the Apostle appears for the first time, in the centre, as it were, of a Pagan population; and it is remarkable that in this wild and inland region we find the old barbarous religion maintaining a lively and commanding influence over the popular mind. In the more civilized and commercial part of the Roman world, in Ephesus, in Athens, or in Rome, such extraordinary cures as that of the cripple at Lystra might have been publicly wrought, and might have excited a wondering interest in the multitude: but it may be doubted whether the lowest or most ignorant would have had so much faith in the old fabulous appearances of their own deities, as immediately to have imagined their actual and visible appear-

Lystra.

---

[d] Acts xiii. 6–12.

[e] Acts xiv. 6–19. There were Jews resident at Lystra, as appears by Acts xvi. 1, 2. Timotheus was the offspring of an intermarriage between a Jewish woman and a Greek: his name is Greek.

ance in the persons of these surprising strangers. It is only in the remote and savage Lystra, where the Greek language had not predominated over the primitive barbarous dialect ' (probably a branch of the Cappadocian), that the popular emotion instantly metamorphoses these public benefactors into the Jove and Mercury of their own temples. The inhabitants actually make preparation for sacrifice, and are with difficulty persuaded to consider such wonder-working men to be of the same nature with themselves. Nor is it less characteristic of the versatility of a rude people, that no sooner is the illusion dispelled, than they join with the hostile Jews in the persecution of those very men whom their superstition, but a short time before, had raised into objects of divine worship.

In the second, and more extensive journey of St. Paul, having parted from Barnabas,⁸ he was accompanied by Timotheus and Silas or Sylvanus; but of the Asiatic part of this journey, though it led through some countries of remarkable interest in the history of Paganism, no particulars are recorded. Phrygia,

Phrygia. which was a kind of link between Greece and the remoter East, still at times sent out into the Western world its troops of frantic Orgiasts; and the Phrygian vied with the Isiac and Mithraic mysteries in its influence in awakening the dormant fanaticism of the Roman world. It is probable that, in these regions, the Apostle confined himself to the Jewish settlers and their prose-

Galatia. lytes. In Galatia, it is clear that the converts were almost entirely of Hebrew descent. The vision which invited the Apostle to cross from Troas

---

' Jablonski, Dissertatio de Lingua Lycaonica, reprinted in Valpy's edition of Stephens's Thesaurus. ⁸ Acts xv. 36 to xviii. 18.

to Macedonia, led him into a new region, where his countrymen, though forming flourishing communities in many of the principal towns, were not, except perhaps at Corinth, by any means so numerous as in the greater part of Asia Minor. His vessel touched at Samothrace, where the most ancient and remarkable mysteries still retained their sanctity and veneration in that holy and secluded island.

At Philippi he first came into collision with those whose interests were concerned in the maintenance of the popular religion. Though these were only individuals, whose gains were at once put an end to by the progress of Christianity, the owners of the female soothsayer of Philippi were part of a numerous and active class, who subsisted on the public credulity. The proseucha, or oratory, of the Jews (the smaller place of worship, which they always established when their community was not sufficiently flourishing to maintain a synagogue), was, as usual, by the water side. The river, as always in Greece and in all southern countries, was the resort of the women of the city, partly for household purposes, partly perhaps for bathing. Many of this sex were in consequence attracted by the Jewish proseucha, and had become, if not proselytes, at least very favourably inclined to Judaism. Among these was Lydia, whose residence was at Thyatira, and who, from her trading in the costly purple dye, may be supposed a person of considerable wealth and influence. Having already been so far enlightened by Judaism as to worship the One God, she became an immediate convert to the Christianity of St. Paul. Perhaps the influence or the example of so many of her own sex worked upon the mind of a female of a different character and occupation. She may have been an impostor, but more probably was a young girl of excited temperament, whose disordered imagination was employed by men of more artful character for their own sordid purposes. The enthusiasm of this "divining" damsel now took another turn. Impressed with the language and manner of Paul, she suddenly deserted her old employers, and, throwing herself into the train of the Apostle, proclaimed, with the same exalted fervour, his divine mission, and the superiority of his religion. Paul, troubled with the publicity, and the continual repetition of her outcries, exorcised her in the name of Jesus Christ. Her wild excitement died away; the spirit passed from her; and her former masters found that she was no longer fit for their service. She could no longer be thrown into those paroxysms of temporary derangement, in which her disordered language was received as oracular of future events. This conversion produced a tumult throughout the city; the interests of a powerful body were at stake, for the trade of soothsaying, at this time, was both common and lucrative. The employers of the prophetess inflamed the multitude. The Apostle and his attendants were seized, arraigned before the magistrates, as introducing an *unlawful* religion. The magistrates took part against them. They suffered the ordinary punishment of disturbers of the peace; were scourged and cast into prison. While their hymn, perhaps their evening hymn, was heard through the prison, a violent earthquake shook the whole building; the doors flew open, and the fetters, by which probably they were chained to the walls, were loosened. The affrighted jailor, who was responsible for their appearance, expected them to avail themselves of this opportunity of escape, and in his despair was about to commit suicide. His hand was arrested by the calm voice of Paul, and to his wonder he found the prisoners remaining quietly in their cells. His fears and his admiration wrought together; and the jailor of Philippi, with his whole family, embraced the Christian faith. The magistrates when they found that Paul had the privilege of Roman citizenship, were in their turn alarmed at their hasty infringement of that sacred right, released them honourably from the prison, and were glad to prevail upon them to depart peacefully from the city.

Thus, then, we have already seen Christianity in collision with Polytheism, under two of its various forms: at Lystra, as still the old poetic faith of a barbarous people, insensible to the progress made elsewhere in the human mind, and devoutly believing the wonders of their native religion; in Philippi, a provincial town in a more cultivated part of Greece, but still at no high state of intellectual advancement, as connected with the vulgar arts, not of the established priesthood, but of itinerant traders in popular superstition. In Athens Paganism has a totally different character, inquiring, argumentative, sceptical, Polytheism in form, and that form embodying all that could excite the imagination of a highly polished people ; in reality admitting and delighting in the freest discussion, altogether inconsistent with sincere belief in the ancient and established religion. *Contrast of Polytheism at Lystra, Philippi, and Athens.*

Passing through Amphipolis and Apollonia, Paul and his companions arrived at Thessalonica ; but in this city, as well as in Berea, their chief intercourse appears to have been with the Jews. The riot by which they were expelled from Thessalonica was blindly kept up by the disorderly populace, instigated by many of the Jewish community, indignant at the apparent countenance given to the Christians by *Thessalonica.*

Jason their chief, who had received them into his house. Having left his companions, Timotheus and Silas, at Berea, Paul arrived alone at Athens.

At Athens, the centre at once and capital of the Greek philosophy and Heathen superstition, takes place the first public and direct conflict between Christianity and Paganism. Up to this time there is no account of any one of the Apostles taking his station in the public street or market-place, and addressing the general multitude.[h] Their place of teaching had invariably been the synagogue of their nation, or, as at Philippi, the neighbourhood of their customary place of worship. Here, however, Paul does not confine himself to the synagogue, or to the society of his countrymen and their proselytes. He takes his stand in the public market-place (probably not the Ceramicus, but the Eretriac Forum[1]), which, in the reign of Augustus, had begun to be more frequented, and at the top of which was the famous portico, from which the Stoics assumed their name. In Athens, the appearance of a new public teacher, instead of offending the popular feelings, was too familiar to excite astonishment, and was rather welcomed, as promising some fresh intellectual excitement: and in Athens, hospitable to all religions and all opinions, the foreign and Asiatic appearance, and possibly the less polished tone and dialect of Paul, would only awaken the stronger curiosity. Though they affect at first (probably the philosophic part of his hearers) to treat him as an idle "babbler," and others (the vulgar, alarmed for the honour of their

---

[h] This appears to be intimated in the expression, Acts xvii. 16. "His spirit was stirred within him when he saw the city wholly given to idolatry."

[1] Strabo, x. 417.

deities) supposed that he was about to introduce some new religious worship, which might endanger the supremacy of their own tutelar divinities; the Apostle is conveyed, not without respect, to a still more public and commodious place, from whence he may explain his doctrines to a numerous assembly without disturbance. On the Areopagus (the Hill of Mars)[k] the Christian teacher takes his stand, surrounded on every side with whatever was noble, beautiful, and intellectual in the older world,—temples, of which the materials were only surpassed by the architectural grace and majesty; statues, in which the ideal Anthropomorphism of the Greeks had almost sanctified the popular notions of the Deity, by embodying it in human forms of such exquisite perfection; public edifices, where the civil interests of man had been discussed with the acuteness and versatility of the highest Grecian intellect, in all the purity of the inimitable Attic dialect, where oratory had obtained its highest triumphs by "wielding at will the fierce democracy;" the walks of the philosophers, who unquestionably, by elevating the human mind to an appetite for new and nobler knowledge, had prepared the way for a loftier and purer religion. It was in the midst of these elevating associations, to which the student of Grecian literature in Tarsus, the reader of Menander and of the Greek philosophical poets, could scarcely be entirely dead or ignorant, that Paul stands forth to proclaim the lowly yet authoritative religion of Jesus of Nazareth.

Paul on the Areopagus

Speech of Paul

---

[k] It has been supposed by some that Paul was summoned before the Court of the Areopagus, who took cognizance of causes relating to religion. But there is no indication in the narrative of any of the forms of a judicial proceeding.

His audience was chiefly formed from the two prevailing sects, the Stoics and Epicureans, with the populace, the worshippers of the established religion. In his discourse, the heads of which are related by St. Luke, Paul, with singular felicity, touches on the peculiar opinions of each class among his hearers; [a] he expands the popular religion into a higher philosophy; he imbues philosophy with a profound sentiment of religion.[b]

It is impossible not to examine with the utmost interest the whole course of this (if we consider its remote consequences, and suppose it the first full and public argument of Christianity against the heathen religion and philosophy), perhaps the most extensively and permanently effective oration ever uttered by man. We may contemplate Paul as the representative of Christianity, in the presence, as it were, of the concentrated religion of Greece; and of the spirits, if we may so speak, of Socrates, and Plato, and Zeno. The opening of the Apostle's speech is according to those most perfect rules of art which are but the expressions of the general sentiments of nature. It is calm, temperate, conciliatory. It is no fierce denunciation of idolatry, no contemptuous disdain of the prevalent philosophic opinions; it has nothing of the sternness of the ancient Jewish prophet, nor the taunting defiance of the later Christian polemic. "Already

---

[a] Paulus summâ arte orationem suam ita temperat, ut modo cum vulgo contra philosophos, modo cum philosophis contra plebem, modo contra utrosque pugnet. Rosenmüller in loc.

[b] The art and the propriety of this speech are considerably marred by the mistranslation of one word in our version, δεισιδαιμονεστέρους—which does not imply reproof, as in the rendering "too superstitious." Conciliation, not offence, of the public feeling, especially at the opening of a speech, is the first principle of all oratory, more particularly of Christian teaching.

the religious people of Athens had, unknowingly indeed, worshipped the universal deity, for they had an altar to the Unknown God.[o] The nature, the attributes of this sublimer being, hitherto adored in ignorant and unintelligent homage, he came to unfold. This God rose far above the popular notion; He could not be confined in altar or temple, or represented by any visible image. He was the universal Father of mankind, even of the earth-born Athenians, who boasted that they were of an older race than the other families of man, and coeval with the world itself. He was the fountain of life, which pervaded and sustained the universe; He had assigned their separate dwellings to the separate families of man." Up to a certain point in this higher view of the Supreme Being, the philosopher of the Garden, as well as of the Porch, might listen with wonder and admiration. It soared, indeed, high above the vulgar religion: but in the lofty and serene Deity, who disdained to dwell in the earthly temple, and needed nothing from the hand of man,[p] the Epicurean might almost suppose that he heard the language of his own teacher. But the next sentence, which asserted the providence of God as the active, creative energy,—as the conservative, the ruling, the ordaining principle,—annihilated at once the atomic theory, and the government of blind chance, to which Epicurus ascribed the origin and preservation of the

---

[o] Of all the conjectures (for all is purely conjectural) on the contested point of the "altar to the Unknown God," the most ingenious and natural, in my opinion, is that of Eichhorn. There were, he supposes, very ancient altars, older perhaps than the art of writing, or on which the inscription had been effaced by time: on these the piety of later ages had engraven the simple words "To the Unknown God."

[p] Needing nothing: the coincidence with the "nihil indiga nostri" of Lucretius is curious, even if accidental.

universe. "This high and impassive deity, who dwelt aloof in serene and majestic superiority to all want, was perceptible in some mysterious manner by man: his all-pervading providence comprehended the whole human race; man was in constant union with the Deity, as an offspring with its parent." And still the Stoic might applaud with complacent satisfaction the ardent words of the Apostle; he might approve the lofty condemnation of idolatry. "We, thus of divine descent, ought to think more nobly of our universal Father than to suppose that the Godhead is like unto gold, or silver, or stone, graven by art or man's device." But this Divine Providence was far different from the stern and all-controlling Necessity, the inexorable Fatalism of the Stoic system. While the moral value of human action was recognised by the solemn retributive judgment to be passed on all mankind, the dignity of Stoic virtue was lowered by the general demand of repentance. The perfect man, the moral king, was deposed, as it were, and abased to the general level; he had to learn new lessons in the school of Christ; lessons of humility and conscious deficiency, the most directly opposed to the principles and the sentiments of his philosophy.

The great Christian doctrine of the Resurrection closed the speech of Paul; a doctrine received with mockery perhaps by his Epicurean hearers, with suspension of judgement probably by the Stoic, with whose theory of the final destruction of the world by fire and his tenet of future retribution it might appear in some degree to harmonise. Some, however, became declared converts; among whom are particularly named Dionysius, a man of sufficient distinction to be a member of the famous court of the Areopagus, and a woman, named Damaris, probably of considerable rank and influence.

At Athens, all this free discussion on topics relating to the religious and moral nature of man, and involving the authority of the existing religion, passed away without disturbance. The jealous reverence for the established faith, which, conspiring with its perpetual ally, political faction, had in former times caused the death of Socrates, the exile of Stilpo, and the proscription of Diagoras the Melian, had long died away. With the loss of independence, political animosities had subsided, and the toleration of philosophical and religious indifference allowed the utmost latitude to speculative inquiry, however ultimately dangerous to the whole fabric of the national religion. Yet Polytheism still reigned in Athens in its utmost splendour: the temples were maintained with the highest pomp; the Eleusinian Mysteries, in which religion and philosophy had in some degree coalesced, attracted the noblest and the wisest of the Romans, who boasted of their initiation in these sublime secrets. Athens was thus, at once, the headquarters of Paganism, and at the same time the place where Paganism most clearly betrayed its approaching dissolution.

From Athens, the Apostle passes to Corinth. Corinth was at this time the common emporium of the eastern and western divisions of the Roman Empire. It was the Venice of the Old World, in whose streets the continued stream of commerce, either flowing from, or towards the great capital of the world, out of all the eastern territories, met and crossed.[a]

Corinth, A.D. 52.

---

[a] After its destruction by Mummius, Corinth was restored, beautified, and colonised by Julius Cæsar. Strabo, viii. 381. For its history, wealth, and commercial situation, see Diod. Sic. Fragm. The profligacy of Corinthian manners was likewise proverbial:—πολὺν οἰκεῖτε τῶν οἴκων τε καὶ γεγενημένων ἀπορρεόντωνδρων. Dio. Chrysost. Orat. 37, v. ii. p. 110.

The basis of the population of Corinth was Roman, of very recent settlement; but colonists from all quarters had taken up their permanent residence in a place so admirably adapted for mercantile purposes. In no part of the Roman empire were both the inhabitants and the travellers through the city so various and mingled; nowhere, therefore, would a new religion spread with so much rapidity, and send out the ramifications of its influence with so much success; and at the same time excite so little observation amid the stir of business and the perpetual influx and efflux of strangers, or be less exposed to jealous opposition. Even the priesthood, newly settled, like the rest of the colony, could command no ancient reverence; and in the perpetual mingling and confusion of all dresses and dialects, no doubt there was the same concourse of religious itinerants of every description.' At Corinth, therefore, but for the hostility

---

' Corinth was a favourite resort of the Sophists (Aristid. Isthm. Athenæus, l. xiii.), and in an oration of Dio Chrysostom there is a lively and graphic description of what may be called one of the fairs of antiquity, the Isthmian Games, which happily illustrates the general appearance of society. Among the rest, the Cynic philosopher Diogenes appears, and endeavours to attract an audience among the vast and idle multitude. He complains, however, "that if he were a travelling dentist or an oculist, or had any infallible specific for the spleen or the gout, all who were afflicted with such diseases would have thronged around him; but as he only professed to cure mankind of vice, ignorance, and profligacy, no one troubled himself to seek a remedy for those less grievous maladies." "And there was around the Temple of Neptune a crowd of miserable Sophists, shouting and abusing one another; and of their so-called disciples, fighting with each other; and many authors reading their works, to which nobody paid any attention; and many poets chanting their poems, with others praising them; and many jugglers showing off their tricks; and many prodigy-mongers noting down their wonders; and a thousand rhetoricians perplexing causes; and not a few shopkeepers retailing their wares wherever they could find a customer. And presently some approached the philosopher,—not indeed the Corinthians; for as they saw him every day in Corinth, they did not expect to derive any advantage from hearing him,—

of his countrymen, the Christian Apostle might, even longer than the eighteen months which he passed in that city, have preserved his peaceful course. The separation which at once took place between the Jewish and the Christian communities in Corinth—the secession of Paul from the synagogue into a neighbouring house—might have allayed even this intestine ferment, had not the progress of Christianity, and the open adoption of the new faith by one of the chiefs of the synagogue, reawakened that fierce animosity which had already caused the expulsion of both parties from Rome, and the seeds of which no doubt rankled in the hearts of many. Here, therefore, for the first time, Christianity was brought under the cognisance of a higher authority than the municipal magistrate of one of the Macedonian cities.

The contemptuous dismissal of the cause by the Proconsul of Achaia, as beneath the majesty of the Roman tribunal; his refusal to interfere, when some of the populace, with whom the Christians were apparently the favoured party, on the repulse of the accusing Jews from the seat of justice, fell upon one of them, named Sosthenes, and maltreated him with considerable violence, shows how little even the most enlightened men yet comprehended the real nature of the new religion. The affair was openly treated as an unimportant sectarian dispute about the national faith of the Jews. The mild' and popular character of Gallio,

Gallio, A.D. 53.

---

but those that drew near him were strangers, each of whom having listened a short time, and asked a few questions, made his retreat, from fear of his rebukes." Dio. Chrys. Orat. viii.

* "Nemo mortalium uni tam dulcis est quam hic omnibus." Senec. Nat. Quaest. 4. Praef. "Hoc plusquam Senecam dedisse mundo. Et dulcem generasse Gallionem." Stat. Sylv. ii. 7. Compare Dion. Cass. lx.

his connexion with his brother Seneca,[*] in whose philosophic writings the morality of Heathenism had taken a higher tone than it ever assumes, unless perhaps, subsequently, in the works of Marcus Antoninus, excite regret that the religion of Christ was not brought under his observation in a manner more likely to conciliate his attention. The result of this trial was the peaceful establishment of Christianity in Corinth, where, though secure from the violence of the Jews, it was however constantly exposed, by its situation, to the intrusion of new comers, with different modifications of Christian opinions. This, therefore, was the first Christian community which was rent into parties, and in which the authority of the Apostle was perpetually wanting to correct opinions not purely Jewish in their origin.

Thus eventful was the second journey of Paul: over so wide a circuit had Christianity already been disseminated, almost entirely by his personal exertions. In many of the most flourishing and populous cities of Greece communities were formed, which were continually enlarging their sphere.

The third journey,[a] starting from the head-quarters of Christianity, Antioch, led Paul again through the same regions of Asia, Galatia, and Phrygia. But now, instead of crossing over into Macedonia, he proceeded along the west of Asia Minor, to the important city of Ephesus.

---

[*] Among the later forgeries was a correspondence between Seneca and St. Paul; and many Christian writers, as unacquainted with the history of their own religion as with the state of the heathen mind, have been anxious to trace all that is striking and beautiful in the writings of the Stoic to Christian influence.

Mons. de Champagny (Les Césars, t. ii. 231, &c., and Appendix, p. 417) has laboured ingeniously, but without success, to work out this theory. M. Dubois Guchan (Tacite et son Siècle) takes the opposite view.

[a] Acts xviii. 23, to xxi. 3.

Ephesus,[x] at this time, may be considered the capital, the chief mercantile city, of Asia Minor. It was inhabited by a mingled population; and, probably, united, more than any city in the East, Grecian and Asiatic habits, manners, and superstitions.[y] Its celebrated temple was one of the most splendid models of Grecian architecture; the image of the goddess retained the symbolic form of the old Eastern nature-worship. It was one of the great schools of magic; the Ephesian amulets, or talismans,[a] were in high request. Polytheism had thus effected an amicable union of Grecian art with Asiatic mysticism and magical superstition: the vender of the silver shrines, which represented the great Temple, one of the wonders of the world, vied with the trader in charms and in all the appurtenances of witchcraft. Great numbers of Jews had long inhabited the chief cities of Asia Minor; many had attained to opulence, and were of great mercantile importance. Augustus had issued a general rescript to the cities of Asia Minor for the protection of the Jews, securing to them the freedom of religious worship; legalising the transmission of the Temple tribute to Jerusalem by their own appointed receivers; and making the plunder of their synagogues sacrilege.[b] Two later edicts of Agrippa and Julius Antonius, proconsuls, particularly addressed to the magistracy of Ephesus, acknowledged and confirmed the imperial decree. From this period, nothing can yet have occurred to lessen their growing prosperity, or to lower them in the estimation

---

[x] Rosenmüller, Das alte und neue Morgenland, 6–50.
[y] Compare Matter, Hist. du Gnosticisme, i. 137.

[a] Ἐφέσια γράμματα.
[b] Ἱεροσυλία, Joseph. Ant. xvi. 6. Krebs, Decreta Romanorum pro Judæis, Lipsiæ, 1778.

of their Gentile neighbours. Among the numerous Jews in this great city, Paul found some who, having been in Judæa during the teaching of John the Baptist, had embraced his opinions, and received baptism, either at his hands or from his disciples, but appear not only not to have visited the mother country, but to have kept up so little connexion with it as to be almost, if not entirely, ignorant of Christ and of Christianity. The most eminent of them, Apollos, had left the city for Corinth, where, meeting with St. Paul's companions, the Roman Jews, Priscilla and Aquila, he had embraced Christianity, and, being a man of eloquence, immediately took such a lead in the community as to be set up by one of the conflicting parties as a kind of rival of the Apostle. The rest of this sect in Ephesus willingly listened to the teaching of Paul: to the number of twelve, they " received the Holy Ghost," and thus became the nucleus of a new Christian community in Ephesus. The followers of John the Baptist, no doubt, conformed in all respects with the customary worship of their countrymen: their peculiar opinions were superinduced, as it were, upon their Judaism; they were still regular members of the synagogue. In the synagogue therefore Paul commenced his labours, the success of which was so great as evidently to excite the hostility of the leading Jews: hence, here likewise, a complete separation took place; the Apostle obtained possession of a school belonging to a person named Tyrannus, most likely a Grecian sophist, and the Christian church stood alone, as a distinct and independent place of divine worship.

Paul continued to reside in Ephesus two years, during which the rapid extension of Christianity was accelerated by many wonderful cures. In Ephesus, such cures were likely to be sought with avidity; but in this centre of magical superstition would by no means command belief in the divine mission of the worker of miracles. Jews, as well as Heathens, admitted the unlimited power of supernatural agencies, and vied with each other in the success of their rival enchantments. The question then would arise, by what more than usually potent charm or mysterious power such extraordinary works were wrought. The followers of both religions had implicit faith in the magic influence of certain names. With the Jews, this belief was moulded up with their most sacred traditions. It was by the holy Tetra-Grammaton,[b] the Sem-ham-phorash, according to the Alexandrian historian of the Jews, that Moses and their gifted ancestors wrought all the wonders of their early history. Pharaoh trembled before it, and the plagues of Egypt had been obedient to the utterance of the awful monosyllable, the ineffable name of the Deity. Cabalism, which assigned at first sanctity, and afterwards power over the intermediate spirits of good and evil, to certain combinations of letters and numbers, though not yet cultivated to its height, existed, no doubt, in its earlier elements, among the Jews of this period. Upon this principle, some of the Jews who practised exorcism attributed all these prodigies of St. Paul to some secret power possessed by the name of Jesus. Among these were some men of high rank, the sons of one of the high priests, named Sceva. They seem to have believed in the

Ephesian magic.

Jewish exorcists.

---

[b] Artapanus apud Euseb. Præp. Evangel. viii. 28. Compare Clemens. Alex. Strom. v. p. 562. It is curious enough that the constant repetition of the mysterious name of the Deity, Oum, should be the most acceptable act of devotion among the Indians, among the Jews the most awful and inexpiable impiety.

superstition by which they ruled the minds of others, and supposed that the talismanic influence, which probably depended on Cabalistic art, was inseparably connected with the pronunciation of this mystic name. Those whom this science or this trade of exorcism (according as it was practised by the credulous or the crafty) employed for their purposes, were those unhappy beings of disordered imagination, possessed, according to the belief of the times, by evil spirits. One of these, on whom they were trying this experiment, had probably before been strongly impressed with the teaching of Paul, and the religion which he preached; and irritated by the interference of persons whom he might know to be hostile to the Christian party, assaulted them with great violence, and drove them naked and wounded out of the house.*

This extraordinary event was not only fatal to the pretensions of the Jewish exorcists, but at once seemed to put to shame all who believed and who practised magical arts, and the manufacturers of spells and talismans. Multitudes came forward, and voluntarily gave up, to be burned, not only all their store of amulets, but even the books which contained the magical formularies.⁴ Their value, as probably they were rated and estimated at a high price, amounted to 50,000 pieces of silver, most likely Attic drachms, or Roman silver denarii, a coin very current in Asia Minor, and worth about 7½d. of our money. The sum would thus make something more than 1600l.

---

* It is not improbable that they may have taken off their ordinary dress, for the purpose of performing their incantation with greater solemnity.

⁴ On the Ἐφέσια γράμματα there are some amusing and instructive observations in Kreuser, Vorfragen über Homeros, p. 112.

DEMETRIUS THE SILVERSMITH.

These superstitions, however, though domiciliated at Ephesus, were foreign; and, perhaps, according to the Roman provincial regulations, unlawful. Yet even the established religion, at least some of those dependent upon it for their subsistence, began to tremble at the rapid increase of the new faith. A collision now, for the first time, took place with the interests of that numerous class who were directly connected with the support of the reigning Polytheism. The Temple of Ephesus, as one of the wonders of the world, was constantly visited by strangers; by a few, perhaps, from religion, by many from curiosity or admiration of the unrivalled architecture; at all events, by the greater number of those who were always passing, accidentally, or with mercantile views, through one of the most celebrated marts of the East. There was a common article of trade, a model or shrine of silver representing the temple, which was preserved as a memorial, or, perhaps, as endowed with some sacred and talismanic power. The sale of these works gradually fell off, and the artisans, at the instigation of a certain Demetrius, raised a violent popular tumult, and spread the exciting watchword that the worship of Diana was in danger. The whole city rung with the repeated outcries, "Great is Diana of the Ephesians." Two of Paul's companions were seized and dragged into the public theatre, the place where in many cities the public business was transacted. Paul was eager to address the multitude, but was restrained by the prudence of his friends, among whom were some of the most eminent men of the province, the Asiarchs.*

margin note: Demetrius, the maker of silver shrines, A.D. 57.

---

* This office appears to have been a wreck of the ancient federal constitution of the Asiatic cities. The Asiarchs were elective, by certain cities, and represented the general league or confederation. They possessed the su-

The Jews appear to have been implicated in the insurrection; and, probably, to exculpate themselves, and to disclaim all connexion with the Christians, they put forward a certain Alexander, a man of eloquence and authority. The appearance of Alexander seems not to have produced the effect that they intended. As a Jew, he was considered hostile to the Polytheistic worship; his voice was drowned by the turbulence, and for two hours nothing could be heard in the assembly but the reiterated clamour, "Great is Diana of the Ephesians." The conduct of the magistrates seems to indicate that they were acting against a part of the community, in whose favour the imperial edicts were still in force. Either they did not yet clearly distinguish between the Jews and Christians, or supposed that the latter, as originally Jews, were under the protection of the same rescripts. Expressing the utmost reverence for the established religion of Diana, they recommend moderation; exculpate the accused from the charge of intentional insult, either against the temple or the religion of the city; require that the cause should be heard in a legal form; and, finally, urge the danger which Ephesus incurred of being punished for the breach of the public peace by the higher authorities,—the proconsular governor of Asia. The tumult was allayed; but Paul seems to have thought it prudent to withdraw from the excited city, and to pursue his former line of travel into Macedonia and Greece.

From Ephesus, accordingly, we trace his course through Macedonia to Corinth. Great changes had

---

preme sacerdotal authority; regulated and presided in the theatric exhibitions. Their pontifical character renders it more remarkable that they should have been favourably disposed towards Paul.

probably taken place in this community. The exiles from Rome, when the first violence of the edict of Claudius had passed away, both Jews and Christians, quietly stole back to their usual residences in the metropolis. In writing his Epistle to the Roman Christians from this place, Paul seems to intimate both that the religion was again peaceably and firmly established in Rome (it counted some of the imperial household among its converts); and, likewise, that he was addressing many Christians with whom he was personally acquainted. As, then, it is quite clear, from the early history, that he had not himself travelled so far as Italy, Corinth seems the only place where he can have formed these connexions.

His return led him, from fear of his hostile countrymen, back through Macedonia to Troas; thence, taking ship at Assos, he visited the principal islands of the Ægean, Mitylene, Chios, and Samos; landed at Miletus, where he had an interview with the heads of the Ephesian community; thence, by sea, touching at Coos, Rhodes, and Patara, to Tyre. Few incidents occur during this long voyage: the solemn and affecting parting from the Ephesian Christians, who came to meet him at Miletus, implies a profound sense of the dangers which awaited him on his return to Palestine. The events which occurred during his journey, and his residence in Jerusalem, have been already related. This last collision with his native Judaism, and his imprisonment, occupy between two and three years.[f]

A.D. 58.

The next place in which the Apostle surveyed the strength and encountered the hostility of Paganism

---

[f] For the period between the years 58 and 61, see the last chapter.

was in the metropolis of the world. Released from his imprisonment at Cæsarea, the Christian Apostle was sent to answer for his conduct in Jerusalem before the imperial tribunal, to which, as a Roman citizen, he had claimed his right of appeal. His voyage is singularly descriptive of the precarious navigation of the Mediterranean at that time; and it is curious that in the wild island of Melita, the Apostle having been looked upon as an atrocious criminal, because a viper had fastened upon his hand, when he shook the reptile off, without having received any injury, was admired as a god. In the barbarous Melita, as in the barbarous Lystra, the belief in gods under the human form had not yet given place to the incredulous spirit of the age. He arrives, at length, at the port in Italy where voyagers from Syria or Egypt usually disembarked, Puteoli. There appear to have been Christians in that town, who received Paul, and with whom he resided for seven days. Many of the Roman Christians, apprised of his arrival, went out to meet him as far as the village of Appii Forum, or a place called the Three Taverns. But it is remarkable that so complete by this time was the separation between the Jewish and Christian communities, that the former had no intelligence of his arrival, and what is more singular, knew nothing whatever of his case.[e] Possibly the usual correspondence with Jerusalem had been interrupted at the time of the expulsion of the Jews from Rome, and had not been re-established with its former regularity; or, as is more probable, the persecution of Paul, being a party and Sadducaic measure, was neither avowed nor supported by the great body of the nation. Those who

---

[e] Acts xxviii. 21.

had visited, and returned from, Jerusalem, being chiefly of the Pharisaic or more religious party, were either ignorant or imperfectly informed of the extraordinary adventures of Paul in their native city: and two years had elapsed during his confinement at Cæsarea. Though still in form a prisoner, Paul enjoyed almost perfect freedom, and his first step was a general appeal to the whole community of the Jews then resident in Rome. To them he explained the cause of his arrival. It was not uncommon in disputes between two parties in Jerusalem, that both should be summoned or sent at once by the governor, especially if, like Paul, they demanded it as a right, to plead their cause before the imperial courts. More than once the High Priest himself had been reduced to the degrading situation of a criminal before a higher tribunal; and there are several instances in which all the arts of court intrigue were employed to obtain a decision on some question of Jewish politics. Paul, while he acknowledges that his conflict with his countrymen related to his belief in Christ, as the Messiah, disclaims all intention of arraigning the ruling authorities for their injustice: he had no charge to advance against the nation. The Jews, in general, seem to have been inclined to hear from so high an authority the real doctrines of the Gospel. They assembled for that purpose at the house in which the Apostle was confined; and, as usual, some were favourably disposed to the Christianity of Paul, others rejected it with the most confirmed obduracy.

But, at this instant, we pass at once from the firm and solid ground of authentic and credible history, upon the quaking and insecure footing of legendary tradition. A few scattered notices of the personal history of Paul may be gathered from the later

A.D. 63.
St. Paul leaves Rome.

Epistles; but the last fact which we receive from the undoubted authority of the writer of the Acts is, that two years passed before the Apostle left Rome.[b] To what examination he was subjected, in what manner his release was obtained, all is obscure, or rather without one ray of light. But to the success of Paul in Rome, and to the rapid progress of Christianity during these two eventful years, we have gloomy and melancholy evidence. The next year after his departure is darkly noted in the annals of Rome as the era of that fatal fire which enveloped in ruin all the ancient grandeur of the Eternal City;—in those of Christianity, as the epoch of the first heathen persecution. This event throws considerable light on the state of the Christian Church at Rome. No secret or very inconsiderable community would have attracted the notice, or satisfied the blood-thirsty cruelty of Nero. The people would not have consented to receive them as atoning victims for the dreadful disaster of the great conflagration, nor would the reckless tyranny of the Emperor have condescended to select them as sacrificial offerings to appease the popular fury, unless they had been numerous, far above contempt, and already looked upon with a jealous eye. Nor is it less clear, that even to the blind discernment of popular indignation and imperial cruelty, the Christians were by this time distinguished from the Jews. They were no longer a mere sect of the parent nation, but a separate, a marked, and

A.D. 64. Burning of Rome.

---

[b] Whatever might be the reason for the abrupt termination of the book of the Acts, which could neither be the death of the author, for he probably survived St. Paul, nor his total separation from him, for he was with him towards the close of his career (2 Tim. iv. 11), the expression in the last verse but one of the Acts limits the residence of St. Paul in Rome, at that time, to two years.

peculiar people, known by their distinctive usages, and incorporating many of Gentile descent into their original Jewish community.

Though at first there appears something unaccountable in this proscription of a harmless and unobtrusive sect, against whom the worst charge, at last, was the introduction of a new and peaceful form of worshipping one Deity, a privilege which the Jew had always enjoyed without molestation; yet the process by which the public mind was led to this outburst of fury, and the manner in which it was directed against the Christians, are clearly indicated by the historian.[1] After the first consternation and distress, an access of awe-struck superstition seized on the popular mind. Great public calamities can never be referred to obvious or accidental causes. The trembling people had recourse to religious rites, endeavoured to ascertain by what offended deities this dreadful judgement had been inflicted, and sought for victims to appease their yet perhaps unmitigated gods.[k] But when superstition has once found out victims, to whose guilt or impiety it may ascribe the divine anger, human revenge mingles itself with the relentless determination to propitiate offended Heaven, and contributes still more to blind the judgement and exasperate the passions. The other foreign religions, at which the native deities might take offence, had been long domiciliated in Rome. Christianity was the newest, perhaps was making the most alarming progress: it was no national religion; it was disclaimed with eager

---

[1] Mox petita diis piacula, aditique Sibyllæ libri, ex quibus supplicatum Vulcano et Cereri Proserpinæque, ac propitiata Juno per matronas, primùm in Capitolio, deinde apud proximum mare, &c. Tac. Ann. xv. 44.

[k] Sed non ope humanâ, non largitionibus principis, aut deûm placamentis decedebat infamia, quin jussum incendium crederetur.

animosity by the Jews, among whom it originated; its principles and practices were obscure and unintelligible; and that obscurity the excited imagination of the hostile people might fill up with the darkest and most monstrous forms.

<small>Probable causes which implicated the Christians with this event.</small> I have sometimes thought it possible that incautious or misinterpreted expressions of the Christians themselves might have attracted the blind resentment of the people. The minds of the Christians were constantly occupied with the terrific images of the final coming of the Lord to judgement in fire; the conflagration of the world was the expected consummation, which they devoutly supposed to be instantly at hand. When, therefore, they saw the great metropolis of the world, the city of pride, of sensuality, of idolatry, of bloodshed, blazing like a fiery furnace before their eyes,—the Babylon of the West wrapped in one vast sheet of destroying flame,—the more fanatical—the *Jewish* part of the community [m]— may have looked on with something of fierce hope, and eager anticipation; expressions almost triumphant may have burst from unguarded lips. They may have attributed the ruin to the righteous vengeance of the Lord; it may have seemed the opening of that kingdom which was to commence with the discomfiture, the desolation, of heathenism, and to conclude with the establishment of the millennial kingdom of Christ. Some of these, in the first instance, apprehended and examined, may have made acknowledgments before a passionate and astonished tribunal, which would lead to the conclusion

---

[m] Some deep and permanent cause of hatred against the Christians, it may almost seem, as connected with this disaster, can alone account for the strong expressions of Tacitus, writing so many years after:—Sontes et novissima exempla meritos.

that, in the hour of general destruction, they had some trust, some security, denied to the rest of mankind; and this exemption from common misery, if it would not mark them out in some dark manner [a] as the authors of the conflagration, at all events would convict them of that hatred of the human race so often advanced against the Jews.

Inventive cruelty sought out new ways of torturing these victims of popular hatred and imperial injustice. The calm and serene patience with which they were armed by their religion against the most excruciating sufferings may have irritated still further their ruthless persecutors. The sewing up men in the skins of beasts, and setting dogs to tear them to pieces, may find precedent in the annals of human barbarity;[b] but the covering them over with a kind of dress smeared with wax, pitch, or other combustible matter, with a stake under the chin to keep them upright, and then placing them to be slowly consumed, like torches in the public gardens of popular amusement,—this seems to have been an invention of the time; and, from the manner in which it is mentioned by the Roman writers, as the most horrible torture known, appears to have made a profound impression on the general mind. Even a people

---

[a] Haud perinde in crimine incendii quam odio generis humani convicti sunt.

M. de Pressensé (t. ii. p. 97) has adopted and followed out this notion. "Ils purlaient sans doute de ces flammes du jugement qui devaient dévorer un monde impie." Compare the whole passage.

[b] Et pereuntibus addita ludibria, ut ferarum tergis obtecti, laniatu canum interirent; aut crucibus affixi, aut flammandi, atque ubi defecisset dies, in usum nocturni luminis urerentur. Tac. Ann. xv. 54. Juvenal calls this "tunica molesta," viii. 235.

tædá incrēbis in illā
Qua stantes ardent, qui fixo gutture fumant
Et latum media sulcum deducit arenā.—
       i. 166.

Illam tandem alimentis ignium illitam et latextam.—Senec. Epist. xix. It was probably thought appropriate to consume with slow fire the authors of the conflagration.

habituated to gladiatorial shows, and to the horrible scenes of wholesale execution which were of daily occurrence during the reigns of Tiberius, Caligula, and Nero, must yet have been in an unusual state of exasperated excitement to endure, or rather to take pleasure in, the sight of these unparalleled barbarities. Thus, the gentle, the peaceful religion of Christ was welcomed upon earth by new applications of man's inventive faculties, to inflict suffering, and to satiate revenge."

The Apostle was, no doubt, absent from Rome at the commencement, and during the whole, of this persecution. His course is dimly descried by the hints scattered through his later epistles. It is probable that he travelled into Spain. The assertion of Irenæus, that he penetrated to the extreme West,¹ coincides with his

---

" Gibbon's extraordinary "conjecture" that the Christians in Rome were confounded with the Galileans, the fanatical followers of Judas the Gaulonite, is most improbable. The sect of Judas was not known beyond the precincts of Palestine. The insinuation that the Jews may have escaped the proscription, through the interest of the beautiful Poppæa and the favourite Jewish player Aliturus, though not very likely, is more in character with the times.

Notwithstanding the doubts of some—of one historian, especially, for whom I feel the utmost respect—few historical facts appear to me to rest on more authentic testimony than the Neronian persecution. The traditionary abhorrence of Nero in the Christian Church, the expectation of his reappearance as Antichrist, which prevailed for two or three centuries, is a curious, to me a strong, confirmation of the fact. It is certainly extraordinary that at so early a period the Christians should be numerous enough and important enough to be charged with such a crime. But it must be remembered that it was the object of all to find victims, however obscure, to glut the popular fury, to appease the angry gods, of whom the Christians were the notorious, the avowed enemies (the most irreligious in days of calamity are seized with paroxysms of religious terror and vengeance), above all, to divert the suspicions of the people, already directed to the highest quarters, to the Emperor himself. It was imputed to Nero that he was utterly indifferent, that he made an indecent theatrical amusement of the ruin of the imperial city and the sufferings of the people. No doubt there were those who brooded over darker charges against him.

¹ The visit of St. Paul to Britain,

intention of visiting that province declared at an earlier period. As it is difficult to assign to any other part of his life the establishment of Christianity in Crete, it may be permitted to suppose, that from Spain his course lay eastward, not improbably with the design of revisiting Jerusalem. That he entertained this design, there appears some evidence; none, however, that he accomplished it.[r] The state of Judæa, in which Roman oppression had now begun, under Albinus, if not under Florus,[s] to grow to an intolerable height; the spirit of indignant resistance which was fermenting in the mind of the people, might either operate to deter or to induce the Apostle to undertake the journey. On the one hand, if the Jews should renew their implacable hostility, the Christians, now having become odious to the Roman government, could expect no protection; the rapacious tyranny of the new rulers would seize every occasion of including the Christian community under the grinding and vexatious system of persecution: and such occasion would be furnished by any tumult in which they might be implicated. On the other hand, the popular mind

---

in my opinion, is a fiction of religious national vanity. It has few or no advocates except English ecclesiastical antiquarians. In fact, the state of the island, in which the precarious sovereignty of Rome was still fiercely contested by the native barbarians, seems to be entirely forgotten. Civilisation had made little progress in Britain till the conquest of Agricola. Up to that time it was occupied only by the invading legionaries, fully employed in extending and guarding their conquests, and by our wild ancestors with their stern Druidical hierarchy. From which class were the Apostle's hearers or converts? My friend Dr. Cardwell, in a recent essay on this subject, concurs with this opinion.

[r] This is inferred from Heb. xiii. 23. This inference, however, assumes several points. In the first place, that Paul is the author of the Epistle to the Hebrews. To this opinion, though by no means certain, I rather incline. But it does not follow that Paul fulfilled his intention; and even the intention was conditional, and dependant on the speedy arrival of Timothy, which may or may not have taken place.

[s] Florus succeeded Albinus, A.D. 64.

among the Jews being absorbed by stronger interests, engrossed by passions even more powerful than hatred of Christianity, the Apostle might have entered the city unnoticed, and remained concealed among his Christian friends; particularly as the frequent change in the ruling authorities, and the perpetual deposal of the High Priest, during the long interval of his absence, may have stripped his leading adversaries of their authority.

Be this as it may, there are manifest vestiges of his having visited many cities of Asia Minor—Ephesus, Colossæ,[t] Miletus,[u] Troas;[x] that he passed a winter at Nicopolis, in Epirus.[y] From hence he may have descended to Corinth,[z] and from Corinth, probable reasons may be assigned for his return to Rome. In all these cities, and, doubtless, in many others, where we have no record of the first promulgation of the religion, the Christians formed regular and organised communities. Constant intercourse seems to have been maintained throughout the whole confederacy. Besides the Apostles, other persons seem to have been constantly travelling about, some entirely devoted to the dissemination of the religion, others uniting it with their own secular pursuits. Onesiphorus,[a] it may be supposed, a wealthy merchant, resident at Ephesus, being in Rome at the time of Paul's imprisonment, laboured to alleviate the irksomeness of his confinement. Paul had constantly one, sometimes many, companions in his journeys. Some of these he seems to have established, as Titus, in Crete, to preside over the young communities; others

---

[t] Philem. 22.
[u] 2 Tim. iv. 20.
[x] 2 Tim. iv. 13. Compare Paley, Horæ Paulinæ.
[y] Titus iii. 12.
[z] 2 Tim. iv. 20.
[a] 2 Tim. i. 16-18.

were left behind for a time to superintend the interests of the religion; others, as Luke, the author of the Acts, were in more regular attendance upon him, and appear to have been only occasionally separated by accidental circumstances. But, if we may judge from the authentic records of the New Testament, the whole Christianity of the West emanated from Paul alone. The indefatigable activity of this one man had planted Christian colonies, each of which became the centre of a new moral civilisation, from the borders of Syria, as far as Spain, and to the city of Rome.

A.D. 66.

Tradition assigns to the last year of Nero the martyrdom both of St. Peter and St. Paul. That of the former rests altogether on unauthoritative testimony; that of the latter is rendered highly probable, I think certain, from the authentic record of the Second Epistle to Timothy. This letter was written by the author when in custody at Rome,[b] apparently under more rigorous confinement than during his first imprisonment; not looking forward to his release,[c] but with steadfast presentiment of his approaching violent death. It contains allusions to his recent journey in Asia Minor and Greece. He had already undergone a first examination,[d] and the danger was so great, that he had been deserted by some of his most attached followers, particularly by Demas. If conjecture be admitted, the preparations for the reception of Nero at Corinth, during the celebration of the Isthmian Games, may have caused well-grounded apprehensions to the Christian community in that city. Paul

---

[b] All the names of the Church who unite in the salutation, iv. 21, are Roman.
[c] 2 Tim. iv. 5, 6, 7.
[d] 2 Tim. i. 12-18. Rosenmüller, however (in loc.), understands this of the examination during his first trial.

might have thought it prudent to withdraw from Corinth, whither his last journey had brought him, and might seize the opportunity of the Emperor's absence to visit and restore the persecuted community at Rome. During the absence of Nero, the government of Rome and of Italy was entrusted to the freed-slave Helius, a fit representative of the absent tyrant. He had full power of life and death, even over the senatorial order. The world, says Dion, was enslaved at once to two autocrats, Helius and Nero. Thus Paul may have found another Nero in the hostile capital; and the general tradition, that he was put to death, not by order of the Emperor, but of the governor of the city, coincides with this state of things.

The fame of St. Peter, from whom she claims the supremacy of the Christian world, has eclipsed that of St. Paul in the Eternal City. The most splendid temple which has been erected by Christian zeal, to rival or surpass the proudest edifices of heathen magnificence, bears the name of that Apostle, while that of St. Paul rises in a remote and unwholesome suburb. Studious to avoid, if possible, the treacherous and slippery ground of polemic controversy, I must be permitted to express my surprise that in no part of the authentic Scripture occurs the slightest allusion to the personal history of St. Peter, as connected with the Western Churches. At all events, the conversion of the Gentile world was the acknowledged province of St. Paul. In that partition treaty, in which these two moral invaders divided the yet unconquered world, the more civilized province of Greek and Roman heathenism was assigned to him who was emphatically called the Apostle of the Gentiles, . while the Jewish population fell under the particular care of the Galilean Peter. For the operations of the latter, no part of the world, exclusive of Palestine, which seems to have been left to James the Just, would afford such ample scope for success as Babylonia and the Asiatic provinces, to which the Epistles of Peter are addressed. His own writings distinctly show that he was connected by some intimate tie with these communities; and, as it appears that Galatia was a stronghold of Judaical Christianity, it is probable that the greater part of those converts were originally Jews or Asiatics, whom Judaism had already prepared for the reception of Christianity. Where Judaism thus widely prevailed, was the appropriate province of the Apostle of the circumcision. While then those whose severe historical criticism is content with nothing less than contemporary evidence, or, at least, probable inferences from such records, will question the permanent establishment of Peter in the imperial city, those who admit the authority of tradition will adhere to, and may, indeed, make a strong case in favour of St. Peter's residence;[e] or his martyrdom at Rome.[f]

---

[e] The authorities are Irenæus, Dionysius of Corinth apud Eusebium, and Epiphanius.

[f] Pearson in his Opera Posthuma, Diss. de Serie et Successione Romæ Episcop., supposes Peter to have been in Rome. The explanation of Babylon as Rome is as old as Clem. Alex. See Routh, f. p. 34. Compare Townson on the Gospels, Diss. 5, sect. v. Barrow (Treatise of the Pope's Supremacy) will not "avow" the opinion of those who argue him never to have been at Rome, vol. vi. p. 189 (Oxford ed. 1818). Lightfoot, whose profound knowledge of every thing relating to the Jewish nation entitles his opinion to respect, observes, in confirmation of his assertion that Peter lived and died in Chaldea,—quam absurdum est statuere, ministrum præcipuum circumcisionis sedem suam figere in metropoli præputiatorum, Româ. Lightfoot's Works, 8vo. edit. x. 392.

If, then, with Barrow I may "bear some civil respect to ancient testimonies and traditions" (loc. cit.), the strong bias of my own mind is to the following solution of this problem. With Lightfoot, I believe that Babylonia was the scene of St. Peter's labours. But I am likewise confident that in Rome, as in Corinth, there

The spent wave of the Neronian persecution* may have recovered sufficient force to sweep away those who were employed in reconstructing the shattered edifice of Christianity in Rome. The return of an individual, however personally obscure, yet connected with a sect so recently proscribed, both by popular odium and public authority, would scarcely escape the vigilant

---

were two communities,—a Petrine and a Pauline,—a Judaising and an Hellenising Church. The origin of the two communities in the doctrines attributed to the two Apostles, may have been gradually transmuted into the foundation first of each community, then generally of the Church of Rome, by the two Apostles. All the difficulties in the arrangement of the succession to the episcopal see of Rome vanish, if we suppose two cotemporary lines. Here, as elsewhere, the Judaising Church either expired or was absorbed in the Pauline community.

The passage in the Corinthians by no means necessarily implies the personal presence of Peter in that city. There was a party there, no doubt, a Judaising one, which professed to preach the pure doctrine of "Cephas," in opposition to that of Paul, and who called themselves, therefore, " of Cephas."

Dum primus ecclesiæ Romanæ fundatores quæro occurrit illud. Acts ii. 10. 'Οι ἐπιδημοῦντες 'Ρωμαῖοι, 'Ιουδαῖοι τε καὶ προσήλυτοι. Lightfoot's Works, 8vo. edit. i. 392.

* As to the extent of the Neronian persecution, whether it was general, or confined to the city of Rome, I agree with Mosheim that only one valid argument is usually advanced on either side. On the one hand, that of Dodwell, that the Christians being persecuted not on account of their religion, but on the charge of incendiarism, that charge could not have been brought against those who lived beyond the precincts of the city. Though as to this point, it is to be feared that many an honest Protestant would have considered the real crime of the Gunpowder Plot, or the imputed guilt of the Fire of London, ample justification for a general persecution of the Roman Catholics. On the other hand is alleged the authority of Tertullian, who refers, in a public apology, to the *laws* of Nero and Domitian against the Christians—an expression—too distinct to pass for rhetoric, even in that passionate writer, though he may have magnified temporary edicts into general laws. The Spanish inscription not only wants confirmation, but even evidence that it ever existed. There is, however, a point of some importance in favour of the first opinion. Paul appears to have travelled about through a great part of the Roman empire during this interval, yet we have no intimation of his being in more than ordinary personal danger. It was not till his return to Rome that he was again apprehended, and at length suffered martyrdom.

police of the metropolis. One man is named, Alexander the coppersmith, whose seemingly personal hostility had caused or increased the danger in which Paul considered himself during his second imprisonment. He may have been the original informer, who betrayed his being in Rome, or his intimate alliance with the Christians; or, he may have appeared as evidence against him during his examination. Though there may have been no existing law, or imperial rescript against the Christians; and Paul, having been absent from Rome at the time, could not be implicated in the charge of incendiarism; yet the representative of Nero,[k] if faithfully described by Dion Cassius,[l] would pay little regard to the forms of criminal justice, and would have no scruple in ordering the summary execution of an obscure individual, since it does not appear that, in exercising the jurisdiction of prefect of the city, he treated the lives of knights or of senators with more respect. There is, therefore, no improbability that the Christian Church in Rome may have faithfully preserved the fact of Paul's execution, and even cherished in their pious memory the spot on the Ostian road watered by the blood of the Apostle. As a Roman citizen, Paul is said to have been beheaded, instead of being suspended to a

Martyrdom of Paul.

---

[k] The remarkable phrase μαρτυρήσας ἐπὶ τῶν ἡγουμένων, used by Clement of Rome, is singularly in accordance with this view. It would have been a strange word to apply to the Emperor, but very appropriate when the imperial authority in Rome was, as it were, in commission; it would answer to "the authorities."

[l] Τοὺς μέντοι ἐν τῇ Ῥώμῃ καὶ τῇ Ἰταλίᾳ πάντας Ἡλίῳ τινὶ Καισαρείῳ ἐκδότους παρέδωκε. Πάντα γὰρ ἁπλῶς αὐτῷ ἐπετέτραπτο, ὥστε καὶ δημεύειν, καὶ φυγαδεύειν, καὶ ἀποκτιννύναι (καὶ πρὶν δηλῶσαι τῷ Νέρωνι) καὶ ἰδιώτας ὁμοίως, καὶ ἱππέας καὶ βουλευτάς. Οὕτω μὲν δὴ τότε ἡ τῶν Ῥωμαίων ἀρχὴ δύο αὐτοκράτορσιν ἅμα ἐδούλευε, Νέρωνι καὶ Ἡλίῳ. Οὐδὲ ἔχω εἰπεῖν ὁπότερος αὐτῶν χείρων ἦν. Dion Cassius (or Xiphilin), lxiii. c. 12.

cross, or exposed to any of those horrid tortures invented for the Christians; and so far the modest probability of the relation may confirm rather than impeach its truth. The other circumstances—his conversion of the soldiers who carried him to execution, and of the executioner himself—bear too much the air of religious romance. Though, indeed, the Roman Christians had not the same interest in inventing or embellishing the martyrdom of Paul, as that of the other great Apostle from whom they derive their supremacy.

APPENDIX TO CHAPTER III.

The deliverance of St. Paul from custody at Rome; his subsequent missionary journey, possibly to Spain, certainly to Greece and Asia Minor; and his second imprisonment, have undergone the severe scrutiny of modern criticism, and have been rejected by very many able writers, of whom Wieseler may be held the best and fairest representative. I am bound to give reasons for my adherence to the old opinion; and the importance of the subject may justify some length in this digression. I will not insist on the difficulty which I find in crowding the whole vast work of conversion, the recorded visits to so many wide-spread Churches, within the limited period in Paul's life before the imprisonment in Rome; still less on the marked and almost generally admitted difference—I. In the style and language between the Epistles acknowledged by all to have been written during the first (?) imprisonment at Rome, those to the Ephesians, Colossians, Philemon (which Wieseler adduces strong grounds for supposing to be that to the Laodiceans), Philippians, and those which are commonly called the Pastoral Epistles. On this difference Baur has mainly rested his denial of the authenticity of these latter Epistles. Wieseler, on the other hand, so little admits it as to ascribe the First Epistle to Timothy to the Apostle's two years' residence in Ephesus (Acts xix., about A.D. 56). In the Pastoral Epistles above fifty words (they are drawn out in Coneybeare and Howson's book) are either not used at all in the older Epistles, or used with some peculiar modification of sense in the later. The whole construction of the style in the Pastoral Epistles, clear, simple, sententious, is in striking contrast with the involved, parenthetical, obscure manner of the addresses to the Churches; obscure, I mean, not from want of clear conception, but from a kind of eager, thronging, press of argument.

II. In the apparently advanced, more developed, at least progressive state of the Churches in the Pastoral Epistles, their more settled constitutions, if I may so speak; the manifest and growing dawn of those divergencies of opinion, not only of Judaising opinion, but the incipient fermentation of those tenets which gradually grew up into the Gnostic heresies: I may add the still worse growing heresies of the unchristian life; the departure from the primitive simplicity, fervour, holiness, discipline, concord; the heresies against the life as well as the faith of the first days. These discrepancies, which I think the ordinary reader may perceive if he will peruse attentively the two classes of Epistles, are altogether inconsistent with the notion that they were written simultaneously. Some time must have elapsed to account both for the variation in the manner of writing and in the state of the Christian world. On these points, however, I do not dwell.

The gist of the question rests mainly, I say, not exclusively, on the concluding verses of the Acts and the last chapter of the Second Epistle to Timothy.

Now, it is generally admitted (Wieseler determines this point without hesitation) that St. Paul arrived in Rome, and commenced his first imprisonment in the spring of A.D. 61. St. Luke thus closes the Book of the Acts of the Apostles: *And Paul dwelt two whole years in his own hired house, and received all that came in unto him. Preaching the kingdom of God, and teaching those things which concern the Lord Jesus Christ.* These two years of what may be called easy, if not honourable, captivity (it is not necessary to inquire what restrictions were placed on his freedom, or what measures were taken for his safe custody) were passed undisturbed, uninterrupted, with free access to all who wished to approach him, and unlimited intercourse with the outer world. There was absolutely no restraint on what we may venture to call his apostolical usefulness. The words of St. Luke, therefore, seem to preclude the supposition of any hearing, trial, or defence during those two years. Why the prosecution was suspended, we know not: whether the Sanhedrin in Jerusalem, which on Paul's arrival at Rome had not sent any deputation or even letters to the Jews of Rome to make good their charge (Acts xxviii. 21), had still neglected to do so, (content, it might be, with ridding themselves of so dangerous an adversary in Jerusalem): whether from changes in the dominant parties, and so in the politics of the Sanhedrin ; or whether the fact may be attributed to circumstances in Rome. It has been suggested that the marriage of Poppæa with the Emperor (Poppæa, as we learn from Josephus, was a Jewish proselyte) towards the close of the two years may have so strengthened the influence of the Jews in Rome as to induce them—galled, perhaps, by the progress of Christianity through the unchecked exertions of Paul—to revive or press on the prosecution. All this, too, is pure conjecture.

These two years bring us to the spring of A.D. 63. In the year and a quarter between this time and the Fire in Rome, July 19, A.D. 64, must have taken place—1st. The trial of St. Paul. At this trial (2 Tim. iv. 16) (I give hereafter my reasons, to me conclusive, for referring this passage to the first, the only recorded trial), though allowed all the privileges of Roman citizenship, Paul was in great danger. He was deserted by all his friends and disciples. He stood alone before the awful tribunal; according to his own strong expression, "*No man stood with me*, but all forsook me." God, however, inspired him with more than ordinary courage, with such power of eloquence, that not only does the accusation entirely fail, but his defence (he did not content himself with rebutting the charges against him, but seized the opportunity of preaching the faith) had considerable effect on the Pagan auditory in raising at least their respect for the religion of Christ. "*Notwithstanding, the Lord stood with me and strengthened me; that by me the preaching might be fully known, and that all the Gentiles might hear.*" The trial ended in his acquittal; "*and I was delivered out of the mouth of the lion.*"

What then became of him on his acquittal? Was he remanded to prison, to be brought up a second time on the same charges before the same tribunal within a few months, condemned to death (as Wieseler supposes, in the beginning of A.D. 64), and executed as a malefactor? The charges were, as we may conclude, insult to the Jewish ceremonies and Temple, which, as Judaism was a lawful religion, were under the protection of the Romans, and (what was a capital offence) provoking a violation of the peace of the empire and stirring up sedition against its authority. There could be no new charges. The interest of the Jews with Poppæa could hardly have so much increased as to bring on such a crisis for a second time. There was nothing to do away with the favourable impression produced on the Romans by his demeanour, eloquence, persuasiveness at the first trial. Remember that the Fire had not taken place; the malice of the Government and the fury of the populace had not yet been excited against the Christians as incendiaries. By what law, by whose judgement then, on what accusation, was he thus, in those yet peaceful times, made a martyr? It is less improbable (and some, I believe, of those who reject the second imprisonment take this view) that he perished in the general massacre of the Neronian persecution. This, however, is contrary to all tradition; and, though in general I have no superstitious respect for tradition, I cannot but think that of such a death, at such a time, under such terrible unforgotten circumstances, tradition would not have been silent.

Now, turn to the last chapter of the Second Epistle to Timothy. That this was the latest Epistle written by St. Paul, all who admit the Pastoral Epistles are agreed. No one can refuse to observe the contrast between the manner in which the Apostle writes of his prospects in the earlier Epistles written from Rome and in this. In the Epistles to the Ephesians, the Colossians, to Philemon, and to the Philippians, there is no apprehension of imminent danger of his life. On the contrary, there is a glowing and sanguine expectation of future success in the propagation of the Gospel (Ephes. vi. 19, 20; Coloss. *passim*, iv. 18; Philemon, 21). In the Philippians a kind of doubtfulness and gentle melancholy appears to have crept over him; it might seem as if his trial were approaching, yet he has good hope of visiting again the Philippian Church (Philip. i. 20, 26). In the Second Epistle to Timothy there is, on the other hand, a calm, deliberate presentiment, almost a prophecy of his imminent, his approaching death. "*He has fought his good fight; he has finished his course; he awaits his crown.*" Yet he can hardly have contemplated immediate, instant martyrdom; for, if so, he would not have summoned Timothy to join him, and to bring with him certain effects and persons who might be useful to him. He was not in actual danger; but manifestly danger was closing around him. Demas, who when he wrote to the Colossians (iv. 14) and to Philemon was with him (named together with the faithful Luke), had now fallen off from him.

Is it probable, is it possible, that all this change can have taken place in the few months between the date of his first trial and that assigned for his death by Wieseler, or even during the year and a quarter before the Fire of Rome? We have to find time also for the writing the Epistle. Indeed, as to the Fire, the charge of incendiarism must have burst as suddenly and unexpectedly on the Christians as the Fire upon the inhabitants of Rome. Are we to suppose that St. Paul wrote this Epistle amid the terror and confusion of those days? Even he would hardly have written so calmly and with such a quiet anticipation of death; still less would he if he had had time allowed in this fierce and hasty persecution. At all events, he could not have summoned disciples to come to him at Rome. This is utterly impossible; I think Wieseler's theory hardly less inconceivable.

But this last chapter of the Second Epistle to Timothy must undergo still closer investigation. It teems with allusions, as it seems—and has seemed to all but comparatively late inquirers—to a recent journey in different parts of Greece and Asia Minor, with notices of different persons encountered during that journey. If it was not after the first imprisonment and the trial, the journey must have taken place above *five years* before; for the going up to Jerusalem was in A.D. 58; the close of St. Paul's captivity in Rome, whether by release or death, A.D. 63. Now,—I. As to the cloak, books, and parchments left at Troas in the care of a certain Carpus. If St. Paul had been lately there, we can conceive his anxiety about them. But after five or six years or longer (see Acts xvi. xx.) it seems hardly to be accounted for. II. Erastus abode at Corinth. This appears to imply that he had recently left Erastus there. "Trophimus have I left at Miletus, sick." This cannot have been five or six years before. With this difficulty Wieseler seems to me to struggle entirely without success. III. The incidents relating to Timotheus are to me equally conclusive. In the Epistle to the Philippians, written, as all agree, from Rome in 61 or 62, Timotheus was with St. Paul at Rome. The Apostle was about to send him to the East (ii. 19, 23). That he did go to the East there can be no doubt, and with a charge of the most solemn responsibility, requiring a long time to organise Churches, to fulfil arduous missions in many places and in many ways. Yet Timotheus is summoned back to St. Paul in Rome (iv. 9). Now, if this Second Epistle was written early—according to Wieseler's theory, A.D. 63—we have St. Paul, engaged in a design not less magnificent than evangelising at least the Roman empire, sending forth, if I may so say, his legate, with instructions to visit, to organise, to correct, to be, as it were, his own vicar, a kind of apostle all over the East among a multitude of distant and wide-spread communities; and then recalling him after so brief a time, when his task could not have approached fulfilment, to Rome, it would appear, to share his own dangers, perhaps to share his own martyrdom. This after a few years is conceivable—a few years of common labour; in less than a few years it is to me utterly incredible.

For all these reasons, I adhere with confidence to the view, as old as Eusebius, if not as old as Clement of Rome, as to the second imprisonment of St. Paul after some years of renewed apostolic labours. I adhere to Eusebius, and differ from some writers of credit, as Pearson, in referring the first answer—the πρώτη ἀπολογία (2 Tim. iv. 16)—to the close of the first imprisonment. Nothing could be more natural than, as danger for a second time was darkening around him, that his mind should revert to his former danger, to the desertion of friends who might again desert him; now that the lion had begun to roar again and to open his threatening jaws, that he should remember how God once had delivered him from the terrors of that lion. Moreover, that he should be permitted, after the Neronian persecution, to make any defence; that he should make a defence even temporarily successful; that he should have been permitted in that defence to preach Christ, and that such preaching of Christ should be heard not unfavourably even by Gentiles, is absolutely inconceivable. For Paul was not at that period, according to his own view, a Jew, arraigned by the Jews of Palestine on some strange, to the Romans unintelligible, questions of their Law, at worst of being the cause, it might be the blameless cause, of riot against the peace of the empire; he was now the ringleader, the notorious, avowed, boastful ringleader of a wicked, hateful sect, convicted, as it was generally believed, of having burned glorious, holy Rome; a sect which the blood-battened magnates and populace of Rome had seen with gloating joy and vengeance exposed to torments at which even they might shudder; mockery added to martyrdom; sewn up in skins, swathed in pitch-vests and set on fire, holding in their agony torches over the voluptuous banquets of senators.

But one word more. How came Paul at Rome? at Rome, at such a time? Because he was the Apostle of Christ—of Christ who died for men. What could be more expedient, what more necessary, than the restoration, the reorganization, the resettlement of the Roman Church, persecuted, scattered, decimated—worse than decimated—by the fierce persecution; of the few faithful, probably most in concealment, whom not less than the profoundest faith could keep from apostasy; not less than that love which Christianity alone inspires could keep from disclaiming their spiritual kindred? And to whom but an Apostle, to whom but to St. Paul, belonged the perilous, the almost desperate office of confronting Rome, glutted but not satiated with Christian blood?—of offering, if necessary, his life, and of leaving his blood of martyrdom as the prolific seed of the future Church in the Imperial City?

END OF VOL. I.

www.ingramcontent.com/pod-product-compliance
Lightning Source LLC
Chambersburg PA
CBHW051240300426
44114CB00011B/815